The Quest for Modernity

The Quest for Modernity

Secular Liberal and Left-Wing Political Thought in Egypt, 1945–1958

Roel Meijer

Routledge
Taylor & Francis Group

LONDON AND NEW YORK

First published 2002
by Routledge
2 Park Square, Milton Park, Abingdon, Oxon OX14 4RN

Simultaneously published in the USA and Canada
by Routledge
711 Third Avenue, New York, NY 10017, USA

Routledge is an imprint of the Taylor & Francis Group, an informa business

© 2002 Roel Meijer

Typeset in Centaur by LaserScript Ltd, Mitcham, Surrey

All rights reserved. No part of this book may be reprinted or
reproduced or utilised in any form or by any electronic,
mechanical, or other means, now known or hereafter invented,
including photocopying and recording, or in any
information storage or retrieval system, without permission in
writing from the publishers.

British Library Cataloguing in Publication Data
A catalogue record of this book is available from the British Library

Library of Congress Cataloging in Publication Data
A catalog record for this book has been requested

ISBN 13: 978-0-7007-1247-2 (hbk)
ISBN 13: 978-1-138-86987-5 (pbk)

For Marianne and Tarik

Contents

Acknowledgements	ix
Introduction	1
Theoretical Background	7
Civil Society and Political Culture under the British Occupation and the Monarchy	14
Civil Society, the State, and New Modernist Trends	21

PART I: THE FORMATION OF MODERNIST POLITICAL THOUGHT

Chapter One: Liberal Reform: The Society of National Renaissance	37
Introduction	37
Political Reform Program	44
Social Reform	51
Conclusion	59
Chapter Two: Authoritarian Socialism: Rashid al-Barrawi	66
Introduction	66
Ideological Sources	70
Laws of Development	77
Reform	82
Conclusion	88

CONTENTS

Chapter Three: Egyptian Communism and the Paradigm of the Front — 96
- Introduction — 96
- International and Local Background — 100
- Formation of the Egyptian Paradigm of the Front — 106
- The Nationalist Revolution — 113
- Reorientation — 119
- Conclusion — 126

PART II: THE RISE OF AUTHORITARIAN MODERNISM

Chapter Four: The Dilemmas of Reform, 1950–54 — 135
- Introduction — 135
- The Failure of Liberal and Revolutionary Reform — 137
- The July Revolution — 146
- The Communists and the July Revolution — 157
- The March Crisis — 162
- Conclusion — 166

Chapter Five: Towards a Modern Society, 1955–57 — 173
- Introduction — 173
- Economic Planning — 178
- Reorientation of the Liberals — 186
- Reorientation of the Communists — 190
- Conclusion — 201

Chapter Six: The Hegemony of Authoritarian Modernism, 1958 — 208
- Introduction — 208
- A Modern Democracy — 212
- The Role of the Intellectual — 218
- Joining a Modern Civilization — 230

Conclusion — 246

Bibliography — 255

Index — 269

Acknowledgments

I wish to acknowledge with gratitude the help I received from my supervisor Ruud Peters in writing this book. I remember the hospitality and stimulating academic atmosphere he and his wife Marlies Weijergang provided for students during his directorship of the Netherlands Institute of Archeology and Arabic Studies in Cairo in 1982–87. The numerous remarkable American and German researchers who frequented the Dutch Institute initiated me into Middle Eastern studies during our desert hikes.

Ken Cuno and Marilyn Booth have been extremely helpful by taking me to "Hajj Muhammad," where I was able to find most of the books of the intellectuals mentioned in this work. I remember with growing nostalgia the garages full of second-hand books stacked to the ceiling one had to burrow through to find the treasures of Egyptian intellectual production of half a century ago. I am grateful for the assistance of Professor Ra'uf Abbas of the History Department of Cairo University, who provided me with several works written by members of the Society of National Renaissance that I would not have been able to obtain otherwise. I am also indebted to many Egyptian intellectuals who spent much of their time answering my questions and providing me with insights into the atmosphere of the 1950s.

I would like to express my gratitude to Professor Kees Versteegh, who appointed me as a lecturer at the University of Nijmegen three years ago. The new insights I gained from lecturing on almost every topic except the one of this book have enriched the present version. To the International Institute for Social History (IISH) I am grateful for hiring me to collect documents of the communist movement in Egypt and the Sudan.

ACKNOWLEDGMENTS

I am especially indebted to Israel Gershoni. His unstinting and exceptionally generous support has made the task of finishing this work less difficult. His work has served as an inspiring example. Thanks also go to the friends I made during the years I was in Egypt: Jan Goldberg, Didier Monciaud, and Ahmad Abdalla. They kept the atmosphere of Cairo alive during the production of this book. Sherif Younes deserves to be particularly mentioned for making an excellent Arabic translation of a previous version of this work.

Without the keen interest, enthusiasm, and financial support of my parents throughout the writing of my dissertation, this work would not have been finished. As contemporaries of the generation I studied in Egypt, I learned from them the basics of modernism in its Dutch social-democratic form.

Above all, I would like to thank Martine van Elk for taking upon herself the arduous task of checking the English in this book. More than just editing the text, she helped me to rethink it. This is remarkable for someone who is a specialist in Shakespeare. Finally, I wish to thank Marianne for her support as my partner for the past ten years.

Introduction

From 1952 to 1958 Egypt experienced a major change in its history as a result of the military takeover and the reform measures that followed. The new regime abolished the monarchy, instated a single-party system, and concentrated power in the hands of the president. The economic power of the large landowners shifted to the middle classes due to land reform, while the nationalization of most foreign assets and the introduction of economic planning ended a century of foreign economic dominance in Egypt. No less spectacular was the change in foreign policy. The Bandung conference and the Czech arms deal in 1955, the defeat of Britain and France during the Suez Canal crisis a year later, and the unification with Syria in 1958 launched Egypt as a new regional and international power. It acquired new ties with its Arab neighbors, the Communist Bloc, and the decolonizing world. Non-Alignment and pan-Arabism became the ideological props of the new rulers.

If these events pulled Egypt into the limelight of international politics, for Egyptians they signified a new dawn. The second half of the 1950s saw an optimism and a self-confidence that were unrivaled in Egypt's history. For the first time in decades, Egyptians believed firmly that their country had taken control of its own destiny and left its past behind. Many were convinced that Egypt had entered a higher historical stage of development and that this was the beginning of the "new era," as the military called it. Ambitious civil engineering projects such as the Aswan High Dam and the Iron and Steel works at Helwan were symbols of the new era, and social engineering projects like land reform were proof of its certain success. It seemed as if Egypt had finally entered the realm of modernity and had caught up with "the spirit of the times" (*ruh al-'asr*).

Half a century later the euphoria of the modernist experience of the 1950s (and 1960s) has evaporated. What remains is the awesome legacy of one of the largest corporatist states outside the former communist world: an authoritarian regime that impedes democratization, a bureaucracy that drains all initiative, an inefficient public sector that absorbs investments, the continued dominance of the military, and a partly nationalized press. Opposition has shifted to the Islamist movement, which categorically rejects the modernist project of state-led development.

Why did Egypt take the authoritarian road to modernity? After all, such a development was not inevitable. In fact, in many ways it was a major reversal of the trend before 1952, when civil society had been diverse and growing. The gradual loss of the monarchy's legitimacy, the decline in popularity of the largest nationalist party, the Wafd, and the gradual British retreat from empire after World War II had laid the foundations for a modern civil society. As part of this process, the press had gained confidence in its critique of the existing order, trade unions had freed themselves from patronage, and the student movement had obtained its independence from party tutelage. Likewise, professional organizations witnessed an unprecedented growth in influence in these years, while political pluralism rose to new heights with the contest between the Muslim Brotherhood and the communist movement.

This study focuses on the role secular intellectuals and political currents of the 1940s played in the transition from the pluralist political system of the monarchy to the authoritarian regime of the Nasserist era. Central to this book is the question why so many prominent intellectuals joined the new regime in the second half of the 1950s, even though most of them had laid the ideological and institutional foundations for a pluralist civil society in the 1930s and 1940s. It also explores how these intellectuals helped shape the ideology of the reformist regime in the years between 1955 and 1958.

I will argue that the answer to these questions lies in the fact that Egyptian society produced two contradictory political traditions during the British occupation and under the monarchy. On the one hand, there was a strengthening of the emerging modern civil society and its independent institutions; on the other, the country witnessed the lagging, but inexorable growth of the sovereign power of the state. The tension between these two trends is reflected in a strong ambivalence in most reformers, whose ideas oscillated between support for democratic reform in order to enhance civil society on the one hand and a complete rejection of such developments combined with the endorsement of the authoritarian transformation of society by the state on the other hand. That this tension was ultimately resolved in favor of state-led reform must be ascribed to the hold of authoritarian modernism on the thought of the reformists dealt with in this study.

Historiography

This study aims to bridge the gap between two fields of research on Egypt that each try independently to come to grips with the transition from the monarchy to the July Revolution of 1952. The first of these is the field of Egyptian intellectual history of the first half of the 20th century. The historiography of intellectual trends in this period reveals several possible several viewpoints, depending when these works were written. Nadav Safran[1] and Afaf Lutfi al-Sayyid Marsot,[2] writing in the 1960s and 1970s, mostly focused on the early liberal intellectuals and their "betrayal" of the liberal cause by taking up Islamic themes. The secular, liberal "democratic experiment" of 1920s is favorably compared to the 1930s, which is seen as the beginning of a new era, leading inevitably to the military dictatorship of the July Revolution. P.J. Vatikiotis took up the same theme, portraying Young Egypt and the Muslim Brotherhood as the ideological harbingers of dictatorship.[3]

In the 1980s this approach was criticized from a Marxist perspective. Concentrating on the social and economic basis of liberal reformist thought, Marxist historians exposed the interests these intellectuals shared with colonialism. Prominent liberal intellectuals such as Ahmad Lutfi al-Sayyid turned out to have a less than democratic outlook.[4] The Marxist analysis of the radical nationalist movements in the 1930s was more mixed. Focusing on the practical political stand of the Muslim Brotherhood and Young Egypt, historians treated these movements as dictatorial, spreading a strong ethnic Egyptian nationalism or an extreme Islamic nationalism. In contrast, the communist movement was regarded as a modern, "progressive" force capable of reversing the development in favor of the authoritarian, corporatist regime that would succeed the "reactionary" monarchy.[5] These historians claim that "betrayal" of the movement takes place when nationalist intellectuals subordinate the cause of the workers and the international outlook of the movement to the nationalism of the military regime.[6]

In the 1980s and 1990s, Israel Gershoni and James Jankowski re-evaluated Egyptian intellectual history and succeeded in putting it back on the map. Their work is based on in-depth research of the content and discourse of the intellectual writings of the period from 1900 to 1945.[7] The theme running through their work is the changing representation of Egyptian national identity, from Egyptian territorial nationalism or "Pharaonism" in the 1920s to Pan-Arabism in the 1930s and 1940s. They analyze the ideas of the Egyptian intellectuals in their own right – not as the ideological precursors of Nasserism. However, despite the advantage of not having an ideological ax to grind – liberal, Marxist, or otherwise – they disregard the relationship between ideas and power, only addressed it in general terms, as for instance in the case of the rise of the *effendiyya* (the middle classes) in the 1930s and the revolt against the elite.[8] Their concentration on the issue of identity brings them to neglect political thought as such.[9] Another problem with the highly informative and stimulating work of both authors is that they tend to lose sight of the diversity of intellectual thought, with the result that much of the differentiation in ideas between intellectuals is lost.

This study should also be situated in the field of political science and political economy. With the exception of the early years of the 20th century and the foundation of Bank Misr, political scientists and political economists who study Egypt have largely neglected economic and political ideas and ideologies.[10] Only recently, in a Gramscian analysis of hegemony, has more attention been given to the issue of political discourse and power.[11] Most political economists analyze political developments as structural developments or as the result of class forces.[12] The exception, linking discourse to power and politics in the broadest sense, has been the interesting work of Timothy Mitchell.[13] However, Mitchell fails to examine the practical effects of ideas. The efficacy of "modernizing" disciplinary forms of power was undermined by the fact that these disciplinary ideas were adopted by intellectuals who focused on the family and maintained their power through patronage and clientalist relations.[14] Mitchell's work also neglects the ambivalent and contradictory effects of idea systems. Disciplinary systems can be both repressive and emancipatory, depending on the political and social context. In other words, a more traditional system of political control like patronage can be exploitative and repressive, while more disciplinary political forms of organizations like those of the communists and the Muslim Brotherhood can be emancipatory.

I will argue that disciplinary systems become invidious when they are imposed by an authoritarian state, and especially by an authoritarian nation-state. With the exception of the Muhammad Ali period at the beginning of the 19th century, the state's power had been curtailed by the British occupation.[15] It was not until the 1920s that the Egyptian nation-state came into being, acquiring greater political sovereignty and power over the Egyptian population in the 1930s and 1940s and achieving absolute sovereignty in 1956. I will argue that the emergence of civil society resulted from the absence of centralized political control, which was divided between the British, the nationalists, and the khedive, and later the monarchy. Its strength under the monarchy explains why many intellectuals had democratic ideas, could express themselves relatively freely, and create the institutions (i.e. the press and private associations) to support them. Their ambivalence towards democratic procedures came about when state-led reform became a real option with the increase of its sovereign power and when civil society and especially political society were increasingly discredited.

This book should be situated somewhere in between these other trends of research into this period in Egypt. In terms of intellectual ideas, I concentrate on secular liberal, socialist, and communist political thought in the period between 1945 and 1958. In that sense, this is a history of political ideas that is based on a close reading of political tracts, newspapers, and publications of these secular political currents in the period 1945–1958. My purpose is to trace political ideas over this transitional period in more theoretical works and in their adjustment to the more practical day-to-day political changes. This in itself produces some unexpected results. First, it shows that there were many intellectuals who were more interested in politics, social change, and social reform than in the issue of identity and national image, which is assumed by many scholars to be paramount in this period. In a time of intense nationalist struggle for independence, it stands to reason that the issue of identity appears in their work, but their treatment of this issue should be read in the context of "modernization" and the country's development. I have therefore made a distinction between what I call the discourse of identity and the discourse of "modernism." The distinction is not that the first is not modern or that these discourses lack common elements; rather in the first the issue of identity predominates and authenticity is the main issue, while in the second identity is subordinated to political, social, and economic reform and the concept of authenticity is mostly distrusted.

On the question of the role of nationalism as an ideology in this period, therefore, I disagree with Israel Gershoni and James Jankowski. Further, I do not believe that there was a general trend from Egyptian nationalism to Pan-Arabism, which, they argue, became predominant in the 1930s and 1940s. In fact, in the case of the modernist currents discussed here, I have found that Pan-Arabism was of secondary importance. For this reason, this study explores the content of "modernism" and its presence in the works of the reformist movement of the 1940s and 1950s, showing how it led Egyptian intellectuals to support the authoritarian regime.

Second, this study demonstrates that, paradoxically, democratic reform, along with its defense of the 1923 Constitution and the parliamentary system, was not dead in the 1930s. Democratic ideas remained more important in Egyptian politics than is usually assumed.[16] Until the March Crisis of 1954 many intellectuals argued for a democratic road to "modernity." Neo-liberals, socialists, and communists were in favor of the retention of the parliamentary system, although they thought it needed drastic reform. Many of them even pinned their hopes on reforming Egypt by means of a more democratic parliamentary system. Their political ideas were, however, ambivalent, contradictory, and constantly changing. While democratic ideas were in evidence in many of these movements, there was also a strong authoritarian streak. Concentrating on state institutions, these thinkers argued for the strengthening of the state as the main agent for the imposition of reforms from above, without consultation of the population, solely controlled by and on the advice of "experts." I link this simultaneous presence of democratic and authoritarian strains in reformist discourse to the existence of a civil society under the monarchy, on the one hand, and the gradual rise of the sovereign state on the other. The first half of this study investigates the contradiction between these democratic and authoritarian forms of modernism in the works of the different intellectual currents that were prominent between 1945 and 1954. The second half of the study analyzes how and why these currents supported the regime in the 1955 to 1958 and helped formulate an ideology of authoritarian modernism. Many secular intellectuals believed that the quest for modernity was being fulfilled by the new regime and that they could assist in this process as "modernizers."

This approach disagrees with the analysis of the communist movement by Marxist scholars. Although the works of Joel Beinin, Zachary Lockman, and Selma Botman are highly informative, their views of the communist movement are open to questioning. It was not the nationalist but the authoritarian modernist strain in the communist movement, along with its conception of modernity, that accounts for its support of the Nasserist regime in the second half of the 1950s. Finally, this study differs from the work done by political scientists and the economists when it comes to the role of ideas in the explanation of economic and political developments. I argue that economic planning was much more important in the first half of the 1950s than is usually assumed and that it became an ideology in its own right. With regard to the new regime, scholars have completely failed to see that economic planning laid the foundation for technocracy as an ideology. Having become an important ideological strain of the regime during its nadir before 1955, in the three following years, planning grew to become the main, formative element of the ideology of authoritarian modernism that legitimized the regime. As a discourse of power, planning created the image of a "modern," rationalizing regime. It was also the main principle behind the destruction of political society, the containment of civil society, and the regulation of economic society. Many intellectuals helped formulate this ideology of modernization in the so-called Bandung period of the entente between intellectuals and the regime, between 1955 and 1958.

In the next section, I will discuss the theoretical concepts of civil society and modernism, followed by a historical account of civil society and modernism in Egypt between 1882 and 1952. The introduction will end with a brief look at the three secular currents that are at the heart of this study.

Theoretical Background

Civil society and the state

Civil society is usually defined as the public space between the household and the state.[17] In eighteenth-century Europe, debate on civil society was conducted primarily in the public sphere, which was free from state interference. The "birth" of the public sphere is directly linked to the emergence of places where people could discuss politics and culture freely and organize themselves independently from state control or aristocratic patronage. Such liberated space was found at coffeehouses, salons, table societies, schools, publishing houses, inns, and independent households, where public debate was allowed to flourish. As part of this movement, a free press came into being that emancipated itself from patronage and depended for its survival on popular sales. According to the ideal, the result of such a development would be a public opinion yielding moral rules with universal validity. Such rules then lay the basis for laws to which both citizens and the state are subject. Parliament, one of the institutional forms of the expanding public space, should check the "natural" tendency of the state to keep its activities cloaked in secrecy. The concept of the citizen and its legal underpinnings in the form of private property and the rule of law buttress the idea of a civil society free from state capriciousness.

Contemporary debate on civil society has elaborated on the notion of public space by demarcating different fields of activity, divided under the headings of civil, political, and economic society. In a democracy, each of these has its own set of functions in relation to the others and to society as a whole.[18] Civil society is defined as consisting of independent, voluntary or civil associations, ranging from social movements, interest groups, and religious groupings to learned societies, publishing houses, schools, and municipal councils.[19] In the form of trade unions, entrepreneurial groups, and journalist and lawyer syndicates, such associations represent the interests of various professions and social groups. These affiliations should be powerful enough to check the infringement of their rights by the state. Most theorists agree that individuals must be free to choose to which association they belong.[20] Civil society must also offer a solid basis for political values related to "civility." As a precondition for democracy, there must be a general sense of responsibility to society as a whole, along with other values that enhance tolerance and thus ensure the peaceful resolution of political conflicts.[21] Broadly speaking, civil society ensures a set of values that form the ethical foundation of political, cultural, and religious pluralism.[22]

Political society constitutes a separate domain, in which political parties and politicians contest each other over the legitimate right to public power and control over the state apparatus. Political society has its own rules of compromise, routinization, and conflict regulation; it is complementary to civil society because it must have its support to democratize politics. Conversely, the task of political society is to translate, articulate, and represent the political demands of civil society. As such, it acts as an intermediary between the state and civil society.[23] For these reasons, political society, as an independent field of activity, functions at its best in a multi-party system.

Most theorists of civil society see a largely independent economic society as prerequisite to democratic development.[24] To what extent the market must be completely free is debatable. Very few scholars believe that an unregulated economy enhances democracy because economic society must be regulated for the benefit of the general public by political and civil society. The state comprises a set of differentiated, autonomous and public institutions, which are territorially centralized and claim jurisdiction over a given territory, including the monopoly over coercion and extraction. On this model, the state should be regulated by political society. According to John Keane, "it requires the state to govern civil society neither too much nor too little; while a more democratic order cannot be built through the state, it cannot be built without the state power."[25]

Threats to civil society and democracy

From the model described above it is clear that the nature of the relations between the civil, political, and economic societies and the state are crucial. Each field has its own tasks so that the other powers are kept in check and the rule of law is guaranteed. Ideally, when this system is routinized, a consensus arises about the values on which society is based and the way in which conflicts are resolved. When boundaries are crossed, however, the system is under threat. Political society, for instance, can jeopardize the independence of civil society through the totalizing impact of radical political ideologies. When this happens, the public good or the interests of the national community override the interests of separate social groups, which lose their autonomy.[26] The growth of civil society may also be limited by economic society, which can impose the exclusive economic interests of a certain social class at the expense of the rights of the population as a whole. In this sense, the state may become detrimental by infringing the rights of civil society. In its most extreme form, state repression can crush civil society, as happened in the Soviet Union, where the political rights of the citizen were abolished.

Studies of the Middle East and Latin America contribute to the debate on civil society by drawing attention to more personalized forms of politics that may impede its development, such as patronage and populism.[27] Patronage hampers the well-being of civil society by maintaining vertical relations of dependence. Populism has the same effect by appealing directly to the "people" and national harmony, bypassing the intermediary organizations of civil society. Both forms of political control and mobilization undermine the attributes that are essential to the preservation of the autonomy of civil society.[28]

In Egypt, analysis of the relations between the state and civil society began in the mid-1980s with the start of tentative liberalization under Hosni Mubarak. Scholars disagree about the force and character of civil society in Egypt. Some are extremely pessimistic. John Waterbury, for instance, even denies the existence of civil society. He holds the view that the ideological content of politics – its "sacred mission" – and the inclination of the bourgeoisie and the intelligentsia not only to cooperate but also to identify with the state have led to a stifling state corporatism, which, he predicts, will soon disappear.[29] Stressing cultural factors, others regard prevalent forms of patriarchy, or neo-patriarchy, patronage, clientalism, populism, and the concomitant vertical relations of dependency as a major threat to civil society.[30] The more optimistic scholars point to encouraging signs of independent organizations and even see Egypt going through a process of civil-society building and democratization.[31]

Whatever these scholars may think about the current situation and the future prospects for civil society in Egypt, no one has looked to the monarchy as the basis of civil society, let alone to the opportunities it presented for a different path to modernity.[32] Most of the works that do take the liberal features of the monarchy seriously tend to view them as the result of the introduction of Western thought and parliamentarianism, locating their heyday in the 1920s.[33] According to this historiography, this trend was over by the 1930s with the rise of radical ideologies, the degeneration of the Wafd, and the autocratic leanings of the monarchy.

Under British occupation and the monarchy Egypt experienced a modern division of the fields of activity between civil, political, and economic society. The so-called liberal experiment of the 1920s and its intellectual achievements were based on the public space created by this division, which gave civil society room for expansion. The explanation for the failure of democracy to develop fully in the subsequent period must be sought in the absence of a strong, sovereign state to regulate and support it. Therefore, contrary to what is generally thought, I argue that the basic political weakness of the period was not the absence of civil society, even though it did remain elitist and exclusive both in social formation and ideology. More important were the types of relations between civil and political society, which were determined by patronage and dependence. It was against the prevalent political culture and the entire social and economic structure associated with it that the new, "modernist" currents protested. By the time civil society began to liberate itself from this tutelage on an extensive scale in the 1930s and 1940s, political society had been discredited. Most reformers intended to dismantle it completely and replace it with state-led development, an option that became increasingly feasible. The failure of political society to make the transition from monarchist pluralism to a more coherent and homogeneous nation-state in a democratic manner between 1919 and 1952 led to the rise of authoritarian alternatives.

Modernity, modernism, and the role of intellectuals

The political transition from a liberal civil society to an authoritarian state was accompanied by a parallel ideological development. I contend that whereas the acceptance of modernity led to the establishment of a modern state and a modern civil society, its radicalization in the 1930s led to the demise of civil society and the establishment of an authoritarian state in the 1950s. Before we can explain this development and the influence of ideas on it in some detail, we must begin by looking at some of the general characteristics of modernism that are relevant to the Egyptian situation.

I use the term modernism for ideologies belonging to modernity during the period in European history that spans roughly from 1800 to 1950.[34] Modernity is usually associated with industrialization, urbanization, the technological revolution, the rise of a mass society, the development of political ideologies, and the establishment of the nation-state. Modernists are those who accept modernity wholeheartedly, while we may say that romanticists react against modernity and try to contain it. In Egypt, modernism as an ideology belongs to the period between 1800 and 1970. In this period Egyptian intellectuals adopted many of the central tenets of modernism and modernity, including its conceptions of time, place, identity, society, and the nation.

In general modernist political and cultural currents refuse to accept the limitations of time. Rather than accepting the boundaries set by the past, modernity is, in the words of Göran Therborn, "the discovery of the future as an open, unbuilt site never visited before, but a place reachable and constructible."[35] Where space is concerned, modernists view the city as the symbol of modernity. They praise the city as the center of change, applaud the possibilities it offers for social mobility, and welcome the continuous flux of ideas and values that the city stimulates. In contrast, the countryside is seen as traditional, stagnant, and backward. Modernists also are confronted with the issue of identity, which becomes problematic with the erosion of traditional values and concepts of solidarity. The idea that there are no more standard values to live by enables modernists to invent and construct identities.[36] In Egypt, the first generation of "modernist" intellectuals of the period from 1900 to 1930 accepted many of the cultural and political forms of modernism, but it was also deeply conservative in other political and especially social matters. Thus, this generation believed that the notable families constituted the nation and that politics could be managed through patronage and clientalism.

In contrast, the second generation experienced the crisis of modernity, its alienation, and its responsibilities to a far greater degree and looked for more encompassing ideas to create a nation. Central to Egyptian thinkers of the 1930s and the 1940s is the realization that modernity involves the emergence of the view of society as to be created and constructed by the state. While the first generation upheld a more traditional idea of community with its strong sense of the past, place, proximity, solidarity, and the central role of the family, the second generation of modernist thinkers accepted a notion of society that implied their acknowledgment of fragmentation, alienation, and distance.[37] Their approach to society is marked by social constructivism, the idea that society is malleable. This is evident in the modernist emphasis on the social sciences as a means of understanding and managing social flux and movement. It should be no surprise that modernists in general eagerly welcome the possibilities of social engineering.[38] One of the central elements in Egyptian society in the second half of the 1950s was the concept of economic planning. In the modernist currents all these elements are combined in a master-narrative of historical emancipation from political, economic, and cultural backwardness to enlightenment and personal and collective development.

What caused a central contradiction between democratic and authoritarian trends in the ideologies of the second-generation modernist intellectuals was that integration could only take place through recognition of citizens' rights. The second-generation modernists were also aware that only an individual who has emancipated himself from the bonds of tradition can function as a full-blown, patriotic citizen in a modern society and that the relations of patronage associated with paternalism and dependence impair this process of emancipation.[39] According to the modernist ideal, citizens should fully accept their responsibilities in civil society with its modern forms of sociability. On the other hand, the second generation was unaware of the dangers of the authoritarian state, with its threat to civil society and to the gradual strengthening of the rights of the newborn citizen.[40] In a colonial society, the state is the central, integrating force that unifies an increasingly fragmented and pluralized society through education, health services, the army, and culture.[41] Once the state acquires full sovereignty and develops bureaucratic means of control, the scope of intervention is potentially endless, and society becomes an object that the state can manage and transform with a view to perfecting it.[42]

The height of the nation-state in Egypt was reached in the 1950s and 1960s when the ideology of "high modernity" exerted a great deal of influence on the military regime. High modernity, according to James C. Scott, claims to speak about the improvement of the human condition with the authority of scientific knowledge. Thus, it implies a radical break with history and tradition. High modernists believe that all human habits and practices – from the structure of the family and patterns of residence to moral values and forms of production – are inherited and hence not based on scientific reasoning. For that reason, they have to be reexamined and redesigned.[43] Progress is objectified and measured by means of a series of preconceived goals that are largely material and quantifiable. Planning and social and civil engineering in tandem reign supreme. At its most extreme, high modernism banishes and suppresses civil society and all sources of independent resistance against central authority.[44]

High modernism never penetrated the state in Egypt in the 1950s and 1960s to the extent that it did in the Soviet Union. The nationalist strain within it contained its capacity to destroy Egyptian indigenous culture and values. Civil society as it had evolved under the monarchy was too strong to be completely erased, although it became partly incorporated into the state. The Egyptian state did, however, adopt many of its features, and its intellectual supporters upheld some of its basic ideological tenets. The secular reformists of the 1940s were the most whole-hearted supporters of a far-reaching rationalization of society, speaking in name of a superior, objective knowledge with universal validity. The new regime not only put an end to their chief frustration about their inability to realize their reforms, it also adopted an ideology of planning that gave a central role to intellectuals. The result was a classic marriage of knowledge and power.

Civil Society and Political Culture under the British Occupation and the Monarchy

The emergence of modern civil society in Egypt, 1882–1919

To understand the rise of authoritarian modernism we need to look more closely at the context in which it developed. The dilemmas faced by intellectuals in the formulation of their reform programs and their political and ideological solutions to these dilemmas can be explained through the emergence of civil society and the political culture that supported it. Radical modernism in Egypt was formulated specifically in opposition to the system of patronage and patron-client relations that had dominated Egypt for so long.

Several factors contributed to the emergence of civil society in modern Egypt at the height of the colonial era, between 1882 and 1914.[45] First, the rivalry with the French until 1904 limited British power over the Egyptian state, and the Capitulations rights put foreign communities outside the purview of British jurisdiction. Second, the British focused initially only on the building of an efficient administration. They were more interested in restoring financial solvability than in developing the country in a more general sense. Third, the principle of indirect rule made the British dependent on Egyptian large landowners, who controlled the countryside and limited the reach of the state. The notables also restricted the power of the British politically as they proved useful in curtailing the autocratic ambitions of khedive Abbas II (1892–1914), the official ruler of Egypt. The result of this division of power was the creation of a social and political space that allowed for private activities that would otherwise have been crushed by the establishment of a modern autocratic state under the khedives.[46]

The foreign communities, i.e. the Greeks, Armenians, Italians, French, British and the Arabic speaking Lebanese-Syrian Christian immigrants, were the first to establish a cosmopolitan civil society in the form of their own churches, missionary schools, hospitals, orphanages, clubs, councils, and other communal organizations.[47] They were followed by the Egyptian notable class, which laid the basis for what Magda Barakat calls the "bourgeois cultural revolution" of private, *ahli* organizations.[48] In this atmosphere of private initiative, schools, scientific associations, geographical associations, student clubs, literary salons, cafés, and other public spaces were established in order to meet and freely discuss culture, scientific developments, and politics. In the absence of state education, khedival and princely patronage led to the founding of a private university in 1908.[49] To expand their following, political parties set up consumer cooperatives and trade unions.[50] The economic ambitions of the Egyptian entrepreneurial class found expression in the institution of the Egyptian Chamber of Commerce in 1913 and the presentation of the national program of development by the Commission of Commerce and Industry in 1918.[51]

The growth of the press supported this vibrant cultural and political climate. Although freedom of the press was a stated policy of the British, the Capitulations regime would have made it difficult to suppress the nationalist press even if they had wanted to do so. As a result the Egyptian press went through one of its most creative periods in history.[52] A wealth of newspapers were founded, including the neutral *al-Ahram* (1876) and *al-Muqattam* (1889), the Pan-Islamist *al-Mu'ayyad* (1889) and *al-Liwa* (1900), and the scientific weeklies *al-Muqtataf* (1884) and *al-Hilal*, as well as several women's journals.[53] Copts participated freely in the new media through their own newspapers *al-Watan* (1877) and *Misr* (1895).[54] The reading public grew to 200,000 and the founding of the Umma Party, the Nationalist Party, and the Reform Party in 1907 turned public opinion into a force to be reckoned with.[55]

Despite its vibrancy, Egyptian civil society had several flaws that severely undermined its strength. An important weakness was its segmentation along foreign and minority lines. Further, the economy was oriented towards the international market and unprotected against foreign imports by tariffs. In addition, almost all commercial and mortgage banks, utility companies, and commercial firms were in foreign hands. Because of the financial priorities of the British administration, which included investing in infrastructure projects, modern education remained extremely inadequate. On the Egyptian side, wealth was concentrated in the hands of large landowners. As a result, modernization was restricted to the Turkish elite, the Egyptian notables, and the small, rising middle classes. Civil society was also confined to the two major cities of Egypt, Cairo and Alexandria. The overwhelming majority of Egyptian population, the *fallahin*, only experienced modernity in limited ways, as the effects of the world market and in the special form it took in a countryside dominated by the *izba'* estates of the notables. These estates were almost completely outside the power of the state and were run as in a capitalist manner in combination with strong coercive enforcement and debt peonage. The ability of the peasants to organize themselves politically was non-existent, and their resistance to this system expressed itself only in occasional revolts.

Due to this economic, social, and political set-up, political methods of control and mobilization during the colonial era were based on patronage and other forms of personal dependence. Not surprisingly, when the first political parties were founded they relied on higher forces, with the khedive patronizing the more radical Mustafa Kamil (1878–1908) and his Watani Party, while the British encouraged the moderate and pro-British Umma Party.

The elitist and paternalistic politics of the time are reflected in the political writings of Ahmad Lutfi al-Sayyid (1878–1963), leader of the Umma Party and admirer of John Stuart Mill. Lutfi al-Sayyid is generally known for his pioneering work in creating a secular Egyptian national identity and rejecting pan-Islam as a political doctrine.[56] Equally important is the fact that he contributed to the separation of the public and private spheres and the limitations imposed on the powers of the ruler. Less known are his political ideas concerning public participation in politics and the restriction of the public sphere. His conservative political attitude was reflected in a deep distrust of "public opinion" (*al-ra'y al-'amm*), which he believed to be dominated by "common people" (*al-'amma*). In his eyes, the common people were ignorant, childish, and led by prejudice and emotion, which stimulated "religious fanaticism" (*al-ta'assub al-dini*).[57] His conclusions were clear: given the irresponsibility of the common people the rule of the country should remain in the hands of the "opinion makers" (*ahl al-ra'y*), whom he defined as large landowners or more generally as "those who have a real stake in society" (*ashab al-masalih al-haqiqiyya*).[58] The notable "families" (*a'ilat*), not the public at large, formed the Egyptian nation, and only they were entitled to citizens' rights.[59]

In contrast, the more populist Watani Party, which upheld pan-Islamist ideas and was supported by the middle classes, put much more store in public opinion. Mustafa Kamil freed himself towards the end of his short life from the patronage of the Khedive Abbas by depending directly on the mobilization of public opinion for the struggle for independence.[60] Mustafa Kamil and the watanists were also active in establishing schools for workers and the elderly as well as hospitals and clinics for broader sectors of society.

Civil society and the political culture of patronage, 1919–1936

Civil society expanded in the period between the Revolution of 1919 and the signing of the Anglo-Egyptian Treaty in 1936. As had been true in the pre-war period, the political division of authority and power between the British, the King, and the nationalist movement allowed civil society to grow. While the British officially divulged their sovereignty over internal affairs in the Unilateral Declaration of Independence, the power gained by Egyptian political society was diluted by the split between the King and the Wafd.[61] Although this situation was conducive to the development of a civil society and political and cultural pluralism, it proved disastrous to political society as well as to the reforms necessary for the formation of a full-fledged nation-state.

The relatively liberal atmosphere of the 1920s allowed for a further increase of private initiative. Under the protection of the 1923 Constitution, a multi-party system was installed and free elections were held. Likewise, the emerging Egyptian economic society seized new opportunities for independent development. Bank Misr was founded in 1920, the Egyptian Federation of Industries in 1922, and provincial Chambers of Commerce flourished in the following years. Towering bankers and industrialists such as Tal'at Harb,[62] Ahmad Abbud,[63] Amin Yahya, and Isma'il Sidqi[64] symbolized the self-confidence of the Egyptian entrepreneurial class. The Agricultural Syndicate was established in this period, and the Cooperative Laws of 1923 and 1927 stimulated the growth of cooperative, with the result that there were no fewer than 538 cooperatives in 1931.[65] In the meantime welfare organizations emerged, and especially Islamic welfare organizations proliferated, laying the basis for the Muslim Brotherhood. The Young Men's Muslim Association (YMMA) was one of the most important associations of the period.[66] The period also saw the advance of the working class and the establishment of numerous trade unions and related associations.[67]

Vital to civil society was the rise of a new generation of Egyptian intellectuals who supported the new institutions. Taha Husayn (1889–1973), Ahmad Amin (1886–1954), Muhammad Husayn Haykal (1888–1956), Salama Musa (1887–1958) Abd al-Qadir Hamza (1880–1973), Isma'il Mazhar (1891–1962), Abbas Mahmud al-'Aqqad (1889–1964) were founders and members of associations, contributed to journals, and participated in the theater and other forms of cultural life in this period. Their lively debates on political, cultural, and economic issues contributed to the expansion of the public sphere.[68] The 1920s and 1930s were also the heyday of the political press. In the elation of the Revolution of 1919, this generation created a new national image that was based entirely on Egypt and the Egyptian personality (*al-shakhsiyya al-Misriyya*).[69]

All the same, political fragmentation and short-lived cabinets made it extremely difficult to develop stable political institutions. Politics under the monarchy remained largely based either on patronage and the building of personal clientelism, or on the alternative of populism – as in the case of the Wafd. The palace in particular compensated for its weak following by creating a clientele through the distribution of largess and patronage. The fact that it regarded Egypt as its personal preserve enhanced its proprietary attitude. It found limitless scope for patronage through its constitutional right to making political and administrative and military appointments. Especially adept at this art was Ali Mahir, who succeeded, as the Head of the Royal Diwan and despite the fact that he was himself a reformer, temporarily in creating a clientele in the army in the 1930s.[70] Institutions that were directly under royal control proved even more pliant. The Azhar, for instance, was mobilized at crucial moments to combat the King's opponents, as happened during the campaigns in 1925 and 1926 against the liberal publications of Ali Abd al-Raziq and Taha Husayn. Likewise, the minority parties that were too weak to combat the Wafd on their own were drawn into the orbit of the monarchy's patronage system. For these parties, patronage was their lifeblood as they themselves amounted to little more than alliances of notable families that used their family networks to mobilize their dependent clients on their estates for elections.[71] In this political culture, the party system was regarded as a means not to carry out a political program and pursue abstract goals but to distribute favors in return for support.[72]

Even the Wafd did not make a great difference in this respect. Although on the whole it had a better reputation as a democratic movement, its effect on the discipline of the population was negligible and its education in liberal politics weak. Its followers were not subject to official party orthodoxy, while its organization lacked both a formal membership and a system of subscriptions. Moreover, an internal democratic structure was almost non-existent. The leadership and the Central Committee made all the decisions and co-opted its new members.[73] Despite the willingness of the Wafd to cater to the demands of the rising new forces, such as the student movement and the trade unions, the party rarely fulfilled its promises and tried to keep patron-client relationships intact.[74] The relations with the trade unions were mostly maintained in order to mobilize their members during elections.[75]

No less consequential to Egyptian political culture were the close relations between political society and economic society. A good example is the way in which large landowners and the textile industry seized the newly acquired tariff autonomy of 1930 to defend their interests behind a high tariff wall. A typical alliance between the agrarian and industrial wings of the ruling elite – a so-called marriage between "cotton and textiles" – was the result.[76] The tremendous power of the landed interests was reflected in the huge sums of public funds that were spent on the protection of large landowners who were in danger of losing their land to foreign mortgage companies.[77] They exerted their influence in parliament to block any plans for land reform. The numbers reflect the extent of social inequality at this time: the largest landowners with over 200 *faddan* (0.42 hectares) were limited to 2000 families; 12,000 families owned 35 percent of the land, while 2.5 million families held five *faddan* or less. In the meantime the land-less class had risen to 1,600,000 million. The expansion of the onerous estate system (*izba*), which gave large landowners almost absolute power over their tenants, continued until 1952.[78] Fear, debt, the *kurbaj* (whip made of Hippopotamus hide), and servility kept the peasant in his place. Due to these economic practices and the economic crisis of the 1930s, the standard of living overall declined by 10 percent between 1914 and 1940.

Elitist and populist political discourse

The power relations of Egyptian political society are obvious in the political discourse of the times. The Wafd was the most vocal political movement. Claiming to express the will of the nation, it made absolutist and exclusive claims to political power.[79] During the period 1925–29, the Wafd even denounced "party politics" (*al-hizbiyya*) as divisive and a hindrance to the unity needed to achieve independence.[80] Through its radical populism, evident in its claim to represent the "lower classes" (*tabaqat al-ruʻaʻ*), the Wafd tried to discredit the Party of the Liberal Constitutionalists.[81]

By contrast, the Liberal Constitutionalists cultivated a strong elitist and paternalistic stand, much of which it had inherited from the Umma Party of Ahmad Lutfi al-Sayyid. Characteristic for this party was the political thought of Muhammad Husayn Haykal, one of its intellectual leaders and editor of its newspaper, *al-Siyasa*. He combined the liberal, Westernized elitism of the Umma Party with its conservative idealization of the familiarity and solidarity of traditional village life and the self-evident authoritarian rule of the notable families. As a member of the cultural elite, he claimed that the superior individual embodied in the *littérateur* should lead Egypt in its emancipation from tradition and antiquated modes of thought.[82] Like Ahmad Lutfi al-Sayyid, he condemned democracy and expressed his disdain for public opinion. He saw rationality and order as concomitant with the rule of the landed classes, whereas revolution and "chaos" (*fawda*) were associated with the Wafd. This elitist attitude can be seen in the idea that direct elections are dangerous and that two-stage electoral procedures "would give the country true representation through differences of opinion and principles."[83] To justify the supremacy of the notable class, he adhered to Social Darwinism. The same elitism is apparent in the political writings of another intellectual leader of the times, Ahmad Amin (1886–1954), who, like Haykal, believed that one of the major tasks of political leaders was to mold public opinion rather than to follow it.[84]

Similar ideas were to be found among spokesmen of economic society. Isma'il Sidqi (1875–1950) expressed its views when he introduced his new autocratic constitution in October 1930 in a letter addressed to the King. In his address he criticized the Constitution of 1923 for not guaranteeing peace and tranquillity and not allowing the country to "direct the nation's affairs successfully through those most qualified for such a task." He called the Wafd an "autocratic party" that exploited the sympathies of the masses and deflected Egypt from the true path of progress. Furthermore, he claimed that the Wafd was incapable of solving the country's problems and developing its resources. In addition to limiting the membership of parliament to the elite through a restrictive electoral law, he proposed to censure the press because it had corrupted the country's morals and impaired its unity.[85]

Not all intellectuals of this period were as politically elitist and socially conservative. Salama Musa[86] and Taha Husyan,[87] for instance, were modernists *par excellence*. This did not mean that they were democrats. Indeed, like Husayn Haykal, Salama Musa thought that the masses were irrational and needed guidance by an elite to prevent them from exploding in a "barbarous" frenzy, as had happened during the Revolution of 1919 and in the Bolshevik revolution.[88] However, in contrast to Haykal, Salama Musa did accept and even called for social change, which would be steered by the new professional elite of the middle classes. Musa was also an enthusiastic supporter of industrialization and mass culture. He viewed cities as centers of renewal and change and industrialization as the harbinger of science, rationality, new technologies, the rise of new classes, and the annihilation of old forms of thought and organization.[89]

Civil Society, the State, and New Modernist Trends

Emancipation from patronage

The 1930s marked a major change in Egypt's political culture and ideology and opened up the way for the reformist ideas of the intellectuals of the 1940s. This period witnessed the beginnings of resistance to the elite's inability to establish a nation-state that was politically independent, socially integrated, culturally homogeneous, and economically beneficial for Egyptians. These years saw the end of the so-called "liberal experiment" and the rise of the Egyptian citizen who demanded his rights from a deficient, occupied, and divided state.

Emancipation from elite society and the call for reform took two forms. On the one hand, a current emerged that revolted against the existing elitist and Westernized system by adopting a radical nationalist or Islamist terminology of anti-Westernism. Though modernist, this current is in many ways comparable to the revolt of Romanticism against the rationalization of the Enlightenment and therefore should be designated as reactionary modernism.[90] This way of thinking was represented by Young Egypt (1930) and the Muslim Brotherhood (1928). These organizations formulated their protests in a discourse of cultural authenticity and identity and emancipated themselves fully from the politics of patronage at the end of the 1930s, when they became political movements. During the Fifth Conference in 1939, the Muslim Brotherhood expressly stipulated, "the avoidance of the hegemony of notables and elders" (*al-buʿd ʿan haymanat al-aʿyan wa al-kubaraʾ*) should be one of the Muslim Brotherhood's five fundamental characteristics.[91]

On the other hand, a current appeared that adopted a program based on clear-cut political and social reform, couched in a secular discourse of emancipation and rationalization. The liberal reformist, socialist, and communist movements that took on the secular discourse of radical modernism aimed to deepen and expand the "liberal experiment." They must be regarded as a direct continuation of the Enlightenment project with all the contradictions this project entailed. Their immediate precursor was Salama Musa and the *Majalla al-Jadida* group. However, whether the demands of these two new modernist currents (whether modernist or reactionary modernist) were based on civil rights, religious values, or on a more radical nationalist identity, they argued for a more inclusive and broader concept of the nation than had prevailed before. Both currents demanded a social and political contract between state and citizen and advocated thorough reform of the prevailing relations between civil, political, and economic society.

Socially the challenge to the elite of the *ancien régime* was led by the rising middle class, the so-called *effendiyya*. Dressed in European style, they were newly educated students, civil servants, teachers, and clerks.[92] The power of this social group derived from its growing numbers and its increasing influence over certain sections of society. Their basis lay in the new possibilities provided through a modern education from the second half of the 1920s on. The doubling of the numbers of doctors, lawyers, and engineers between 1927 and 1947 was reflected in the founding of syndicates of medicine, journalism, and engineering in the period.[93] The reading public involved in the formation of public opinion increased dramatically as well. Daily newspaper circulation grew from 180,000 in 1928–29 to 500,000 in the second half of the 1940s.[94] Israel Gershoni and James Jankowski have computed that the number of "writers and journalists" grew from 1,200 to 8,200 in the period between 1937 and 1947.[95]

Civil society was further enhanced by the rise of the working class and the emergence of an independent trade union movement after the fall of the Wafd government in 1937.[96] Growing self-reliance and self-consciousness were expressed in a struggle for greater independence from interference by non-labor organizations.[97] The first independent labor newspaper *Shubra* was published in 1942, the same year trade unions were legalized. In 1944 workers of the Cairene neighborhood Shubra entered the political arena during general elections for the first time by putting forward their own candidate.[98] The student and worker demonstrations against the government in 1945–46 should be regarded as a direct continuation of the student demonstrations in 1935, which forced the government to form a coalition and reinstate the Constitution of 1923.[99]

The increasing resistance to patronage espoused by the two ideological currents of the 1930s and 1940s enhanced the pluralist and independent character of civil society during the second half of monarchical rule. Their organizational strength, internal discipline, and efficient means of mobilizing their own resources undermined the hold that traditional political society had on them. While their ability to start their own press furthered their independent character, their middle-class and worker background promoted the diversity of civil society. Finally, the ideological homogeneity propagated by both movements would give rise to the uniformity and cohesion necessary for the establishment of the nation-state.

Factors undermining civil society, 1936–1952

At the same time, it is clear that the greater pluralism and independence of civil society was not sufficient in itself for the establishment of a democratic society. In fact, it led to more internal strife, undermined the monarchy, and made the institutionalization of civil virtues difficult. Several factors explain this outcome. Without the legal channels to express themselves, influence, transform, and eventually take over political society, leading representatives of civil society were unable to push for necessary reforms. Once the new movements became independent, they posed a threat to the status quo, and a clash became inevitable. The student and worker movement of 1945–46, the suppression of the Muslim Brotherhood in 1948, the unilateral abrogation of the 1936 Anglo-Egyptian Treaty in 1951, and the subsequent guerrilla struggle along the Suez Canal were signs of the monarchy's inability to control and integrate the new forces of political, social, and cultural-ideological emancipation.

The cohesion and the strength of the new organizations of civil society were further weakened on account of the split into two completely opposed discourses of reform and projects of national unity and emancipation. Although it is by now clear that the discourse of cultural identity, as expressed in a dichotomy between East and West, or "Easternism," does not necessarily exclude a democratic stance, it did not actively support democracy either.[100] The discourse of authenticity is not renowned for proposals to strengthen the 1923 Constitution. Instead it rejected parliamentarianism as "partisanship" (*hizbiyya*) leading to internal division and sought solutions in the creation of the nation through cultural unity, moral rectitude, obedience, and self-sacrifice.[101] Politics was regarded as a moral problem rather than a practical one.

The secular movements in general rejected extreme forms of the politics of identity as irrational. While liberals regarded the discourse of authenticity as a diversion from more important concerns such as political reform, democratization, and unification of the country, Marxists equated it with instilling a false consciousness in the workers and the middle class, while socialists evaluated it as irrelevant and a distraction from real issues. To the secular political mind, extreme identity politics were "reactionary," a misconceived attempt to turn the clock back to the Middle Ages. That the issue of identity, especially in its religious form, was not "scientific" made it suspect.

In the meantime, the state was able to harness its sovereignty in the 1930s and 1940s. The Anglo-Egyptian Treaty of 1936 and especially the Conference of Montreux a year later meant that the Egyptian state had secured full sovereignty over foreign residents. Their privileged position was terminated, and for the first time they became subject to Egyptian laws and taxation. In 1938 further steps were taken to Egyptianize society, when private schools became subject to control of and inspection by the Ministry of Public Education. In the field of economics, similar measures were promulgated in 1942–43 when Arabic was declared the official language of all written business communications and in 1947 when Law No. 132 restricted the power of foreign capital.[102] The growing power of the state was also reflected in the means used to impose new regulations. An important step in this regard was the foundation of the Ministry of Social Affairs in 1939. The Ministry was designed to correct the social crisis and alleviate poverty, while at the same time it was assigned the task to control civil society. The first laws regulating voluntary organizations and the co-operative movement were promulgated in 1945.

Contrary to expectations, the elite failed to profit from the expansion of the state's sovereignty. What undermined the use of the enhanced administrative force over the citizens was the political elite's loss of legitimacy, a development that became increasingly significant, as the new social classes that had gained power demanded a new state-citizen relationship. The regime's position was seriously undermined by the February 1942 incident, which fatally damaged the position of the King and the Wafd, the lost war with Israel in 1948, and the inability to achieve full independence from the British and instate social justice. The regime finally lost the support of the army and thereby the capacity to repress the oppositional civil society. The complete political impasse between the Fire of Cairo in January 1952 and the July Revolution of 26 July showed that neither the state, through traditional political society, nor the new civil society were capable of breaking the deadlock. In the subsequent period, with the establishment of the independent state, the reformist intellectuals could finally begin to realize their modernist program.

New reformist currents

This study focuses on three secular political currents and their representatives, whose ideological changes can be followed continuously over the period between 1945 and 1958: the liberal Society of National Renaissance, the socialist Rashid al-Barrawi, and the communist movement. The study is divided into two parts. In part one I have concentrated on the more theoretical and broader aspects of the ideas of these political currents as they developed in the period between 1945 and 1950. The Society of National Renaissance will be examined in chapter one. This group of liberal intellectuals sprang up as an informal association of friends in 1936, was officially founded after World War II, and became one of the most important liberal think tanks of the era until it was dissolved in 1949, although its members played an important role during the entire transitional period. The liberal reform program of the Society of National Renaissance is remarkable for its completeness and extensiveness as well as for the internal tensions between its emancipatory and repressive elements. In contrast to its reform of the parliamentary system, which was meant to buttress civil society, its writings on social reform reinforced the power of the state and its means of surveillance and control. The two conflicting tendencies within the Society laid the basis for the divergence of the political stands of its members after the new regime took power. While some of them joined the July Revolution at an early stage, others remained opposed to it and played a prominent part in the opposition during the March Crisis of 1954.

Rashid al-Barrawi, who has been selected as the representative of the socialist current, will be discussed in chapter two. His work shows a strong etatist-reformist strain of "administrative socialism" derived from the British Labour Party. It contains a deep mistrust of civil society and a firm belief in the state as the embodiment of rationality. This trend is underlined by his historical interpretation of the middle classes as the vanguard of history. Although Rashid al-Barrawi's work also displays a certain tension between democratic and state-led reform, many tendencies in his work foreshadow his later support for the regime and make clear why he joined the new regime at an early stage. After the military takeover, he became the spokesman of the Permanent Council for the Development of National Production (PCDNP) and director of the Industrial Bank, both institutions of the "new era." In these capacities, he was at the forefront of state building and played an important role in paving the way administratively and ideologically for the state to become a dominant player before 1955.

Chapter three analyzes the communist movement and the ideological tensions in the communists' more theoretical work. Comparatively, the communist movement may have had more difficulty resolving the dilemma between reform form above and below than the other reformists. To a far greater extent than the liberals or the socialist al-Barrawi, the communist movement supported civil society in practice through its ties with the independent trade union movement. The tactic of the national front meant that it regarded parliamentary democracy as a means by which the workers movement could emancipate itself and lead Egypt to independence. And yet, in stark contrast to its defense of civil society, the communists supported the new regime after Bandung conference and the Suez Canal crisis. This dualism should largely be ascribed to the modernist strain in communism and its support of state-led development. Once it had accepted the regime as a modernizing agency, the communist movement had a vast ideological repertoire at its disposal to justify state intervention in the economy and abolish the multi-party system.

Part two of the study deals less with theoretical issues and focuses more on the attitudes these thinkers adopted towards the new regime that came to power in July 1952. Chapter four concentrates on the transitional period between 1950 and 1954, which began with the Wafd's electoral victory and ended with the March Crisis. In my discussion of this period I analyze the vagaries of the liberal current not only by discussing the Society of National Renaissance, but also by following the politics of the daily newspaper *al-Misri* and the weekly *Ruz al-Yusuf*. A comparison of these two publications further highlights the dilemma and the different fates of the liberals. Encouraging democratic reform until the March Crisis itself, liberals were constantly adjusting their ideas to the circumstances, and even briefly called for a dictatorship to carry out reforms leading to democracy. In this chapter I also look at Rashid al-Barrawi's legitimization of the new regime in authoritarian modernist terms. Finally, the chapter considers the attitude of the communist movement towards the regime.

In chapters five and six, which should be read together, I assess the contribution the reformist intellectuals made to the formulation of authoritarian modernism in the three year period between 1955 and 1958. Chapter five concentrates mostly on the gradual move towards support for the new regime and the reaction of the intellectuals to Egypt's foreign policy successes after 1955. However, I will argue in the first part of the chapter that the main reason for their support was the new regime's modernization program and its "rationalization" of Egyptian society — projects that were under way from 1952 onwards. Only in the second half of the 1950s did younger generation of reformist Egyptian intellectuals have the feeling that Egypt was entering into a stage of modernity. One of the primary reasons for this belief was that the regime had adopted an ideology of planning and control over society that seemed to supplant the corruption, chaos, and irrationality of civil society under the monarchy. To what extent this conviction was correct remains largely immaterial. From the available evidence it is clear that Egyptians were enthusiastic about planning and that planning as an ideology has obvious links with the defeat of the pluralist forces during the March Crisis in 1954. How economic planning was institutionalized and spread as the ideology of the new technocracy will be illustrated through the career and writings of Rashid al-Barrawi.

Chapter six analyzes the final establishment of the hegemony of authoritarian modernism. I demonstrate its force through the pervasive influence of planning in the form of the concept of "guided democracy"; the purposeful creation of a collective national image; the emergence of the intellectual as "modernizer"; the totalizing character of Marxist historiography in creating a master-narrative of development and modernization; an example of the positivist character of philosophy in support of modernization; and, finally, the "discovery" of the rest of the developing world by Egyptian intellectuals as represented in travel literature. The Soviet Union and China were upheld in this literature as models of emulation on account of their "rational" character. I will demonstrate that contrary to most interpretations of the 1950s, which regard the period as marked by an ideological vacuum, it had its own distinctive ideology. The prevalent ideology of the second half of the 1950s was based on an authoritarian version of modernization theory, in which the state played the role of modernizer with the reformist intellectuals at the helm. The unlimited optimism of the 1950s found its clearest expression in authoritarian modernism.

Notes

1. Nadav Safran, *Egypt in Search of Political Community: An Analysis of the Intellectual and Political Evolution of Egypt, 1804–1952* (Cambridge, Mass.: Harvard University Press, 1961).
2. Afaf Lutfi al-Sayyid Marsot, *Egypt's Liberal Experiment: 1922–1936* (Berkeley: University of California Press, 1977).
3. P.J. Vatikiotis, *The History of Egypt: From Muhammad Ali to Sadat* (London: Weidenfeld and Nicolson, 1969) and *Nasser and His Generation* (London: Croom Helm, 1978).
4. Walid Kazziha, "The Jaridah-Umma Group and Egyptian Politics," *Middle Eastern Studies* 13 (1977), 373–85.
5. Joel Beinin and Zackary Lockman, *Workers on the Nile: Nationalism, Communism, Islam and the Egyptian Working Class, 1882–1954* (London: I.B. Tauris, 1988); Selma Botman, *The Rise of Egyptian Communism, 1939–1970* (Syracuse: Syracuse University Press, 1988); Selma Botman, "Egyptian Communists and the Free Officers: 1950–54," *Middle Eastern Studies* 22 (1986), 350–66.
6. Joel Beinin, "The Communist Movement and Nationalist Political Discourse in Nasirist Egypt," *The Middle East Journal* 41 (1987): 568–84, and his *Was the Red Flag Flying There? Marxist Politics and the Arab-Israeli Conflict in Egypt and Israel, 1948–1965* (London: I.B. Tauris, 1990).
7. See especially Israel Gershoni and James Jankowski, *Egypt, Islam and the Arabs: The Search for Egyptian Nationhood, 1900–1930* (Oxford: Oxford University Press, 1986) and *Redefining the Egyptian Nation, 1930–1945* (Cambridge: Cambridge University Press, 1995).
8. See for instance the introduction to *Redefining the Egyptian Nation*, 1–31.
9. This criticism does not apply to James Jankowksi's first book, *Egypt's Young Rebels "Young Egypt": 1933–1952* (Stanford: Hoover Institution Press, 1975) and Israel Gershoni's recent article, "Egyptian Liberalism in an Age of 'Crisis of Orientation': al-Risala's Reaction to Fascism and Nazism, 1933–39," *International Journal of Middle East Studies* 31 (1999), 551–76.
10. See for instance Eric Davis, *Challenging Colonialism: Bank Misr and Egyptian Industrialization, 1920–1941* (Princeton: Princeton University Press, 1983).

INTRODUCTION

11 Kirk Beattie, *Egypt during the Nasser Years: Ideology, Politics and Civil Society* (Boulder: Westview Press, 1994).
12 The most conspicuous example is John Waterbury, *The Egypt of Nasser and Sadat: The Political Economy of Two Regimes* (Princeton: Princeton University Press, 1983).
13 Timothy Mitchell, *Colonising Egypt* (Cambridge: Cambridge University Press, 1988).
14 See for instance the analysis of the ideas of liberal Egyptian intellectuals at the turn of the century by Walid Kazziha, and Charles Wendell, *The Evolution of the Egyptian National Image: From Its Origins to Ahmad Lutfi al-Sayyid* (Berkeley: University of California Press, 1972).
15 For the disciplinary system implemented in the army under Mehmed Ali, see Khalid Fahmy, *All the Pasha's Men: Mehmed Ali, His Army and the Making of Modern Egypt* (Cambridge: Cambridge University Press, 1997). For an extensive analysis of patronage and clientalism in mid-century Egypt, see Ehud Toledano, *State and Society in Mid-Century Egypt* (Cambridge: Cambridge University Press, 1990), 94–107.
16 This study also differs from the excellent work by Joel Gordon, *Nasser's Blessed Movement: Egypt's Free Officers and the July Revolution* (Oxford: Oxford University Press, 1992), which analyzes the period between 1952 and 1954 as a power struggle.
17 I have based this general section on civil society mainly on the anthologies edited by Michael Walzer, *Toward a Global Civil Society* (Providence: Berghahn Books, 1995) and John Hall, *Civil Society: Theory, History, Comparison* (Cambridge: Polity Press, 1995), as well as on general works such as John Keane, *Democracy and Civil Society: On the Predicaments of European Socialism, the Prospects for Democracy, and the Problem of Controlling Social and Political Power* (London: Verso, 1988) and Edward Shils, *The Virtue of Civility: Selected Essays on Liberalism, Tradition, and Civil Society*, edited by Steven Grosby (Indianapolis: Liberty Fund, 1997). For a useful historical overview of the concept of civil society see John Ehrenberg, *Civil Society: The Critical History of an Idea* (New York: New York University Press, 1999). For a stimulating historical-philosophical analysis see Jürgen Habermas, *The Structural Transformation of the Public Sphere: An Inquiry into a Category of Bourgeois Society*, translated by Thomas Burger (Cambridge: Polity Press, 1989).
18 I have adopted the distinction between civil, political, and economic society in particular from Juan J. Linz and Alfred Stepan, *Problems of Democratic Transition and Consolidation: Southern Europe, South America, and Post-Communist Europe* (Baltimore: The John Hopkins University Press, 1996), 7–15.
19 Keane, 14–15.
20 Víctor Pérez-Díaz, "The Possibility of Civil Society: Traditions, Character and Challenges," in Hall, 98.
21 Shils, 63–102.
22 Christopher G. A. Bryant, "Civic Nation, Civil Society, Civil Religion," in Hall, 143; and Shils, 63–102.
23 Linz, 9–10.
24 Michael Walzer, "The Concept of Civil Society," in Walzer, *Civil Society*, 12–13.
25 Keane, 23.
26 Adam B. Seligman, "Animadversions upon Civil Society and Civic Virtue in the Last Decade of the Twentieth Century," in Hall, 204–6 and 209; Walzer, 14–15.

27 See, for instance, Nicos Mouzelis, "Modernity, Late Development and Civil Society," in Hall, 224–50; Hisham Sharabi, *Neopatriarchy: A Theory of Distorted Change in Arab Society* (Oxford: Oxford University Press, 1988).
28 Pérez-Díaz, 84.
29 John Waterbury, "Democracy without Democrats?: The Potential for Political Liberalization in the Middle East," in *Democracy without Democrats? The Renewal of Politics in the Muslim World*, edited by Ghassan Salamé (London: I.B. Tauris, 1994), 23–47.
30 For a recent debate on the topic: Michael C. Hudson, "The Political Culture Approach to Arab Democratization: The Case for Bringing It Back in, Carefully," in *Political Liberalization and Democratization in the Arab World, Vol. 1: Theoretical Perspectives*, edited by Rex Brynen, Bahgat Korany, and Paul Noble (Boulder: Lynne Rienner, 1995), 61–76, and, in the same volume, Lisa Anderson, "Democracy in the Arab World: A Critique of the Political Approach," 77–92. See for the most extensive research on informal political ties, Robert Springborg, "Sayed Bey Marei and Political Clientalism in Egypt," *Comparative Political Studies* 42.3 (1979): 259–88 and Robert Springborg, "Patterns of Association in the Egyptian Political Elite," in *Political Elites in the Middle East*, edited by G. Lenzsowski (Washington DC: American Enterprise Institute, 1975), 83–108. Also, Clement Henry Moore, "Authoritarian Politics in Unincorporated Society," *Comparative Politics* 6.2 (1974): 193–218.
31 The most optimistic analyses of the prospects of civil society have been presented in two volumes edited by Augustus Richard Norton entitled *Civil Society in the Middle East* (Leiden: E.J. Brill, 1995). See the contributions in Volume One by Saad Eddin Ibrahim, "Civil Society and the Prospects for Democratization in the Arab World," 27–54 and Mustapha Kamel al-Sayyid, "A Civil Society in Egypt?," 269–94. Robert Bianchi, *Unruly Corporatism: Associational Life in Twentieth-Century Egypt* (Oxford: Oxford University Press, 1989) does pay attention to civil society, but regards it as having been incorporated by the state at an early stage. Lately the phenomenon has been given more attention, and the pluralist character of the monarchy has been recognized. See Magda Barakat, *The Egyptian Upper Class between Revolutions, 1919–1952* (Reading: Ithaca Press, 1998), who describes the rise of the civil society of the upper class; Brynjar Lia points to the proliferation of Islamic civil institutions in the interwar period in *The Society of the Muslim Brothers in Egypt: The Rise of an Islamic Mass Movement, 1928–1942* (Reading: Ithaca Press, 1998). See also Robert Vitalis, *When Capitalists Collide: Business Conflict and the End of Empire in Egypt* (Berkeley: University of California Press, 1995). Vitalis gives a diversified picture of Egyptian business circles at the time.
32 Mustafa Kamil al-Sayyid, *al-Mujtama wa al-siyasa fi Misr. Dawr jama'at al-masalih fi al-nizam al-siyasi al-Misri, 1952–1981* (Cairo: Dar al-Mustaqbal al-'Arabi, 1983) completely neglects the monarchy. The same applies to Moheb Zaki, *Civil Society & Democratization in Egypt, 1981–1994*. Cairo: Konrad Adenauer Stiftung and The Ibn Khaldun Center, 1995.
33 For the classic historical analysis of liberalism and its prospects during the monarchy see Marsot and Vatikiotis.
34 This period is usually described as modernity in the postmodern debate. For informative publications on this topic see, for instance, Bryan S. Turner, ed., *Theories of Modernity and Postmodernity* (London: Sage Publications, 1990); Mike

Featherstone, Scott Lash, and Roland Robertson, eds., *Global Modernities* (London: Sage Publications, 1995); Marshall Berman, *All That Is Solid Melts into Air: The Experience of Modernity*, 6th ed. (London: Verso, 1991); David Harvey, *The Condition of Postmodernity*, 3rd ed. (Cambridge: Blackwell, 1990); Jan Nederveen Pieterse, *Empire and Emancipation: Power and Liberation on a World Scale* (London: Pluto Press, 1990), Gerard Delanty, *Social Theory in a Changing World: Conceptions of Modernity* (Cambridge: Polity Press, 1999); Gerard Delanty, *Modernity and Postmodernity: Knowledge, Power and the Self* (London: Sage Publications, 2000), and Zygmunt Bauman, *Legislators and Interpreters: On Modernity, Post-Modernity and Intellectuals* (Cambridge: Polity Press, 1987).
35 Göran Therborn, "Routes to/through Modernity," in Featherstone, 126.
36 David McCrone, *The Sociology of Nationalism: Tomorrow's Ancestors* (London: Routledge, 1998), 33.
37 Delanty, *Modernity*, 116.
38 Delanty, *Social Theory*, 11.
39 Therborn, 130–31.
40 Nederveen Pieterse, 6.
41 McCrone, 52.
42 James C. Scott, *Seeing Like a State: How Certain Schemes to Improve the Human Condition Have Failed* (New Haven: Yale University Press, 1998), 92.
43 Scott, 93.
44 Scott, 101–2.
45 For a similar argument see Barakat, 63.
46 Guilain Denoeux, *Urban Unrest in the Middle East: A Comparative Study of Informal Networks in Egypt, Iran and Lebanon* (Albany: State University of New York Press, 1993), 63–70.
47 See Gudrun Krämer, *The Jews in Modern Egypt, 1914–1952* (London: I.B. Tauris, 1989), 68–115, and Alexander Kitroeff, *The Greeks in Egypt, 1919–1937: Ethnicity and Class* (Oxford: Ithaca Press, 1989).
48 Barakat, 62–71.
49 Donald M. Reid, *Cairo University and the Making of Modern Egypt* (Cambridge: Cambridge University Press, 1990), 28–30.
50 B. L. Carter, *The Copts in Egyptian Politics* (London: Croom Helm, 1986), 48–50.
51 Rober T. Tignor, *State, Private Enterprise and Economic Change in Egypt, 1918–1952* (Princeton: Princeton University Press, 1984).
52 Abbas Kelidar, "The Political Press in Egypt, 1882–1914," in *Contemporary Egypt: Through Egyptian Eyes: Essays in Honour of P.J. Vatikiotis*, edited by Charles Tripp (London: Routledge, 1993), 1–21. See also Ami Ayalon, *The Press in the Arab Middle East: A History* (Oxford: Oxford University Press, 1995), 39–46 and 50–62.
53 Beth Baron, *The Women's Awakening in Egypt: Culture, Society, and the Press* (New Haven: Yale University Press, 1994).
54 Carter, 43–7.
55 Kelidar, 13.
56 Wendell, 238.
57 Wendell, 232 and 235.
58 Ahmad Zakariyya Shilaq, *Hizb al-Ahrar al-Dusturiyyun, 1922–1953* (Cairo: Dar al-Ma'arif, 1982), 105 and Walid Kazziha, 377–9 and 381.
59 Wendell, 285.

60 Arthur Goldschmidt Jr., *Modern Egypt: The Formation of a Nation-State* (Boulder: Westview, 1988), 47. See also Arthur Goldschmidt, Jr., "The Egyptian Nationalist Party: 1992–1919," in *Political and Social Change in Modern Egypt: Historical Studies from the Ottoman Conquest to the United Arab Republic*, edited by P.M. Holt (Oxford: Oxford University Press, 1968), 308–33.
61 Elie Kedourie, "The Genesis of the Egyptian Constitution of 1923," *The Chatham House Version and Other Middle-Eastern Studies* (Hannover: University Press of New England, 1984), 160–7; Tariq al-Bishri, "Sira' 'ala al-Sulta," in his collection of articles *Dirasat fi al-Dimuqratiyya al-Misriyya* (Cairo: Dar al-Shuruq, 1987), 55–77.
62 See Davis.
63 See Vitalis.
64 Malak Badrawi, *Isma'il Sidqi 1875–1950: Pragmatism and Vision in Twentieth-Century Egypt* (Richmond: Curzon Press, 1996).
65 James B. Mayfield, "Agricultural Cooperatives: Continuity and Change in Rural Egypt," in *Egypt from Monarchy to Republic: A Reassessment of Revolution and Change*, edited by Shimon Shamir (Boulder: Westview Press, 1995), 90.
66 Lia, 54–60. See for more on voluntary benevolent organizations, Morroe Berger, *Islam in Egypt Today: Social and Political Aspects of Popular Religion* (Cambridge: Cambridge University Press, 1970), 90–126.
67 Beinin and Lockman, 110–20.
68 The literature on the heyday of the so-called liberal experiment is vast. See Marsot; and Janice Terry, *The Wafd, 1919–1952: Cornerstone of Egyptian Political Power* (London: Third World Centre, 1982).
69 Gershoni and Jankowski, *Egypt*.
70 Tripp, 56.
71 Shilaq, 118–26; also, Marius Deeb, *Party Politics in Egypt: The Wafd & its Rivals, 1919–1939* (London: Ithaca Press, 1979), 77–9.
72 Vitalis, 76.
73 Selma Botman, *Egypt from Independence to Revolution, 1919–1952* (New York: Syracuse University Press, 1991), 58–60.
74 Beinin and Lockman, 105.
75 Ellis Goldberg, *Tinker, Tailor and Textile Worker: Class and Politics in Egypt, 1930–1952* (Berkeley: University of California Press, 1986), 69.
76 Tignor, 109–11.
77 'Asim al-Disuqi, *Kibar mallak al-aradi al-zira'iyya, wa dawruhum fi al-mujtama al-Misri* (Cairo, 1975), 174–210.
78 James B. Mayfield, "Agricultural Cooperatives: Continuity and Change in Rural Egypt," in Shamir, 82–5.
79 Marsot, 57; Deeb, 73.
80 Deeb, 181.
81 Deeb, 180.
82 Charles D. Smith, *Islam and the Search for Social Order in Modern Egypt: A Biography of Muhammad Husayn Haykal* (Albany: State University of New York Press, 1983), 42.
83 Smith, 74.
84 William Shepard, "The Dilemma of a Liberal: Some Political Implications in the Writings of the Egyptian Scholar, Ahmad Amin (1886–1954)," in *Modern Egypt: Studies in Politics and Society*, edited by Elie Kedourie and Sylvia Haim (London: Frank Cass, 1980), 84–97.

85 Badrawi, 64–75.
86 Vernon Egger, *A Fabian in Egypt: Salamah Musa and the Rise of the Professional Classes in Egypt* (Lanham: University Press of America, 1986).
87 See for an analysis of Taha Husayn as a modernist, Abdelrashid Mahmoudi, *Taha Husain's Education: From the Azhar to the Sorbonne* (Richmond: Curzon Press, 1998).
88 Egger, 91.
89 Egger, 80.
90 See Partha Chatterjee, *The Nation and Its Fragments: Colonial and Postcolonial Histories* (Princeton: Princeton University Press, 1993), 3–34.
91 Lia, 140.
92 Gershoni and Jankowski, *Redefining*, 11.
93 Donald M. Reid, "The Rise of Professions and Professional Organizations in Modern Egypt," *Comparative Studies in Society and History* 10 (1974): 24–57.
94 Ayalon, 81.
95 Gershoni and Jankowski, *Redefining*, 13.
96 Beinin and Lockman, 225–54.
97 Beinin and Lockman, 239.
98 Goldberg, 33.
99 Haggai Erlich, *Students and University in Twentieth-Century Egyptian Politics* (London: Frank Cass, 1989), 116–23; and Ahmad Abdalla, *The Student Movement and National Politics in Egypt* (London: Saqi Books, 1985), 39–43.
100 See Israel Gershoni, "Rejecting the West: The Image of the West in the Teachings of the Muslim Brotherhood, 1928–1939," in *The Great Powers in the Middle East, 1919–1939*, edited by Uriel Dann (New York: Holmes and Meier, 1988), 370–91; Israel Gershoni, "Imagining the East: Muhammad Husayn Haykal's Changing Representations of East-West Relations, 1928–1933," *Asian and African Studies* 25 (1991): 209–51.
101 See Gershoni and Jankowski, *Redefining*, 2–7; James P. Jankowski, *Egypt's Young Rebels*, 56–71; Richard P. Mitchell, *The Society of the Muslim Brothers* (New York: Oxford University Press, 1969), 218–20.
102 Thomas Philipp, "Copts and Other Minorities in the Development of the Egyptian Nation-State" in Shamir, 131–50.

◆ PART I ◆

The Formation of Modernist Political Thought

◆ CHAPTER ONE ◆

Liberal Reform:
The Society of National Renaissance

Introduction

The Society of National Renaissance (Jama'at al-Nahda al-Qawmiyya) was the liberal answer to the crisis of the 1930s. The Society's main platform was its defense of the parliamentary system based on the Constitution of 1923. The major contribution of the new liberals to Egyptian political thought was a liberal reform program that claimed to be able to solve the political and social crisis of the 1930s and 1940s and provide an alternative to the politics of communal identity. The new liberals believed that the twin processes of political reform, the "deepening" of the political system on the one hand and social "integration" of new sections of the population into the nation on the other, would turn Egypt into a modern nation-state. The historical turning point that prompted their initiative was the signing of the Anglo-Egyptian Treaty in 1936. They interpreted this event as the end of the era of patronage and populism that had dominated the nationalist struggle since 1919. To them, it inaugurated the beginning of a new era that would be completely dedicated to reform and the modernization of Egypt. Faithful to their liberal and enlightened background, they understood this process primarily in terms of a greater rationalization of Egypt's political and social structure.

The social reforms that were intended to "integrate" the excluded sections of society resulted in a new liberalism that differed in crucial respects from the liberalism of the beginning of the last century. Significantly, after two decades of mismanagement of the country, the new liberals had lost faith in the class of notables as the country's saviors. The elite's conceptions of its own role in society and its relations with other classes were considered outdated. Thus, the new liberals abandoned the notion that political rights should be limited to the leading notable families, propounded at the beginning of the century by the Umma Party and its newspaper *al-Jarida*.[1] They also rejected the idea that power should be the prerogative of the superior individual, as argued in the 1920s by leading liberals like Muhammad Husayn Haykal (1888–1956). These tenets were replaced by the more inclusive concept of the abstract citizen and equal rights in representation.[2] The new liberals were equally critical of the discourse of character and its moralistic legitimization of the leading role of the elite,[3] and, for that matter, of Social Darwinism, with its advocacy of the survival of the fittest as a justification for social inequality and the privileged position of the notables.[4]

The ideological shift was also apparent in their lack of praise for the communitarian values of village life and the concomitant support of traditional relations of authority, so prominent in the romantic social conservatism of some of the early liberals.[5] They regarded especially paternalism and the related phenomena of patronage and clientalism as major obstacles to the modernization of Egyptian political and social relations. These "traditional" relations of dependency, the new liberals argued, had to be replaced by "modern" administrative institutions that would establish a direct link between the state and the citizen. They believed that in return for a basic livelihood, education, and economic well-being, the citizens would pledge their primary allegiance directly to the nation-state. It was assumed that the gradual emancipation from personal dependence on patronage would result in a greater ability on the part of the citizens to pursue their individual interests, organize themselves in horizontal organizations, rely on contractual relations, and establish independent political parties. Eventually, this would lead to the creation of a vibrant civil society strong enough to counter the power of the state and contain the reach of primordial ties, of which paternalism was a leftover.

The ingenious attempts by the new generation of liberals to forge a new, more inclusive society were not just prompted by idealism. They were as much the result of the insight that Egypt was changing rapidly economically, socially, and culturally. These changes had to be controlled and directed to prevent social and political conflict from bringing down the existing liberal system. Sociological theories of cohesion and control were adopted to regulate the increasing social disaffection. Similarly, the new liberals felt that "social differentiation," which was regarded as the source of Egypt's problems, had to be countered by the establishment of national institutions. Such institutions would instill shared values, a sense of common identity, and uniform standards of social comportment into the newly integrated population. In the struggle against alienation, nationalism was only a secondary means to securing unity and homogenization. While the liberals rejected the more elitist forms of liberal nationalism such as Pharaonism mostly on the grounds of their ineffectuality,[6] they also opposed the new, radical, nationalist mass politics of the 1930s as counterproductive and misleading in its sloganeering (*sha'arat fadfada*).[7] Reconfirming the preponderance of politics over culture, they ardently believed in the efficacy of "rational" reform over the mass mobilization of the people on the basis of the politics of identity.[8] Not surprisingly, for a group that believed that Egypt had gained its independence in 1936 and had finally left the rhetoric of nationalism behind, the economic and cultural struggle against Western imperialism did not figure at all in the liberal program of the Society. Typically, one member of the Society commented that the student and workers movement of 1945–46 was a waste of time because it had not led to fruitful reforms.[9]

While this social reform program was designed to integrate the different social classes into the nation, the complementary political reform of "deepening" aimed at incorporating these classes into the body politic and inculcating liberal values. Like the political reforms of Ahmad Lutfi al-Sayyid and other early liberal reformers at the beginning of the century, a major part of the program of the new liberals was meant to increase the powers of the legislative assembly at the expense of the prerogatives of the King. After having acquired independence after the signing of the Anglo-Egyptian Treaty Egypt the Society believed Egypt should concentrate on amending the Constitution of 1923 and giving it a more liberal character. In contrast with the previous generation, however, this attempt to shift the balance of power in favor of parliament was not intended to benefit the class of notables. Instead, it was part of the larger project of incorporating the new classes into the political system and broadening the scope of civil society as the guarantee of this system. It was time to create a strong and well informed public opinion. The weakness of this program was that it could only be implemented if the old political system was able to absorb the new social forces, a process that depended on its ability to reform itself and accommodate the social and political demands of the new classes. As neither the King, the minority parties, nor, as later would become apparent, the Wafd were willing to accept reforms that affected them and lead to integration and deepening, liberals were increasingly forced to look for other ways of realizing their ideas.

As the 1940s wore on, liberalism acquired a more authoritarian character. Although it still concentrated on political reform, the significance of control and surveillance became more marked. The reason for this was that instead of "withering away" after 1936, as the liberals had predicted, the nationalist movement was becoming more radical. The student and workers' demonstrations of 1945–46, the radicalization of the Muslim Brotherhood and the activities of its terrorist wing, the first Arab-Israeli war of 1948, the guerrilla warfare along the Suez Canal in 1951, and the Cairo fire of January 1952, reflected an increasing discontent with the prevailing colonial domination and socioeconomic situation. The more this struggle combined with social issues and endangered the position of the social elite, the harder it became to discuss matters in a rational fashion and agree on compromises. Consequently, integration and deepening had to be accompanied by a far-reaching "rationalization" of society through bureaucratic means. Caught in the paradox of creating and controlling civil society through administration, liberalism was inevitably faced with the question at which point social reform would begin to jeopardize its democratic character. This paradox, common to the doctrine of liberalism, is much more pronounced in environments that are not conducive to its introduction.[10]

The upshot of this "social turn" was that the character of the new avant-garde changed considerably from that of the previous generation. The leader of the modern era was no longer the elitist *littérateur* with the highest degree of intellectual acumen and a perfect awareness of the literary tastes of the West. Neither was it the lawyer of the early part of the century, despite the large amount of attention paid to legal reform in the Society. Instead, the new professional classes, recruited from the *effendiyya* and untainted by wealth, would act as guide on the liberal road to modernity. Social engineers, the ultimate rationalist designers and creators of societies, were the heroes for these liberals. Regarded as the new elite, they were given special authority in planning society on account of their superior knowledge and insight into the processes of social change. The statutes of the Society reflect this new elitism. They foreshadow the predominance of technocracy in the 1950s, for instance, by expressly forbidding political debate (*al-jadl al-siyasi*).[11]

In this chapter, I begin by giving an account of the background of the Society of National Renaissance and the biographies of its leading members, paying particular attention to the role they played in the Egyptian political debate before the July Revolution. Then, the program of the organization and the intellectual influences on the Society will be analyzed. The main focus, however, will be on the internal logic of the liberal discourse of the Society and the way in which its different parts fit together to form a comprehensive reform program of social "integration" and political "deepening." First, we will see how parliament is regarded as a model of politics and of education with the purpose of disseminating certain attitudes and habits that are deemed essential to building a liberal society. Second, I trace the demarcation lines drawn between the state and private initiative and discuss the Society's argument that it is the state's task to establish a nation-state by imposing social discipline on the newly integrated classes and instilling a common national consciousness and identity. These sections demonstrate the problems experienced by Egyptian liberalism. I focus on the difficulties involved in the creation of a "modern" liberal society based on a completely new sense of time, space, and identity with new norms of self-discipline and self-regulation, without succumbing to etatism and sacrificing political rights, such as the right to resist reform and new ordering. The chapter ends with the social reform program of the Society and an evaluation of its influence on other reformist groups in Egyptian society.

Origins

The Society of National Renaissance was one of the most productive and interesting liberal think tanks of the 1930s and 1940s. To underline its task of enlightening the general public and raising the level of political consciousness, the Society published a series of studies dealing with pressing issues, ranging from agrarian and political reform to Egypt's Sterling balances, its position in international law, and its foreign policy.[12] At the same time, the series was an important avenue for lobbying the elite. It tried to impress upon its elite readership the necessity of social reform to bring the country "in accordance with the spirit of the age."[13] But this elitist character was also its main limitation. The Society sought its strength in its intellectual brilliance and the force of its arguments rather than in the power of numbers. As a result, its membership was confined to nine founding members during the early phase of its development, between 1939 and 1944, a number that expanded to twenty-three when the Society gained a firm footing after the World War II.[14] Nevertheless, in complete contradiction with its own aim to strengthen civil society, a 1949 proposal to reestablish the Society as a political party was rejected.[15]

The driving force of the Society was an even smaller group of liberals, whose autobiographies give insight into their social and educational backgrounds and the political relations they maintained. Mirrit Butrus Ghali (1908–1991), the most active member of the Society and author of several leading works on political and agrarian reform, belonged to the famous Coptic Butrus Ghali family, which had a long history of involvement in liberal politics. His great-uncle was assassinated in 1910 when in office as Prime Minister, while his father Najib had been Minister of Agriculture.[16] Mirrit Butrus Ghali himself had been elected to parliament twice and was known as author of the book *The Policy of Tomorrow*, which formed the basis of the Society's liberal program.[17] Ibrahim Bayumi Madkur (1902–199?), who worked closely with Mirrit Butrus Ghali on several publications, had a distinguished career as an academic and well-known political adviser. His involvement in politics was also a family tradition. He inherited his father's Wafdist seat in the Senate in 1937, but later became an independent when the party opposed his land reform laws.[18] Muhammad Zaki Abd al-Qadir (1908–1982), the third leading figure of the Society, was a journalist, owner of the Society's publishing house, and editor-in-chief of its monthly, *al-Fusul*. In the 1940s he became a journalist for *al-Ahram* and began writing his famous column *Nahwa al-Nur* (*Towards the Light*). He ran for parliament as an independent candidate twice, first in 1945 for the district south of Zaqaziq, where he had grown up, and again in 1950 for Rawd al-Faraj in Cairo. Both times he was defeated.[19]

The elitist character of the Society was further enhanced by the group's close social and political relations with the older generation of liberal politicians, in spite of their different conceptions of liberal principles. Several prominent liberals even helped to found the Society. They include Ahmad Lutfi al-Sayyid (1878–1963), the founder of liberalism at the beginning of the century and rector of Cairo University since 1925, Ali al-Shamsi, president of the board of directors of Egypt's acting Central Bank, al-Bank al-Ahli, who inspired the economic studies of the Society, and Baha al-Din Barakat, another well known liberal and former Minister of Education, who had written several interesting works on politics.[20]

Many of the connections between the two generations of liberals dated from the early careers of the young members of the Society. Ibrahim Bayumi Madkur, for instance, had become well acquainted with Ahmad Lutfi al-Sayyid after 1935, when he was appointed lecturer in Islamic Philosophy at the Faculty of Arts at the University of Cairo. He had frequented the Muhammad Ali Club with him and had joined him on a number of trips abroad. In his autobiography, he repeatedly mentions the well-known members of the older generation with whom he socialized and whom he admired for their sagacity, such as Mustafa Abd al-Raziq, Ahmad Amin, and Amin al-Khuli.[21]

Muhammad Zaki Abd al-Qadir maintained even closer ties with the intellectual giants of the previous generation. After his graduation from law school at the end of the 1920s, he had worked for the first three years of his career as a journalist for *al-Siyasa*, which he has described as "the leading newspaper in thought, culture, politics and literature."[22] As a staff member, he had been on intimate terms with Husayn Haykal and Taha Husayn (1889–1973).[23] In this environment, he had also acquired first-hand experience of the "illiberal" aspects of the Liberal Constitutionalists. He would later analyze these in his classic historical defense of the 1923 Constitution, *The Disaster of the Constitution* (1955).[24] Most importantly, he had developed a distaste for the leading professional politicians of the Party of the Liberal Constitutionalists, such as Muhammad Mahmud (1878–1941), whose dictatorial political style he ascribed to Mahmud's absolute power as large landowner over his tenants on his estate (*'izba*) in Upper Egypt. Muhammad Zaki Abd al-Qadir held such politicians directly responsible for destroying the democratic experiment in Egypt. He believed that what he called the *buyutat* (grand families), whose whole existence hinged on personal patronage and maintaining a system of dependent clients, had undermined Egyptian politics. He claimed that it was this class that collaborated with the Palace to oust the Wafd and establish the first non-parliamentary regime in 1928.[25]

Partly on account of their aversion to what they regarded as traditional forms of authority and power, the new generation of liberals respected other reformers, such as Ali Mahir and Fahmi Nuqrashi, although they might be considered less than liberal and worked within the prevalent patronage system. Ibrahim Bayumi Madkur admired Ali Mahir for being one of the few politicians who was able to debate objectively in the Senate without letting party politics and interests interfere.[26] Even such forceful characters as

Isma'il Sidqi, the strong man, who had replaced the Constitution of 1923 with his own highly dictatorial one in 1930, was praised for his courage by someone like Muhammad Zaki Abd al-Qadir, perhaps the most consistent liberal of the whole group, who had worked as editor for his newspaper, *al-Sha'b*.[27] It shows both the desperation and the elite nature of the members of the Society that they looked to these non-democratic insiders of the political system for the implementation of their social reforms. Mirrit Butrus Ghali and Ibrahim Bayumi Madkur even joined the second government of Ali Mahir in September 1952, after the military had taken over power.

Nonetheless, several members of the Society remained faithful to their democratic principles throughout this period. Muhammad Zaki Abd al-Qadir, for instance, unreservedly condemned the banishment of the Muslim Brotherhood by Prime Minister Nuqrashi in 1948, arguing that an organization cannot be held responsible for the aberrant activities of the most radical and uncontrolled section of its members.[28] Wahid Ra'fat (1901–1984), professor in international law and the Society's legal expert, was even nominated to become Prime Minister during the March Crisis of 1954. Consistently the Society condemned the existing political system and its patronage system.

Political Reform Program

The program of the Society of National Renaissance

In October 1945 the Society of National Renaissance published a fourteen-page program, followed in December 1946 by the official announcement of the statutes, which clearly exhibit the cerebral and neutral, "scientific" character of the foundation.[29] The first article of the statute lays down that the Society would "work to create an enlightened public opinion and direct national attention towards a correct understanding of the problems of the nation, whether they are political, social, or economic; and that it will provide solutions for these problems through study and research and present views undistorted by political bias." The second article states the Society's intention to "draw up a program which will realize the aspirations of the nation in creating a renaissance (*nahda*) and progress; and that it will complete political and economic independence and raise the standard of living." Finally, the statute stipulates, "the Society is independent from political parties and that political debates are prohibited."[30]

A mere summary of the points of the reform program of the Society does not capture the full extent of its internal logic, ultimate goals, and contradictions. Despite the limited clout of the Society and its social and political restrictions, its scope and ambitions were vast. The objective that the organization set itself was to establish a democratic society in Egypt. What makes this effort unique is that it uncovers the principles that were at the root of that society. All its political, social, and economic reforms ultimately had one purpose: the transformation of the Egyptian personality and the creation of the Egyptian citizen. In other words, the Society's members aimed to instill in the Egyptian population a sense of order and proper conduct that they regarded as the basis of a modern society. Individualism, self-regulation, and the concomitant qualities of sobriety, diligence, and discipline were deemed essential for bringing Egypt "in accordance with the spirit of the age."[31] Economically, this liberal reform program meant that Egyptians would have to engage diligently in profitable pursuits, calculate the risks involved, and act as entrepreneurs. Politically, it entailed the priority of democratic procedures over patronage and authority and of major issues over rhetoric.

Although the language in which the reforms were couched was moderate and the argument carefully worded, the liberal program of the Society of National Renaissance was far-reaching, even totalitarian in its consequences. It entailed a chain of reforms that interacted in different fields of activities that had to be (re)ordered to ensure the instilment of civil conduct. In principle, no aspect of life remained sacred and secluded; the opening up of society and its "enlightenment" (sometimes literally, as in the case of modern housing) was seen as natural and justified in the name of development and modernization. Society as a whole was systematically and meticulously analyzed to replace "backward" conduct and rules with values of earnestness, honesty, diligence, and responsibility. A hierarchy of social levels was identified. Attributing to each level its own regulations and functions, the program imposed values and models that were regarded as conducive to development. The central liberal institutions and politicians formed the top of the hierarchy. Their task would be to spread liberal values among the population and present themselves as models of modern rational conduct. The lowest level consisted of the *fallahin*, who were to be integrated into the new system of values through model villages. If precise rules of conduct had to be formulated for parliamentarians and political parties concerning the technique of debating and the drawing up of laws, the same applied to the *fallahin* on a lower level: they would be instructed in matters of hygiene, the value of property and the basic rules of order.

There was, however, a major contradiction in the liberal program of reform, as we have seen. Although their intention was to establish a self-regulating civil society, the members of the Society of National Renaissance also advocated the implementation of reforms by the state. The stronger the state became, the more it would encroach upon the prerogatives and the hoped for self-regulating functions of civil society. On the one hand, these liberals realized that the state had to penetrate society, open it up, and impose discipline and order, so that the population could be integrated into society as a whole on the level of economics, education, and the military. On the other hand, they argued that civil society should be self-regulatory and democratic and that the infringement of the state should be limited. Liberal reform could only succeed if private institutions could be convinced to reform themselves and if the power of the state could be controlled by a parliament whose powers would have to be enlarged at the expense of the executive power. Due to the elitist character of the Society, its members were never able to resolve the contradiction that a liberal society would have to be produced by an authoritarian state imposing its reforms from above.

Ideological influences

It is not clear exactly which thinkers have influenced Mirrit Butrus Ghali and Ibrahim Bayumi Madkur, the two most prominent members of the Society of National Renaissance. Considering the widely diverging autobiographies of Muhammad Zaki Abd al-Qadir and Muhammad Bayumi Madkur, we can only come up with an educated guess.[32] Generally, we can detect the influence of John Stuart Mill (1806–1873) and the utilitarian philosophy of Jeremy Bentham (1748–1832). The impact of Mill's thought on the Society's model of parliament is obvious.[33] Yet, the sociology of Emile Durkheim (1858–1917), which had been taught at Cairo University since 1925, exerted a more direct influence. Mirrit Butrus Ghali must have come into contact with Durkheim's ideas either there or in France, where he studied political science and international law.[34] Ibrahim Bayumi Madkur mentions following a sociology course at the Sorbonne, and Muhammad Zaki Abd al-Qadir's interest in social engineering in the 1930s also derives from a sociological approach to social problems.[35] Their overall approach in solving the problem of social dislocation and explaining the function of education confirms the influence of French sociology on this particular Egyptian group of liberal thinkers.[36]

These members of the Society took from Durkheim their rejection of biological and geographical factors as determinants of social development in favor of a functionalist, sociological approach in which every aspect of society is related to a larger whole.[37] This is true for their support of the notion of intermediate institutions in which citizens must organize themselves to give meaning to their lives and prevent the state from crushing private initiative, although this is also a general liberal tenet.[38] Durkheim's argument that the collective consciousness (*conscience collective*) is crucial to keeping society together and countering social differentiation, is transformed by Mirrit Butrus Ghali and Ibrahim Bayumi Madkur into the concepts of the "national spirit" (*al-ruh al-wataniyya*) and the "national consciousness" (*al-shu'ur al-qawmiyya*).[39] Its association with morality and moral obligation is one of the central themes of the liberal reform program of the Society. These two Egyptian reformers would therefore be wholly in agreement with Durkheim when he states that the social and moral disorder of modern societies are indicative of their failure to institute new regulative controls to replace traditional authority.[40]

Corruption of the political system

The two most important books on political institutions by members of the Society of National Renaissance are Mirrit Butrus Ghali's *The Policy of Tomorrow* (published in 1938) and *Government Institutions: A New Order, a New Life*, by Mirrit Butrus Ghali and his friend and associate Ibrahim Bayumi Madkur.[41] The latter book must be regarded as a sequel to the first, on which it elaborates. First distributed to politicians in a limited edition in 1943, the book could not be published until the lifting of censorship in 1945, when it was printed by Dar al-Fusul. Both works present parliament as the model of modern conduct.

In *The Policy of Tomorrow* Mirrit Butrus Ghali describes in Durkheimian terms what he believes to be the main problem of Egyptian politics: public institutions, like the constitution, the administration, and the judiciary, persist only if supported by the spirit of those communities for which they have been established.

They cannot properly discharge their function except with the cooperation and actual participation of those communities.[42] He tries to explain the gap between the two by pointing to the imposed character of these institutions, being derived from Western Europe and lacking indigenous roots. In contrast to those intellectuals who uphold a discourse of authenticity, Mirrit Butrus Ghali does not assert, however, that Western institutions in themselves are not universal. He argues that they are alien because Egypt was not as advanced as Europe when they were instituted: "Since the historical development which transformed absolute rule into a democratic system, has not completely taken place in Egypt, democracy is a strange system with us, a system transplanted to a milieu unprepared for it and lacking the elements necessary for its maintenance and growth." The disparity can be overcome by creating a "political public opinion" and giving the Egyptians "a true social and political education."[43] Within the Enlightenment paradigm, a nation can only become civilized by establishing an enlightened and stable, independent public opinion. A mature public opinion and national consciousness, together with a strong and firm social system and economic resourcefulness, are, Mirrit Butrus Ghali believes, the foundations of modern democratic societies such as Great Britain and France.[44] In Egypt there are no such foundations, a deficiency that is partly ascribed to the malfunctioning of the parliamentary system.

Mirrit Butrus Ghali castigates the Egyptian political parties for failing to integrate the population into the parliamentary system and raise its political consciousness. In *The Policy of Tomorrow*, he accuses them of being "disorganized," and "inexperienced in matters of state and democratic procedure." Apart from the Wafd, he writes, "there are no real Egyptian parties that we may speak of; for those so-called political parties have no proclaimed exact policy regarding national life, no constant idea regarding the forms and methods of government, and no outlined schemes for economic and social reconstruction." Instead, the political system in Egypt is based on the "politics of personalities and of personal ulterior motives."[45] The unprincipled character of Egyptian political parties is also reflected in the choice of unqualified political candidates, who are mostly sought among relatives and friends. In *Government Institutions*, the word *mujamala* is used to denote this phenomenon. Although literally the word means politeness, amiability, and courteousness, it has the connotations of a lack of principles and a predisposition for bribery and corruption. According to the authors, "*Mujamala* is the most pervasive affliction of our private and public life."⁴⁶ In party politics it means that candidates are chosen arbitrarily, not based on clear lines of distinction, such as personal "competence" (*kaf'*) and "expertise" (*khibra*).

Mirrit Butrus Ghali and Ibrahim Bayumi Madkur argue that old traditions and institutions have acquired new outer forms and have lodged themselves within the framework of the Constitution of 1923, undermining its modern character and function, as was the case with so many other aspects of the then present regime. The authors describe this process of corruption as the conflation of *'asabiyya* (i.e. relations based on tribal relations) with *hizbiyya* (i.e. relations based on modern multi-party system). This corruption of new forms by old attitudes and values of patronage and dependence erodes democratic procedures. For instance, blood relations and special interests turn debates between candidates in elections into violent clashes, rallies become a show of physical force, and elections are often won by intimidation rather than being characterized by the prevalence of reason and the possibility of a rational choice between different options.⁴⁷ The authors complain that "extremism" (*tatarruf*), "exaggeration" (*ghuluw*), and "extravagance" (*israf*) often reign supreme where rationality is called for. Flattery and outrageous promises, not intended to be kept, are shored up by extravagance, in the form of presents, huge rallies, or conspicuous consumption.⁴⁸

This lack of public spirit and non-adherence to abstract principles, Mirrit Butrus Ghali points out, also affects the administration, which is subordinated to politicians' personal goals to such an extent that it seems as if it is "the property of the political parties." There are no clear procedures for the selection and appointment of public officials, nor does there seem to be a sense of social responsibility. During elections, the administration provides no services, as it is "annexed to the action of parties and follows their trail." Due to the corruption of the administration, the public has become convinced that no weight is attached to any right as such, and "only personal intervention and great influence could avail in such matters." Mirrit Butrus Ghali concludes, "tyranny and instability in administrative affairs prevent [...] the political, social, and economic growth of the nation."⁴⁹

Parliament as model of conduct and discipline

In opposition to this corrupted liberal system, Mirrit Butrus Ghali and Ibrahim Bayumi Madkur propose a political system in which parliament is the central organ of society and the expression of the will of the population. Parliament should not only provide for "guidance" (*irshad*) and "education" (*ta'lim*) in practical procedures and moral behavior.[50] It should also present an exemplary model of conduct: "It protects the general interest, renounces personal advantages, and radiates divine justice and peace in the election district and the rest of the country, as it does under the dome of parliament."[51] The central reform on which this political program hinges is the principle of ministerial responsibility and the elimination of "obscurity" (*ghumud*) in the relations between the legislative and the executive, which the king abuses to his advantage.[52] Mirrit Butrus Ghali and Ibrahim Bayumi Madkur condemn all those who support the executive power of the king for their old-fashioned ideas based on "traditions that are not in harmony with the new system." The reformers state that this is an excellent example of how "the power of the past not only is found in forms and traditions, but extends to principles and articles of the constitution which have the purpose to root out this past and to free itself from its bonds."[53]

However, legal reforms alone cannot bring about major changes. The survival of the parliamentary system as a rational model for politics is above all dependent on the reform of the political parties themselves. As Mirrit Butrus Ghali states in *The Policy of Tomorrow*, "no advance can be hoped for unless it be under the light of fully elaborated cultural, economic, and social programs, which can only be the work of political parties."[54] Opportunism and favoritism would therefore have to be substituted by principles and clear rules. The "multi-party system" (*hizbiyya*) is the only rational means to channel politics, when people belonging to different movements can organize themselves around common political principles and programs that should be directed towards "reform" (*islah*) and the "renaissance" (*nahda*). Flexibility and adaptability "in accordance with the needs of the nation" are indispensable in achieving these goals.[55] In that sense, Mirrit Butrus Ghali claims, the multi-party system should be a "school" (*madrasa*) where public consciousness is formed and problems are studied.

In agreement with the general moral and educational purpose of the parliamentary system, Mirrit Butrus Ghali and Ibrahim Bayumi Madkur's model politician is an expert and educator. He stands above selfish interests and has the welfare of the nation at heart. As "there is no other method for recovery than through expertise (*khibra*)," an important criterion in the selection of candidates for political parties and elections should be his professional qualities.⁵⁶ Procedures should be introduced to determine the qualifications of the candidate:

> What is a candidature but a testimony (*shahada*), an exam, and a proof of integrity (*tazkiya*); a testimony before a court of the public opinion in order to support the candidate and help him win his case for election; and a proof of integrity before a leader or political party for whom he offers his services to the public and declares himself capable of fulfilling them?⁵⁷

The outcome of these reforms finds its apogee in elections. They are the most important vehicle for instilling democratic ideals into the people. Again, the two reformers use the metaphor of the school and strong moral language to explain the process and underline their message: "Elections are the school (*madrasa*) of the people and the means of educating (*tarbiyya*) the public opinion." Mutual respect, the "personal dignity" (*karama shakhsiyya*) of the candidates, and their "individual independence" (*al-istiqlal al-fard*) are essential to democracy. Only free and honest elections can give the country's citizens the feeling that they have equal rights and that their policy of choice is being carried out. Elections also have the important function of strengthening nationalist sentiment. They are a demonstration of nationalism, or, in the words of the authors, "the *hajj* to the *Ka'ba* of the *umma*."⁵⁸ Any infringement of the electoral process is not only a crime against a particular party, but also a crime against "virtue" (*fadila*) and the morality and intelligence of the nation.⁵⁹

Social Reform

Public and private spheres and the issue of social discipline

Having established the central function of the parliamentary system as an exemplary model of political conduct, the next step for the reformers is to define the demarcation lines between the government and civil society and to formulate the specific tasks of government. Despite its liberal character and the emphasis on creating a mature citizenship and a responsible government, it is exactly at this juncture that the major tensions in the Society's program are revealed. If the ideals of a true civil society and a new moral community are the main points of focus, and self-discipline and responsibility are the basis for the new moral order, the role of the state versus the responsible citizen remains ambiguous in most of the writings of the members of the Society. Reasoning from their liberal background they demand that the state execute reforms to establish a civil society. At the same time they try to keep the state at bay and restrict its range of activities.

The liberal dilemma remains largely hidden in *The Policy of Tomorrow*. Mirrit Butrus Ghali rejects state intervention for two reasons. First, he believes that it is a "prevalent illusion [...] that if government would improve its methods and carry out its functions with perfect rectitude, it would automatically become capable of meeting the present economic shortage with success."[60] Second, he is of the opinion that the demands for income redistribution, which became one of the most important reasons for state intervention in Europe in the 1930s, are only applicable in Western Europe. There, the issue of distribution of wealth arose, "under the assumption that the national wealth was large enough to guarantee a fair standard of living." He argues that the Egyptian situation is different: "Our economic and social difficulties are only the result of the shortage of national resources and the incapacity of these resources to meet the needs of the people." From this argument, he concludes, "the question of distribution plays, therefore, only a insignificant role in them."[61] Adhering to nineteenth-century liberalism, he proclaims that the economy is the preserve of civil society: "we shall hardly ever suggest measures which would call for government intervention in the economic machine, especially where the law of supply and demand is involved. If we ever do so, it should be carried out with the utmost caution and after exhaustive scrutiny."[62]

If on this liberal model of development the state confines itself to non-economic sectors of society, it does not follow that its only task is the maintenance of law and order. One of the important differences with the previous generation of liberal politicians is the role that members of the Society of National Renaissance assign to the state in creating a responsible citizenship as a precondition for economic development and political stability. Areas of government concern are the "major social and cultural problems, like national education and development of the national spirit, which may actually be even more important and more grave than the former [economic problems], although at times they do not call for attention and press for urgent solutions."[63] Indeed, government officials should "devote themselves to the development of [the] national spirit among the people, which is their task *par excellence.*" Once government reform programs are implemented, the ultimate goal of the liberal reform program will have been fulfilled, and *"every individual would carry out his national obligation willingly without any need for check and control."*[64] Therefore, government intervention is seen as key to accomplishing the liberal ideal of a self-regulatory society. The extent and character of such intervention, however, partly undermines the liberal reform program, as is most apparent in the section on housing.

Mirrit Butrus Ghali singles out three areas of activity in which the state has a major role to play: public health, public education, and housing. The first two are perhaps less remarkable than the last, as the most perceptive of the older generation of liberals had already become interested in these topics, particularly education, by the end of the 1930s.[65] Nevertheless, his goals regarding health and education are not the same as those of the previous generation. Now, health and education are perceived as conducive to "social progress" and promoting "the national spirit" among the *whole population*, and especially of course among the lower classes – a task that had become the responsibility of the government *"par excellence."* In a functional society in which all parts depend on each other, these three special spheres of life of the lower classes have to be integrated and "civilized."

Housing and social dicipline

The most revealing and innovative section of *The Policy of Tomorrow* deals with housing. All the objectives of the liberal program in its more authoritarian form as means of "normalization" come together in the introduction to this section.[66] As the spearhead of the government's civilizing goals, "housing is one of the first problems which should attract the attention and receive the care of state authorities." The basic tenets of the liberal housing policy (printed in italics) are enumerated as follows: (1) "Housing is a fundamental element in human life and *a sign of a people's real wealth and prosperity."* In addition, (2) "It is always an indication of the *level of social development and civilization* of a people." Furthermore, (3) "The improvement of housing conditions is a very effective means of *developing national consciousness* in the ranks of the people, generally, and among the peasantry in particular." Moreover, (4) "If a house is cherished by a person and is the object of his care and pride, this person will thereby come to *recognize the social order* and to *respect the rights of his brethren* and compatriots." Thus, (5) "It promotes his *national spirit*." And, finally, (6) "No doubt, Egypt would make *a great step towards progress* and *social stability* if we could improve the housing conditions of towns and villages in such a way as would *satisfy the modern requirements of health and comfort*."[67]

Mirrit Butrus Ghali's ideas on housing reveal the depth of his will to change Egyptian society into a "modern" society. Prevalent housing conditions symbolize for him the backwardness of Egyptian traditional society. Its enclosed character prevents the peasantry from participating in modern society and becoming modern citizens at the behest of the civilizing efforts of the state:

> The thousands of villages and estates in which the greatest numbers of people live consist of small, low-roofed mud houses, devoid of paint or furniture and closed to the purifying rays of the sun. A part of the house, despite its limited size, is devoted to the animals; the peasant's whole family has to sleep in proximity to them. All houses are built close to one another without order or planning and have neither grounds nor gardens.[68]

As is typical for his early writings, Mirrit Butrus Ghali gives a "special agency" the task of drawing up and carrying out the reconstruction program, and not the government itself, which "is certainly not the best agency for such necessary constructive work in towns and villages." True to his nature as a modern social engineer of high modernism, he asserts that the *tabula rasa* created by fire offers the best opportunity for executing the plans of the Housing and Reconstruction Institute.[69] The Institute, he writes, should seize those villages that are destroyed every year by fire with the aim of "rebuilding the village along modern lines, meeting the requirements of social progress in our country."[70]

The degree to which a semi-governmental institute, like the Housing and Reconstruction Institute, is given the power to interfere in the minute details of the daily life of the villagers, is especially clear in the presentation of the model village, designed for the purpose of maintaining control and order. Avoiding the uniformity of the monotonous grid plan, a model village should be concentrated around a little circle "from which radiate streets and houses." The circle, the main square, would be "a sort of center of the village," harboring the main public services, such as fresh water supply, a general clothes-washing pool, and a drinking trough for animals. As such the circle functions as a place where "persistent social guidance and supervision of order and cleanliness would create in the inhabitants some feeling of pride in their reconstructed village and houses and some inclination and will to keep them well-ordered and clean." The purpose of this surveillance is to "promote in them national consciousness and social responsibility." Thus, the Institute's job is not finished with completion of the construction of the village. Its duties include the general supervision of domestic and social life in the villages; it would also be "concerned with the village house furniture and equipment and would assist villagers in obtaining them."[71]

The same method is to be applied to the industrial quarters. Encouraged to construct housing units for workers, industrial companies should create industrial "estates" on modern principles, equipped with public baths, a pharmacy, and playgrounds. In this manner, writes Mirrit Butrus Ghali, "we would avoid the isolation of workers in quarters reserved for them which alone might create in them the feeling of class differentiation and stimulate their resentment towards the social system."[72]

Creating a national consciousness

So far we have seen how Mirrit Butrus Ghali's reform program works from the most abstract level of conceptualization to the most detailed, practical level of realization. We have seen how the spheres of influence are divided between the state and the private sector. The economic field is open to private initiative, while the state is given the responsibility for civilizing the population. Certain sections such as housing are delegated to special institutes, and semi-government institutions are allowed to intervene to a large extent in the daily life of the rural and urban poor, with the intention of drawing them out into the open and integrating them into national life.

However, the state's task of integration is only complete when a national consensus is established and the population has acquired a "national consciousness," one of the main ingredients of a mature public opinion, together with a democratic attitude. It is clear that what the liberal reformers have in mind is the process of ideological homogenization and necessary to the establishment of the nation-state.[73] The problem in Egypt, Mirrit Butrus Ghali points out, is that a single concept of the nation, which forms the basis for a national consciousness, is neither well-developed nor widely shared by the population. Even after the 1919 Revolution, the "national spirit has not pervaded all classes and individuals." The rural population in particular does not participate in the national life of the country: "These people miss all the advantages of the stir and enthusiasm of nationalistic feelings and for all intents and purposes, they are dead as regards healthy nationalistic life. The right to vote has not educated them. Illiteracy, a low standard of living, poverty, and ill-health all add to their incapacity to develop an interest in public affairs." Both a weak militaristic spirit and the absence of a civil spirit among members of the educated classes have hindered the spread of national consciousness.[74]

The existence of highly divergent concepts of nationalism among the Egyptian intelligentsia is, according to Mirrit Butrus Ghali, no less damaging to the development of national consciousness. In fact, he claims, they "may seriously prejudice the nation's future." Especially threatening to liberal institutions is that "with the extension of education, this difference will spread to the ranks of the whole nation; and the conflict now raging among the educated alone would envelop the whole people." He goes on to condemn all the existing political ideologies for endangering the development of a national consciousness. Their basic flaw, he claims, is their one-sidedness, their selectivity in concentrating on one aspect of Egyptian history and character at the expense of the whole.[75]

This is neither the first nor last time in the political and cultural history of Egypt that the solution to ideological conflict is sought in commissioning an "able and competent historian" to rewrite national history and present it to the reader in an "exact and clear form."[76] In keeping with the objectivist, scientific approach of the Society of National Renaissance, Mirrit Butrus Ghali states, "it is therefore our duty to define and delimit the diverse factors and elements which make up our national consciousness and to draw with perfect clarity the ideal to which it points." This brings him to the conclusion,

> that we should therefore help the nation and encourage the people to grasp the national idea completely and wholly so that they may then be capable of making use of foreign culture and of accepting its influence without fear or danger. Otherwise, it will sweep their national being away or at least weaken their national structure ... Blind resistance to everything that may come to us from the outside is the certain acknowledgement of our own incapacity and is a withdrawal from the progress and movement of the world.[77]

Completely in accordance with his own rationalism and the cosmopolitanism of the Egyptian elite, Mirrit Butrus Ghali's ultimate definition of Egypt's national character is ephemeral and strangely lacking in substance, especially considering the fact that it is meant to homogenize the population and pose an alternative to the ideologies of nationalist and Islamist movements. Despite his affirmation of the representation of the Egyptian nation in its history, language, religion and literature, and despite the statement that "we belong to neither East nor West," he defines Egypt's character as open and linking different continents.[78]

Agrarian reform

The best-known section of the reform program of the Society of National Renaissance was its agrarian reform proposal. By the time the Society had drawn up its overall reform program in 1945, the deteriorating political and social situation had made it clear to most liberals that reforms could no longer be limited to "civilizing" society by presenting models of conduct, disciplining the lower classes, and producing a national consciousness. Reform now had to include the social structure if the liberal ideal of the self-regulatory society were to be established. Although the Society's reform plan has often been regarded in isolation or compared to other agrarian reform plans, it is closely connected with the Society's overall modernist reform program.[79] This program is reflected in the idea that relations that prevail in the countryside should be changed to bring Egypt "more in accordance with the spirit of the age and its demands."[80]

The necessity of reforming the socioeconomic agrarian structure was first emphasized in Mirrit Butrus Ghali's book *Agrarian Reform: Property, Rent, Labor*, published in 1945.[81] The ideas that are propounded in the book reflect those of the members of the Society, who had widely discussed its contents and endorsed them. This is even more remarkable because even though most of the members of the Society were large landowners themselves, this social class is identified as the main obstacle to progress. Large landowners are accused of losing their grip on rural areas and shrinking from "their mission (*risala*), that is the duty of every landowner to remain among his people and take part in their life and culture."[82] They have become absentee landowners who see their land as just another investment and are no longer interested in rural society itself. As a consequence, writes Mirrit Butrus Ghali, they have lost their civilizing function. He concludes, "large landownership is a form of property that does not comply with our special circumstances; one large estate deprives hundreds of rural families of their right to economic independence and social stability."[83]

Even more important for the development of liberal thought is the direct connection that Mirrit Butrus Ghali makes between agrarian reform and industrial growth, a connection not yet made in *The Policy of Tomorrow*. He now realizes that industry and agriculture should be more thoroughly integrated with and adjusted to each other in order to attain balanced economic and social progress. Therefore, the reforms he proposes in this work are generally designed to discourage large landownership, stimulate the transfer of capital from land to industry, create employment opportunities in industry for the surplus rural population, and insure reasonable rents and wages as a result of decreasing pressure on the land. None of these goals, he states, will be attained unless the government intervenes.[84]

The question remains what measures the government should take.[85] Mirrit Boutros Ghali warns that reform should keep in mind that "land has an important role to play in retaining the social system and the enhancement and promotion of the national renaissance (*nahda*) in all its aspects."[86] Social justice is the principle on which land reform should rest.[87] For this reason he appeals to the social conscience of the landed classes: "Our generation should take this to heart and sacrifice itself for the respect of the nation and the execution of our duties."[88] He envisions a transformation of society that would be achieved over a long period of time to give the ruling class the opportunity to adjust and reform itself along the lines of the bourgeois model that the Society has set up for it. Large landowners would have the choice between becoming real agricultural entrepreneurs, living on the land and improving agricultural efficiency and productivity, on the one hand and investing their capital in industry and transforming themselves into an industrial bourgeoisie on the other.[89]

Despite the bold thrust of the Society's arguments, the proposed reforms are extremely moderate: "One to one and a half million rural inhabitants (family of five) will acquire economic independence and the necessary measure of social stability in order to create a firm class of small farmers."[90] The most significant and controversial proposition put forward is the distribution of large estates. Mirrit Butrus Ghali suggests setting the maximum at 100 *faddan*. As expropriation is considered too "drastic a measure" (*tadbir 'anif*), distribution of land would be attained through natural means, that is by law of inheritance. No landholder with land larger than 100 *faddan* would be allowed to buy land. Thus, through inheritance the large estates would dwindle in the course of time, while progressive taxation would encourage the landholders to sell their land and invest their money in industry. All this is based on the premise "that we want a reform and a transformation, not a revolution and a replacement [of the system]."[91] He affirms that the measures the Society proposes are in the service of the general interest, for "it is the duty of the government in the interest of society to guarantee land to as many farmers as possible."[92]

The proposal to set a maximum for rents and wages is perhaps the most important of the liberal reforms, because it would practically curtail the power of the large landowners over the rural population. In effect, Mirrit Butrus Ghali writes, the rents should not be allowed to exceed twice the land tax, while wages are determined by commission.[93] To prevent absenteeism and the practice of renting large stretches of land to intermediaries who re-rent the land to small tenants, laws are proposed to prohibit landowners from renting more than 10 *faddan* to one person.[94] In addition, the duration of the lease would be extended to a minimum of three years, to enable the tenant to plan and improve the fertility of the soil.[95] Mirrit Butrus Ghali reckons it will take twenty-five years for the reforms to come to fruition. By that time, he predicts, smallholdings will have increased by 120 percent, large landownership will have halved, and landholdings under 3 *faddan* will remain the same.[96] Of greater consequence are the establishment of a new middle class and the encouragement of industry for which a whole new internal market will have opened up.

Conclusion

The program of the Society of National Renaissance was primarily an attempt on the part of a small group of liberals to reform society with the purpose to socially "integrate" the excluded classes and politically include them through a "deepening" of the political system. The Society was radical in its attempt to reform Egyptian society. It was modernist in its trust in the efficacy of politics, the rule of law and the impact of social engineering. The reforms it promoted were aimed at creating a new citizen who would be formally educated, culturally homogenized, and economically employed in accordance with the new demands of the nation-state. The new citizen would be imbued with a sense of modern universal rules of "rational" conduct based on a linear and regular sense of time and a geometrical sense of space. Fully carried out, the proposed reforms would emancipate the citizen by freeing him from the "darkness of superstition," the degrading poverty of the estate (*izba*), and the debilitating subjection to the large landowner. At the same time, they would clamp the citizen in a grid of bureaucratic rational conduct that was drawn up and controlled by the state, whose reach and power gradually extended into the deepest recesses of individual conduct. The reforms exposed the general dilemma of Egyptian liberalism of the 1940s. Attempting to implement political and social reform, with the purpose to create a strong public opinion and an independent civil society, it was increasingly forced to rely on state and other institutional means of control and surveillance. This dilemma became all the more acute during the 1940s when the trust of the Society in the capacity of existing political society to implement reforms was eroded and reformers had to look to the state to carry out authoritarian reforms against vested interests.

The weakness of the Society lay in its dependence on the ruling elite to carry out its reforms. Unable to establish its own political party and use political pressure, the Society had to rely on the power of its arguments to convince large landowners and industrialists of the need for a political, social, and economic transformation. In this the Society completely failed, as is apparent from the fate of the agrarian reform proposals in the 1940s. In 1944, senator Muhammad Khattab submitted an agrarian reform law very similar to the one Mirrit Butrus Ghali would draw up a year later. Although the law was at first accepted by the Social Affairs Committee of the Senate, the government opposed it, and a majority of senators voted to return it to the Committee of Agrarian Affairs. The Senate finally rejected the proposed law on 16 June 1947.[97] Ibrahim Bayumi Madkur submitted another proposal for land reform on 23 February 1948. It was directly modeled on Mirrit Butrus Ghali's booklet, and it was promoted in *al-Fusul*, all to no avail.[98] In this respect, it is interesting to note the topics that the Society did not address. For one thing, the Society's program completely neglected the rise of independent trade unions. Neither was the Society at any time involved in the radicalized nationalist movement after the Second World War. Mirrit Butrus Ghali even regarded the year 1946, which saw the most violent clash between the regime and the radical nationalist movement, as a lost year because it had diverted attention away from internal reform to the nationalist issue.[99]

The reform program of the Society was more important when it comes to the influence of its ideas on parliamentary reform. Its proposals to reform the Constitution of 1923 as the basis of Egyptian democracy in particular have been more influential than is commonly assumed. These ideas of the Society had the greatest impact on middle-class, socialist intellectuals. Despite the absence of a formal organization, these individuals in turn had a significant influence in the press and the new civil society that emerged in the 1930s, in which they were well represented. The newspaper *al-Misri*, under the editorship of Ahmad Abu al-Fath (b. 1917), was one source of liberal reform proposals; the weekly *Ruz al-Yusuf* was another.[100] The left wing of the Wafd, al-Tali'a al-Wafdiyya, with its newspaper *al-Wafd al-Misri*, also belonged to this movement, although it was politically more oriented towards the communist movement.[101]

The Society was to exert considerable influence on these groups through its monthly *al-Fusul*, which became a popular magazine in the 1940s and 1950s. Many journalists who would acquire fame later on and leading opinion-makers of *Ruz al-Yusuf*, such as Ahmad Baha al-Din (1927–1996), Fathi Ghanim (1924–2000), and Adil Thabit, served their apprenticeship at *al-Fusul*, where they were exposed to the liberal influence of its editor-in-chief, Muhammad Zaki Abd al-Qadir. *Ruz al-Yusuf* was to adopt many democratic notions of reformist liberalism. Like the Society, *Ruz al-Yusuf* had a long history of struggle for independence from the traditional parties in the 1930s.[102] In contrast to the Society, however, it succeeded in becoming a formidable, independent, and much more radical force in its own right. Once Ihsan Abd al-Quddus (1919–1991) was appointed editor-in-chief and Ahmad Baha al-Din and Fathi Ghanim joined the board of editors, the journal became one of the strongest forces for liberal and socialist reform in the 1950s. With *al-Misri* and liberal and social-democratic intellectuals like Wahid Ra'fat (1901–1984), *Ruz al-Yusuf* defended the Constitution of 1923 and the liberal rights against military dictatorship during the March crisis. It was not until after 1955, following their defeat and with the success of Nasser's independent foreign policy, that the liberal reform program was superseded by a completely different one. Just like the Society, these currents too struggled with the problem of creating a liberal society and being increasingly forced to rely on authoritarian means to achieve that goal.

Notes

1 Walid Kazziha, "The Jarida-Umma Group and Egyptian Studies," *Middle Eastern Studies* 13 (1977): 373–85.
2 Charles Smith, *Islam and the Search for Social Order in Modern Egypt: A Biography of Muhammad Husayn Haykal* (Albany: SUNY Press, 1983), 48.
3 For the Egyptian discourse of character, cf. Timothy Mitchell, *Colonising Egypt* (Cambridge: Cambridge University Press, 1988), 104–11; for a comparison with the British discourse of character see Stefan Collini, *Public Moralists: Political Thought and Intellectual Life in Britain, 1850–1930* (Oxford: Clarendon Press, 1991), Chapter 3, "The Idea of Character: Private Habits and Public Virtues," 91–118, and Richard Bellamy, *Liberalism and Modern Society: An Historical Argument* (Cambridge: Polity Press, 1992), Chapter 1, "Britain: Liberalism Defined," 9–57.
4 Smith, *Islam*, 46.
5 Charles Smith, "The Intellectual and Modernization: Definitions and Reconsiderations: The Egyptian Experience," *Comparative Studies in Society and History* 22 (1980): 525–8.
6 For the standard analysis of the phenomenon of Pharaonism see Israel Gershoni and James Jankowski, *Egypt, Islam and the Arabs: The Search for Egyptian Nationhood, 1900–1930* (Oxford: Oxford University Press, 1986).
7 Ra'uf 'Abbas, *Jama'at al-Nahda al-Qawmiyya* (Cairo: Dar al-Fikr, 1986), 42.
8 For the standard analysis of radical cultural nationalist movements see Israel Gershoni and James P. Jankowski, *Redefining the Egyptian Nation, 1930–1945* (Cambridge: Cambridge University Press, 1995).
9 Tariq al-Bishri, *al-Haraka al-siyasiyya fi Misr, 1945–1952* (Cairo: Dar al-Shuruq, 1982), 184.
10 Bellamy, 39. The comparison of the adaptation of liberalism to different circumstances in France and especially Italy with Egypt is enlightening. See his chapters on France and Italy, 58–156.
11 'Abbas, 50.
12 The books published by Dar al-Fusul are: Mirrit Butrus Ghali, *al-Islah al-zir'a. al-milkiyya, al-ijar, al-'amal* (Cairo, 1945); Mirrit Butrus Ghali and Ibrahim Bayumi Madkur, *al-Adat al-hukumiyya: Nizam jadid, hayah jadida* (Cairo, 1945); Ahmad Ibrahim, *al-Bank al-markazi* (Cairo, 1949); Sana Laqani, *Arsida istirliniyya* (Cairo, 1949); Wahid Ra'fat, *Misr wa-l-nizam al-duwwaliyya* (Cairo, 1949); Wadi' Faraj, *al-Siyasa al-kharijiyya* (Cairo, 1949); Wadi' Faraj, *Misr wa al-ittifaqat al-duwwaliyya* (Cairo, 1949).
13 Mirrit Butrus Ghali, *al-Islah*, 3.
14 The original members at the founding of the Society were: Ibrahim Bayumi Madkur, 'Abd al-Malik Hamza, Muhammad Zaki 'Abd al-Qadir, Muhammad 'Abd al-Rahman Nasir, Mirrit Butrus Ghali, Wadi' Faraj, and Yahya al-'Alayali. See 'Abbas, 45.
15 'Abbas, 49.
16 Donald Malcolm Reid, "Archeology, Social Reform and Modern Identity among the Copts," in *Entre réforme sociale et mouvement national: Identité et modernisation en Égypte (1882–1962)*, edited by Alain Roussillon (Cairo: CEDEJ, 1995), 329–31.

17 Mirrit Boutrus Ghali, *Siyasat al-ghadd. Barnamij siyasi wa iqtisadi wa ijtima'i* (Cairo: Matba'a al-Risala, 1938). It was translated by Isma'il R. el Faruqi as *The Policy of Tomorrow* (Washington, DC: American Council of Learned Societies, 1953). I have used this translation throughout.
18 Muhammad Bayumi Madkur, *Ma'a al-ayyam: Shay' min al-dhikriyyat* (Cairo: Kitab al-Hilal, 1990), 117, 128–37.
19 Muhammad Zaki 'Abd al-Qadir, *Mudhakkirat ... wa dhikriyyat* (Cairo: n.p., n.d.), 114–20.
20 Baha al-Din Barakat, *Safahat min tarikh* (Cairo: Dar a-Hilal, 1960).
21 Madkur, *Ma'a al-ayyam*, 85–7, 116, 121.
22 Muhammad Zaki 'Abd al-Qadir, *Aqdam 'ala al-tariq* (Cairo: al-Mu'assasa al-Misriyya al-'Amma li-l-Ta'lif wa l-Nashr, 1967), 182.
23 'Abd al-Qadir, *Aqdam*, 104.
24 Muhammad Zaki 'Abd al-Qadir, *Mihnat al-dustur, 1923–1952* (Cairo: Kitab Ruz al-Yusuf, 1955).
25 'Abd al-Qadir, *Aqdam*, 175, 226–7.
26 Madkur, *Ma'a al-ayyam*, 156.
27 'Abd al-Qadir, *Aqdam*, 276.
28 'Abd al-Qadir, *Mudhakkirat*, 67–8.
29 'Abbas, 65–9.
30 'Abbas, 50.
31 Butrus Ghali, *al-Islah*, 3.
32 Madkur, *Ma'a al-ayyam*, 'Abd al-Qadir, *Mudhakkirat*, and 'Abd al-Qadir, *Aqdam*.
33 John Stuart Mill, *Representative Government*, in *Utilitarianism, On Liberty and Considerations on Representative Government* (London: J.M. Dent & Sons Ltd, 1972), 175–393.
34 Letter from Mrs. Gertrude Butrus Ghali to the author dated 30 January 1993.
35 'Abd al-Qadir, *Aqdam*, 315.
36 See Bellamy's chapter "France: Liberalism Socialized," 58–104.
37 Ernest Wallwork, *Durkheim: Morality and Milieu* (Cambridge MA: Harvard University Press, 1972), 31. Robert A. Nisbet, *The Sociology of Emile Durkheim* (London: Heinemann Educational, 1975), 16–7, 32 and 67.
38 Nisbet, 135 and Wallwork, 116.
39 Wallwork, 37–8.
40 Wallwork, 83.
41 Mirrit Butrus Ghali and Ibrahim Bayumi Madkur, *al-Adat al-hukumiyya: Nizam jadid, hayah jadida* (Cairo: Dar al-Fusul 1945).
42 Boutros Ghali, *Policy*, 3.
43 Boutros Ghali, *Policy*, 5.
44 Boutros Ghali, *Policy*, 8.
45 Boutros Ghali, *Policy*, 6.
46 Butrus Ghali and Madkur, *al-Adat*, 66.
47 Butrus Ghali and Madkur, *al-Adat*, 69.
48 Butrus Ghali and Madkur, *al-Adat*, 70–3.
49 Boutros Ghali, *Policy*, 11–3.
50 Butrus Ghali and Madkur, *al-Adat*, 74.
51 Butrus Ghali and Madkur, *al-Adat*, 48.
52 Butrus Ghali and Madkur, *al-Adat*, 34.
53 Butrus Ghali and Madkur, *al-Adat*, 36.

54 Boutros Ghali, *Policy*, 7.
55 Boutros Ghali, *Policy*, 6.
56 Boutrus Ghali and Madkur, *al-Adat*, 82.
57 Boutrus Ghali and Madkur, *al-Adat*, 66.
58 Boutrus Ghali and Madkur, *al-Adat*, 62–3.
59 Boutrus Ghali and Madkur, *al-Adat*, 74.
60 Boutros Ghali, *Policy*, 49.
61 Boutros Ghali, *Policy*, 49.
62 Boutros Ghali, *Policy*, 50.
63 Boutros Ghali, *Policy*, 16.
64 Boutros Ghali, *Policy*, 17. Italics added.
65 Taha Hussein, *The Future of Culture in Egypt* (New York: Octagon Books, 1975), 29 and 49–55.
66 See for similar examples of "normalization" in the nineteenth century, Mitchell.
67 Boutros Ghali, *Policy*, 68. See also Michel Foucault, *Power/Knowledge: Selected Interviews and Other Writings, 1972–1977*, edited by Colin Gordon (New York: Pantheon Books, 1980), 103–6.
68 Boutros Ghali, *Policy*, 68.
69 James C. Scott calls this the ideal of the social engineer of high modernism: "At its most radical, high modernism imagined wiping the slate utterly clean and beginning from zero." *Seeing Like a State: How Certain Schemes to Improve the Human Condition Have Failed* (New Haven: Yale University Press, 1998), 94. Also, cf. chapter 3 "Authoritarian High Modernism," 87–102, for a full analysis of the phenomenon.
70 Boutros Ghali, *Policy*, 70–2.
71 Boutros Ghali, *Policy*, 73.
72 Boutros Ghali, *Policy*, 73–5.
73 Ernest Gellner, *Nations and Nationalism* (Oxford: Blackwell, 1983), 53–62.
74 Boutros Ghali, *Policy*, 99–100.
75 Boutros Ghali, *Policy*, 102–3.
76 Boutros Ghali, *Policy*, 104.
77 Boutros Ghali, *Policy*, 105–8.
78 Boutros Ghali, *Policy*, 110. Italics in the original translation.
79 Gabriel Baer, "Egyptian Attitudes Towards Land Reform, 1922–1955," in *The Middle East in Transition: Studies in Contemporary History*, edited by W. Laqueur (London: RKP, 1958), 92.
80 Butrus Ghali, *al-Islah*, 3.
81 Butrus Ghali, *al-Islah*, 3. First published by the publishing house of the Society of National Renaissance, Dar al-Fusul, it was later reissued in French by *L'Egypte Contemporaine*. Mirrit Ghali Bey, "Un programme de reforme agraire pour l'Egypte," *L'Egypte Contemporaine* 38 (January–February 1947): 3–66.
82 Butrus Ghali, *al-Islah*, 4.
83 Butrus Ghali, *al-Islah*, 57.
84 Butrus Ghali, *al-Islah*, 72–3.
85 Butrus Ghali, *al-Islah*, 14.
86 Butrus Ghali, *al-Islah*, 15.
87 Butrus Ghali, *al-Islah*, 22.
88 Butrus Ghali, *al-Islah*, 13.
89 Butrus Ghali, *al-Islah*, 58.

90 Butrus Ghali, *al-Islah*, 33.
91 Butrus Ghali, *al-Islah*, 60.
92 Butrus Ghali, *al-Islah*, 58.
93 Butrus Ghali, *al-Islah*, 80 and 83.
94 Butrus Ghali, *al-Islah*, 74.
95 Butrus Ghali, *al-Islah*, 75.
96 Butrus Ghali, *al-Islah*, 91.
97 Baer, 91.
98 'Abbas, 106–9; for a reproduction of the law proposal, 221–47. Butrus Ghali's support of the proposal can be found in "al-Islah al-zira'i," *al-Fusul* 44 (February 1948): 26–8.
99 al-Bishri, *al-Haraka al-Siyasiyya fi Misr, 1945–1952* (Cairo: Dar al-Shuruq, 1983), 184.
100 See chapter 5.
101 Isma'il Muhammad Zayn al-Din, *al-Tali'a al-Wafdiyya wa al-haraka al-wataniyya, 1945–1952* (Cairo: al-Hay'a al-Misriyya al-'Amma li-l-Kitab, 1991).
102 Fatima al-Yusuf gives an account of the conflict between the Wafd and *Ruz al-Yusuf* in *Dhikrayat* (Cairo: Kitab Ruz al-Yusuf, 1953), 155–216.

◆ CHAPTER TWO ◆

Authoritarian Socialism: Rashid al-Barrawi

Introduction

Rashid al-Barrrawi (1907–1987) was one of the most important intellectuals of the period 1945–55, who continued on the socialist modernist trajectory of Salama Musa (1887–1958).[1] Turning the modernist project into a clear ideology, he expressed the aspirations of the rising middle class intellectuals and reformers who yearned for a radical break with the past without having to go through either a right-wing, authoritarian or a left-wing, communist revolution. His works reflect their frustrations with the existing system, which had produced privilege, enormous differences of income, insufficient employment opportunities, and increasing class conflict. For the new middle classes, the reforms of the Society of the National Renaissance were too elitist and too mild, envisioning a long process of transition at best. The liberal emphasis on education and gradual transformation of society was couched in terms that were too legalistic. This reflected the more enlightened elite's intention to modernize Egyptian society painlessly – though thoroughly – by integrating both the large landowners and the lower classes into the emerging nation-state. Rashid al-Barrawi proposed reforms that contrast sharply with the Society's argument for the establishment of a self-regulatory democratic order built on the liberal values of self-discipline and self-control. He presented a socialist program that could be realized within a limited time frame and that insured a social transformation for the direct benefit of the *effendiyya*. Its drawback was to reverse the growing independence of civil society and reduce the scope of parliamentary politics, which had been such an important part of the liberal agenda. Al-Barrawi's diagnosis of

Egypt problems was typical of the modernism of the 1940s in that it combined economic and political factors and gave a total picture of the ills of society and its cure. He argued that the interpenetration of political and economic society had led to corruption, waste of national resources, repression, and exploitation. As a result, Egypt was still in a backward phase of its history in which large landowners ruled the country and foreign interests blocked its development. Insofar it had a modern civil society it represented chaos, disorganization and the conflict of interests, while political society was corrupt and dominated by economic interests of the large landowners, the British and the emerging industrialists. The prevailing political culture based on patronage and clientalism prevented Egyptian citizens from demanding their rights.

Rashid al-Barrawi's contribution to the resolution of Egypt's political and socioeconomic problems was his promotion of the state as the embodiment of "rationality" and the perfect instrument of social transformation. Technocracy was to find in Rashid al-Barrawi one of its foremost spokesmen in the 1940s, and, in that sense, he should be regarded as one of the most important precursors of the Nasserist state, for which he helped pave the way ideologically.[2] Central to al-Barrawi's thought is his support for revolution from above, technocratic rationalization of the economy through planning, and politics as "administration." He voiced his absolute belief in the progressive forces of science, expertise, efficiency, and the power of numbers in the language of extreme socialist modernism. This accounts both for the popularity of his writings and for his use of an unambiguous vocabulary of class.

For these reasons, Rashid al-Barrawi was one of the first Egyptians to help formulate the discourse of authoritarian modernism. His writings initiated and encouraged the use of words that constituted this discourse, such as "supervision" (*ishraf*), "co-ordination" (*tansiq*), and "planning" (*tawjih* or *takhtit*). But the scope of his work was much broader. His originality lies equally in his appropriation of the master narrative of national emancipation and liberation for the middle class. He casts this class as a new force, capable of discerning the laws of history and leading Egyptian society into a more advanced stage of historical development, in which the contradictions of the monarchy would be dissolved by the creation of an overarching, rational, and transformative state. Al-Barrawi's career, a perfect integration of theory and praxis, exemplifies the extent to which his worldview anticipated and formed future ideology. He was one of the few intellectuals who joined the new military regime from the beginning, helping to formulate its ideology of modernization as well as shape and implement its policies.

Al-Barrawi did not come up against the dilemma between reform and democracy, faced by the members of the Society of the National Renaissance. Until the military take-over in 1952, the radical nationalist movement was still in its innocent phase, when it did not have to make crucial choices between the demands of democracy and development. All the same, in spite of Rashid al-Barrawi's enthusiasm for an etatist transition, there is a tension in his work. It is to a certain extent still marked by a conflict between technocratic authoritarianism and democratic liberal socialism. The purpose of this chapter is to trace the main components of Rashid al-Barrawi's political thought in the period prior to the July Revolution. It discusses the sources of his administrative socialism and the ways in which he constructed his theory of modernization, central to his *The Military Coup in Egypt*.

Biography

Rashid al-Barrawi was a self-made man who was proud of his achievements. They were almost entirely the result of his own endeavors, without the help of his family or inherited wealth. He was born on 7 March 1907 in a lower-middle-class family in Mit Ghamr, one of the larger towns in the delta. Graduating from a college for primary teachers in 1927, he started his career as a schoolteacher. He learnt English at the British Council in Cairo, and, after following summer courses for several years at the London School of Economics, acquired a BA in history in 1936 and an MA four years later. In the meantime he had been appointed as an English teacher at the prestigious Khedive Isma'il Secondary School in Cairo.[3] His British degrees enabled him to obtain a lectureship at the Cairo University in 1940. There he started out as a historian of economics, perhaps partly under the impression that with the Egyptianization of the university he could take the place of foreign professors in the field, like A. E. Crouchley. During the war, he wrote his dissertation on the Egyptian economy during the Fatimid period, a remarkable subject for someone who was primarily interested in contemporary politics and economic development.[4] In 1947, Rashid al-Barrawi succeeded in switching to the Faculty of Commerce. The Faculty's social orientation in its demands for reform, such a prominent feature of political thought after Second World War, was expressed in its official journal.[5]

During the following years, al-Barrawi became a well-known publicist and popularizer of socialist ideas. By translating the classics of socialist thought, writing works on the history of socialism, and applying socialist ideas to the Egyptian situation, he promoted the advance of the discourse of radical modernism in Egypt. He was a pioneer in many of these fields. Besides writing an economic history of Egypt,[6] he translated Lenin's *Imperialism the Highest Stage of Capitalism*,[7] Karl Marx's *Capital*,[8] Lev Leontev's *The Political Economy of Socialism*,[9] a selection of writings by Friedrich Engels,[10] and Alfred Bonné's *State and Economics in the Middle East*.[11] In addition, he published two works on socialism, one co-authored with Ahmad Nazmi Abd al-Hamid, a colleague at the Faculty of Commerce.[12] He also wrote the first Egyptian book on economic planning.[13]

That Rashid al-Barrawi was able to continue his work in the increasingly polarized and repressive political climate of the 1940s and early 1950s and advocate internal economic and political reforms[14] attests to his ability to keep a "scientific" distance from party politics.[15] Other writings that contributed to his fame dealt with world peace.[16] This gave him the opportunity to expound his theory of history and international development.[17] At the beginning of the 1950s, his "neutral stand" was so successful that even the monarchist newspaper *al-Zaman* employed him as a regular contributor, presumably in an effort to acquire a more modern reputation.

The July Revolution of 1952 changed all this, and for the first time Rashid al-Barrawi was able to release his pent-up frustrations by carrying out his reform proposals. The military gave him the assignment to draw up the land reform law of September 1952. In subsequent years he became one of the regime's most important ideologues as well as one of its foremost administrators in the new "revolutionary" institutions, such as the Permanent Council for the Development of National Production (PCDNP) and the Industrial Bank. These institutions were important symbols of the new revolutionary era and the ideology of modernization from which the regime drew much of its legitimacy.

At the same time, the July Revolution enabled al-Barrawi to produce many publications that supported the new regime by incorporating its policies into his evolutionary modernist scheme of history. Convinced that the new regime's measures were not only historically necessary, but also preordained, he presented them as the march of science and progress through history. Boldly, he heralded the middle classes, the *effendiyya* of the 1930s, as the vanguard of this movement. By rationalizing society, he claimed, they brought Egyptian society to a higher historical stage, or, in other words, created circumstances in Egypt that were "compatible with the spirit of the age."[18] In this respect, his analysis of the coup d'état in *The Military Coup in Egypt*, one of the classics of the period, represents a trend that both academic and communist Egyptian historians would emulate in the second half of the 1950s. After the Bandung conference of 1955, most left-wing intellectuals began to support the regime and adopted the vocabulary and master narrative of authoritarian modernism.[19]

Ideological Sources

Authoritarian socialism

Any attempt to understand Rashid al-Barrawi's thought must begin by disentangling its main components and tracing their origins. British socialism exerted the greatest influence on al-Barrawi. Within British socialism two distinct and contrasting doctrines have been prevalent since its foundation. In al-Barrawi's time, one can discern on the one hand a current of thought that was based on the concepts of organization and efficiency. The adherents of the autocratic tradition were represented by Sidney (1859–1947) and Beatrice Webb (1858–1943) and the Fabian Society to which the Webbs belonged. They believed that supervision and control are required for society to be organized properly and scientifically, with the elimination of all waste (or inefficiency) and the defects that had dominated British economic and political life. The democratic tradition, on the other hand, principally followed the thought of Harold Laski (1893–1950). It upheld the ideals of liberty, individual and social fulfillment, and moral regeneration. The achievement of these ideals did not necessarily presuppose the rise of a controlling public authority since this could have negative consequences that were sometimes regarded as more important than the cure of iniquity.[20]

It is clear from his works that during his stay in Great Britain in the 1930s Rashid al-Barrawi was inspired by both strands of British socialism. Of the two Webbian socialism had the greatest impact on him.[21] As several researchers have pointed out, Webbian thought was atypical of British socialism because its roots are not in the radical non-conformist tradition of dissenting Protestantism, but in the scientific spirit of Jeremy Bentham's Utilitarianism and the positivism of Auguste Comte (1798–1857).[22] Bentham's principle of utility, the idea that in all activity the objective is and should be the maximization of individual and social happiness, was a potent force of rationality. For him, utility serves to replace "sinister interests," as represented by the dominance of the common law, the Church, corporations, local customs, and aristocratic privilege.[23] Al-Barrawi saw these concepts as highly relevant to Egypt, which was dominated by special interests, such as large landownership, the monarchy, and foreign companies, that did not have the general welfare of the population at heart.

The positivist and collectivist inclinations of the Fabian Society, derived from Comte, were important to independent intellectuals like Rashid al-Barrawi.[24] Positivism attracted many intellectuals on account of the idea that an elite of social scientists can manage the transition to the positive phase. They are to "reconstruct" the social order to achieve a higher stage of industrial and scientific progress. Revolutionary change can be avoided, according to this theory, if the development of society is managed properly. This argument was enhanced by the view of society as a "social organism," which evolves through a process of increasing differentiation and integration, demanding ever more coordination to insure "functional adaptation."[25] Logically, considering this technocratic analysis of change, socialism entailed for the Webbs no more than the transition of private to public ownership.[26] The main rationale for the collectivization of the means of production is the belief that the state is far more competent than private initiative in engendering progress. With the means to establish special technical institutes for "scientific management" at its disposal, a state led by "disinterested experts"[27] could direct and command society as "a great productive army" or a "vast machine"[28] that would overcome "narrow working class interests."[29]

Rashid al-Barrawi based most of the etatist part of his discourse of modernism on Webbian and Fabian socialism. Efficiency, instrumental rationalism, collectivism, anti-capitalism, industrialization as a means of rationalizing and modernizing society, bureaucratic control, and technocracy embodied in the "expert" are topics that pervade his work. Three specific aspects of al-Barrawi's thought that reinforce its overall autocratic socialist tendencies stand out. The first is Sidney Webb's theory of "rent," founded on the Ricardian-Benthamite, Utilitarianist critique of the privileged position of the British landed class, the so-called leisure class. To Sidney and Beatrice Webb, the theory of rent formed "the very corner-stone of collectivist economy."[30] Its premise is the notion that all income above a certain minimum from land and labor as well as capital and ability (i.e. education) should be considered rent and therefore unjustifiable income. This authorizes the expansion of the state as the only neutral coordinating institution, which thus acquires enormous powers of taxation.[31] By adopting the Fabian extension of the Ricardian theory of rent to all economic sections of society, Rashid al-Barrawi laid the groundwork for a general reform program in which the state becomes the agent of modernization.

Second, we can perceive the presence of Webbian thought in al-Barrawi's ambivalence towards Marxism. Although he has translated Marx's *Capital*, al-Barrawi was not a Marxist. His admiration for Marx concerned primarily his dialectical conception of historical development, in which each phase of history is superseded by a higher phase of progress.[32] He also accepted a materialist and economistic view of history, in which the superstructure reflects economic conditions and the forces of production determine the character of society.[33] However, he rejected the argument that the contradiction between the forces of production and the relations of production must necessarily find a new equilibrium through violent revolution. Faithful to Fabianism, al-Barrawi believed that the state could implement reforms to circumvent a revolution and that the intelligentsia, the experts, and the middle classes represented progressive forces against the irrationalism of the leisure class.[34]

The third and most important aspect of the Webbs's thought that would deeply influence Rashid al-Barrawi is their collectivist rationalist socialism, which evolved into the concept of a planned economy. Having grown disillusioned with the possibility of reforming capitalism through parliament during the economic crisis of the 1930s, the attention of the Webbs turned to the Soviet Union. After visiting the Soviet Union in the early 1930s, they published one of the most extensive accounts of the Soviet Union available in the West at that time, *Soviet Communism: A New Civilisation* (1935).[35] The Five Year Plan, first put into practice in 1928, seemed to them the epitome of the ordered, rational, and technocratic society that they had advocated for so long. Al-Barrawi's interest in the Soviet Union and especially in a planned society was further stimulated by a stream of books that expressed admiration for the Soviet Union, published in Great Britain during and shortly after the Second World

War. He reworked the information in these books and incorporated it in his own book on the planned economy, thereby making an important and well-reasoned contribution to the image of the Soviet economy as an alternative model of development.[36] Rashid al-Barrawi was one of the foremost propagandists of planning, which would become a central prop of authoritarianism in the 1950s.

Democratic socialism

Until the July Revolution the highly technocratic influence of the Webbs on Rashid al-Barrawi's concept of modernity, based on efficiency and order with the state as overarching agent of change and power, was partly checked by the pluralism of Harold Laski. In Laski's 1925 seminal work *A Grammar of Politics*, al-Barrawi found a more ethical and principled conception of socialism, in which rationality and the fulfillment of human potential are more balanced.[37]

Several elements of Harold Laski's thought turn up in Rashid al-Barrawi's writings before the July Revolution. Just prior to the last general elections in Egypt, held in December 1949, al-Barrawi published his famous booklet *Free Opinions*, written with the intention to admonish the Wafd to establish a welfare state in order to stave off the revolution. Seemingly in complete contradiction with his admiration for the etatism of the Webbs, al-Barrawi shows himself in *Free Opinions* in favor of a large measure of decentralization and the strengthening of private groups and particularly of economic associations such as trade unions and professional associations.[38] Following Laski, al-Barrawi believed that society should be federal and pluralistic rather than hierarchical. He did not go so far as to plead for the distribution of economic power, and, in contrast with Laski, he did not associate "economic democracy" with the concentration of power in trade unions, but identified it with the social welfare policy of the state.[39] Still, al-Barrawi was in agreement with Laski in his belief that man should do what he deems morally right and that he could only be obedient if what is asked of him is consonant with his ethical standards.[40]

In *A Grammar of Politics* the state is presented as the only institution capable of mitigating and abolishing social inequality. As such, it is "the keystone of the social arch" and "the co-ordinating factor in the community."[41] Yet, Laski's central principle is the fulfillment of the individual, whose basic rights are abused by capitalism. He sees it as the state's task to defend and promote these rights. Consequently, Laski argues, "the State is not itself an end, but merely the means to an end, which is realized only in the enrichment of human lives. We are, that is to say, subjects of the State, not for its purpose, but for our own."[42] The doctrine of individual rights not only provided Rashid al-Barrawi with the means to criticize the Egyptian state and the economic and social system that it supported before 1952. It also helped him to transcend the limits of the liberalism of the previous generation and to give democratic reform a more certain footing than neo-liberals like Mirrit Butrus Ghali could. Yet, it is clear from his writings that in the end the collective transcends the rights of the individual.

Intellectually, *Free Opinions* is an adaptation of Harold Laski's basic ideas as presented in *A Grammar of Politics* to the Egyptian situation. The booklet stresses the rights of the citizens in their relations with the state, and it delimits the responsibility of the state towards its citizens.[43] *Free Opinions* begins with a definition of democracy. The first and foremost element of democracy is the guarantee of "welfare" or "happiness" (*sa'ada*), which is as much a sign of progress as of real well-being. Al-Barrawi describes for instance treatment in a hospital, social security, compulsory education, and public utilities as signs of progress because they are an expression of the state's interest in its citizens. Secondly, democracy guarantees the "equality" (*masawah*) of all citizens, defined in social democratic terms as guaranteed equal opportunities. Finally, democracy requires the right to freedom, i.e. the freedom of work, movement, and expression, and the freedom to form a political party and print whatever one wants. Freedom is ultimately restricted, however, because it is subordinate to the "common good" (*maslahat al-jama'a*), the "general welfare," and "prosperity" (*rifahiyya*).[44] In true socialist manner, the final purpose of these principles, says al-Barrawi, is the "realization of welfare" (*idrak al-sa'ada*).[45]

The welfare state

Rashid al-Barrawi was not only influenced by theoretical debates within British socialism; he was also very interested in its practical programs when, after the electoral victory of 1945, the Labour Party laid the foundations for the welfare state. Two topics that fascinated him were the Beveridge Plan and Labour's nationalization program. Al-Barrawi had studied at the London School of Economics in the 1930s, when William Beveridge was its director. His personal acquaintance with the institution that was founded by Sidney Webb must have sparked his interest in *Social Insurance and Allied Services*, or the Beveridge Plan, which was drawn up in 1942.

For al-Barrawi, the Beveridge Plan and its comprehensive social security, which covered health problems, unemployment, and old age, represented the pinnacle of civilization.[46] Its huge popularity during the Second World War in Great Britain, its means of enforcement, and the ideas behind it, strengthened al-Barrawi's vision of the state as the agent of change and social peace. All social reformers in Egypt in this period had the Beveridge Plan uppermost in their minds.[47] This is especially true of Rashid al-Barrawi, who constantly reiterated the main points of Labour's social security program that were implemented by the government between 1945 and 1951.[48] In addition to the nature of the plan itself, we may look for an explanation of al-Barrawi's interest in the fact that its originator, Beveridge, was the quintessential a-political, technocratic civil servant, whose thought, like the Webbs's, was dominated by a belief in an impartial, benevolent, educated elite.[49]

Labour's nationalization program was the linchpin of Rashid al-Barrawi's enthusiasm for the state as the agent of change and control. The reasons given for nationalization were especially important. Characteristically, Labour saw efficiency as one of the main justifications for the nationalization of aging industries, such as the coal mines and the railways, that had "failed the nation." With regard to the Bank of England and Cable and Wireless, the emphasis was on planning, for these institutions had to be integrated into a new national policy of investment and re-equipment.[50] In almost all of these cases Labour introduced a corporate model, and internal democratization was very limited.[51] The impact of these measures on countries like Egypt, where the economy was still dominated by foreigners or by the "parasitic" large landowners and monopolists, was tremendous. In the eyes of the more radical political forces, the program legitimized the nationalization of foreign firms. Egyptian intellectuals regarded the denial by the British Labour government of the right of the Iranian government to nationalize the oil industry in 1951 as a remarkable piece of hypocrisy.

Lenin's theory of imperialism

Having taken a program of etatist reform from the Webbs and a program for revolt from Laski, Rashid al-Barrawi still lacked an economic theory that would explain Egypt's position in the world and justify reform. He found it in Lenin's *Imperialism, the Highest Stage of Capitalism* (1916), which he had translated into Arabic in 1945.[52] Undoubtedly, *Imperialism, the Highest Stage of Capitalism* was one of the most influential political tracts in Egypt during this period. The popularity of the book must be regarded as a sign of the rise of a radical nationalist movement and of the economistic, secular trend within it, of which Rashid al-Barrawi was a leading exponent. Despite its inadequate historical analysis when it was published in 1916,[53] the work provided the middle classes and the disgruntled Egyptian intelligentsia with a convincing explanation of the history of Western interference in Egypt and an uncanny resemblance to the reality of daily life. In post-Second World War Egypt, with its disenchantment with ruling political parties and the economic system, the book provided a theoretical basis to the growing tendency to equate capitalism with imperialism and ascribe the retardation of the Egyptian economy to the domination of foreign firms. As a country with one of the highest rates of foreign investment in the world, Egypt seemed to illustrate Lenin's theory of the monopoly capitalist phase of imperialism, in which bank capital and industrial capital merge to form "finance capital."

Lenin's theory of the decay and degeneration of capitalism held a special appeal for radical Egyptians. In chapter seven of *Imperialism, the Highest Stage of Capitalism*, Lenin describes imperialism's degradation: "Like all monopoly, this capitalist monopoly inevitably gives rise to a tendency to stagnation and decay." He goes on to explain, "monopoly prices become fixed, even temporarily, so the stimulus to technical and, consequently, to all progress, disappears to a certain extent, and to that extent, also, the economic possibility arises of deliberately retarding technical progress."[54] Monopoly capitalism creates a class of "bondholders" (or rentiers), those who live by "clipping coupons," who take no part whatsoever in production, and whose profession is idleness. Lenin concludes, "the rentier state is a state of parasitic, decaying capitalism."[55]

Rashid al-Barrawi and other economists of his generation placed increasing emphasis on the idea of monopoly capital as a retarding force. For instance, Ali al-Gritli, one of the most important Egyptian economists of the 1960s, condemned cartelization in *The Structure of Modern Industry in Egypt* (1948) as "inimical to further industrialisation and to the interests of the people." He states that it ossifies the industrial structure and "delays the adoption of new techniques lest they adversely affect the value of existing investments." On this basis, Al-Gritli concludes, "in the special circumstances of Egypt the case against monopoly is particularly strong and the evils of exploitation are especially glaring owing to the prevalent poverty and appalling inequality of wealth."[56]

Laws of Development

Defining "backwardness" and "progress"

Rashid al-Barrawi's theory of history is remarkable because it is pieced together from highly diverse sources and because he tries to set up an economic interpretation of Egyptian history and explain its backwardness in comparative terms. In its radical modernism thrust it is revolutionary. Al-Barrawi was one of the first to divest himself of the more nationalist interpretation that had been standard practice and search for a concept of history based on quasi-neutral, universal, historical "laws" that dictate the development of every country throughout world history. He treats history as a process of continuous development, a dialectical unfolding of human potential, in which each stage of history is transcended by a higher stage. Technology is the motor of historical change,[57] while, in true Fabian fashion, the middle classes are the vanguard of history and the hero of al-Barrawi's narrative. Following the general myth of the Enlightenment, al-Barrawi sees middle-class rationalism as the most important weapon against absolutism, the privileges of the aristocracy, and the power of the church.[58]

Rashid al-Barrawi discerns three levels in world history on which the clash between the forces of progress and reaction has expressed itself since the rise of capitalism in the eighteenth century. On the economic level, unbridled capitalism, which developed into monopoly capital in the nineteenth century, has been opposed by democratic forces, which have tried to control it and transform it for the benefit of the general good. On the ideological level, this conflict has unfolded between the forces of "order" (*nizam*), "control," and "direction" (*tawjih*), and the forces of "chaos" (*fawda*) and "disturbance" (*idtirab*). The third level is constituted by the struggle between the reactionary, nationalist and the progressive, internationalist forces.[59] Not all endeavors to transcend the limitations of capitalism have been successful, writes al-Barrawi. He sees Italian Fascism and German Nazism as failed attempts to escape from the chaos of capitalism. The reason for their failure, he states, is that they believed imperialism could solve the population problem and that they revered war as the ultimate expression of the national will.[60]

Compared to Germany and Italy, the Soviet Union has, according to Rashid al-Barrawi, been more successful in harnessing the forces of history to overcome the basic contradictions of the capitalist world. The Soviet Union represents for him in many respects an example for the "backward" parts of the world, from which he draws general rules.[61] In his opinion, the sources of Russia's backwardness at the end of the 19th and the beginning of the 20th century are comparable to those of many contemporary colonies and semi-colonies. As was the case for the Soviet Union, he claims that the secret of development lies in the creation of a strong state that can enforce planning and industrialization over and against indigenous, landed, and foreign commercial interests.

Rashid al-Barrawi's general theory of "backwardness" (*ta'akhkhur*) is contained in his analysis of the origins of the Russian Revolution. His theory of underdevelopment stresses first the detrimental role of the ruling classes, to whose it advantage it was "to keep a reserve of cheap labor and preserve a situation of semi-slavery, thereby blocking the advancement of the agrarian productive forces and thwarting the application of advanced methods."[62] Secondly, al-Barrawi holds that Western capitalist investments aggravated the retardation of the development of the socioeconomic structure. Attracted on advantageous terms, foreign investment was unable to promote real development because it had already reached the parasitic stage of finance capital, as described by Lenin. As a result, profits were exported, workers became more impoverished, and trade between the countryside and towns did not increase sufficiently. Despite rapid industrialization, the Soviet Union remained basically an exporter of raw materials. In these circumstances, the middle classes were unable to push through a revolution and the 1905 revolution failed:

> Foreign capital found that it was in its interest to support the Czar and his following against liberal opinion [*ara hurra*],[63] and endeavored to destroy the constitutional system, out of fear of the representatives of the people and especially of the middle classes, who would probably affect foreign interests and prevent Russia from becoming a source of high profits for foreign capital."[64]

Rashid al-Barrawi shows himself a wholehearted supporter of the Russian revolution and its high modernism.[65] For him, the Russian revolution was the only avenue to the transcendence of underdevelopment, not because of its violence, but because of its policy of centralized development. He praises the communist leadership for its ruthless determination to transform society in all its aspects: "their eyes were focused on one goal: the rupture of the links with the past concerning philosophy, economic systems, social circumstances, cultural values, and age old traditions."[66]

His full support of the centralizing tendencies of the state is underlined in his condemnation of the brief period in which workers and peasants controlled production. Following the Webbs, he treats this period as an illustration of the collision of selfish interests with the needs of society as a whole. The workers' "supervision" (*ishraf*) over their own labor at the beginning of the revolution only led to arbitrariness and a lapse of discipline. "Coordination" (*tansiq*) and "direction" (*tawjih*) were lacking. Similarly, he argues, the production of the peasantry declined after they divided the property of the *kulaks* among themselves. As a result of self-supervision, the economy ground to a halt and cities were bereft of food.[67] In these circumstances, the state was forced to nationalize industries, for, writes al-Barrawi, "nationalization was also a guarantee that workers would get used to the system and would obey orders and implement assignments that the state gave in order to organize industry."[68] Likewise, he regards collectivization in agriculture as the ideal mode of maximizing production and disciplining the peasantry.

Rashid al-Barrawi's highest praise is reserved for the period after 1928 when the plans for the first five years were put into practice, during the so-called period of "socialism in one country." "Waste" (*tabdid*), "extravagance" (*israf*), and "backwardness" (*ta'akhkhur*) were eliminated during this time, says al-Barrawi.[69] The Gosplan insured that the Soviet economy was "directed" (*tawjih*), that the production of different goods was "harmonized" (*tansiq*), and that consumption was "organized" (*tanzim*). The result was that consumption and production were "balanced" (*tawazun*). Thus, al-Barrawi claims, capitalism, which is based on the chaos of personal decisions, was substituted by a plan that organized production like "a chain in which the shackles are linked together."[70] But planning in itself does not lead to development. Only in connection with industrialization and especially heavy industry would planning lead to modernization, or the complete transformation of the Egyptian person into a modern rational being:

Industrialization is one of the most important means of getting rid of obsolete opinions and systems, and carries within its folds elements that promote courage and efforts to work for the future, while it terminates dangerous social illnesses, such as favoritism (*mahsubiyya*), bribery (*rashwa*), corruption (*fasad*), extravagance (*israf*), indifference (*khumul*); indeed, it will stimulate us to enact social legislation in order to raise the standard of living and implement the necessary social and other types of reform.[71]

The origins of Egyptian backwardness

Rashid al-Barrawi and Muhammad Hamza Ulaysh were the first Egyptians to write a comprehensive economic history of Egypt. The work was entitled *The Economic Development of Egypt in the Modern Era* and published in 1944.[72] Other books on the subject had been published before, but most had been written by foreigners, like A.E. Crouchley and François Charles-Roux, who either worked for the government or had close ties with foreign firms in Egypt.[73] Moreover, none of these studies were theoretical or interpretative. The only other Egyptian who published in the field of economic history, Muhammad Fahmi Lahita, a senior colleague of Rashid al-Barrawi, wrote books in praise of Fu'ad I.[74] It was not until the end of the monarchy that he applied himself to more daring genres.[75] At the time official historical studies coming out of the university were dominated by the conservative historian Muhammad Shafiq Ghurbal (1894–1961).[76] He stimulated Ali al-Gritli, the prominent economic historian, to research the economic history of Egypt during Muhammad Ali's reign.[77] But he himself produced only a small monograph in praise of the reigning Muhammad Ali family, at the time of the publication of the study by al-Barrawi.[78] The only other Marxist works of economic history were written by members of the communist movement, like Ahmad Rushdi Salih (see chapter 3).

In *The Economic Development of Egypt in the Modern Era* Rashid al-Barrawi and Muhammad Hamza Ulaysh attempt to apply al-Barrawi's general theories of development to Egypt. It is also a preliminary study for *The Military Coup in Egypt*. The work probes the reasons why "poverty" (*faqr*), "disease" (*marad*), and "ignorance" (*jahl*) were still prevalent in Egypt. Its innovation was to consider economics as the key to the Egyptian renaissance (*al-nahda al-Misriyya*). Although the analysis is perhaps not very original at this early stage, its economistic approach in combination with a nationalist master narrative is an important departure from the standard historiography.

As is typical of the nationalist, anti-Ottoman historiography that characterizes the modernist school, al-Barrawi and Hamza Ulaysh believe modern history started with the French Occupation of Egypt in 1798. The authors call it, "a turning point in Egyptian history on the political, the social, and the economic level."[79] They describe the economic situation before the French occupation as deplorable and stagnant, comparable to the Middle Ages in Europe. Muhammad Ali (1805–48), whom they regard as the founder of modern Egypt, would later emulate the methods by which French scientists surveyed Egypt and planned its development. In defense of Muhammad Ali, they treat the monopoly system as the only way for the state to establish an Egyptian industry, expand transport, and develop trade.[80]

Rashid al-Barrawi and Muhammad Hamza Ulaysh condemn the enforced specialization in cotton production under the British occupation because they believe that Egypt missed a crucial opportunity to industrialize, which would have meant the difference between becoming a rich, developed country, comparable to European countries, and remaining a backward country. They write that this was the result of a deliberate policy by the British, who prevented Egypt from developing economically through the use of tariffs and other political and economic instruments. Consequently, Egypt's economic and social structure was distorted.[81] Industrial investment was actively discouraged, bankrupting existing industries, which meant that for a while Egypt was even de-industrializing and losing its technological expertise.[82] The upshot, write al-Barrawi and Hamza Ulaysh, was that Egypt was left totally dependent on cotton production and foreign investment.[83]

The two authors tread a more independent path with their comparison between Russia before the revolution and Egypt's economic situation before 1919. But they fail to give an account of the rise of class differences in Egypt and the development of the skewed relations between the indigenous dominant classes, the *a'yan*, and the British. They only mention in passing the creation of large landownership and the impoverishment of the *fallahin*. Aside from the publication of the *Report of the Commission on Commerce and Industry* in 1918 and the establishment of Bank Misr in 1920, the authors regard the tariff reform of 1930 as the real turning point because it enabled the state to stimulate industry actively and render an economic renaissance (*nahda*) possible.[84]

Rashid al-Barrawi and Muhammad Hamza Ulaysh are convinced that the Second World War presented a crucial opportunity for developing Egypt's potential. Just like the previous war, industry expanded on a considerable scale, the percentage of the population working in industry increased, and government control grew. At the same time, the war made it abundantly clear that the present political regime was incapable of coping with the situation. *The Economic Development of Egypt in the Modern Era* criticizes the government for not holding down inflation or organizing a rationing system for the poor, and letting profits soar for the rich. In the chapter "Some Problems of Tomorrow," the authors express their belief that changes will have to be made if the regime wants to survive. They warn ominously, "without doubt the transition from war to peace demands an attentiveness not to make mistakes that are difficult to mend. Not one moment does it seem that those responsible realize this."[85] Drastic reform would be necessary if the regime wished to make the transition to a higher phase of history successfully.

Reform

Introduction

After the Second World War, Rashid al-Barrawi became a well-known social reformer, who took part in major debates on the subject. During this period he kept his radicalism, expressed in his more theoretical books, in check and gained access to the more respectable newspapers like *al-Ahram* and the weekly *al-Fusul*. Until the burning of Cairo by rioting crowds on 26 January 1952, his own theories of history must have kept him constantly anxious about the growing confrontation between a radicalized nationalist movement and a regime that was unable to carry out reforms and establish a stable society. While the monarchy was totally incapable of even contemplating reform, the nationalist movement concentrated on mass revolution through the streets and "chaotic" and uncoordinated revolt with the aim of destroying the state. Only an etatist program of planning, collectivization, and mass industrialization, imposed from above, could guarantee development, al-Barrawi believed.

Agrarian reform

Like all reformers, Rashid al-Barrawi was acutely aware that the basic obstacle to modernization, democratization, and industrialization was the social structure of rural society. The social and economic relations in the countryside prevented the rural lower classes from participating in society and creating a strong Egypt that could function in the modern world. The three classic afflictions of Egypt at this time, "ignorance" (*jahl*), "poverty" (*faqr*), and "sickness" (*marad*) were nowhere more conspicuous than in the countryside. It is interesting to analyze al-Barrawi's description of agrarian reform in some detail because it shows the difficulty of expressing criticism at the time and it underlines his technocratic tendencies, already pointed to in the previous sections.

A chapter added in the 1945 edition of *The Economic Development of Egypt in the Modern Era* presents its readers with a short agrarian reform program, which, with Mirrit Butrus Ghali's, was one of the first to raise the issue in Egypt.[86] Rashid al-Barrawi and Muhammad Hamza Ulaysh cite almost the same statistics as Mirrit Butrus Ghali, based on the 1940 figures of the Ministry of Agriculture.[87] However, they draw a conclusion from these figures that is different from Mirrit Butrus Ghali's. By including the number of owners, the statistics are much more dramatic as they reveal not only the poverty in the countryside, but also the enormous discrepancy in wealth: about 0.8 percent of the landowners own half the land. On the basis of this information, the authors determine that such inequality would be impossible to maintain once the peasantry becomes more educated and more aware of its deplorable position. In tune with their failure to mention class interests, they discuss different proposals for reform, without really taking a position, although they seem to be in favor of sequestration of land above 100 *faddan*. For the rest, they propose a number of supporting measures such as imposing a minimum level of land reform, strengthening agrarian co-operatives, reclaiming of land.

In 1948, Rashid al-Barrawi mentions agrarian reform for the second time, in a little tract entitled *Our Social Problems: Poverty, the Peasant, Nationalization, the Workers*.[88] This time, he presents his agrarian reform program in greater detail, relating it to other aspects of his overall reform program. He clearly speaks out in favor of land reform and sets the maximum amount of land to be owned at 50 *faddan*. Over that figure, all land should be sequestrated. Citing statistics from 1944, he makes the following simple calculation of the way in which the land should be distributed. All the owners of an amount of land over 50 *faddan*, that is 12,132 owners, possessing a total of 2,430,084 *faddan*, should be dispossessed; 12,132 x 50 *faddan* equals 606,600 *faddan*. This amount is subtracted from 2,430,084 *faddan*, which means that 1,823,484 *faddan* is available for distribution. In addition, 300,000 *faddan* will be made available for distribution over the following five years by land reclamation. Another source of land is the ministry of religious domain (*awqaf*), which has 180,000 *faddan* at its disposal. Thus, a total of 2,303,484 *faddan* can be distributed, which is almost half of all agricultural land in Egypt, covering 5,873,206 *faddan*. The land available for reform should be distributed over 3/4 million members of the two poorest categories of landowners, especially those farmers with less than 2 *faddan*.[89]

It is unclear how exactly this distribution is to take place, and why Rashid al-Barrawi has arrived at the figure of 3/4 million of the poorest landowners to receive 4 *faddan*, even though he acknowledges that landowners with less than 1 *faddan* alone amount to 1,792,530 persons. Nevertheless, compared with Mirrit Butrus Ghali's proposals, Rashid al-Barrawi's agrarian reform program *is* radical. If one follows his plan, more than 2 million *faddan* could be distributed within a few years, while Butrus Ghali's plan does not really specify the amount of land available for distribution to the lowest categories of landowners; nor does it set a time schedule. The only part of the land reform about which Butrus Ghali is specific is land reclamation, covering slightly over 1 million *faddan*, a project that would take decades to complete.

Typically, Rashid al-Barrawi's main motive for land reform, like the reform proposals of the Webbs or those of the Society of National Renaissance, was not so much social justice, although social reform and combating poverty were certainly important issues. Rather, he seems to have been inspired by the ideal of the modernization of society. This is evident from his constant reiteration of the importance of economic efficiency and economies of scale, which are central themes in his work. For instance, the importance of institutionalizing expertise in committees in the Ministry of Agriculture is strongly emphasized.

In the same vein, agrarian reform has its main rationale in technological improvement. Al-Barrawi believes that the dangers of fragmentation and inefficiency can only be counteracted by cooperatives and the consolidation of small plots into large agrarian collectives along the lines of the Soviet Russian model. However, to make his reform more acceptable to the middle classes, al-Barrawi dropped the demand for the nationalization of land. The solution that he proposes is to join plots of 5 *faddan* together to form large tracts of land measuring 1,000 *faddan*, which should be worked as a unit, thus allowing for the use of the latest machinery and the most efficient form of organization, as in a factory. In this collectivized cooperative, the state would provide for houses, schools, and hospitals.[90]

In the meantime, agrarian reform had attracted the attention of the United Nations and the British Labour government. Not surprisingly, they argued for reform in the same technocratic manner as al-Barrawi, who had taken his modernist, reformist vocabulary from the West. Doreen Warriner's evocative description of Egypt's poverty in *Land and Poverty in the Middle East* (1948) played a key role in placing land reform on the political agenda in Western countries, especially during the Cold War.[91] Her main thesis was that Egypt had become "over-populated" after the First World War when population growth had begun to outstrip the expansion of cultivation. Using W. Cleland's figures,[92] Warriner estimated that one-fifth of the labor force might be able to maintain the current volume of production. With the introduction of machinery, ten percent of Egypt's peasants could do the same amount of work. Warriner describes how falling real income per head, increasing costs of living, and deplorable housing lead to undernourishment and disease, making the conditions of the *fellah's* life "morally degenerate," an "unrelieved horror."[93]

The solutions proposed by Warriner resemble Rashid al-Barrawi's: land reclamation, industrialization, and, most importantly, land reform. The strengthening of the internal market, a precondition for industrialization, depends on land reform.

> From the standpoint of management, the reform of land-ownership would be easier to carry out in Egypt than in any other country ... But nowhere are political obstacles greater. The Egyptian "pashas" are cotton lords, big business men controlling large fortunes, who hold the entire country in their grip and are utterly opposed to any measure which would raise the level of the cultivators.[94]

Coming from the same intellectual origins as Rashid al-Barrawi, Doreen Warriner's influential book undoubtedly strengthened the call for land reform in the 1940s and 1950s in Egypt and elsewhere.

The July Revolution and the Spirit of the Age

The Military Coup in Egypt, published at the end of 1952, almost six months after the military took power, is the highpoint of Rashid al-Barrawi's historical writing. Despite his contacts with the military and especially Gamal Abd al-Nasser, *The Military Coup in Egypt* follows logically from his earlier writings. The basic purpose of the book is to demonstrate that the military takeover was in fact a modernist revolution that would propel Egypt into the twentieth century and let the country catch up with the rest of the world:

> What has been established ..., as will be seen from the following chapters and in the light of what has already been achieved, is that it has been a wide-scale revolt against the economic, social and political state of affairs, aiming at radical changes with the object of bringing about conditions compatible with the spirit of the age and the aims of the community.[95]

In this work, al-Barrawi combines the Fabian, Marxist and Leninist terminology with which he had struggled in his economic and historical studies over the past decades. He incorporates these concepts confidently in his broad and sweeping narrative, which acquires its authority from objective "laws of history." These laws are part of the march of Reason, which overcomes "backwardness," ignorance, corruption, vested interests, patronage and clientalism, and all those forces that are allied with the *ancien régime*, to ensure the "greatest good to the greatest number."[96] Although the terminology of the technocratic revolution "from above" is conspicuously absent, al-Barrawi clearly presents the military as essential to the new "rational" transition to modernity: "formerly, demonstrations, riots and barricades were the principal aspects of any revolution. Nowadays, such antiquated methods have become ineffective and it has become necessary for the success of a revolution that it should be undertaken by regular armed forces."[97]

Rashid al-Barrawi's book turned out to be a more successful exercise in modernist historiography than *The Economic Development of Egypt in the Modern Era*. This is because for the first time he provides his plot with high drama, peopling the book with villains, the "reactionaries," and heroes, the representatives of "progress," who are locked in a class struggle for historical dominance. In this narrative, the "new middle classes" are the protagonists, representing a rising force in history.

The references to al-Barrawi's earlier work are obvious, and the basic historical problem of Egypt is now stated clearly:

> It is the nature of the bourgeoisie that it should spare no effort in destroying feudalism. But in the case of Egypt, however,

there was a strange anomaly. The bourgeoisie, in their quest for social prestige according to the social prestige of the day, began to acquire land and so were directly interested in the maintenance of the obsolete feudal system.[98]

As had been the case in Russia, the Egyptian bourgeoisie, which led the 1919 revolution, had betrayed its goals, according to al-Barrawi. He defines these goals as the liberation from foreign rule, the abolition of Capitulations, and the establishment of the constitutional system to check the authority of the palace and the influence of large landowners.[99] Besides its feudalization, al-Barrawi points specifically to the Tariff Agreement of 1930, the Anglo-Egyptian Treaty of 1936, and especially the 1937 Montreux Conference, as important contributions to what he sees as the degeneration of the middle classes. Whereas the first of these international agreements allowed the state to limit internal competition, the second made all inhabitants of Egypt equal before the law and stimulated the cooperation between Egyptian and foreign capital.[100] The result was the metamorphosis of the "old middle classes" into the "bourgeoisie," and subsequently into the supporters of "big monopolist capitalism." The villains in this scenario are Isma'il Sidqi, Hafiz Afifi, Ali Mahir, politicians who were closely related to the Palace and the financial and "feudal" interests and who persuaded the "bourgeoisie" to join the existing alliance between the feudal classes, the Palace, and the British.[101]

Al-Barrawi's own addition to the construction of this plot is the application of the Russian historical trajectory, previously described in his book *Five Year Plans* (1948), and the Fabian concept of the "new middle class" to the Egyptian historical context. He discerns a general law in the Egyptian and Russian narrative of development: if a class failed to achieve its "historic mission," that is, to supplant a backward system by a more advanced one, "another [class] was bound to rise and destined to carry the bright torch of progress."[102] According to this historical law, the new middle class would inherit the task of completing the revolution from the higher bourgeoisie. The members of this group had after all discredited themselves by blocking economic progress through their position as monopoly capitalists. They had also hampered the democratic process by abrogating the 1923 Constitution and preventing the achievement of independence through their alliance with the Palace, the feudal class, as well as the British.[103]

It was Rashid al-Barrawi's task to provide the regime with political and social legitimation. In light of this, his representation of a new middle class, whose responsibility it is to lead Egypt to a new historical stage, is not just an academic exercise. It gives insight into the nature of the popular alliance that supported the new regime, according to al-Barrawi. He includes among the *effendiyya* lower government employees, the majority of the professionals, students at the universities, artisans, and traders. Further, he assures his readers that they are "most revolutionary" because they are "inimical to British imperialism, Palace absolutist pretensions, feudal and capitalist privileges." Moreover, the new class has inherited the leadership of the nationalist movement from the bourgeoisie because it is able "to enlist the support of the laboring classes in towns, together, though on a very modest scale, with the sympathy of the rural population."[104] This progressive alliance, under the leadership of the new middle class, is pitted against the reactionary alliance.

Although al-Barrawi's analysis of Egypt's history is majestic, it is also revealing for what it leaves out. He conveniently forgets to mention the great diversity of and splits between the middle classes, which may explain why none of the many organizations that represented the *effendiyya*, such Young Egypt, the communists, and others, failed to take power. By imagining the new class as an entity, it acquires a tangibility it did not have. This conforms to the wishes of al-Barrawi and his interest in building a state machinery that would override all "special interests" of the reactionary alliance. By including all capitalist groups into this reactionary alliance, he also gave the state the authority to nationalize and sequester its property as well as that of the large landowners.

Conclusion

During the second half of the 1940s Rashid al-Barrawi became one of the major representatives of the discourse of modernism. His works advocated a different road to modernity than that of the liberals of the Society of National Renaissance. Instead of strengthening civil society, he supported the strengthening of the state as the main instrument of change and progress. Only the state could overcome the chaos of civil society, resolve the conflict of interests of political society, and promote the general interest of the nation-state. Foreshadowing his later backing of central planning, for al-Barrawi the state embodied rationality and the unlimited capacity for social and civil engineering, while the middle classes represented the new presence that would lead Egypt to a new dawn and a new future.

The origins of Rashid al-Barrawi's ideas concerning the modernization paradigm are not difficult to trace. Following Salama Musa, he gathered most of his ideas from the British Labour Party and more particularly from the Fabian Society, which represented the new combination between power and knowledge in the service of the emancipation and progress of the working and middle classes. He added to this knowledge his own experience in Great Britain and theories of economic development or underdevelopment, as they would later be called.

Rashid al-Barrawi's originality lies in his blending of different ingredients in a convincing meta-narrative of reform and progress in which the rising class of the *effendiyya* of the 1930s and 1940s is given the role of the vanguard of the national struggle for independence and social and economic development. In opposition to the dichotomy between Western materialism and Eastern spiritualism characteristic of the discourse of authenticity upheld by the Muslim Brotherhood and Young Egypt,[105] al-Barrawi posited a counter-discourse of modernization that centered on the dichotomy between progress and reaction. He presented the middle classes as the progressive force in this struggle while the landed and industrial interests were its reactionary foes. According to al-Barrawi the middle classes were the true nation, not because they belonged to the "leading families" (*a'ilat*) or "those who have a real stake in society" (*ashab al-masalih al-haqiqiyya*), as had been the case for the liberals of the previous generation, or because they were more authentic, but because they were better educated, worked for their income, and in general understood the contemporary world better. This applied *a fortiori* to middle class intellectuals. Independent from the patronage and corruption of the elite, they could claim to be the real "opinion makers" (*ahl al-ra'y*). From a vantage point of superior knowledge, they were able to discern the universal economic and social laws that ruled Egyptian society, show the nation its future, and lead it to modernity. Science, knowledge, and expertise were the monopoly of this new class and could be wielded to combat the prejudices and narrow interests of the ruling class that kept the country in a state of backwardness. Poverty (*faqr*), disease (*marad*), and ignorance (*jahl*), the three classic afflictions causing Egypt's state of backwardness, could be eliminated if the new middle classes ruled the country.

Rashid al-Barrawi believed that the merger of knowledge and power necessary to reform could be achieved if the middle classes seized state power and used it to modernize Egyptian society. Although al-Barrawi was himself a product of the emerging civil society and the relative protected sphere of the University of Cairo, he associated rationality with the state and not with the greater independence and strengthening of civil society. As an advocate of authoritarian modernization, he was one of the promoters of what James C. Scott calls "high modernism." His concept of history was largely future-oriented, deterministic, instrumentalist, and emancipatory, leading ruthlessly to national progress, which was objectified and reified by being expressed mainly in quantifiable units of production and material development. Above all Rashid al-Barrawi's high modernism is expressed in his absolute belief in the complete malleability of society. Industrialization and land reform were the means to create and discipline a new Egyptian who would live, produce, and create rationally according to modern rules and objectives. The different aspects of his version of modernity came together in the concept of planning and the state's complete control over society. The tension in his political thought between democratic and authoritarian means to achieve modernity were dissolved after the July Revolution in favor of the latter.

Notes

1 Vernon Egger, *A Fabian in Egypt: Salamah Musa and the Rise of the Professional Classes in Egypt, 1909–1939* (Lanham: University Press of America, 1986). Also, Ibrahim A. Ibrahim, "Salama Musa: An Essay on Cultural Alienation," *Middle Eastern Studies* 15 (1979): 346–57.
2 See for a discussion of the technocratic character of the Nasserist state, Nazih N. M. Ayubi, *Bureaucracy and Politics in Contemporary Egypt* (London: Ithaca Press, 1980), Chapter 3, "New Political Order, New Organizational Facts," 157–270. Ayubi stresses the technocratic character of the regime by pointing to its dependence on "science," its "technicality," and the "organizational," "administrative," and "efficiency" aspects of its rule, which involved the domination of administration over politics. Even though he describes the "pragmatic" and "empirical" nature of the regime's political leadership, Ayubi nonetheless repeats the cliché that the regime did not have any specific political ideology.
3 Biographical information is obtained from the register of the University of Cairo and a personal interview with Salah al-Din Namiq, a close personal friend and colleague of Rashid al-Barrawi, on 27 October 1989.
4 Rashid al-Barrawi, *Halat Misr al-iqtisadiyya fi 'ahd al-Fatimiyyin*. The work was brought out in Cairo in 1948 by the publishing house that published almost all of Rashid al-Barrawi's books, Maktabat al-Nahda al-Misriyya.

5 *Al-Iqtisad wa al-ijtima'* was the official journal of the Faculty of Commerce for which, beside Rashid al-Barrawi and other junior reformist economists like Abd al-Raziq Hasan, more established figures wrote, such as Muhammad Fahmi Lahita. Their articles on reform can be found in Nos. 11 and 12 of *al-Iqtisad wa al-ijtima'* 1945.
6 Rashid al-Barrawi and Muhammad Hamzat 'Ulaysh, *al-Tatawwur al-iqtisadi fi Misr fi al-'asr al-hadith*, 2nd ed. (Cairo: Maktabat al-Nahda al-Misriyya, 1945).
7 V. I. Linin, *al-Isti'mar a'la marahil al-ra'smaliyya*, translated by Rashid al-Barrawi (Cairo: Maktabat al-Nahda al-Misriyya, 1945).
8 Karl Markis, *Ra'smal*, vol. 1 and vol. 2., translated by Rashid al-Barrawi (Cairo: Maktabat al-Nahda al-Misriyya, 1947). Although in Arabic there are two volumes, in fact only the first volume of *Capital* was translated.
9 A. Liyuntif, *al-Iqtisad al-siyasi*, translated by Rashid al-Barrawi (Cairo: Maktabat al-Nahda al-Misriyya, 1946).
10 Fridrik Injilz, *al-Tafsir al-ishtiraki li al-tarikh: Mukhtarat min Fridrik Injilz*, translated and introduced by Rashid al-Barrawi (Cairo: Maktabat al-Nahda al-Misriyya, 1947).
11 A. Buni, *al-Dawla wa al-nuzum al-iqtisadiyya fi al-Sharq al-Awsat*, translated by Rashid al-Barrawi (Cairo: Maktabat al-Nahda al-Misriyya, 1950).
12 Rashid al-Barrawi, *al-Nizam al-ishtiraki min al-nahiyyatayn, al-nazariyya wa al-'amaliyya* (Cairo: Maktabat al-Nahda al-Misriyya, 1951). Rashid al-Barrawi and Ahmad Nazmi 'Abd al-Hamid, *al-Nizam al-ishtiraki: 'Ard, wa al-tahlil, wa naqd* (Cairo: Maktabat al-Nahda al-Misriyya, 1946).
13 Rashid al-Barrawi, *Mashru'at al-sanawat al-khams* (Cairo: Maktabat al-Nahda al-Misriyya, 1948).
14 For economic reforms, see Rashid al-Barrawi and 'Ali Dalawir, *Mushkilat al-ijtima'iyya: Al-Faqr, al-fallah, al-ta'mim, al-'ummal* (Cairo: Maktabat al-Nahda al-Misriyya, 1948) and for political reforms, see Rashid al-Barrawi, *Ara' hurra* (Cairo: Maktabat al-Nahda al-Misriyya, 1949).
15 Personal interview with Salah 'al-Din Namiq, 27 October 1989.
16 Rashid al-Barrawi, *Nahwa 'alam jadid aw tatawwur al-fikra al-duwaliyya*, (Cairo: Maktabat al-Nahda al-Misriyya, 1945). Also, Rashid al-Barrawi, *al-Tariq ila al-salam: Bahth fi tanzim al-'alaqat al-duwwaliyya* (Cairo: Maktabat al-Nahda al-Misriyya, 1949).
17 Rashid al-Barrawi, *Mashru'at al-difa' 'an al-Sharq al-Awsat* (Cairo: Maktabata al-Nahda al-Misriyya, 1952). Rashid al-Barrawi, *al-Kutla al-islamiyya* (Cairo: Maktabat al-Nahda al-Misriyya, 1952). Rashid al-Barrawi *Harb al-bitrul fi al-Sharq al-Awsat* (Cairo: Maktabat al-Nahda al-Misriyya, 1950). Rashid al-Barrawi, ed., *Mushkilat al-Sharq al-Awsat* (Cairo: Maktabat al-Nahda al-Misriyya, 1948). Rashid al-Barrawi, ed. *Dirasat fi al-Sudan wa iqtisadiyyat al-Sharq al-Awsat* (Cairo: Maktabat al-Nahda al-Misriyya, 1951).
18 Rashed El-Barawy, *The Military Coup in Egypt: An Analytic Study* (Cairo: The Renaissance Bookshop, 1952), 21.
19 El-Barawy, *Military Coup*. The book is a translation of the Arabic version, Rashid al-Barrawi, *Haqiqat al-inqilab al-akhir fi Misr* (Cairo: Maktabat al-Nahda al-Misriyya, 1952).
20 W. H. Greenleaf, "Laski and British Socialism," *History of Political Thought* 2 (1981): 577.
21 Louis Awad believes that the two forces that had influenced Rashid al-Barrawi were Harold Laski and Marxism: "It is difficult to say what Rashed el-Barrawy,

an economic publicist, really wanted, for while he translated *Das Kapital* he agitated for Harold Laski and the Welfare State." Louis Awad, "Cultural and Intellectual Developments in Egypt Since 1952," in *Egypt Since the Revolution*, edited by P. J. Vatikiotis (London: George Allen and Unwin, 1968), 154.

22 E. J. Hobsbawm, *Labouring Men: Studies in the History of Labour* (London: Weidenfeld and Nicolson, 1964), 252–5. And Peter Wittig, *Der englische Weg zum Sozialismus: Die Fabier und ihre Bedeutung für die Labour Party und die englische Politik* (Berlin: Duncker & Humblot, 1982), 252. See also Peter Beilharz, *Labour's Utopias: Bolshevism, Fabianism, Social Democracy* (London: Routledge, 1992), 51–92.
23 W. H. Greenleaf, *The British Political Tradition*, vol. I, (London: Methuen, 1983), 248 and 252.
24 Wittig, 89–97.
25 Sidney Webb, "The Basis of Socialism," in *Fabian Essay* (1889) cited in Wittig, 93.
26 Wittig, 141.
27 Sidney Webb, *The Necessary Basis of Society*, Fabian Tract No. 159 (1911), cited in Wittig, 273.
28 Sidney Webb, *Socialism, True or False*, Fabian Tract No. 5 (1894), cited in Wittig, 161.
29 Sidney and Beatrice Webb, *What is Socialism?* (1913), cited in Wittig, 174
30 Sidney and Beatrice Webb, *The History of Trade Unionism* (1894), cited in Wittig, 135.
31 See for an analysis of the Ricardian and Fabian theories of rent, Wittig, 135–8 and A. M. McBriar, *Fabian Socialism and English Politics 1884–1918* (Cambridge: Cambridge University Press, 1966), 29–47.
32 Introduction written by Rashid al-Barrawi for his translation of *Capital, Ra'smal*, I. For a translation of al-Barrawi's introduction and other information about the translations of *Capital* in Arabic, see also: Stefan Wild, "'Das Kapital' in arabischer Übersetzung," in *Festgabe für H. Wehr*, edited by Wolfdietrich Fischer (Wiesbaden: Otto Harrassowitz, 1969). For Rashid al-Barrawi's analysis of Marxism, see al-Barrawi, *Nizam*, 22–49.
33 Al-Barrawi, *Nizam*, 103.
34 Al-Barrawi, *Nizam*, 122.
35 Sidney and Beatrice Webb, *Soviet Communism: A New Civilisation* (London and New York: Longmans, 1935).
36 The works that Rashid al-Barrawi cites in *Mashru'at al-sanawat al-khams* on the Soviet Union are: Maurice Dobb, *Soviet Planning and Labour in Peace and War* (1942), Christopher Hill, *Lenin and the Russian Revolution* (1947), and an anthology edited by G. D. H. Cole, *Our Soviet Ally* (1945).
37 Harold Laski, *A Grammar of Politics* (London: George Allen & Unwin, 1925).
38 Al-Barrawi, *Ara' hurra*.
39 Laski, 55–6.
40 Laski, 23–37.
41 Laski, 72 and 82.
42 Laski, 88.
43 Rashid al-Barrawi, "Hadha sawt al-sha'b fa-istami'u ilayhi," *al-Ahram*, 11 January 1950.
44 Al-Barrawi, *Ara' hurra*, 6–14.
45 Al-Barrawi, *Ara' hurra*, 15.

46 Rashid al-Barrawi, "al-Hizb al-musaytira 'ala aqdar Biritaniya wa khitatuhu fi tatbiq al-ishtirakiyya," *al-Fusul* 78 (March 1951): 24–9.
47 Personal interview with 'Abd al-Raziq Hasan on 2 October 1989.
48 Al-Barrawi, *Nizam*, 147–81.
49 José Harris, *William Beveridge: A Biography* (Oxford: Clarendon Press, 1977), 314–5. See also Harriet Jones, "Beveridge's Trojan Horse," *History Today* (1992): 44–9.
50 K. O. Morgan, *Labour in Power, 1945–1951* (Oxford: Clarendon Press, 1984), 95.
51 Morgan, 97–108.
52 Linin, *Isti'mar*.
53 See for a critique of Lenin's theory of imperialism: B. Warren, "About-Turn: Lenin's Imperialism," *Imperialism, Pioneer of Capitalism* (London: Verso, 1980), 48–83.
54 V. I. Lenin, "Imperialism, the Highest Stage of Capitalism," *Selected Works*, Vol. I (Moscow: Foreign Language Publishing House, 1946), 717.
55 Lenin, "Imperialism," 719.
56 A. A. I. El-Gritly, "The Structure of Modern Industry in Egypt," *L'Égypte Contemporaine* 38 (1948): 525–7.
57 Al-Barrawi, *Nizam*, 22–47.
58 Al-Barrawi, trans., *Tafsir*, 1–18. And al-Barrawi, *Tariq*, 9–11 and 28–9.
59 Al-Barrawi, *Tariq*, 79.
60 For al-Barrawi's analysis, see al-Barrawi, *Nahwa*, 141–57; in addition to al-Barrawi, *Tariq*, 108–9 and 162–9.
61 Al-Barrawi, *Mashru'at*, 11.
62 Al-Barrawi, *Mashru'at*, 28.
63 It is interesting to note that Rashid al-Barrawi wrote a pamphlet with the same title in 1949.
64 Al-Barrawi, *Mashru'at*, 60.
65 See for the analysis of the high modernist quality of Lenin's political discourse, James C. Scott, *Seeing Like a State: How Certain Schemes to Improve the Human Condition Have Failed* (New Haven: Yale University Press, 1999), Chapter 5, "The Revolutionary Party: A Plan and a Diagnosis," 147–79.
66 Al-Barrawi, *Mashru'at*, 64.
67 Al-Barrawi, *Mashru'at*, 84–96.
68 Al-Barrawi, *Mashru'at*, 106.
69 Al-Barrawi, *Mashru'at*, 199.
70 Al-Barrawi, *Mashru'at*, 196.
71 Al-Barrawi and Hamzat 'Ulaysh, 297.
72 The Egyptian economic historian Ali Barakat regards *al-Tatawwur al-iqtisadi fi Misr fi al-'asr al-hadith* as "one of the first analytical economic historical works [in Egypt]." 'Ali Barakat, "Fi tariq ila madrasa ijtima'iyya fi kitabat tarikh misr al-hadith," *al-Fikr* 5 (1985): 58.
73 A. E. Crouchley, *The Investment of Foreign Capital in Egyptian Companies and Public Debt* (Cairo: Government Press, 1936). Also, A. E. Crouchley, *The Economic Development of Modern Egypt* (London: 1938). François Charles-Roux, *La production du coton en Égypte* (Paris: Colin, 1908). Crouchley's writings remained the standard work on industrial development in Egypt until 'Ali al-Gritli's thesis was published in 1948. A. A. I. El-Gritly, "The Structure of Modern Industry in Egypt," *L'Égypte Contemporaine* 38 (1948): 363–582.

74 Muhammad Fahmi Lahita was one of the first Egyptian professors at the Faculty of Commerce. He started to publish in 1922. The most important works that he wrote in the period between 1945 and 1952 are published as: *Tarikh Fu'ad al-awwal al-iqtisadi. Misr fi tariq al-tawjih al-kamil*, 3 vols. The works were brought out by Maktabat al-Nahda al-Misriyya in 1945 and 1946.
75 Muhammad Fahmi Lahita, *al-Nizam al-naqd bayna al-ra'smaliyya wa al-ishtirakiyya*, 2 vols. (Cairo: Maktabat al-Nahda al-Misriyya, 1950).
76 See for an analysis of Shafiq Ghurbal's work, Youssef M. Choueri, "Muhammad Ali and the Sphinx: Shafiq Ghurbal's Histories of Egypt," *Arab History and the Nation-State: A Study in Modern Arab Historiography 1820–1980* (London: Routledge, 1989), 65–114.
77 'Ali al-Jritli, *Tarikh al-sina'a fi Misr fi al-nisf al-awwal min al-qarn al-tasi' 'ashar* (Cairo: Dar al-Ma'arif bi-Misr, 1952).
78 Shafiq Ghurbal, *Muhammad 'Ali al-Kabir* (Cairo: Dar al-Ihya' li-l-Kutub al-'Arabiyya, 1944).
79 Al-Barrawi and Hamzat 'Ulaysh, 24.
80 Al-Barrawi and Hamzat 'Ulaysh, 29–63.
81 Al-Barrawi and Hamzat 'Ulaysh, 106–27.
82 Al-Barrawi and Hamzat 'Ulaysh, 148–9.
83 Al-Barrawi and Hamzat 'Ulaysh, 173–9. There is a remarkable resemblance between Rashid al-Barrawi's theory of underdevelopment and those of the *dependencia* school. See Bjorn Hettne, *Development Theory and the Three Worlds* (Burnt Mill: Longman, 1990), 82–7.
84 Al-Barrawi and Hamzat 'Ulaysh, 242.
85 Al-Barrawi and Hamzat 'Ulaysh, 289.
86 Al-Barrawi and Hamzat 'Ulaysh, 289–96. Gabriel Baer, "Egyptian Attitudes Towards Land Reform, 1922–1955," in *The Middle East in Transition: Studies in Contemporary History*, edited by W. Laqueur (London: RKP, 1958), 93.
87 Al-Barrawi and Hamzat 'Ulaysh, 290.
88 Rashid al-Barrawi, *Mushkilatuna al-ijtima'iyya. al-Faqr, al-fallah, al-ta'mim, al-'ummal* (Cairo: Maktabat al-Nahda al-Misriyya, 1948).
89 Al-Barrawi, *Mushkilatuna*, 30–1. Any discrepancy between the statistics of 1940 and the figures presented in *Mushkilatuna* is due to the fact the figures in *Mushkilatuna* are based on the national statistics of 1944.
90 Al-Barrawi, *Mushkilatuna*, 32–8; al-Barrawi, *Mashru'at*, 448–52.
91 Doreen Warriner, *Land and Poverty in the Middle East* (London and New York: Royal Institute of International Affairs, 1948).
92 W. Cleland, "A Population Plan for Egypt," *L'Egypte Contemporaine* 30 (May 1939): 461–84.
93 Warriner, 39.
94 Warriner, 48–9.
95 El-Barawy, *Military Coup*, 21.
96 El-Barawy, *Military Coup*, 47.
97 El-Barawy, *Military Coup*, 49.
98 El-Barawy, *Military Coup*, 73.
99 El-Barawy, *Military Coup*, 52–3.
100 El-Barawy, *Military Coup*, 69.
101 El-Barawy, *Military Coup*, 69–74.
102 El-Barawy, *Military Coup*, 105.

103 El-Barawy, *Military Coup*, 148–82.
104 El-Barawy, *Military Coup*, 80.
105 See Israel Gershoni, "Rejecting the West: The Image of the West in the Teachings of the Muslim Brotherhood, 1928–1939," in *The Great Powers in the Middle East, 1919–1939*, edited by Uriel Dann (New York: Holmes and Meier, 1988), 370–91; Israel Gershoni, "Imagining the East: Muhammad Husayn Haykal's Changing Representations of East-West Relations, 1928–1933," *Asian and African Studies* 25 (1991): 209–51.

◆ CHAPTER THREE ◆

Egyptian Communism and the Paradigm of the Front

Introduction

After it had almost disappeared a decade earlier, the Egyptian communist movement went through a revival at the end of the 1930s, becoming the most prominent secular, modernist movement. Its modernism was expressed in its orientation to the future, its enthusiasm for movement and change, and its promotion of social transformation and cultural innovation. The communists accepted industrialization, urbanization, and the accompanying alienation, which were incorporated into a meta-narrative of progress leading to emancipation from social, economic, and cultural oppression. In general, the movement was disciplined and ruled by a strong ideology. The modernism of the communist movement appealed to intellectuals and others who revolted against the socially and politically exclusive, elitist system of the monarchy. Intellectually it gave them the vocabulary with which to explain the world and understand their own society, while channeling their moral outrage about injustice and offering a political program for change. That all this had a basis in science and in indisputable laws of social and economic change gave the communist movement the authority with which to combat its opponents. Moreover, the international dimension convinced the communists that they fought for a cause that far transcended their personal lives. The modernity of the communists was also partly based on their claim to constitute the intellectual elite and the nationalist vanguard.

In true modernist fashion, these ideas gave the members of the communist movement a new identity. Theirs was not an identity based on a discourse of authenticity or national essence; rather it was formed on the basis of movement and in the struggle for national liberation and modernization. The issue of identity was also related to the conflict between generations, which Egypt was experiencing for the first time in history during this period.[1] Because so many of its members were young university students, the Egyptian communist movement played an important role in youthful resistance against parental and traditional authority. The modernist thrust of communism enabled its followers to rebel against patriarchy and the confines of tradition. More positively, it gave individuals the opportunity to develop their artistic, creative, and scientific potential and to transcend the boundaries of their social or ethnic environment.

Revolt and emancipation, the essence of the communist movement, can therefore be seen on the three interlinked and mutually reinforcing levels of family, politics, and nation. The revolt against the oppressiveness of patriarchy and paternalism in the family was matched and enhanced by the struggle for emancipation from patronage and clientalist relations in politics and civil society as well as by the struggle for national independence from foreign oppression and exploitation. A final attraction of the movement was its Western orientation. In contrast to "Easternism" and the discourse of authenticity, the communist movement had the advantage that it condemned Western economic imperialism even as it retained its Western cultural and political orientation. Its revolutionary and progressive character allowed the communist movement to take the leadership over the nationalist movement away from the secular liberalism of the 1919 Revolution, while keeping a strong Western cultural orientation. This process of "overcoming" allowed the communists to leave Egyptian national identity largely undefined and to concentrate on reform and modernization.[2]

Initially, the communist movement recruited its members especially among the non-Egyptian minorities (Greeks, Armenians, Italians, and Jews with different backgrounds), among members of organizations of Egyptian civil society (such as the trade union movement) that struggled for independence from patronage, and at later stage among Egyptians in the less traditional, often higher or middle classes and artistic milieus who had more than casual contact with Western culture and political debate. In its diversity, the communist movement faced different political, economic, and social developments that turned out to be incompatible in the end. On the one hand, it caught the tail end of the colonial era and the fading cosmopolitan culture of the non-Egyptian minorities and the Egyptian upper- and middle classes.

This enabled the communists to create a radical modernist movement that could lead the transition to a nation-state. On the other hand, they could not prevent the demise of both groups. The establishment of the nation-state spelt the end of foreign minorities and ultimately of communism itself. No less contradictory were the communist relations with civil society. While taking advantage of the existence of a relatively well-developed civil society and a strong public sphere, both of which it helped to expand, the communist movement ended up supporting the establishment of an authoritarian state.

Although communism was an international ideology, it had to adapt itself partly to local circumstances. When communism was introduced in Egypt, the popular front in France was in existence, and its program proved highly influential in Egypt. More than a tactic to acquire political power, the popular front was an ideological program that supplied the terminology and logic for Egyptian communists to integrate Egypt conceptually into a "modernist," universal scheme of history. Transposed to Egypt, this universal program became a mold into which the Egyptian political, economic, and cultural situation was forced. At the same time it allowed considerable tactical and ideological leeway. The model of the popular front provided universal standards that enabled a comparison of the complex indigenous situation with other countries in the world with similar "forces of progress" and "reaction." In a broader sense it offered not only a theory of development and an explanation for Egypt's "backwardness," but also strategies for reaching a stage of full modernity. Thus, while identifying the agrarian classes as "feudalists," the industrial class as "monopolists," and the Muslim Brotherhood and Young Egypt as "fascists organizations" – comparable to the Nazis and fascists in league with German and Italian capital – the strategy of the popular front allowed the communists to portray themselves as a revolutionary movement that held the keys to independence and social and economic development.

At the same time the front strategy also implied that the communist movement could not reach its goals alone. In the then current historical stage it needed the cooperation of other organizations and classes. For that reason, the popular front tactic gave rise to a more democratic stance ideologically. This enhanced the growth and independence of civil society at the end of the 1930s and during the 1940s. The communists supported the struggle of the trade unions, the student movement, and cultural and other associations to free themselves from the patronage and control of "bourgeois" and "feudal" parties, but at the same time they did not reject the parliamentary system and the 1923 Constitution, as was the case for Young Egypt and the Muslim Brotherhood. Many communist organizations even proposed to work together with the Wafd and acknowledged its relatively "progressive" character as well as its traditionalism.

I will call the ideology and political tactic of the popular front in Egypt the "paradigm of the front." In the broader history of the communist movement as a whole, it is closely tied up with the "two-stage revolution," i.e. first the bourgeois and then the socialist proletarian revolution, and it is usually regarded as a part of a moderate program of change, despite the Comintern background of the strategy. For this reason, I also refer to it as the communist "minimum program." The more authoritarian strain in the communist movement, or its "maximum program," usually associated with the strategy of the "single-stage revolution," was embodied especially in the ideas of the "dictatorship of the proletariat" and "class against class," which were based on the notion that the stage of the bourgeois revolution had been passed.

Despite its backing of civil society, the communist movement resembled the other modernist currents in its deep ambivalence towards democratic and authoritarian reform. Although both tendencies within the communist movement supported the trade unions, many points in the general "modernization" program worked in favor of an authoritarian modernism in which the state played a dominant role. Specific aspects of communism that promoted an overall authoritarianism were the support for a centralized economy, the growth of the public sector, the idea of industrialization as the equivalent of modernization, agrarian collectivization, and the concept of planning. Even the minimum program did not alter the political content of the communist modernist project, for in the end it led to the movement's backing of the military once it was recognized as the "national bourgeoisie." Eventually, the authoritarian modernization program gave rise to the communist movement's endorsement of the Nasserist regime.

In this chapter, I will analyze the way in which the European model of the popular front was transposed and adjusted to the Egyptian situation. I will focus on the paradigm of the front and the "minimum" and "maximum" programs of the Comintern. The strategy of the front is important for it set the terms of the debate on how to analyze the Egyptian situation and how to formulate the movement's tactics first towards the Wafd and later towards the military as the representatives of the "national bourgeoisie." Moreover, it also determined the model of Egyptian reality that communist intellectuals would construct. The paradigm of the front was central to their analysis of Egyptian history, economics, social structure and ultimately to their vision of the future.

International and Local Background

The international dimension

The "minimum program" of the international communist movement derived from the Seventh and last Congress of the Comintern, which was held in 1935, whereas the "maximum program" had the upper hand before that date. The main difference can be found primarily in the attitude of the communist movement towards the bourgeoisie and nationalism. Although the Egyptian communist movement of the second wave was not a member of the Comintern, it was heavily influenced by the strategy of the Comintern. The popular front in France and the united front in China in particular were instrumental in supplying the terminology for creating the paradigm of the front.

In the seven Comintern congresses held between 1919 and 1935 different policies were adopted towards the (national) bourgeoisie. Whereas a more lenient policy was promoted during the First Congress, a harsher approach towards the nationalist bourgeoisie was backed in the theses of the Fourth Congress of the Comintern (1922), which seemed to be in agreement with the critical attitude of the Indian communist M. N. Roy towards the national bourgeoisie. He had stated that, "the ruling classes among the colonial and semi-colonial peoples are unable and unwilling to lead the struggle against imperialism in so far as that struggle assumes the form of a revolutionary mass movement."[3] For the first time "young proletarians of the colonies" were advised to fight for an independent position within the "anti-imperialist united front" to become its leading force. This new strategy was laid down in the "dual tasks" of the communist parties, which were first, to "fight for the most radical possible solution of the tasks of a bourgeois-democratic revolution, which aims at the conquest of the political independence;" and second, to "organize the working and peasant masses for the struggle for their special class interests, and in doing so exploit all the contradictions in the nationalist bourgeois-democratic camp."[4]

The Sixth Comintern Congress (1928) resulted in a further hardening of the Comintern attitude towards all collaboration with other political organizations and classes both in Europe and in the dependent, colonial areas. In Europe it inaugurated the so-called Third Period tactics, which were laid down in the maximum program. It was argued that after periods of world revolution, followed by a stabilization of capitalism, the world economy had entered a third period, which was characterized by a crisis of capitalism and a consequent radicalization of the masses. The political corollary of this diagnosis was summed up in three slogans, "class against class," the labeling of social democrats as "social fascists," and the "united front from below," which meant the creation of a united front of socialist and communists workers without signing collaborative agreements with socialist leaders. This policy of confrontation with the social-democratic parties was to have disastrous consequences for the development of European history. In Germany it eventually helped Hitler seize power in January 1933.[5] In France the CPF declined and became marginalized. The rejection of the nationalist movement in the dependent countries also weakened the communist movement, as was the case in Egypt, where the communist party was crushed in a direct conflict with the Wafd government.

Several factors helped the Comintern change its policy during the Seventh Congress in July 1935 and adopt a minimum program. Within the Comintern the Bulgarian communist Georgi Dimitrov, the hero of the Reichstag trial, who had become a member of the political secretariat of the Comintern executive committee in 1934, raised his voice against the Third Period tactics and in favor of collaboration with social democrats. In July 1934 he challenged "the wholesale qualification of social-democracy as social-Fascism" and as "the chief social prop of the bourgeoisie." He called for "a united front from above and below" instead.[6]

Meanwhile, developments in France forced a change. On 6 February 1934 a right-wing demonstration ended in a bloody collision with the police, which left fifteen dead. The left regarded this as a direct threat to the Republic and a sign of the advance of fascism in France. In this light, the struggle for a socialist revolution was gradually subordinated to the defense of democracy and the mobilization of as many people as possible against the fascist threat. In October 1935 the CPF submitted a program that was designed to create "a broad front" extending "to trade unions of workers, and to the masses belonging to co-operative groups of peasants, artisans, small traders and other elements of the middle classes."[7] Remarkable about the popular front was not only that the CPF expressed its willingness to collaborate with the socialists, but also that the *petite bourgeoisie* and *les classes moyennes* were included in the broad anti-fascist strategy in the form of the Radical Party.[8] The program drawn up by Comité du Rassemblement Populaire for the July 1935 demonstration against fascism was clearly a minimum program. It was directed against fascism, and the capitalist foe was limited to 200 families who owned the country's major banks and monopolies. Speculation about a socialist revolution was abandoned or subdued.[9] On the basis of this minimum program the popular front of Socialist Party, the Radical Party, and the CPF won a landslide victory in May 1936. For the first time in French history a government was formed by a socialist premier, Leon Blum. The CPF supported the government, but did not join it. During the previous July the Seventh Comintern Congress had already endorsed the popular front strategy.

A direct consequence of the popular front strategy was the infusion of the communist movement with a considerable dose of nationalism, or what Julian Jackson calls the "reappropriation of the symbols of the Republic."[10] During the popular front period, the Marseillaise, the tricolor, and 14 July were regarded as a part of the national heritage in which the CPF participated and which it defended against fascism. Before, these symbols had been seen as chauvinistic. For the CPF this was a new means of integrating itself into French society.[11]

Beside the French popular front, the Chinese united front also inspired the Egyptian communist movement. The interest in the Chinese united front in Egypt is apparent in translations by different Egyptian communist organizations of Mao Zedong's booklet *On New Democracy*, in which he expounds his ideas on the bourgeois revolution.[12] Of special importance for Egyptian theorizing on its stage of history was Mao Zedong's description of China as a semi-colonial and semi-feudal society. The translations, which were disseminated in mimeographed form, would only be published officially by the communist publishing house Dar al-Nadim in 1957, during the so-called Bandung period, together with a whole series of other books on China.[13] Among these was *People's China*, a history of China written by Muhammad Awda.[14]

The tendency to adopt a minimum program was enhanced by developments in China, when in 1935 the Seventh Comintern Congress called for the formation of an "anti-imperialist united front" in China after the Japanese invasion. Despite this new policy, however, the Chinese Communist Party grew increasingly ambivalent towards the bourgeoisie, which it held responsible for the massacre of the Shanghai workers by Chiang Kaishek in April 1927.[15] Mao Zedong argued, for instance, that besides having "a revolutionary quality at certain periods and to a certain degree, because China is a colonial and semi-colonial country which is a victim of aggression," the bourgeois class was "extremely flabby economically and politically," and had "a proneness to conciliation with the enemies of the revolution."[16] From these developments Mao drew the conclusion that the proletariat, the intelligentsia, and the other sections of the petty bourgeoisie formed the backbone of the struggle against the Japanese invasion and the future revolution.[17]

The second wave in Egypt

The second wave of the Egyptian communist movement came about in the second half of the 1930s after the disbandment of the Egyptian Communist Party and was strongly influenced by these French and Chinese developments. At first it was an exclusively foreign and *mutamassir* (i.e. of Egyptianized foreigners) affair of primarily francophone and Jewish residents in Egypt who had attended the French *lycée*. There, they had undergone the influence of several teachers who were communist sympathizers. At the end of the 1920s or the beginning of the 1930s, a group was founded that was called Les Essayistes. The poet Georges Henein (1914–1973) was to become its most illustrious member. Other members were the poet Anwar Kamil (1913–1991), Ramsis Yunan, and the painters Kamil Tilmisani and Fu'ad Kamil. Les Essayistes published the journal *L'Effort* and had strong links with the surrealist movement of André Breton. After Georges Henein had established an independent group called Art et Liberté, he published another francophone journal called *Don Quichotte* to which the later communist leaders Henri and Raoul Curiel contributed. In January 1940 Art et Liberté finally published the first socialist journal published in Arabic, entitled *al-Tatawwur* (*Development*). The group around Georges Henein was to play a subordinate but highly creative role in the second half of the 1940s, mostly in the field of literature and art, but also, on account of its minority (Trotskyite) tendencies, because of its criticism of the more authoritarian, Stalinist, high modernist strain in Egyptian communism.[18]

Another source of the second wave was the Ligue Pacifiste, an organization that was established in 1934 by the Swiss Paul Jacot Descombes and which was affiliated with the Rassemblement Universel pour la Paix, a pre-popular front organization in France. Almost all the future Jewish leaders of the communist movement were members of this group. Neglecting the internal Egyptian situation, the union was exclusively oriented towards international political developments, such as the popular front, the Spanish Civil War, and the Italian invasion of Ethiopia. For this reason, Raoul Curiel, Marcel Israel (b. 1913), and Hillel Schwartz established an independent group, the Democratic Union, which was more oriented towards Egypt, in 1939. During the war this group would in turn be divided into what would later become three separate communist organizations that would play an important role in the communist movement: the Egyptian Movement for National Liberation (EMNL, in Arabic: *al-Haraka al-Misriyya li-l-Taharrur al-Watani*, acronym: HAMITU), led by Henri Curiel (1914–1978); Iskra (The Spark) led by Hillel Schwartz, and a smaller group called Liberation of the People (*Tahrir al-Sha'b*), under the leadership of Marcel Israel. A fourth organization, known as the New Dawn group, after its publication *The New Dawn* (*al-Fajr al-Jadid*), was also established in this period. It was headed by three Jews, Ahmad Sadiq Sa'd (1919–1988), Yusuf Darwish (b. 1910), and Raymond Duwayk (1918–).[19]

The predominance of Jews, who often came from rich cosmopolitan backgrounds, was clear proof of the integrative orientation of the movement.[20] In contrast, minorities who could still find support within traditional political parties were not strongly represented in the communist movement. For instance, very few Copts joined the communist movement, with the exception of Georges Henein, Ramsis Yunan, Fawzi Girgis, Anwar Abd al-Malik, and a few others.[21] Although Jews would later be involved in the most radical communist organizations, such as the Voice of the Opposition (Sawt al-Mu'arada), it is perhaps not surprising that this group on the whole adopted the most integrationalist minimum program of the Comintern. As long as they showed themselves willing to build a modern Egyptian nation-state, they believed that there would be a place for them, despite their previous relations with foreign and *mutamassir* interests.

Nevertheless, the issue of nationalism and therefore the issue of identity were to pose a problem from the very beginning and would constitute one of the main distinctions between the different communist organizations. HAMITU accepted nationalism not only as an ideology but also as an organizational principle. In prison Henri Curiel had come to realize that a communist movement had no future in Egypt without becoming fully Egyptianized. Adopting the principle of "Egyptianization" (*tamsir*) as well as accepting the need for "proletarization" (*ta'mil*), he established a cadre school on the estate of his father and recruited among Egyptian intellectuals, as well as attracting trade union leaders to the communist movement. In a sense, the inclusion of nationalism in the communist modernist program was a means of appropriating it politically and neutralizing it. Egyptian nationalism was integrated in and subordinated to the communist program. The communist movement was perfunctorily involved in the modernist attempt to create a national image. And so its national image always remained bloodless and subordinated to the ideas of social movement, economic change, and cultural freedom of expression. Its orientation towards the future instead of looking for an Egyptian "essence" and identity also colored its interpretation of the country's history. Its preoccupation with finding historical laws and its strong economic, reductionist bent was not compatible with a quest for cultural authenticity.

Some sections of the communist movement, like Iskra, even rejected Egyptianization as "chauvinistic." Most of its members belonged to the foreign cosmopolitan community or to the Egyptian intelligentsia, like Shuhdi Atiyya al-Shafi'i and Anwar Abd al-Malik. A highly intellectual organization, the emphasis was on conducting debate, disseminating Marxist theoretical knowledge, and adapting it to the Egyptian situation. Iskra's best-known institution was the House of Scientific Research (Dar al-Abhath al-'Ilmiyya), which organized seminars and lectures and played an important role in attracting Egyptian intellectuals to Marxism. The New Dawn group stood in between the two other organizations, limiting the number of Jewish Egyptians to the original three founders and spreading Marxist ideas through its different publications, as well as organizing a trade union movement along independent lines. Through its numerous organizations and by means of its countless publications, periodicals, pamphlets, and leaflets, the movement further extended the reach of critical debate and the public sphere and sharpened critical awareness of civil society.

Communist modernist discourse consisted primarily in determining the specific place Egypt occupied within the international march to modernity. As the strategy of the communist movement was based on its conception of Egypt's historical stage of development, much depended on determining the "laws of history." The modernist, "scientific" legitimacy and justification of the movement depended largely on this process. For that reason, most organizations concentrated at first on translating classic Marxist literature into Arabic. Especially in the earlier period, a tremendous effort was put into translating left-wing literature from French and English. The *Green Books Series (Silsilat al-Kutub al-Khadra')*, published by HAMITU, was an important source for making translations of Lenin and Stalin available.[22] The House of the Dawn (Dar al-Fajr), affiliated with the People's Liberation, concentrated mostly on translating popular Marxist literature that was more accessible to the general public. The owner of the publishing house, Mustafa Munib, translated most of the works himself.[23] Meanwhile, Dar al-Fajr stimulated a general awareness of the international context in which Egypt found itself, by publishing booklets on the Indian and Indonesian nationalist movements.[24] It also brought out a scathing attack by Salama Musa — generally regarded as a modernist precursor by communists — on press censorship in Egypt and the publishing permit system, which restricted the founding of independent newspapers and journals.[25]

However, the primary means of establishing a communist strategy was to apply Marxist theories to Egyptian society itself and rewrite the country's history. The New Dawn group was particularly successful in this respect. Its publishing house, the Twentieth-Century Publishing House (Dar al-Qarn al-'Ishrin), brought out a series of books on Egyptian history,[26] the agrarian question,[27] political-economy,[28] and culture.[29] These works reflect the New Dawn group's attempt to formulate an extremely mild political attitude.[30] Iskra's major contribution to strengthening Marxist discourse was its manifesto, *Our National Goals*, by Shuhdi Atiyya al-Shafi'i and Muhammad Abd al-Ma'bud al-Jubayli, which is perhaps the most succinct adaptation of the Comintern program of the popular/united front to Egypt and which reflects the ideas of the whole communist movement at the time.[31]

Formation of the Egyptian Paradigm of the Front

False consciousness

Before examining the political strategy of the front, we must first consider the various ways in which it acquired an ideological form and how the paradigm of the front was adapted to Egyptian circumstances. As was the case for liberal and socialist thinkers, the Egyptian communist movement too had to adjust universal theories and international strategies developed elsewhere and formed into a "paradigm of the front" with an eye to specific local conditions. One of the major concerns of the communist movement was its critique of what it regarded as "reactionary thought" (*afkar raja'iyya*). By relating ideology to class interests and not simply treating it as an expression of tradition that can be overcome through rationalism and economic development, the communist movement identified nationalist discourse as false consciousness. Ideological critique became a considerable weapon in the attack on both conservative liberal discourse and the discourse of authenticity, which were viewed as deliberate means of misleading society and taking it off its course towards national and class emancipation.

The best example of a politico-cultural critique of the older generation was written by Abu Sayf Yusuf (b. 1922) in his *On Marxist Philosophy: An Answer to al-'Aqqad*. In his book, Abu Sayf Yusuf starts off by criticizing the political role of Abbas Mahmud al-Aqqad, who had once been a nationalist and a supporter of the Wafd and "unfortunately has strayed from the path of freedom."[32] Abbas Mahmud al-'Aqqad (1889–1964) belonged to the same generation as Husayn Haykal and had, like Haykal, taken an important part in formulating the discourse of authenticity, by writing a famous series on Muhammad and the Rightly-guided caliphs. Based on the idea that, "in every class society the values of the ruling class are dominant," Abu Sayf Yusuf's second line of attack is to relate the discourse of authenticity to the preservation of the socio-economic structure of Egypt, asserting that values are an "instrument" (*adah*) in the hands of the ruling class by which they can portray the social structure as a natural order and defend their interests.[33]

The full range of Abu Sayf Yusuf's critique, however, becomes apparent when he links the discourse of authenticity to Young Egypt and the Muslim Brotherhood, parties he consistently designates as "fascist." It is a clear sign of the influence the paradigm of the front exerted on Egyptian communist thinking at this point. As mass movements, they are assigned a heavy responsibility in defending the existing capitalist system. Instead of analyzing society, he asserts, they mislead the people through religion and resort to "theater" (*masrah*). Although he believes that morals and principles play an important social role, he states that social and political problems are more important while "organizing real life in a proper way must be based on rationality (*'aql*) and science (*'ilm*), which is the precondition for spiritual and moral renewal (*tajdid*)."[34] Thus, emphasizing the classic creed of Enlightenment and rationality, he writes that the more one understands "the development of the human condition and the discovery of natural laws, the more man is capable of understanding the social situation and the more he is capable of liberating himself."[35] This ideal is contrasted with the passivity of religion and faith in irrational forces, which ultimately support foreign domination and repression.

Reinterpreting history

An essential aspect of the process of defining the communist position, culturally and historically both in time and in space, can be found in the application of Marxist concepts to Egyptian history. Egyptian Marxist historiography went through its most creative period in the 1940s and 1950s, and Ahmad Rushdi Salih's work on Lord Cromer is perhaps one of the best-documented and best-reasoned interpretations of early Egyptian Marxism. In his introduction to *Cromer in Egypt: Pages from Egypt's Modern History*,[36] Ahmad Rushdi Salih outlines the task of the left-wing historian, which is to apply with rigor the highly abstract Marxist historical thinking in order to understand Egyptian history and find universal laws in the specific historical development of the country.[37]

The way in which Ahmad Rushdi Salih sets about writing the first communist history of Egypt is revealing of the ideological vacuum in which Egyptian communists found themselves and of their need to construct a history from scratch. Lacking an indigenous tradition of materialist historical writing, Ahmad Rushdi Salih is forced to look to foreign literature on the subject, which he finds in the British anti-imperialist literature of the turn of the twentieth century. Wilfred Scawen Blunt's book on the Urabi revolt,[38] Theodore Rothstein's *Egypt's Ruin: A Financial and Administrative Record*,[39] as well as Elinor Burns's *British Imperialism*,[40] which he had translated for the New Dawn's publishing house,[41] serve as examples for his own book as well as providing him with the necessary material. Another, more theoretical influence is Lenin's theory of imperialism.

Not surprisingly, the main theme of Ahmad Rushdi Salih's work is the idea that international capitalism in the form of imperialism has determined the course of Egyptian history in the nineteenth century. The financial insolvency of khedives Saʿid and Ismaʿil is a major topic. Rushdi Salih treats the Urabi revolution (1881–82) as a class struggle of landlords against foreign occupation; he regards parliament as the arena of the class struggle, while monopoly capital and especially finance capital – with special reference to *Egypt's Ruin* and *British Imperialism* – take up much of the first half of the book.[42] In the second half, Rushdi Salih describes how Egypt was gradually transformed to the advantage of British capitalist interests under the rule of Lord Cromer (1882–1905), who stimulated foreign investment in cotton production, the infrastructure, and the building industry. Meanwhile, de-industrialization insured Britain of an important export market for its industrial products.

Like Rashid al-Barrawi, Ahmad Rushdi Salih does not evaluate British imperialism wholly negatively, despite the exploitation under Cromer. In fact, a central theme of left-wing modernism, as of liberal modernism, was that the British had contributed to Egypt's progress by pulling it into the mainstream of world development, thereby ending a long history of stagnation and decadence under the Ottoman Empire. He admits that, "the cultural reforms and the material renaissance, and the formal developments have positive aspects. We do not deny that these [...] have enabled [Egypt] to acquire an advanced position in relation to the countries surrounding it that have not taken part in the economic and social exchange with developed capitalism."[43] Western imperialism, he argues, integrated Egypt into international capitalism and terminated its "feudal isolation" and "autarky." More importantly, imperialism evoked its own demise in a dialectical manner, by producing a national bourgeoisie and the rise of the nationalist movement led by Mustafa Kamil at the start of the twentieth century.

As the first Egyptian-Marxist analysis, *Cromer in Egypt* is remarkable for its originality, especially if one realizes that Ahmad Rushdi Salih was not a historian by profession. Basing his study on the yearly reports of Cromer, he makes clear that the British Governor-General was incapable of containing the forces evoked by his own policy. The rise of the indigenous bourgeoisie, the budding of the working class, and the introduction of new ideas set Egypt on a course of national liberation. Ultimately, Ahmad Rushdi Salih comes out in favor of the emergence of Egyptian "bourgeois" civil society at the beginning of the twentieth century.

Agricultural reform

Ahmad Sadiq Sa'd's work, *The Problem of the Peasant*, takes up where Ahmad Rushdi Salih left off, as it describes the history of agrarian relations from the beginning of this century to the end of the Second World War.[44] Like Rushdi Salih's study, *The Problem of the Peasant* was written to explain why the peasant had been prevented from participating in a modern society and kept in a state of utter backwardness. It also proposes a means of integrating him in society and making him socially and politically conscious through a complete transformation of rural society.

In a larger context, however, *The Problem of the Peasant* reflects the New Dawn group's policy of support for the bourgeois nationalist revolution and the front strategy. This is apparent in Ahmad Sadiq Sa'd's comment on Mirrit Butrus Ghali's book *Agrarian Reform* and Muhammad al-Khattab's reform proposals in the Senate. Sadiq Sa'd welcomes these proposals, which he regards as "a faithful expression of the frustration of some of the intellectuals of the middle classes with the apparent crisis," but he sees them as too restricted. In typical modernist fashion, he states that the task of "liberal intellectuals," that is left-wing intellectuals, is to support these ideas and to take them to a "higher, and more complete level." What Ahmad Sadiq Sa'd believes to be lacking in these proposals is the courage to put the agrarian problem in a broader theoretical framework that takes the political and economic circumstances into account.[45] He adds that the liberal reformers "do not realize that Egyptian society does not only show faults, but that its basis is severely ill and that this weakness will lead to its immanent demise."[46]

The theoretical innovation and broadening proposed by Ahmad Sadiq Sa'd amounts to placing the agricultural economic and social development within the context of capitalist and imperialist intervention in Egypt. His basic contention is that imperialism has kept agriculture underdeveloped and that it has prevented an Egyptian "economic and democratic renaissance" (*al-nahda al-iqtisadiyya wa-l-dimuqratiyya*). The main source of retardation, he writes, is the "monopoly" (*ihtikar*) of the large landowners who have held this position from the time of Muhammad Ali onwards. Using David Ricardo's theory of rent and his critique of the "leisure class," Sadiq Sa'd regards the large landowners as a "parasitic class" (*al-tabaqa al-tufayliyya*) which is allowed to increase its income without contributing to the economic development of the country.[47]

While the New Dawn group was the only organization to carry out an extensive study of the agrarian question, all communist organizations adopted the same terminology in describing the agrarian structure. Both the New Dawn group and Iskra described Egyptian agrarian socio-economic relations as "feudal," loosely defined by Ahmad Sadiq Sa'd as pertaining to "a backward economic system that does not exist any longer in most countries and no longer has any influence except in those countries that are not sufficiently developed and that retards economic life in these countries."[48] In accordance with the paradigm of the front, the use of the term feudalism points to the belief that Egypt must first go through a democratic, capitalist phase before a socialist revolution can follow. It also implies that large landownership was regarded as one of the biggest enemies of the nationalist movement of which the communist movement claimed to be the vanguard.[49]

Because the communist reform proposals were geared to promoting capitalism as a stage on the road towards socialism, they were more radical than Mirrit Butrus Ghali's program. The agrarian reforms planned by the New Dawn group and Iskra consisted essentially in transforming the small-scale peasant economy into a large-scale modernized economy based on the use of the most recent techniques and agricultural machines. Like Rashid al-Barrawi's agrarian reform, these proposals were high modernist, following the examples of the Kolchoz system in the Soviet Union and extensive agriculture in the United States. Such forms of agrarian production were seen as scientific and not based on the exploitation and self-exploitation to which the Egyptian peasant was forced. The ultimate purpose of agrarian reform was to destroy the "reactionary" landlords, who dominated Egyptian politics.[50] It would have meant a massive migration to the cities, and, in contradiction with their support of civil society, the introduction of a completely inefficient agrarian system run by the state.

Economic reform

On the whole, the communist analysis of capitalism and the industrial bourgeoisie strengthened its belief in the paradigm of the front and the concept of the bourgeois democratic revolution. Yet, there are also signs of ambivalence in this analysis, such as the idea that, in fact, there does not exist a bourgeois to execute such a revolution and that therefore the state would have to take over the task of accomplishing economic and social progress. Adapting the Comintern line to the Egyptian situation, the New Dawn group held the view that Egypt had witnessed a development in the industrial sector that was characteristic of semi-developed countries and consisted of three parts. First, from the founding of Bank Misr in 1920, industrial capitalism had been dominated by finance capital. Second, indigenous capitalist and financial interests had gradually been incorporated into international monopoly capitalism during the 1930s, a development that was reflected in their reactionary attitude towards the nationalist movement.[51] Third, indigenous agrarian and industrial/financial interests had formed an internal coalition that was represented politically by the coalition governments of the Party of the Liberal Constitutionalists and the Sa'di Party.

Further evidence of its ambivalence towards a bourgeois revolution and towards civil society can be seen in the communist movement's adoption of the negative conceptions of capitalism and imperialism found in Lenin's *Imperialism, the Highest Stage of Capitalism*. For instance, Ahmad Sadiq Sa'd calculated that only ten percent of foreign investments was in industry; the rest was in mortgage banks, transport, agriculture, and oil.[52] The communists condemned especially the interpenetration of political and economic society through governmental protection of monopolies and cartels. Anwar Kamil cites the sugar agreement and tariff protection of textiles as the main examples of exploitation.[53] The Anglo-Egyptian Treaty of 1936 was regarded as a means of protecting these interlocking interests. This was one of the main reasons for the communist movement to protest vehemently against Isma'il Sidqi's attempt to retain the military alliance with Western capitalist countries in 1946.

Nevertheless, compared with their severe critique of the three-pronged coalition against progress, the industrial policy of the New Dawn group and Iskra was not as severe as might have been expected. In agreement with the minimum program of the front, it was directed at winning over the national bourgeoisie, but this category is never defined or even identified. Iskra, which avoided the use of the term monopoly capitalism as much as possible, was careful to present its industrialization program, like its agrarian reform, as a standard program, beneficial to economic development and similar to programs that had been implemented in capitalist countries. Both organizations pointed out that the nationalization of foreign companies, such as the Suez Canal and public utilities, in the form of railroads, tramways, gas and electricity concessionaires, did not mean that private initiative was rejected. In this regard, it was crucial what form of government would prevail. The manifesto of Iskra emphasized, "the capitalist system can play a large role in Egypt in our [economic] renaissance, on condition that a democratic government controls and directs it," an indication that the communist movement supported reform by the state but that the government had to be democratic.[54]

All the communist groups advocated state intervention through economic planning. The modernist quality of the economic program of the communist movement and the state's role in it was especially notable in the propaganda for heavy industry. The communists regarded the establishment of heavy industry as an absolute precondition for economic renaissance: "Only this industry can truly liberate us from imperialism and our economic ties with it."[55] Iskra assigned to the state the task of drawing up an overall industrial program that would strike a balance between heavy industry (like chemicals, mining, iron and steel) on the one hand and light industry, such as the textile and shoe industry, on the other. The New Dawn group believed that the state should develop an industrial policy to restructure and reform the present monopolies to the advantage of society as a whole.[56]

On the whole, communist organizations did not object to foreign investment, as long as the state controlled the economy and imposed certain conditions. The New Dawn group even regarded foreign investment as inevitable. Rejecting the slogan "economic evacuation" (*jala' iqtisadi*) of more radical groups, Ahmad Sadiq Sa'd warned that Egypt did not have the financial means to develop its industry and expand its infrastructure on its own.[57] In the optimistic phase of the communist movement, Iskra even regarded the World Bank as a means of acquiring the funds that were necessary for development.[58]

The Nationalist Revolution

The strategy of the front

The demand for democratization was an essential ingredient of the paradigm of the front. In theory, democratization was synonymous with the nationalist movement of which the communist movement now considered itself the vanguard. The idea was that with increased democratic rights for the people, the degree of independence would also be greater, for the people formed a barrier against foreign penetration. In accordance with the teleological concept of history, the communists saw national history as a narrative of continuous growth for the nationalist movement and of the concomitant expansion of democracy. This meant that in the new phase of the nationalist movement after 1945, a front consisting of all the progressive forces would be established to realize the radical nationalist program. As the New Dawn group put it, "the only guarantee that the nationalist goals will be fulfilled is the expansion of democratic rights."[59] The same sentiments were expressed in the manifesto of Iskra.[60]

In general, following the popular/united front strategy, the Egyptian communist organizations of this period defended liberal rights and the increase of power of the legislative at the expense of the executive.[61] In typical evaluations of parliamentary democracy of the time, a progressive historical line can be discerned.[62] And yet, even as the radical nationalist movement agreed with the Wafd in its condemnation of the minority parties, it nonetheless considered the Wafdist concept of democracy as too limited: "It is wrong to think that the democratic system is restricted to parliament. The parliamentary system is inadequate if it does not extend to all aspects of life."[63]

In this manner, independence, democracy, and the integration of larger groups of the population were linked. In 1945 the New Dawn group still believed that new organizations such as the Workers Committee for National Liberation and the National Committee for Students and Workers could be incorporated into the parliamentary system.[64] The group recognized that despite its limitations the present democratic system was the only means of improving the lot of the workers.[65] Eventually, through reform, the popular movement could become the dominant force.[66] Despite these ambitions, the integration of a larger section of the population turned out to be more difficult than expected, which in part a consequence of the communist movement's dependence on the Wafd.

As a result of the absence of a clearly defined concept of the national bourgeoisie, relations between the different communist groups and the Wafd were fraught with ambiguity and contradiction. On the one hand the communist movement still considered the Wafd as the only traditional party that supported democracy and could give the new social and political forces the opportunity to participate in politics and make their demands felt. The Wafd remained the only mass party that could win free elections and was susceptible to popular pressure. The communists hoped that support of the Wafd and the establishment of a Wafd government in the new post-war circumstances would help launch a national democratic revolution. On the other hand, the communist movement was sufficiently aware of the increasing role in the Wafd of the conservative and, in their eyes, even reactionary class of large landowners, represented by Fu'ad Siraj al-Din, whose growing power was gauged by the Wafd's willingness to arrive at a negotiable compromise with the British and by the continuing predominance of a conservative social philosophy based on harmony and patronage.

This ambiguity is obvious in the position of the New Dawn group. Because the New Dawn group did not feel the time had come yet to establish an independent communist party, it was the most willing to work with and within the Wafd. Its strategy was aimed at strengthening the left wing of the Wafd, the so-called Wafdist Vanguard (al-Tal'a al-Wafdiyya), which was led by Muhammad Mandur, editor of the dailies *al-Wafd al-Misri* and later *Sawt al-Umma*. Thus, it was hoped that the Wafd could be tied to the radical nationalist movement, while the communist movement could find a way to be integrated into the broader, historical nationalist movement and transform its program from within.[67]

This attitude towards the Wafd comes to the fore in an article by Muhammad Amin (a pseudonym for Raymond Duwayk) in *al-Fajr al-Jadid* of July 1945, a few months before the upsurge of the nationalist movement. The author reiterates the Wafd's contribution to the nationalist movement by connecting independence with democratic rights. At the same time, however, Amin criticizes the leadership of the Wafd, which "does not present a true reflection of the classes and social layers [in society], especially of the peasants, the workers, and the democratic vanguard of the Egyptian intelligentsia." Moreover, several of the leading figures in the Wafd were not considered democratic at all. Raymond Duwayk concludes, "the interest of the nation demands more democracy than the Wafd is willing to implement." He believed that the rising consciousness of the population would in the long run lead to the formation of workers' and popular parties. In this sense, the communists did support civil society at this point.[68]

In practice, support for the Wafd from 1945 to 1946 depended on its concrete policy towards the minority governments of Mahmud Fahmi al-Nuqrashi and Isma'il Sidqi. As long as the Wafd demanded new elections and rejected the 1936 Treaty, it found the New Dawn group behind it. But when it began to insist on taking part in the delegation that Isma'il Sidqi formed to negotiate with the British, the Wafd was severely criticized.[69] Support of the Wafd was further eroded when the critique of "national capitalism" gained adherents.[70]

Iskra displays a similarly ambivalent attitude towards the Wafd. In *Our National Goals* the Wafd is described as "the party that is the least willing to compromise (*tahadun*) with imperialism and that has the most support from the people."[71] But the Wafd is no longer identified with the nationalist movement. Iskra argued that whenever the Wafd assumed governmental responsibility, it disappointed the expectations of the people, with the result that a rift had appeared between the two. This growing alienation between the Wafd and the people, the manifesto states, enabled imperialism to use the minority parties for its goals.[72] The conclusions drawn from this analysis differ from the conclusions of the New Dawn group. Although Iskra did include the Wafd in a national front strategy and worked together with the Wafdist Vanguard during 1945–46 in the National Committee of Workers and Students, it kept a greater distance from the Wafd as a whole.

Finally, the front strategy of HAMITU is equally unclear where the Wafd is concerned. In his memoirs Henri Curiel describes the Wafd as a democratic force that has withstood fascism. The position of HAMITU concerning the front is generally described as "the national democratic line," which is defined by Selma Botman as

> meaning essentially that it supported national liberation from occupation and the inauguration of a truly democratic system [...] Curiel's idea was to establish a united front whose center was the working class but whose adherents were also members of the social-democratic and reformist organizations. In that way he hoped to attract sympathizers from both the petty and national bourgeoisie.[73]

The National Democratic Front of 1945–46

The paradigm of the front was put into action during the autumn of 1945, when students belonging to HAMITU, Iskra, the Wafdist Vanguard, and other left-wing organizations formed student committees that later became the Preparatory Committee for the National Committee of Students. Meanwhile the communist organizations organized trade union activities, and the New Dawn group, the WCNL, HAMITU, and Iskra organized the Congress of Private Sector Trade Unions. When the government suppressed the Shubra al-Khayma textile workers' union in December and instated a military occupation of Shubra al-Khayma, the student movement and the workers' movement coalesced into a broad front of workers and students. On 9 February 1946 the student committees held a general conference at Cairo University during which resolutions were adopted demanding the termination of negotiations with Britain, the abrogation of the 1936 Treaty, and the immediate evacuation of British troops from Egypt and the Sudan.

The radicalization of the students and the strikes at Shubra al-Khayma found their climax on 18 and 19 February when the National Committee of Workers and Students (NCWS) was formed. In the NCWS, the trade unions, dominated by HAMITU and Iskra, were strongly represented. The NCWS called for a general strike on 21 February, which was designated as "Evacuation Day." On that day a crowd of 40,000 to 100,000 rallied at the Opera Square in Cairo. Repression by the British army left 23 dead and 121 wounded. On 4 March another general strike was announced, but the turnout was less great. The immediate result of the demonstrations was the replacement of Premier Nuqrashi by Isma'il Sidqi.

It was Isma'il Sidqi who suppressed the radical nationalist movement of 1945–46. On 11 July, all left-wing organizations were outlawed, like Iskra's House of Scientific Research and the New Dawn group's Committee of Spreading Modern Culture as well as the Twentieth-Century Publishing House. In addition, several newspapers were suppressed, such as the Wafdist Vanguard's *al-Wafd al-Misri*, HAMITU's *Umm Durman*, and the New Dawn group's *al-Fajr al-Jadid* and *al-Damir*.[74]

Islamism is fascism

The immediate result of the collision of the radical nationalist movement with the government was a strengthening of the paradigm of the front with regard to the relations with the Muslim Brotherhood and Young Egypt. The conflict originates in the struggle between both currents for hegemony over the nationalist movement. In this conflict, the Muslim Brotherhood tried several tactics, ranging from boycotting the committees and calling for re-elections to finally seceding from the National Committee of Workers and Students after 21 February. With Young Egypt, the Muslim Brotherhood created a separate organization, called the National Committee (al-Lajna al-Qawmiyya), which received support from Prime Minister Isma'il Sidqi and was consequently condemned by the communist movement as a "fascist" organization.

In 1947 HADITU, the successor of HAMITU, published *The Muslim Brotherhood in the Balance*, a scathing attack on the Muslim Brotherhood by Muhammad Hasan Ahmad.[75] Although his analysis might be considered extreme, other remarks made by Iskra in *Our National Goals* and articles written in *al-Fajr al-Jadid* confirm that this was the general attitude towards the Muslim Brotherhood and Young Egypt and put into perspective the communist movement's concept of history and society. Typically, parallels are drawn with European history in the 1930s and 1940s. The general theme is the deception of the masses and the undermining of the nationalist/democratic movement through the dissemination of a false consciousness. The logic of the paradigm of the front casts the Muslim Brotherhood and Young Egypt in the role of fascist and Nazi movements, which misled the population in the interests of the monopoly capitalism. Thus, Abu Sayf Yusuf sees the fact that Ali Mahir and Aziz al-Misri patronized Young Egypt in the 1930s as the first link between government circles and fascist organizations.[76] The ties between the National Committee and Isma'il Sidqi in February 1946 are presented by Ahmad Rushdi Salih as a direct continuation of these relations.[77] As in Germany, Yusuf writes, the ruling classes had succeeded in attracting intellectuals from the middle classes "to anesthetize the population and distract its attention from reality."[78] Thus, fascism managed to profit from the "despair" (*ya's*) that prevails in times of crisis, as had been the case in Europe during the 1930s. Instead of demanding higher wages and better standards of living, the attention of the population is distracted by racist issues in Germany and religious ones in Egypt. Yusuf asserts that the reactionary character of the Muslim Brotherhood is attested to by its ideology, "which gives a fully detailed program of a spiritual and ideological return to the Middle Ages."[79]

In line with this overall view, Muhammad Hasan Ahmad writes that a basic mistake in the political thought of the Brotherhood was that it confused political issues with religious ones. The Muslim Brotherhood's main strategy of deception was to concentrate on moral issues like prostitution, the "mingling" of the sexes, corruption, and the licentiousness of the liberal press, instead of analyzing the crisis of capitalist society.[80] He argues that the absence of a clear analysis of the economic and social relations in society leads to contradictory and disastrous policies. While the socio-economic structure is left intact, because the Brotherhood's principal values are based on religion and Islamic solidarity ("As long as the proprietor is a Muslim, the Muslim Brotherhood is required to support and help him"), such a stance endangers the unity of the nationalist movement in its discrimination of Copts and Jews.[81] For the same reason, he writes, the condemnation of British imperialism is confused. Not imperialism as such, but Christian imperialism is condemned.[82] Moreover, Western society is attacked for precisely those qualities that Hasan Ahmad views as the "modern" elements of civilization, i.e. its sciences, laws, art, and culture. Hasan Ahmad concludes that for these reasons the ideology of the Muslim Brotherhood never rules out a compromise with British imperialism, a suggestion that is supported by the alliance between the Brotherhood, the "semi-feudal" classes, and both indigenous and foreign monopoly capitalism.

Reorientation

Unity, factionalism, and radicalization

The failure of the national democratic revolution to materialize had grave consequences for the communist movement and led to an organizational and ideological transformation. The optimistic phase of the communist movement was over, and a period of self-reflection and self-criticism began. The ideological crisis manifested itself in a general hardening of ideology and a greater influence of the maximum program.

The conclusion that several communist organizations drew from the failure of the 1945–46 upsurge was that it was imperative to join forces and organize themselves illegally. After several smaller groups had merged with Iskra and HAMITU, among whom the Liberation of the People, the two larger organizations merged to form the Democratic Movement for National Liberation (al-Haraka al-Dimuqratiyya li-l-Taharrur al-Watani, acronym HADITU) in May 1947. From the start, the different political cultures of the two main organizations, their dissimilar membership, organizational forms, and traditions, which had consolidated over the past years, were a source of friction and factionalism. This resulted in a debate about strategy.

The origins of the debate on strategy dated back to the period prior to unity. In April 1947 Iskra, or the Unified Vanguard (as it was then called), established the newspaper *al-Jamahir*. Many of its most prominent Egyptian intellectuals were staff members. Shuhdi Atiyya al-Shafi'i (1912–1960) was the political editor, Anwar Abd al-Malik (b. 1925) and Muhammad Sid Ahmad (b. 1928) belonged to the foreign affairs editorial board, and Sa'd Zahran contributed to the student page.[83] On 21 April 1947 Shuhdi Atiyya al-Shafi'i launched his first campaign for reorganization of the communist movement in an editorial entitled "The People Want a Party ... of a New Kind." He explains why they do and claims that a new leadership of the working class has arisen.[84] It is clear from this text that the vocabulary and the direction of his thought have changed compared to *Our National Goals*, the liberal manifesto of Iskra, which he co-wrote. The new party that would unite all the communist organizations would become the vanguard of the nationalist movement. In an alliance with the Wafd, the new party would play a dominant role.[85]

What stimulated the debate on strategy was the fact that the foundation of HADITU in July 1947 as the result of the merger between Iskra/United Vanguard and HAMITU fell short of the expectations of the group around Shuhdi Atiyya al-Shafi'i. When Shuhdi Atiyya al-Shafi'i lost his seat in the Central Committee during reorganization, he staged a revolt in HADITU and recruited members for a separate faction, the Revolutionary Bloc (al-Takattul al-Thawri). Although the Revolutionary Bloc was launched before Henri Curiel's famous working paper "The Line of the National and Democratic Forces" was distributed in the Central Committee at the beginning of 1948, this document served as a pretext for a direct attack on the old leadership, its ideology, and its organization of the communist movement.

Shuhdi Atiyya al-Shafi'i reacted by drawing up a report of seventy pages entitled "Here Is the Egyptian Communist Organization that We Want to Create." He criticized HADITU for being bourgeois in its outlook and made up of intellectuals, students, and members of the petty bourgeoisie. Identifying it as a movement of national democratic forces, he charged HADITU with being "uniquely capable of weakening the class struggle by dispersing its militant forces over diversified fields of action."[86] He called for greater participation of workers, the termination of the section system, and the introduction of the cell as the basic unit of organization.[87] The Revolutionary Bloc left HADITU, but does not seem to have played any further role of significance. With the imposition of martial law in May 1948 most of its members were arrested. At the end of 1948 Shuhdi Atiyya al-Shafi'i himself was arrested and sentenced to seven years imprisonment.[88]

All the same, Shuhdi Atiyya al-Shafi'i's opposition to the Central Committee initiated a phase of general dissolution. The most extreme groups at this time were the Voice of the Opposition (Sawt al-Mu'arada) and Towards A Bolshevik Organization (Nahwa Munazzama Bulshifiyya). The Voice of the Opposition called for one hundred percent workers in the organization and drew parallels between the history of the Russian Socialist Party and recent events in the Egyptian communist movement. Basing themselves on Lenin's *The Necessities of the Russian Democratic Socialists*, its members believed that at this stage in Egyptian history the historical split between Mensheviks and Bolsheviks would reoccur.[89] The relations between Egyptian capitalists and imperialism did not allow for the further development of capitalism. The stage of history that Egypt had attained, therefore, demanded a socialist revolution (or in other words the single-stage revolution and the implementation of the maximum program).[90] These ideas would have meant the end of the strategy of the alliance with the Wafd in a national democratic front. In addition, HADITU suffered heavy losses from the imposition of martial law in May 1948 and the arrests of many of its members. The New Dawn group, renamed the Workers' Vanguard, seems to have survived this period in much better shape, without splitting up and with fewer arrests on account of its secretive nature.

The Communist Party of Egypt

The trend towards ideological doctrinism was to find a new equilibrium in the establishment of the Communist Party of Egypt in 1950. In spite of what the name might suggest, the CPE did not become the exclusive communist organization in Egypt. The reason for its late founding was that its founding members, Fu'ad Mursi (1925–1990) and Isma'il Sabri Abdallah (b. 1924), had been engaged in studies in France during the nationalist upsurge in 1945–46 and the disaster of the Palestine Partition Resolution. The CPE presented, therefore, a new start without the euphoria and deception of the 1946 upsurge. In fact, it could benefit from the dissatisfaction that HADITU had generated among its Egyptian members. By drawing up a clear program and establishing a classic communist organization as the vanguard of the working class, it appealed to the demands for clarity and order on the part of members of the older organizations. The official sanction of the French Communist Party added to its adopted status as heir to the earlier communist movement.[91] Important members of HADITU, such as Mustafa Tiba, Sa'd Zahran, and Da'ud Aziz, joined the two founding members after they had come back to Egypt in 1949.[92]

Before the founding of the CPE in January 1950, Fu'ad Mursi wrote a historical and political analysis of Egyptian society on which the strategy of the CPE was based. This work, *The Development of Capitalism and Class Struggle in Egypt*,[93] is one of the rare documents that, on account of length and depth of analysis, give an important insight into communist thought in Egypt in the late 1940s. It is conspicuous for its rigorous logic and somewhat pedantic attitude because, although Fu'ad Mursi was destined to become one of the most important communist leaders, he was not yet twenty-five when he wrote it. Rather than standing out for its innovative investigation, it is revealing of the ways in which the communist movement got bogged down in its modernist pretension to "scientific" analysis of history.

In the first part, after a lengthy historical account, Fu'ad Mursi describes how World War II inaugurated a new phase in Egyptian history, drawing the dividing lines much more clearly between the two opposite camps. Industry expanded, the petty bourgeoisie became "an independent entity," although it declined in wealth and status; inflation rose, while the working class became a force in itself, and the bourgeoisie had to take drastic measures to defend its interests. In 1945–46, writes Mursi, it became clear that the bourgeoisie had abandoned the nationalist struggle and that the working class had taken over as the vanguard of the nationalist movement. Referring to the desperate policies of the Nuqrashi government in 1947–48, Mursi claims that the bourgeoisie had erected a state apparatus to instill terror in the working class in defense of its interests. Within the Wafd, he says, the "big bourgeoisie" took over from the liberal middle classes and suppressed all demands for democracy. For this reason, he notes, it is not surprising that in these circumstances "fascist" groups like the Muslim Brotherhood arose.[94]

With regard to the all-important class relations and alliances after the Second World War, Fu'ad Mursi discerns three developments. The first concerns the role of the bourgeoisie, which betrayed its "historical task" of establishing a democracy and leading the country to national independence as well stimulating economic progress. In a world that is divided into two camps, the one "a democratic and peaceful camp led by the Soviet Union" and the other "an imperialist camp of imperialist wars led by the United States," the bourgeoisie succumbed to the imperialist camp.[95] As he sees it, the second development is the rise of the working class as the "only revolutionary class" capable of struggling against feudalism and imperialism. Finally, reflecting the classic Marxist distrust, Fu'ad Mursi describes the middle classes as vacillating between the workers' movement and the bourgeoisie, mostly choosing to support the latter. The conclusions that Mursi draws from these developments are evident: only a communist party can lead the revolution by organizing the working class, isolating the bourgeoisie, and winning over the petty bourgeoisie.[96]

In the second part of *The Development of Capitalism and Class Struggle in Egypt*, Fu'ad Mursi criticizes the political line of HADITU as right-wing opportunism and that of the Voice of Opposition as left-wing opportunism. He attacks the first for attributing revolutionary potential to all democratic nationalist classes and including them in the nationalist struggle. Instead, Mursi states that only a proletarian revolution can bring about a socialist society. He feels that the HADITU policy would focus exclusively on the anti-imperialist struggle, neglecting the internal enemy and the ultimate goal of the struggle, which is the proletarian revolution. By concentrating on establishing a "national front," right-wing opportunism disregarded in his opinion the establishment of an Egyptian communist party and the achievement of the dictatorship of the proletariat. Likewise, he says, an organization like the New Dawn group directed too much of its energies towards the Wafd.[97] Mursi is especially contemptuous of the right-wing belief in democracy, parliamentary reform, and the possibility to pressurize the government into abolishing martial law.[98]

Fu'ad Mursi takes all these deviations as signs of the communist mistrust of the revolutionary capacity of the working class. In accordance with the principles of Bolshevism, he professes his belief in the revolutionary force of the workers, who could become, in spite of their relatively small numbers, the leading revolutionary force when led by a communist party that enlarges its consciousness and shows it the way. Mursi does not, however, dispense with the two-stage revolution entirely, although he limits it to the bare minimum.

Communist Dissidents

Apart from the factions that split off from the larger communist organizations, there were smaller groups and individuals on the fringe of these larger organizations, who mostly remained independent. Many of these individual intellectuals joined the communist movement during the 1930s when it was not yet strictly organized and no attempts had been made to impose a certain discipline on thought and conduct. Two of these lonely individuals were Abd al-Mughni Saʿid and Anwar Kamil. The interest of their work ensues mostly from their ability to shed a different light on mainstream political thought and the left-wing discourse of modernity, so they serve as a counterpoint. In many ways they argued against the trend within the communist to instill order and discipline. They also warned against the authoritarian streak in the communist movement and its desire to emulate the Soviet Union and its Five Year Plans.

As we have seen, Anwar Kamil (b. 1913) was a member of the surrealist group in the Egyptian left-wing movement in the 1930s. He joined Georges Henein's group of surrealist painters and poets in 1936, Art et Liberté, and wrote for its magazine *L'Effort*. Together with members of other groups, like Marcel Israel's People's Liberation, he founded the first Arabic socialist-libertarian newspaper *al-Tatawwur* in January 1940. In 1942 several members of this group established the Socialist Front, which organized the campaign to get Ramsis Yunan a seat in parliament during the general elections two years later. Anwar Kamil's major contribution to socialist thought were his pamphlets entitled *The Problem of the Workers in Egypt* (1941),[99] *Zionism* (1944),[100] *No Classes ...!* (1945),[101] and *Opium of the People* (1948).[102]

No Classes ...! is remarkable for its directness and its unabashed indictment of the class structure of Egyptian society. In its directness it is not overburdened with theoretical considerations or political strategy, a feature from which so many other communist documents of this period suffer. *Opium of the People* is a much more ambitious book. It is conspicuous for its unconventional stand in relation to the Egyptian communist movement. Contrary to most communist tracts, which are, despite their adherence to liberal rights, imbued with a collectivistic strain, *Opium of the People* is highly individualist, almost anarchist. In its critique of Stalinism, the book can be seen as a continuation of ideas of Henein's surrealistic movement and an example of extreme libertarian modernism, which is rarely found in Egypt's communist movement after 1945. Anwar Kamil's motto is "eternal development and continuous change." His tract is directed against "idols," which, he asserts, hamper individual emancipation and block the continuous progress of humanity. In his crusade against both conservative and left-wing conventions, Kamil castigates all the sacred, more authoritarian modernist tenets of the Egyptian left-wing movement as it had become after 1946. He warns that exploitation will not end by abolishing private property: "It can even be strengthened until [profits] reach astronomical heights of which the capitalist cannot even dream and equality remains afterwards a dream that beguiles the eyelids and never sees the light of the day."[103] Neither does the introduction of public property in his view guarantee a good administration and the termination of the "chaos of production," which was the common designation of capitalism at the time. Kamil criticizes socialists for worshipping the state, comparing their concept of "the state above all," with Young Egypt's slogan, "Egypt above all." Contrary to communist belief, he asserts that it is the state and its power that lead to increased exploitation and the creation of "incredible differences" of income.

Anwar Kamil reserved his most vehement attack for the spread of Soviet communism, which he calls the new "religion" from Moscow. Kamil was one of the few who spoke out against Soviet communism at the time and pointed out its deficiencies. Although he recognizes that the Soviet Union had made huge strides in developing itself over the past half-century, he claims that this had been done at an enormous cost, such as the reign of terror, press censorship, suppression of democratic rights, and the expansion of Russian imperialism after the Second World War in Iran and Eastern Europe. The unsuitability of the Soviet Union as an example was underlined, he writes, with its acceptance of the Palestine Partition Plan.[104]

Abd al-Mughni Sa'id (b. 1915) is in many ways the opposite of Anwar Kamil. Although he had become a socialist in the 1930s and had contributed to *al-Tatawwur*, befriending the surrealist painter Fu'ad Kamil, who designed the jacket of his *The World Between Two Wars*, he left the magazine because of its libertarian morals, and what he believed to be its irreligious and even anti-religious content.[105] Abd al-Mughni Sa'id was one of the few Egyptian socialists who were shocked and repulsed by the cosmopolitan character of the communist movement in the 1930s and during the Second World War. With acrimony, he remembers one of his first encounters with a group of communists, when he collided with one of its female members, who insulted him. He was not the only one to feel this way. The Free Officer Khalid Muhyi al-Din was also repulsed from becoming a member of Iskra in 1947 on account of its offensive stance on religion. Not until Ahmad Fu'ad, the contact between the

Free Officers and the HADITU, had reassured him of HADITU's neutrality on matters of religion, was Khalid Muhyi al-Din willing to re-establish relations with the communist movement.[106]

Abd al-Mughni Sa'id's unique ideological make-up made such a solution impossible. Offering perhaps the first example of a phenomenon that would become common at the end of the 1940s and the beginning of the 1950s, he actively tried to combine Islam and rationalist socialism into one whole.[107] His primary motivation was a deeply-felt nationalism that prevented him from accepting communist rationalism, which only regarded nationalism as part of a worldwide struggle against imperialism and monopoly capital. In *The World Between Two Wars*, a well-documented account of modern international history, he argues that in the Soviet Union, local circumstances and nationalism have brought about communism.[108] Because he believed that communist internationalism was only a means to harness nationalist movements to the interests of the Soviet Union, he argued in favor of remaining neutral during the war.[109] His modernist outlook, however, prevented Abd al-Mughni Sa'id from embracing the ideas of the Muslim Brotherhood. He saw the Brotherhood as unwilling to come to terms with the modern world and examine it. Having studied economics at the Faculty of Commerce in 1935–1938, he became interested in the most modernist of disciplines, economic planning, and he would write one of the first Egyptian books on the subject.[110]

Conclusion

The communist movement was by far the most important promoter of modernist political ideas in Egypt. Through its analysis of the country's economy, social structure, and foreign relations, it identified the forces that produced and hampered progress and backwardness. It made a tremendous effort to apply Marxist analysis to the Egyptian political and economic situation and define Egypt's position in world history. In its ambition to provide a comprehensive analysis, the communists explained how economics, social structure, and culture interacted to keep Egypt in a semi-feudal state of development. Like most communist movements elsewhere, it was characterized by economic reductionism, especially in its view of the Muslim Brotherhood. Due to its ideological modernism, the movement failed to see culture and religion as a separate and independent variable or to recognize that it shared a common cause with the upholders of the discourse of authenticity, who also formed a modern and modernizing current struggling against patronage and clientalism.

On the whole, however, the concepts espoused by the communist movement were evidence of a moderate outlook. Despite its modernist proclamation of a new dawn, most communist proposals were inordinately moderate and highly sensible. Land reform, larger state control over the economy, and social reform may have been radical at the time in Egypt, but elsewhere they were common. Only after repression grew severe and infighting turned particularly vicious and even debilitating after 1948 did the movement become gradually more unbalanced. The extremism of Voice of the Opposition and the Revolutionary Bloc in demanding that a workers' Party lead the nationalist movement and the pretensions of the Egyptian Communist Party showed that the communist movement could easily become isolated and lose contact with reality.

As far as the authoritarian versus democratic modernist content of the works examined in this chapter is concerned, the contradictions are obvious. While portraying the workers as the vanguard of the nationalist movement and the hope for the future, these authors reveal their extreme ambivalence towards the Wafd, arguing for cooperation despite the fact that it was seen as a source of corruption and a representative of traditional politics. In general, however, the movement supported the growth of civil society and the reform of political society. Not until the rise of the radical groups and the bolshevization of the movement is the "one-stage revolution" promoted. More important is the long-term role assigned to the state and the image of the future of Egypt. While the French popular front and the Chinese revolution were important examples that helped determine the movement's political strategy and its relations with the "national bourgeoisie," the Soviet Union remained influential as the model of a new rational economy based on central state planning, with large kolkhoz-type agrarian production and massive industrialization. In the end, it would be up to the state to produce the new Egyptian and see to Egypt's entrance into modernity. The high modernist aspects of the communist ideology, giving rise to the movement's support for an authoritarian revolution from above, would weaken it once it thought that the "national bourgeoisie" had taken over power in the second half of 1950s. Until that time, the communist movement would continue its debate on the historical phase in which Egypt found itself and the tactics it should adopt. Interestingly, as we have seen at the end, important signs of the time to come would emerge from the margins of the movement, as communist-surrealist and Trotskyite dissidents warned against the etatist tendencies in the works of the Egyptian communists.

Notes

1 See Raoul Makarius, *La jeunesse intellectuelle d'Egypte au lendemain de la deuxième guerre mondiale* (Paris: Mouton, 1960).
2 In this chapter I argue that the communist movement was primarily a modernist movement that was torn between a democratic and an authoritarian strain in its ideology and practice. This contradiction explains why the movement eventually supported Nasser after 1956. Joel Beinin and Selma Botman believe that the communist movement started out as a cosmopolitan movement but that under the influence of Egyptian intellectuals, who took over power after 1948, nationalism and anti-imperialism gained strength, as opposed to internationalism and support of the workers' struggle. For Beinin and Botman, this explains the movement's support for the Nasserist regime after the Suez Canal crisis. See Joel Beinin, "The Communist Movement and National Political Discourse in Nasirist Egypt," *The Middle East Journal* 41 (1987): 568–84; Joel Beinin, *Was the Red Flag Flying There? Marxist Politics and the Arab-Israeli Conflict in Egypt and Israel, 1948–1965* (London: I.B. Tauris, 1990); Selma Botman, *The Rise of Egyptian Communism, 1939–1970* (Syracuse: Syracuse University Press, 1988); Selma Botman, "Egyptian Communists and the Free Officers: 1950–54," *Middle Eastern Studies* 22 (1986), 350–66.
3 J.P. Haithcox, *Communism and Nationalism in India: M.N. Roy and Comintern Policy, 1920–1939* (Princeton: Princeton University Press, 1971), 32.
4 Fernando Claudin, *The Communist Movement: From Comintern to Cominform* (London: Peregrine Books, 1975), 267.
5 E. H. Carr, *Twilight of the Comintern, 1930–1935* (New York: Pantheon Books, 1982), 45–103.
6 Carr, 128–9. See also for this period Jonathan Haslam, "The Comintern and the Origins of the Popular Front, 1934–1935," *Historical Journal* 22 (1979), 677–83.
7 Carr, 197.
8 Julian Jackson, *The Popular Front in France: Defending Democracy, 1934–38* (Cambridge: Cambridge University Press, 1988), 37.
9 Jackson, 47–9.
10 Jackson, 40.
11 Irwin M. Wall, *French Communism in the Era of Stalin: The Quest for Unity and Integration, 1945–1962* (Westport, CT: Greenwood Press, 1983), 16. See also E.J. Hobsbawm, *Nations and Nationalism Since 1780: Programme, Myth, Reality* (Cambridge: Cambridge University Press, 1992), 145–50.
12 Mau Tse-Tung, "On New Democracy," (January 1940) *Selected Works of Mau Tse-Tung*, Vol. II (Peking: Foreign Language Press, 1965), 339–84. Raymond Stambouli translated *On New Democracy* from the French into Arabic for HAMITU. See Gilles Perrault, *Un homme à part* (Paris: Bernard Barrault, 1984), 178. The New Dawn group was for a while called People's Democracy under

the influence of Mau Zedong's *On New Democracy*, which it had translated as well. See Rif'at al-Sa'id, *Tarikh al-munazzamat al-yasariyya al-Misriyya, 1940–1950* (Cairo: Dar al-Thaqafa al-Jadida, 1976), 311. According to Mustafa Tiba, the Communist Party of Egypt, established in 1950, was also influenced by the Chinese revolution. See Mustafa Tiba, *al-Haraka al-shuyu'iyya al-Misriyya 1945–1965: Ru'ya dakhiliyya* (Cairo: Sina' li-l-Nashr, 1990), 60.
13 Maw Tsi Tunj, *al-Dimuqratiyya al-jadida*, translated by Yusuf Ahmad (Cairo: Dar al-Nadim, 1957).
14 Muhammad Awda, *al-Sin al-sha'biyya* (Cairo: Dar al-Nadim, 1955).
15 Stuart Schram, *Mau Tse-tung* (Harmondsworth: Penguin Books, 1967), 74, 80–1 and 86. See also Stuart Schram, *The Political Thought of Mau Tse-tung* (Harmondsworth: Penguin Books, 1969), 40–1.
16 Mau Tse-tung, *Works*, 349.
17 Mau Tse-tung, *Works*, 356.
18 A short biography of Georges Henein has been written by Sarane Alexandrian: *Georges Henein* (Paris: Éditions Seghers, 1981). For Georges Henein's early political activities see pages 10–37.
19 The most extensive accounts of the organizational history of the Egyptian communist movement in this period are: Rif'at al-Sa'id, *Tarikh al-munazzamat al-yasariyya al-Misriyya, 1940–1950* (Cairo: Dar al-Thaqafa al-Jadida, 1976), 119–205; Tareq Y. Ismael and Rifa'at el-Sa'id, *The Communist Movement in Egypt, 1920–1988* (Syracuse, N.Y.: Syracuse University Press, 1990), 32–54; Selma Botman, *The Rise of Egyptian Communism, 1939–1970* (Syracuse, N.Y.: Syracuse University Press, 1988), 6–16; Tariq al-Bishri, *al-Haraka al-siyasiyya fi Misr, 1945–1952* (Cairo: Dar al-Shuruq, 1983), 75–91.
20 Gudrun Krämer, *The Jews in Modern Egypt, 1914–1952* (London: I.B. Taurus, 1989), 172–82.
21 B.L. Carter, *The Copts in Egyptian Politics* (Beckenham: Croom Helm, 1986), 110–3.
22 Al-Sa'id, *Tarikh*, 355–6.
23 Most of the books seem to have been pirated as the author is not mentioned or only partially. See for instance, in the booklet *Taqaddum al-insan (The Progress of Man)*, which was translated by Mustafa Munib and represents a typical example of the historical thinking of that time, which propounded that human history had started with slavery and progressed through feudalism and capitalism to socialism. Other books he translated are *Comrade Stalin* in addition to *Marriage and Family in the Soviet Union* and *Marxism and War*.
24 A. Palmer, *al-Hind*, translated by Mustafa Munib (Cairo: Dar al-Fajr, 1946) and 'Abd al-Mun'im al-Ghazali, *Indunisiya al-mujahida* (Cairo: Dar al-Fajr, n.d.).
25 Salama Musa, *Hurriyyat al-'aql fi Misr* (Cairo: Dar al-Fajr, [1945]).
26 Ahmad Rushdi Salih, *Krumir fi Misr: Safahat min tarikh Misr al-hadith* (Cairo: Dar al-Qarn al-'Ishrin, 1945).
27 Ahmad Sadiq Sa'd, *Mushkilat al-fallah* (Cairo: Dar al-Qarn al-'Ishrin, 1945).
28 Ahmad Sadiq Sa'd, *Ma'sat al-tamwin* (Cairo: Dar al-Qarn al-'Ishrin, 1945).
29 Abu Sayf Yusuf, *Hawla al-falsafa al-Markisiyya: Radd 'ala al-'Aqqad* (Cairo, Dar al-Qarn al- 'Ishrin, 1946).
30 Salih, *Krumir*, 10.
31 Shuhdi 'Atiyya al-Shafii'i and Muhammad 'Abd al-Ma'bud al-Jubayli, *Ahdafuna al-wataniyya* (Cairo: Matba'at Risala, October 1945).

32 Abu Sayf Yusuf, *falsafa*, 4.
33 Yusuf, *Hawla*, 26.
34 Yusuf, *Hawla*, 30. Italics added
35 Yusuf, *Hawla*, 19.
36 Salih, *Krumir*, 1–5.
37 Salih, *Krumir*, 10.
38 Wilfrid Scawen Blunt, *Secret History of the English Occupation of Egypt: Being a Personal Narrative of Events* (New York: Alfred A. Knopf, 1922).
39 Theodore Rothstein, *Egypt's Ruin: A Financial and Administrative Record* (London: Cliffords Inn, 1910).
40 Elinor Burns, *British Imperialism in Egypt* (London: The Labour Research Department, Colonial Series No. V., 1928).
41 Ilinur Birnz, *al-Isti'mar al-Biritani fi Misr* (Cairo: Dar Qarn al-'Ishrin, 1946).
42 Salih, *Krumir*, 26–35.
43 Salih, *Krumir*, 60.
44 Ahmad Sadiq Sa'd, *Mushkilat al-fallah* (Cairo: Dar al-Qarn al-'Ishrin, 1945).
45 Ahmad Sadiq Sa'd, "al-Islah al-zira'i. bi-qalam Mirrit Ghali," *al-Fajr al-Jadid* No. 7 (16 August 1945). Republished in Ahmad Sadiq Sa'd, *Safahat min al-yasar al-misri fi 'a'qab al-harb al-'alamiyya al-thaniya, 1945–1946*, introduced by 'Abd al-'Azim Ramadan (Cairo: Maktabat Madbuli, 1976), 161–4. See also Ahmad Sadiq Sa'd, "Mulahazat 'ala tahdid al-milkiyya al-zira'iyya bi-munasabat 'ard mashru' Khattab bak 'ala majlis al-shuyukh," *al-Fajr al-Jadid* No. 5 (16 July 1945). Republished in Sa'd, *Safahat*, 157–60.
46 Sa'd, *Mushkilat*, 20.
47 Sa'd, *Mushkilat*, 27–44.
48 Sa'd, *Mushkilat*, 47.
49 *Ahdafuna*, 55.
50 *Ahdafuna*, 55–58.
51 Ahmad Sadiq Sa'd, "Tatawwur Misr al-ra'smali 1919–1945," *al-Fajr al-Jadid* No. 13 (16 November 1945). Republished in Sa'd, *Safahat*, 176–82.
52 Ahmad Sadiq Sa'd, "Yajib an nuqabil al-ra'smal al-ajnabi bi-shurut," *al-Fajr al-Jadid* No. 12 (11 January 1945). Republished in Sa'd, *Safahat*, 171–75.
53 Anwar Kamil and Lutfallah Sulayman, *Ukhruju min al-sudan* (Cairo: Matbu'at al-Duhama', May 1947).
54 *Ahdafuna*, 52.
55 Ahmad Sadiq Sa'd, "Yajib an nahmi sighar al-muntijin," *al-Fajr al-Jadid* No. 18 (22 January 1946). Republished in Sa'd, *Safahat*, 189–94.
56 Sa'd Makawi, "Misr wa-l-siyasa al-sina'iyya," *al-Fajr al-Jadid* No. 1 (16 May 1945). Cited in Rif'at al-Sa'id, *al-Sihafa al-yasariyya fi misr, 1925–1948* (Cairo: Maktabat Madbuli, 1977), 128.
57 "Jala' iqtisadi am dimuqrati," *al-Fajr al-Jadid* No. 38 (12 June 1946). Republished in Sa'd, *Safahat*, 210–15; and Ahmad Sadiq Sa'd, "Yajib an nuqabil al-ra'smal al-ajnabi bi-shurut," *al-Fajr al-Jadid* No. 12 (1 November 1945). Republished in Sa'd, *Safahat*, 171–75.
58 *Ahdafuna*, 50.
59 Ahmad Sadiq Sa'd, "Fi qadaya al-tahrir al-watani wa-l-dimuqratiyya. Ta'dil al-mu'ahada al-Misriyya al-Injliziyya," *al-Fajr al-Jadid* No. 6 (1 August 1945). Republished in Sa'd, *Safahat*, 62–5.
60 *Ahdafuna*, 48.

61 Ahmad Sadiq Sa'd, "al-Taharrur min al-isti'mar al-Biritani wa-l-mufawadat al-haliyya," *al-Fajr al-Jadid* No. 26 (20 March 1946). Republished in Sadiq Sa'd, *Safaha*, 106–9.
62 Ahmad Sadiq Sa'd, "Dawr al-jamahir fi al-haraka al-wataniyya wa-l-mufawadat al-haliyya," *al-Fajr al-Jadid* No. 29 (10 April 1946). Republished in Sa'd, *Safahat*, 118–22.
63 *Ahdafuna*, 61.
64 Ahmad Sadiq Sa'd, "Limadha nutalib bi-ijra' intikhabat," *al-Fajr al-Jadid* No. 25 (13 March 1946). Republished in Sa'd, *Safahat*, 100–5.
65 Ahmad Sadiq Sa'd, "Hal nulghi al-ahzab," *al-Fajr al-Jadid* No. 20 (2 June 1946). Republished in Sa'd, *Safahat*, 84–8.
66 Ahmad Sadiq Sa'd, "Hawla maqal yajib nuqabil al-ra'smal al-ajnabi bi-shurut," *al-Fajr al-Jadid* No. 14 (6 December 1946). Republished in Sa'd, *Safahat*, 183–4.
67 Ahmad Sadiq Sa'd, "Hawla maqalat al-duktur Mandur," *al-Fajr al-Jadid* No. 38 (12 June 1945). Republished in Sa'd, *Safahat*, 134–7.
68 Raymond Duwayk, "al-Dimuqratiyya al-Misriyya bayna ansariha wa-a'da'iha," *al-Fajr al-Jadid* No. 5 (16 July 1945). Cited in al-Sa'id, *Safahat*, 134.
69 Jean Pierre Thieck, "Communistes et mouvement national en Égypte (1945–1946)," *Passion d'Orient* (Paris: Éditions Karthala, 1992), 77–8.
70 Ahmad Sadiq Sa'd, "al-Sha'b daman intisar harakatiha al-wataniyya," *al-Fajr al-Jadid* No. 22 (20 February 1946). Republished in Sa'd, *Safahat*, 90–2.
71 *Ahdafuna*, 47.
72 *Ahdafuna*, 48.
73 Botman, *Rise*, 47.
74 Beinin and Lockman, *Workers*, 340–4.
75 Muhammad Hasan Ahmad, *al-Ikhwan al-muslimin fi al-mizan* (Cairo: n.p., n.d.).
76 Abu Sayf Yusuf, "al-Muthaqqafun fi mahabb al-fashiyya," *al-Fajr al-Jadid* No. 27 (27 March 1946). Photocopy of the collection of Salah Isa.
77 Ahmad Rushdi Salih, "Wahdat al-wataniyya hiyya al-hadaf lijan am jabha wataniyya wahida?" *al-Fajr al-Jadid* No. 24 (6 March 1946). Photocopy of the collection of Salah Isa.
78 Yusuf, "al-Muthaqqafun."
79 Yusuf, "al-Muthaqqafun."
80 Ahmad, 13–21.
81 Ahmad, 43.
82 Ahmad, 30–35.
83 Al-Sa'id, *al-Sihafa*, 169–70. See for an account of this period Sa'd Zahran's memoirs cum political analysis of Egyptian politics, Sa'd Zahran, *Fi usul al-siyasa al-Misriyya. Maqal tahlili naqdi fi al-tarikh al-siyasi* (Cairo: Dar al-Mustaqbal al-'Arabi, 1985), 106–22.
84 Mahmud Hamdi (Shuhdi 'Atiyya al-Shafi'i), "Yurid al-sha'b "izban ... min naw' jadid," *al-Jamahir* 21 April 1947. Cited in al-Sa'id, *al-Sihafa*, 190.
85 Al-Sa'id, *al-Sihafa*, 192–93.
86 Cited in Botman, *Communist*, 93.
87 For Rif'at al-Sa'id's account of this episode, see al-Sa'id, *Tarikh*, 413–20.
88 Salah Isa, "Ightiyal Shuhdi 'Atiyya al-Shafi'i: 'Abd al-Nasir wa-l-shuyu'iyyun. Shuhur al-'asal wa sanawat al-sidam," Part I, *al-Yasar* No. 6 (August, 1990), 17.
89 Al-Sa'id, *Tarikh*, 422–23.
90 Cited in Botman, *Communism*, 97.

91 Salah Isa, "Tibta hayyan wa maitan ya rafiq Khalid," *al-Yasar* No. 8 (August 1990), 33–35.
92 See for an interesting account of the reasons for one of the prominent Egyptian members of HAMITU to defect to ECP, Mustafa Tiba's political memoirs: Tiba, *al-Haraka*, 33–54.
93 Fortunately this long lost document has been published after Fu'ad Mursi's death in 1990 by his friend Da'ud 'Aziz: Fu'ad Mursi, *Tatawwur al-ra'smaliyya wa kifa' al-tabaqat fi Misr* (Cairo: Kitabat al-Misri al-Jadid, 1990).
94 Mursi, 42–4.
95 Mursi, 51.
96 Mursi, 57.
97 Mursi, 62–9.
98 Mursi, 73–95.
99 Anwar Kamil, *Mashakil al-'ummal fi Misr* (Cairo: n.p., 1941).
100 Anwar Kamil, *al-Sahyuniyya* (Cairo: n.p., 1944). According to Bashir al-Siba'i, this pamphlet was an abridged edition of a British communist Reynab, entitled *Anti-Semitism and the Problem of Zionism*, which was translated and published in Lebanon in 1943. This booklet was in its turn based on Kautsky's book on anti-semitism. See Bashir al-Siba'i "Hawla ma yusamma bi 'al-trutskiyya al-Misriyya' bayna 'amay 1938–1948," *Tarikh Misr bayna al-manhaj al-'ilmi wa-l-sira' al-hizbi* (Cairo: Dar Shuhdi, 1987), 405.
101 Anwar Kamil, *La tabaqat ...!* (Cairo: n.p. 1945).
102 Anwar Kamil, *Afyun al-Sha'b* (Cairo: Matba'at al-Risala, 1948).
103 Kamil, *Afyun*, 20–1.
104 Kamil, *Afyum*, 31–69.
105 See 'Abd al-Mughni Sa'id's memoirs: *Asrar al-siyasa al-Misriyya fi rub' qarn* (Cairo: Kitab al-Hurriyya, 1985), 55–8.
106 Khalid Muhyi al-Din, *Wa al-ana atakallam* (Cairo: Markaz al-Ahram, 1993), 66.
107 Perhaps the most famous example of the combination of Islam and socialist rationalism is the book written by Khalid Muhammad Khalid, *From Here We Start*, translated by Isma'il R. el Faruqi (Washington, D.C.: American Council of Learned Societies, 1953). It was originally published as *Min huna nabda'* (Cairo: Dar al-Nil li-l-Tiba'a, 1950).
108 'Abd al-Mughni Sa'id, *al-'Alam ba'da harbayn* (Cairo: Dar al-Nil li-l-Tiba'a, 1947), 44.
109 'Abd al-Mughni Sa'id, *Asrar*, 75–8.
110 'Abd al-Mughni Sa'id, *Nahwa al-rushd al-iqtisadi. Dirasa shamila li-nazariyyat al-tarshid wa wasa'ilihi* (Cairo: Dar al-Nil li-l-Tiba'a, 1950).

♦ PART II ♦

The Rise of Authoritarian Modernism

◆ CHAPTER FOUR ◆

The Dilemmas of Reform, 1950–54

Introduction

The previous three chapters have presented an analysis of the programs of the secular reformist movements in Egypt. One of the main challenges for modernism in Egypt in the 1930s and 1940s was to establish a nation-state that would incorporate the excluded social classes into the reformed political and social structures through social "integration" and political "deepening." A crucial aspect of this project was to establish "rational" social and political relations, regulated by clear rules and laws.

For the younger generation of Egyptian liberals, socialists, and communists, clarity of definitions and roles was particularly important in the fields of state-society relations and the separation of private and public spheres, which is generally regarded as the precondition for the expansion of civil society and the rationalization of the state. This generation intended to remove politics from the patronage of the large landowners, the minority parties, and the Palace and turn it into a public activity, open for debate, subject to scrutiny, and centered on parliament. Such a shift would put an end to the interpenetration of economic and political society, which had led to widespread corruption. It would turn the state into an instrument for the "common good."

This chapter analyzes the dilemma of the reformist political currents during the period that began with the electoral victory of the Wafd and ended with final defeat of the democratic option with the March Crisis in 1954. It first provides an account of the the tortuous fate of Egyptian liberalism during these four years. The liberal dilemma will be highlighted not through the works of the members of the Society of National Renaissance alone. I also turn to other representatives of liberal thought in Egyptian politics, such as the newspaper *al-Misri*, the magazine *Ruz al-Yusuf*, and especially their editors Ahmad Abu al-Fath (b. 1917) and Ihsan Abd al-Quddus (1919–1990). The conflict between self-reform of political parties and reform "from above" by the state can be seen in the deep divisions this period opened up among the ranks of the liberals.

A second major narrative strand in this chapter concerns the socialist-etatist intervention, represented by Rashid al-Barrawi. Although he too was inspired by a desire for clarity and order, al-Barrawi focused mainly on applying these principles with an eye to ending the colonization of politics by large landowners and capitalists. At the same time, he was less concerned than the liberals with the adverse consequences of the expansion of state power. He felt that the state, as the embodiment of rationality, stood for modernity and could absorb civil society, which in itself had no special function once the social and economic reforms demanded by the middle classes had been put into effect. Faced with a choice between a multi-party system and state-imposed reform, Rashid al-Barrawi clearly favored the second. He was one of the first intellectuals and "experts" to join the new regime and legitimize it in modernist terms as the representative of the "new middle classes." This chapter explores the ways in which Rashid al-Barrawi may be seen to offer the perfect combination of modernist theory and praxis. It will show how his political language of emancipation of the middle classes steered the ideology and politics of the new regime. In the next chapter we will see how his discourse of planning helped form the state ideology of developmentalism and contributed to the consolidation of the new regime.

The third subject of this chapter is the communist movement and its attitude towards the military after July 1952. In the throes of the debate on the nature of the middle class and its role in the revolutionary transition of Egypt from a semi-feudal society to a modern society, the communist movement was continuously torn between adopting a the "minimum program" of support of the nationalist revolution and co-operating with the "petty bourgeoisie" or opposing this class on the basis of the "maximum program." Both strategies were marked by a strong ambivalence regarding democratic change. While the first position implied the support of civil society, the defense of parliamentary system, the upholding of the rights of independent trade unions, freedom of the press, and civil rights, it could also mean support for the military to implement reform from above as long as it was done in a broad nationalist front. In contrast, though it involved a negative attitude towards a military dictatorship and an emphasis on a proletarian revolution, the maximum program did not enhance the democratic option because of its rejection of a front and a parliamentary system.

This chapter analyzes these three reformist political movements during several crucial phases characterized by different means to impose reforms. The first phase was inaugurated by the Wafd's electoral victory in January 1950, when all reformist currents pinned their hopes on the Wafd's capacity for self-reform as a last chance to save the 1923 Constitution and parliamentary democracy. Such optimism proved unfounded, and the activist reformers briefly supported violent methods of enforcing social change during the struggle with the British over the Suez Canal in 1951. The third phase saw a search for a "temporary" dictatorial solution to the problem of reform. This precarious ideological turn finally led reformers to support the July 1952 military takeover. During the next year and a half, the ways of the reformers split. While Rashid al-Barrawi joined the new regime, most turned against it and opposed it openly during the March Crisis. The debates in books, newspapers, magazines, and pamphlets cast a special light on the development of political thought in the period. They reveal the dilemmas faced by reformists due to the special circumstances in which they found themselves and to which they had to adjust. The last phase occurred during the March Crisis itself when a last-ditch effort was made to install a democratic system.

The Failure of Liberal and Revolutionary Reform

The liberal press and reformist networks

Central to democratic reform was the expansion in civil society of independent political, social, and economic organizations that had freed themselves from the tutelage of the political parties. In Egypt the trend towards greater independence had begun at the end of the 1930s. In fact, these networks of associations, clubs and newspapers and other associations that influenced public opinion had gradually begun to overlap and reinforce each other to such an extent that they formed networks and became strong enough to help topple the old regime.

One such network of associations, political groups, newspapers and personal relations that was to play an important role in the growth and defense of civil society was formed around the daily newspaper *al-Misri*. Founded in 1937 by the Abu al-Fath brothers as the first daily actually published by Egyptians, *al-Misri* gradually grew into Egypt's largest daily during the next decade. As it depended upon popular sales instead of patronage, *al-Misri* could pursue its own course, independent from political parties.[1] After Ahmad Abu al-Fath became editor-in-chief in July 1946, the paper took a more critical stance, at first towards the minority governments and the autocratic tendencies of the monarchy, but later also towards the Wafd. The liberal, mildly left-wing, nationalist attitude of the daily in the 1940s is equally evident in its condemnation of all proposals for military pacts with Great Britain or the United States, its favorable disposition towards nationalization of foreign firms, and its neutral if not sympathetic accounts of strikes and other social issues.[2]

The network around *al-Misri* extended both upward to the established Egyptian bourgeoisie during the 1930s and 1940s and downward to the oppositional groups that were gradually coming about after the Second World War. The two Abu al-Fath brothers were themselves important businessmen, involved in major investment operations of the time, such as the electrification of the Aswan Dam.[3] The older of the two, Mahmud Abu al-Fath (b. 1894), became one of the first presidents of the journalists' syndicate. Originally established in 1941 as an employers' syndicate, the journalists' syndicate was supposed to establish professional ethics and exert self-censorship.[4] But it grew into a more independent institution with the delegitimization of the monarchy, a process to which the press would be crucial. Ahmad Abu al-Fath, who was to become an important political figure in this period, built his support among the younger generation of liberal intellectuals and joined the reformist left-wing of the Wafd, the Wafdist Vanguard (al-Tali'a al-Wafdiyya).

The links between the Wafdist Vanguard and the communist group the New Dawn (al-Fajr al-Jadid), which was very close to the Wafd, extended *al-Misri*'s network even further in a left-wing direction. In 1947, the Wafdist Vanguard and the New Dawn group established a joint project with the short-lived weekly *Rabitat al-Shabab*.[5] Through the New Dawn, the network also included the independent trade union movement. In addition, Ahmad Abu al-Fath entertained close relations with Gamal Abd al-Nasser.[6]

The weekly *Ruz al-Yusuf* was the center of another essential cluster of networks that supported reform an the extension of civil society. Although linked by numerous ties to *al-Misri*, *Ruz al-Yusuf* formed its own system of networks. The magazine had been founded in 1924 by the actress Fatima al-Yusuf. Like all reformist institutions, it experienced a clash with the Wafdist leadership when it started to steer an independent course in 1935.[7] The Wafd's official severance of its ties with *Ruz al-Yusuf* enabled it to adopt an independent stance and become a force in its own right. In August 1945, its status as an independent mouthpiece of the new *effendiyya* was confirmed when Fatima al-Yusuf appointed her son, Ihsan Abd al-Quddus, editor-in-chief at the early age of twenty-six.[8] During the following years, *Ruz al-Yusuf* succeeded in becoming perhaps the most creative and original political and cultural medium of the modernist generation. Courageous, undogmatic, and humorous (most conspicuously in the often hilarious political cartoons by Abd al-Sami'), *Ruz al-Yusuf* developed into one of the foremost press organs promoting liberal political and social reform.

At the same time, however, *Ruz al-Yusuf* was prone to the typical ambivalence of liberal reformist movements. To some degree this was a result of the tolerant atmosphere among its editorial staff. The "family" (*al-usra*), as it was called, attracted all types of reformers, from Muslim Brotherhood member Sayyid Qutb (1906–1966) to Marxist Mahmud Amin al-Alim (b. 1923). But in part the weekly also reflected the dilemmas of all modernist reformers, especially in the long editorials by Ihsan Abd al-Quddus, which put their stamp on *Ruz al-Yusuf*. The exuberance of his populist tendencies was balanced by a more principled, social-democratic analysis when highly talented journalists such as Ahmad Baha al-Din (1927–1996) and Fathi Ghanim joined the staff as columnists in 1952 and 1955 respectively. Their sober attitude can undoubtedly be traced to their previous apprenticeship at *al-Fusul*, where they had undergone the political influence of the Society of National Renaissance in the person of Muhammad Zaki Abd al-Qadir. Through these liberal relations and left-wing contacts, *Ruz al-Yusuf* became a mainstay of Egyptian civil society.

Apart from *al-Misri* and *Ruz al-Yusuf*, numerous other networks and institutions upheld reform. Increasingly, the universities became centers of reform as the younger generation acquired positions in which its members were free to assert their ideas. Evidence of the force of these circles and individuals is the appointment of Rashid al-Barrawi in July 1951 as the leading columnist of the monarchist daily newspaper, *al-Zaman*. Before, he had contributed to *al-Ahram*, where Muhammad Zaki Abd al-Qadir supported his reformist appeals. From his articles in *al-Misri* after the revolution, it is clear that al-Barrawi also maintained good relations with Ahmad Abu al-Fath and the Wafdist Vanguard. Like Ahmad Abu al-Fath, he was in close contact with Gamal Abd al-Nasser, through his appointment at the Military Academy, where he taught economics.[9]

The clearest indication of the new force of reformist modernism, however, was its penetration of the bulwark of its main competitor for the support of the new generation, the discourse of authenticity. At the end of the 1940s, a gray area developed between the two discourses. Most significantly, this was reflected by the changing of the name Young Egypt into the Socialist Party of Egypt (SPE) in October 1949.[10] As a result of the expansion of the discourse of political and social reform, there was a marked rapprochement between former left-wing and liberal adversaries. A similar trend took hold in the Muslim Brotherhood, where after the February 1949 murder of Hasan al-Banna (1906–1949) a socialist orientation became evident as its members sought closer ties with secular reformist circles.[11] Finally, by the end of the 1940s, the reformist agenda had also spread to the minority parties. The best example of this is the case of Sayyid Mari' (b.), a young member of the Sa'di Party, who would join the revolution at an early stage and later become minister of agriculture.[12]

The failure of democratic reform

The electoral victory of the Wafd in January 1950 gave new currents the opportunity to exert power and expand their discourse. Naturally, the Wafdist Vanguard, supported by *al-Misri*, believed that the opportunity to press for reform had finally come. The party was strengthened in this belief when several of its most prominent members, Ahmad Abu al-Fath, Aziz Fahmi, and Muhammad Mandur (1907–), were elected to parliament for the first time. Even though the Vanguard was underrepresented in the higher echelons of the party hierarchy and the conservative leadership prevented its members from acquiring portfolios, it became a force to be reckoned with within the central Wafdist organizations. When the Wafd's electoral victory was announced, the communist movement too anticipated a change for the better. Socialists like Rashid al-Barrawi regarded it as the last opportunity to achieve an orderly transition to a welfare state and carry out etatist reform.[13] Even Muhammad Zaki Abd al-Qadir of the Society of National Renaissance, who was very skeptical of the transformative powers of the Wafd, ran for parliament as an independent because he believed that under Wafdist tutelage parliament could at least become a forum where reformers could promote their ideas.[14]

These expectations were soon proven wrong. As the road to reform through potentially democratic institutions was blocked, the first step towards authoritarianism was taken. Almost immediately after its electoral victory, the Wafd made it clear that it would not realize key liberal reforms or push back the powers of the monarchy in favor of parliament. Instead, the Wafd tried to placate the Palace by acquiescing in its constitutional privileges and bowing to its political demands. As a result, the party was now identified with a monarchy that was increasingly perceived as corrupt and decadent and that symbolized everything modernists abhorred in Egypt.[15]

Ironically, these failures were greatly aggravated by the one promise that the Wafd did try to keep: the creation of a relatively liberal political climate. Just after the elections, freedom of the press was reinstated, and in May 1950 the government repealed martial law. Political prisoners who had been arrested during the rule of the minority government were released. This gave independent public and political institutions much more room to expand their activities. Unfortunately for the Wafd, however, these activities were increasingly directed against the government. The now unmuzzled press provided a release for growing dissatisfaction with the party's policies.

The arms scandal especially had the effect of undermining the monarchy. *Ruz al-Yusuf* led the investigation into the affair. From his first telegram, printed on 20 July 1949 and entitled "The Criminals of the Palestine War Should Be Brought to Trial," until his arrest in June 1950, Ihsan Abd al-Quddus published a series of articles in *Ruz al-Yusuf* in which he accused high officers in the Egyptian army of having bought defective arms for the Palestine War.[16] He implied not only that the acquisition of these arms had led to the Egyptian defeat, but also that the monarchy, as the main responsible agent, was incompetent, corrupt, callous, and unfit to rule. The absolutist and sinister character of the Palace was further emphasized when it prevented high officials and important politicians from investigating the case. The Wafdist support for the monarchy in covering up the affair eventually confirmed the image of the decadence of the entire political and economic system and made *Ruz al-Yusuf* into an important symbol of the modernist reformist movement.[17]

The reformist press became a formidable influence on public opinion, turning it against the monarchy and the Wafd. At the forefront of the modernist onslaught against the *ancien régime* were, along with *Ruz al-Yusuf*, the communist daily *al-Malayin* and its weekly *al-Katib* (published by HADITU), *al-Misri* and its weekly issue *al-Jumhur al-Misri*, *al-Daʿwa* (the daily of the Muslim Brotherhood), as well as *al-Ishtiraki* (published by the SPE).

The failure of the popular revolution

On 8 October 1951 the Wafd government finally gave in to the pressure of the nationalist movement and abrogated unilaterally both the Anglo-Egyptian Treaty and the Sudanese condominium. This opened up the way for guerrilla warfare against the British base along the Suez Canal, which had been one of the chief demands of the radicalized nationalist movement since the failure of United Nations mediation in 1947. Even *Ruz al-Yusuf* championed the armed struggle now that democratic reform had failed. One day after the announcement, Ihsan Abd al-Quddus wrote:

> The decrees that have been issued by the government ... are faithful expressions of the revolution that we have called for for so long. That the government has undertaken to implement these measures has made it a revolutionary government, and all of us are with it, unified in self-sacrifice and struggle (*jihad*) as long as the gates of the struggle are open.[18]

Other representatives of the reformist movement, like Ahmad Abu al-Fath and Rashid al-Barrawi, expressed themselves in similar terms.[19] In the fervor of the first weeks, the offices of *Ruz al-Yusuf* and *al-Misri* even served as recruiting stations and centers of organization for the guerrilla struggle against the British troops along the Suez Canal.

Disillusionment was inevitable. The weakness of the reformists even meant that they had to rely on the Wafd to support a mass popular uprising though the Wafdist government had no intention of mobilizing the population against the British. After all, this was a time when these organizations could turn the guerrilla fighters against the tottering establishment. In December 1951 Ihsan Abd al-Quddus wrote, in an article entitled "The Government for us ... or the Government against us,"

Since the abrogation of the Treaty and the announcement of a state of enmity between Egypt and Great Britain, I have demanded that the people alone carry complete responsibility and that the government provide the possibility for the people to carry responsibility ... Where is the armed revolution that will engulf Egypt as a whole and mobilize its youth, financial means, and resources? ... Where is the leader of the revolution?[20]

At the end of the article, he quite rightly concludes, "the government is more anxious about the revolutionary stirrings of the people than it is afraid of the British, especially when the people are armed."

On 26 January 1952 an angry mob set cinemas, foreign clubs, hotels, government buildings, and other symbols of foreign dominance on fire. The burning of Cairo demonstrated the failure of the plan to mobilize the people and organize the revolution "from below." Neither internal reform nor popular pressure had succeeded in bringing about radical social reform or in breaking the stalemate between the traditional political forces of the King, the Wafd, and the British. Although Egypt's political impasse created the opportunity for new forces to make themselves felt, it did not bring about the new, regulated, and controlled form of politics envisioned by most reformers.

In search of a "benevolent dictatorship"

The sacking of Cairo was a sobering experience for all democratic reformers. They felt that with the reinstatement of martial law and censorship and with the dismissal of the Wafd, the last opportunity for change had been missed. Most held the British responsible for the disastrous course of events.[21] For instance, Ihsan Abd al-Quddus believed the British had intentionally mobilized reactionary forces to set fire to Cairo in order to sow "dissension" (*fitna*).[22]

The seven chaotic months prior to the July revolution were marked by instability. In this lull before the storm, liberals looked desperately for other ways to realize their program. In this climate Rashid al-Barrawi reminded his readers of Muhammad Ali's reign (1805–1848), when Egypt had progressed "under the government of an enlightened ruler, who brought about an exemplary revolution that pulled the country from the darkness of the Middle Ages into the light of the modern era." A savior like Muhammad Ali, he wrote, would have to have "a vision and far-sightedness, and be capable of knowing the spirit of the age, discerning the demands of the community, and basing his policy on implementing reforms that comply with that spirit."[23]

In light of the search for an alternative solution to the present political crisis, it was not surprising to find Rashid al-Barrawi and other radical intellectuals welcoming the Ali Mahir cabinet when it was installed on 27 January 1952. Ali Mahir belonged to the old guard of politicians who had tried to create a monarchist, corporatist state in Egypt for the first time at the end of the 1930s.[24] Nevertheless, he was acceptable to Rashid al-Barrawi in the circumstances because he was a reformer, albeit a conservative one. His government could be a bulwark against chaos: "The nation will not be able to reach its political, economic, and social goals unless it unifies its efforts and focuses on productive work that is not interrupted by confusion (*idtirab*) and characterized by instability."[25] Ihsan Abd al-Quddus went even further in praising Ali Mahir as the only uncorrupted, pure (*nazih*) politician.[26] Like al-Barrawi, he entertained the hope that Ali Mahir would carry out reforms to overcome the divisions between the classes. In the clearest expression of what would become the new line of liberal reformers, he argued that Egypt needed a temporary dictatorship, "a dictatorship for the people, a dictatorship for freedom, a dictatorship that moves forward, not one that moves backward."[27]

At a time when prime ministers succeeded each other rapidly without achieving stability or initiating reform, the entire debate on the subject of social change was complicated by the fact that right-wing reformers also marched under banner of the dictatorship. After the fall of the Wafd government, reform was confused with the concept of the "purification" (*tathir*) of public life from corruption, and the question became whether purification should take precedence over national "liberation" (*tahrir*).[28] This issue, which lay dormant while Ali Mahir maintained working relations with the Wafd, became acute when Naguib al-Hilali succeeded him on 1 March, disbanded parliament, and declared purification his official policy. Al-Hilali's cabinet, which lasted until 29 June, posed the threat of a right-wing, reformist, authoritarian dictatorship under the aegis of the monarchy.

Ihsan Abd al-Quddus saw al-Hilali's policy of giving priority to purification and "combating corruption" (*muharabat al-fasad*) as a pretext for drawing attention away from the British occupation.[29]

The al-Hilali episode strengthened Ihsan Abd al-Quddus and other reformers in the belief that the political crisis in Egypt could only be solved by a left-wing, reformist dictatorship: "If – in these circumstances – there is hope that a ruler exists who is faithful to himself without [the limitations of] a constitution, then I would be the first to ask al-Hilali to rule without a constitution and postpone the elections and put in place a "benevolent dictatorship" (*diktatura saliha*)."[30]

The reformist reactions to al-Hilali demonstrate the depth of the dilemma between the use of undemocratic means to create a democratic society and a more passive approach, leaving the initiative to adversaries. At base, this conundrum stemmed from the liberals' organizational weakness and their failure to develop a civil society powerful enough to execute its program through democratic channels. Having helped push the monarchy to the brink, the liberals were incapable of putting through their own reforms. Their preference for a democratic, inclusive solution was unrealistic so long as the conservative forces within the Wafd remained predominant. A "benevolent dictatorship," on the other hand, might prove to be uncontrollable. To prevent such a dictatorship from seizing power and severing it ties with the population, it would have to be a temporary regime that imposed reform from above, to eliminate the "grand families" (*buyutat*).[31] Afterwards, this regime would have to step back, leaving a modernized country with a truly democratic, rationalist, political system. In short, in spite of their reservations, liberals ended up supporting the notion of a benevolent dictatorship, in the belief that it would create the preconditions for the expansion of a liberal, civil society.

Aware of the dangers posed by benevolent dictatorship, reformers took great pains to demonstrate that they had not reneged on their democratic principles. Ihsan Abd al-Quddus repeatedly asserted the central liberal principle that Egypt's problems did not originate in the 1923 Constitution itself, but in the fact that the country had not known a true democracy because emergency laws had been in force for most of the past twelve years.[32] Despite his etatist inclinations, the same line of argument can be found in Rashid al-Barrawi's articles in *al-Zaman*. Confirming the need for accountability and democratic procedures, al-Barrawi opposed right-wing suggestions to abolish the multi-party system and proposed instead to strengthen it by founding new political parties.[33] The suspension of democracy, even temporarily, was at this point in time unacceptable to al-Barrawi because it was "self-defeating," as earlier experiences with dictatorship, under Isma'il Sidqi and Muhammad Mahmud in the 1920s and 1930s, had shown.[34] As recently as one month before the military takeover, al-Barrawi regarded a multi-party system possible if political parties adapted their programs, principles, and means to the "spirit of the age."[35] By adopting "a modern mentality" (*al-'aqliyya al-jadida*), political organizations could regain contact with the people and integrate it into the political process.[36]

The al-Hilali government was what ultimately caused many liberals to call for more authoritarian means of reform. Ahmad Abu al-Fath, the editor-in-chief of *al-Misri*, who had contacts with the military, wrote in his memoirs at the time that he had lost all hope of a better future unless the army took over.[37] The widespread opposition against the al-Hilali government had led the Free Officers to advance the date of their planned coup d'état to February. In a pamphlet that reflects their cooperation with the communist HADITU at the time, they expressed complete adherence to the prevalent analysis that the al-Hilali government, with its attempt to substitute "purification" (*tathir*) for "liberation" (*tahrir*), was an Anglo-American plot.[38] Eventually it took the interlude of the Husayn Sirri government (from 2 through 22 July) and the threat of Naguib al-Hilali's return for the officers to seize power.

The July Revolution

The benevolent dictatorship at last?

The military takeover on 23 July 1952 forced the liberal reformers to face the consequences of their call for a benevolent dictatorship for the first time. The banishment of King Faruq on 26 July 1952, the abolition of titles, and other symbolic measures marking the demise of the *ancien régime* were hailed in true reformist fashion as harbingers of the "new era" (*al-'ahd al-jadid*). For all reformist political currents these measures fulfilled the hopes of the benevolent dictatorship they had been calling for since the Cairo fire. However, at an early stage it would become clear that the course of events was pointing in a less liberal direction. The State Council ruled in the Regency Case on 31 July in favor of "revolutionary jurisprudence" as opposed to the reinstatement of the former Wafdist parliament. This was a first, ominous sign. Nor did the way in which political purification was carried out under Ali Mahir (the first prime minister after the military takeover) or his opposition to social reforms bode well for a democratic, liberal, reformist transition. The September arrests of leading political figures like Fu'ad Siraj al-Din and Abd al-Hadi, albeit no favorites of the reformers, seemed to undermine the hopes for a peaceful transition to democracy even further.

On the whole, these events provoked two kinds of reactions as reformers differed in their assessment of the character and depth of the necessary reforms to be imposed by the military. On the one extreme were the liberals who were primarily interested in political reform. They regarded the banishment of the King as the long awaited liberal revolution that would finally shift power from the executive to the legislative powers and expand an ordered civil society. Such a shift, they believed, had been the original intention of the Constitution of 1923, which had never been realized because of the King's abuse of power. They argued that a reformed parliament would be able to put through further political and social reforms.

On the other extreme, there were those who hoped that the military itself would realize a far-reaching program of social reform to eliminate the large landowners, the "feudal" class, and replace it with the new middle classes, who would inherit the revolution. Such a social revolution would have to be completed before democratic elections could be held. In between these two extreme positions, many combinations were possible. No one predicted, however, that the military would remain in power. When this turned out to be the case, those reformers in favor of keeping the military in power wanted to expand the "revolution" to turn it into an economic and etatist revolution as well, while the liberals clamored for the army's immediate return to the barracks.[39]

Al-Barrawi's moment

Rashid al-Barrawi clearly belonged to the category that propagated a social revolution. In an article published in *al-Zaman* on 4 August, he expressed his ideas for the first time since censorship had been lifted. King Faruq had already been banished and the new era had been proclaimed, but the monarchy was still intact and no drastic social measures were anticipated under the conservative premiership of Ali Mahir. In this context al-Barrawi became one of the most forceful advocates of a social revolution within the boundaries of the "revolution from above." He urged the military leaders to take the opportunity to bring about such a revolution:

I do not think that I am exaggerating or overoptimistic if I say that the aim of the new era, as an expression of the will of the people, is to create a new society on a solid basis and a healthy foundation of social justice so that forms of excessive luxury and corruption will cease to exist and their grounds for existence will be destroyed, and that the necessary financial means for implementing various reform projects will be in abundance.

He continues by explicitly rejecting the use of a progressive tax to restrict the number of landholdings above a certain size because this measure would spare the large landowners, whom he regards as the enemies of progress:

Let us look at the last proposal to set a maximum for landholdings. We see that the biggest source of corruption in this country and the greatest obstacle to the right reforms and the most powerful force that corrupts the parliamentary and party system is this feudal class, which owns vast stretches of land. This class has opposed general taxes for a long time. In addition, this class has made the inheritance tax a farce, while it has also blocked the establishment of trade unions for agrarian laborers and opposed the dissemination of primary education. Moreover, it has dominated the countryside which has enabled it to obstruct free elections and control the political establishment and use the legislative and the executive branches according to its whims and for its own purposes and interests.

The members of this class are all, he concludes, "absentee landowners who exert no effort to obtain their income." Implied throughout is their elimination as a class.[40]

The article had an immediate effect: Rashid al-Barrawi was contacted by Ahmad Hamrush, a Free Officer of lower rank and member of HADITU, and invited to attend a meeting of the Revolutionary Command Council (RCC). There he was given the opportunity to explain his views on land reform. He met with stiff opposition from some RCC officers, the Minister of Economy, Abd al-Jalil Imari, and Ali Mahir, who would later accuse him of being a communist. However, he did receive support from Gamal Abd al-Nasser, his colleague at the Military Academy, and Khalid Muhyi al-Din, a former student of his at the Faculty of Commerce. Although land reform had never been a concern in the pamphlets of the Free Officers, all agreed on its necessity in the end, and they set the maximum amount of land to be owned at 200 *faddan*.[41]

Rashid al-Barrawi was not the only reformer to enter the fray to try to influence the new regime's socioeconomic policy. In mid-August Mirrit Butrus Ghali published his *Report on the Economic and Social Crisis*, in which he presented a much more conservative program to the military. According to Butrus Ghali, the Egyptian economy suffered from "imbalance" (*ikhtilal al-tawazun*), which prevented the eternal problems of and ignorance (*jahl*), poverty (*faqr*), and sickness (*marad*) from being solved.[42] Mirrit Butrus Ghali's recommendations not only showed that his thinking had remained unaffected by the growing influence of left-wing modernist discourse; they also displayed a limited perceptiveness with respect to the changed political circumstances after the banishment of the King. Recognizing the need for a more equitable distribution of income, he denied that this would solve Egypt's basic economic problem, which he defined as the necessity to increase production. Referring to his *Agrarian Reform: Property, Rent, Labor*, he stated that strengthening the social position of the peasant, raising the rent, and creating an internal market were important effects of land reform, but claimed that they were ultimately not enough to remedy the "imbalance."[43] Land reform, Butrus Ghali concluded, should be limited to the proposals he had drawn up seven years earlier.[44]

Of the two major reformers, Rashid al-Barrawi was given the assignment to draw up the land reform law. *Al-Misri* published the new proposal on 12 August 1952. Despite the high limit of 200 *faddan* as the maximum amount of land that could be owned by one individual, the proposal met initially with strong opposition from the Wafd. Only after Ahmad Abu al-Fath had brought Fu'ad Siraj al-Din and Rashid al-Barrawi together and after much internal wrangling did the Wafd acquiesce in his land reforms in its second program, published on 23 September.[45]

Indicative of the influence that the modernist reformers acquired within the new regime were the appointments that were made in this period. Mirrit Butrus Ghali became Minister of Rural Affairs, while his associate, Ibrahim Bayumi Madkur, became Minister of Reconstruction and Rehabilitation during a cabinet shuffle on 5 September. One day later the Ali Mahir cabinet was dismissed, to be replaced by the Muhammad Naguib cabinet, which consisted primarily of the youth faction of the Nationalist Party. Fathi Radwan came to hold the office of Minister of State, and Nur al-Din Tarraf became the new Minister of Health. The two former members of the Society of National Renaissance were later assigned positions in the Permanent Council of Social Services (al-Majlis al-Da'im al-Khadamat al-Ijtima'iyya), one of two newly established institutions of the revolution. Rashid al-Barrawi was appointed spokesman of the other, the Permanent Council for the Development of National Production (al-Majlis al-Da'im li-Tanmiyat al-Intaj al-Qawmi), and president of the Industrial Bank. In the following years, al-Barrawi would become one of the most important policy planners and propagandists of the technocratic revolution for the regime, while the liberal reformers were involved in organizing its institutions and carrying out its plans.

Defining the revolution

Rashid al-Barrawi's efforts to bring about a social revolution were not limited to land reform. He also used his journalistic talents to push the "revolution" forward, by defining it in modernist terms and explaining its "laws." In an article published on the day that Ali Mahir was dismissed, he urged the new regime to press on with the revolution and not let it slip away. Now that the first condition for revolution had been fulfilled with the banishment of the King, he argued, a revolutionary period would have to follow, in which a "complete transformation" (al-tahawwul al-shamil) would take place. The land reforms would be just the beginning because "reformist revolutions do not believe in partial measures or halfhearted solutions." Encouraging his readers to have faith in the military "because they are sons of the people," he nevertheless called upon the military to clarify the goals of the revolution.[46] He would return to the subject on 12 September, three days after the land reform law was enacted. This time he boasted that he had been the first to have named the military takeover a "great revolution" (al-thawra al-kubra), comparable to other world revolutions such as the English, French and Russian revolutions. This evaluation was based on the "decisive events" between 23 and 26 July, which had led to "rectification" (tashih) of the economic, political, and social situation.[47]

Ihsan Abd al-Quddus reacted to the revolution in much the same way; he applauded the beginning of a new era and urged the military to complete the revolution. His immediate reaction to the revolution was to call it a vindication of his concept of the benevolent dictatorship and of the importance of "men above law."[48] With the abdication of the King, Egypt had entered a "new era," but he warned that this in itself was not enough: "When we liberate ourselves from the past, we should not only liberate ourselves from the person of the King but from a certain system and certain discreditable methods of subjection as well as a certain repressive psychology."[49]

The debate on the nature of the political transition was also conducted in the political books of the period. Once again Rashid al-Barrawi takes precedence over his contemporaries. The most famous version of the argument for the military takeover as a social, high-modernist revolution is presented in his classic analysis of the July Revolution, *The Military Coup in Egypt*, published in October 1952.[50] In this work, as we have seen in chapter two, Rashid al-Barrawi musters his wide knowledge of world history and socialism as well as the rhetoric of the grand narrative to buttress his thesis that the revolution is the "logical outcome of history" in favor of the "new rising middle classes." As such, he claims, the revolution marks a new, higher stage in Egyptian history, just as the 1919 Revolution had initiated an earlier, lower phase of history. Through the military takeover Egypt had finally entered the realm of modernity, a transition that could only be made through socioeconomic change: "What has been established [...] is that it has been a wide-scale revolt against the economic, social, and political state of affairs, aiming at radical changes with the object of bringing about conditions compatible with the spirit of the age and the aims of the community."[51]

Another classic of the time demonstrates that modernist authoritarianism had not yet carried the day. In his *Faruk as King*, Ahmad Baha al-Din defends the basic liberal-democratic platform and the installment of civil society, and he demands that the military comply with constitutional rules.[52] He is highly skeptical of the effects of land reform, which he believes are not worth the name of revolution. Neither is he as preoccupied as al-Barrawi with the march of history as a sequence of different systems of class domination. The force of *Faruk as King* lay elsewhere, in its moral defense of civility and democratic principles. The book is an indictment of the decadence, irresponsibility, and repression of the *ancien régime* and its elitism, patronage, clientalism, and sycophancy. Ahmad Baha al-Din describes how, as the largest landowner who stood at the apex of this feudal system, King Faruq ran the country like his personal estate, denying his subjects their rights as citizens.[53] He assumes that the end of Faruq's reign spells the beginning of a civil society in which the rule of law is supreme, freedom of the press unhampered, and in which rational debate will prevail. In this sense, he combines the liberalism of the Society of National Renaissance with the liberal current in British socialism, of which he was an admirer.

A third remarkable analysis of the July revolution written shortly afterwards is *It Is Time The People Know*, by Abd al-Mughni Sa'id.⁵⁴ The difference between the other two authors and Abd al-Mughni Sa'id is that the latter goes beyond the definition of the goals of the nationalist movement in secular terms only as the realization of a society based on an efficient economy and a more equal social structure or as the realization of a society based on the rule of law. For Abd al-Mughni Sa'id, a modern Egyptian society must also be authentic and derive from its Islamic heritage. In his view, it was precisely the Westernization of the different generations of political leadership that had prevented them from liberating the country.⁵⁵ Disillusioned by his own experiences with the left-wing movement in Egypt since the end of the 1930s, he believed that the new generation had also failed in carrying out the goals of the nationalist movement. Despite its awareness of the "spirit of the age," it represented a "misleading dawn" (*al-fajr al-kadhib*), he felt, because its modernist nationalism originated in the West and therefore could not give rise a "nationalist personality" (*shakhsiyya qawmiyya*), which is the precondition for national liberation.⁵⁶

The solution Abd al-Mughni Sa'id urges upon the new military rulers is to combine elements from the discourses of modernism and authenticity. He argues that an Egyptian renaissance can only be based on a new Islamic awareness (*idrak islami jadid*), which will create harmony between Western and Arabic culture by eliminating Western corruption, hypocrisy, and avarice, while adopting Western modern "situations" and "systems." At the forefront of this new culture will be the "new middle classes" of technicians and managers, whose policy is based on a combination of socialist "planning" (*tarshid*) and authentic cultural values that are "in accordance with the circumstances of the country" and with "our mentality."⁵⁷ The state has to impose this Islamic socialism, abolish the old parliamentary system, and disband the political parties.⁵⁸ In light of these ideas, it is not surprising that Abd al-Mughni Sa'id was instrumental to establishing the corporatist state.

Against the benevolent dictatorship

As had been the case under the monarchy, political "purification" (*tathir*) continued to provoke vehement controversy among liberals and in the end alienated them from each other, because it was imposed on the political parties from above and used for specific interests.

At the start of the takeover, Ihsan Abd al-Quddus, who was closely allied with the military and had even advised them to appoint Ali Mahir to the position of Prime Minister,[59] strongly came out in favor of purification of political parties. Despite previous disappointments in their ability to carry through self-purification, he had pinned all his hopes on the old political parties, especially the Wafd, to reform themselves in the new circumstances. Purification of the old guard, which belonged to a "corrupt class" (*tabaqa fasida*), would give the "culturally conscious class" the chance to take the reins and turn the traditional parties into modern ones based on modern programs, which accepted change and reform. Only then could a renaissance (*nahda*) and a "new era" begin. But in order for the Wafd to purify its parliamentary organization and elect a new leadership, it had to acknowledge its own corrupt past and adopt the "new consciousness" (*al-wa'y al-jadid*). Until that time, a return to civil government was ruled out: "[the army] has not liberated the country from Faruq to give it to Fu'ad Siraj al-Din and Uthman Muharram."[60] He reiterated, "this does not mean that I do not demand a return to the constitution, but I want the task that has been begun and has not yet been executed to be finished."[61]

However, Ihsan Abd al-Quddus began to have his doubts about the course of events when the whole project of self-imposed purification seemed to fail as the political parties were unwilling to dismiss their old leaders. At the end of August, this led to his desperate plea for reformers to take the initiative, because otherwise the military would.[62] When the land reform law came into effect and the Ali Mahir cabinet fell, he applauded these developments, but asserted that in themselves social reforms were not sufficient. Political reform of the parties would confirm the power of the new middle classes more quickly and would be more effective in inducing the army to return to the barracks.[63]

By that time other reformers had lost their faith in the intentions of the military and were clamoring for a return to parliamentary rule. Ahmad Baha al-Din is a typical example of those reformers who argued for a democratic, political and a social revolution, but did not believe it could be brought about by the military. In a matter of days after the coup d'état, he warned the military that the constitution was the only protection against the abuse of power, calling it "the green oasis, whose shadow protects us against sudden changes." The constitution, he pointed out, provided for a parliament, limited powers, civil rights, and the freedom of the press.[64] In a typical instance of a liberal interpretation of history, Ahmad Baha al-Din describes how history has led inevitably to a final victory of the constitution over the King.[65]

During the following months Ahmad Baha al-Din came to realize that the constitution might not be victorious in the end, a realization which is apparent in his suspicions about the true nature of purification. He became convinced that those who propagated purification and "revolutionary jurisprudence" were, like Naguib al-Hilali and other previous reformers under the monarchy, the least interested in restoring democracy.[66] He condemned the Party Reorganization Law as reactionary, because it was left to the Minister of the Interior to decide who was corrupt and which parties should be allowed to exist.[67] No less fierce was his denunciation of the supporters of a one-party system. Pointing to Turkey, he tried to prove that thirty years of rule by Ataturk had left the country completely impoverished.[68]

Ahmad Abu al-Fath shared this anxiety about the democratic outcome of the benevolent dictatorship. On 16 August, he launched a campaign against purification and for the immediate return to parliamentary life in his journal *al-Misri*. The campaign opened with an article by Ibrahim Tal'at. Careful to praise the military for banishing the King and opening up a new future, Ibrahim Tal'at tries to win the officers over by blaming their advisers for misleading the nation and pursuing their own non-democratic, political goals. He accuses them of "working the public opinion and spreading false rumors... that parliamentary life is not suitable for the present times" and warns against the call for a "just dictatorship" (*diktatura 'adila*) until the political parties has purified themselves.[69] The following week, Ahmad Abu al-Fath continued the campaign by declaring the military "pure" (*mukhlis*) while emphasizing their promise to retreat from politics and hold elections in February.[70]

The turning point came on 7 September after the arrest of sixty-four prominent politicians of the old guard. In a series of articles entitled "Where To?" Ahmad Abu al-Fath announced that he intended to inform the public of his grave doubts about the turn of events. He believed that the implementation of purification was especially detrimental to democratic procedures. Instead of going along halfheartedly with a policy that has poisoned relations within the party, he writes, the Wafd should have resisted outside interference by reforming its anti-democratic structure, after which internal elections could have been held to appoint a new leadership.[71]

Two days later, when Ahmad Abu al-Fath published the following article in the series, Ali Mahir had already replaced Muhammad Naguib as Prime Minister and a new cabinet had been installed. The subsequent enactment of the Party Reorganization Law only strengthened Ahmad Abu al-Fath's determination to resist purification. In opposition to the increasing powers the military arrogated to themselves and to the whole idea of a revolution from above, he condemns the military's intentions of realizing a "reformist revolution" (al-thawra al-islahiyya). Instead, he states, the people demand the restoration of their sovereignty.[72] In the third and last article of the series, he finally declares himself a resolute opponent of the military's involvement in politics. The fundamentally anti-democratic and hierarchical structure of the army, he argues, disqualify it as a political instrument.[73] These articles show that Ahmad Abu al-Fath had taken the side of the Wafd against the regime, which had tried to impose on the party a new leadership in which Ahmad Abu al-Fath and Ibrahim Tal'at would have figured prominently.[74]

Indicative of the rift among the liberals was the publication of an article by Rashid al-Barrawi in *al-Misri* that came out on the same day that Ahmad Abu al-Fath published his definitive rejection of a military regime. In it, al-Barrawi shows his support for a reformist revolution and still professes his faith in the democratic promises of the military, arguing that it had been Ali Mahir who was responsible for purification.[75] But on 26 September he would come out in support of the inevitability of a period of repression, because, like the French revolution, the Egyptian revolution had to go through a stage of "murderous vilification" (al-ta'na al-qatila) of the feudal and absolutist system. Both revolutions were brought forth by the people and served their interests against the "hostile reactionary elements" (al-'anasir al-raj'iyya al-mu'adiyya). It would not be until after Egypt had gone through this violent phase that a true democracy could be installed. For this reason, al-Barrawi calls upon Egyptian intellectuals to keep faith in the revolution and help support and direct it.[76]

A political party for the military

Despite the growing anxiety among liberals about the power that the military were usurping, they agreed on a common platform when increasingly harsh measures were taken to suppress a pluralist society at the end of 1952. This platform was based on a compromise between those who were in favor of a minimum political revolution and those who supported a maximum social revolution.

The compromise, first voiced on the pages of *Ruz al-Yusuf*, consisted of the integration of the military into a parliamentary system, by encouraging the officers to resign from the army and to found a political party that would participate in free elections.[77] The rationale behind this scheme was that the military had become the "instrument" (*adah*) of the nationalist movement and that none of the existing political parties represented the principles of the new era. By transforming themselves into a political party the military could defend the revolution and the principles it stood for.[78]

This scheme was also appealing in that it gave an important role in politics to the intellectuals and the representatives of the new middle classes, who regarded themselves as the rightful heirs of the revolution. Ihsan Abd al-Quddus wrote, "The form of the state will not become clear unless the new era is represented by a new party to which the peasants, the workers, and the intellectuals (*ashab al-ra'y*) belong and which gives expression to the principles of the revolution, its opinions, and goals."[79] During the transitional period, it was stipulated, a new constitution had to be drawn up and the population would be prepared for new elections in an atmosphere where freedom of the press and other civil liberties were guaranteed. The liberal compromise was to remain the platform of most liberal currents until the March crisis in 1954. It represented an alternative to all the repressive measures of the new regime, such as the abolition of a multi-party system in January 1953, the establishment of the Liberation Rally as the sole political party, censorship of the press, the repression of free opinion, and the harassment and arrests of opponents of the regime.

Instrumental in maintaining pressure on the government and resisting repression were the networks that were established in this period which supported an independent civil society. They were the expression of the liberal hope for democratization and liberalization. The most conspicuous form of solidarity were the contributions made by Ihsan Abd al-Quddus and Ahmad Abu al-Fath to each other's periodicals. By mobilizing liberals against the regime, in spite of the reintroduction of censorship in October, the liberal networks formed a common front against both the regime and the other important molder of public opinion, the *Akhbar al-Yawm* group, which supported the regime's suppression of the Wafd and the abolition of the parliamentary system. But these networks were not exclusively for liberals; often communists and liberals could join in one network. For instance, Abd al-Azim Anis and Mahmud Amin al-Alim published their famous series on modern Egyptian culture in *al-Misri* in 1954,[80] while *Ruz al-Yusuf* increasingly encouraged communist and left-wing intellectuals to contribute. Conversely, liberals such as Ahmad Abu al-Fath and Ahmad Baha al-Din wrote in *al-Ghad*, the monthly of HADITU, in protest against the repressive measures of the regime.[81] On a more practical basis, liberal lawyers defended communists who were brought to trial.

Another fruitful network of liberals and Marxists was formed by the liberal journalists Ahmad Baha al-Din and Adil Thabit, the Wafdist Muhammad Mandur, the Marxist economist Abd al-Raziq Hasan, and the young socialist historian Muhammad Anis. Before being banned in January 1953, the group published two books in their *Kitab al-Muwatin* series, which contained a passionate plea for political pluralism by Muhammad Mandur and a severe critique of the government's conservative economic policy by Abd al-Raziq Hasan.[82] In political terms this resistance to the military had only symbolic value. Yet, the fact that the majority of modernist intellectuals withheld the legitimization of the new regime did make a difference, although from January 1953 until March 1954 all forms of public resistance in the form of publications were banned.

The Communists and the July Revolution

Front with the military

The relations between the Free Officers and the communist movement, and especially HADITU, were as intricate as the relations with the liberals. HADITU was the only communist organization that had recruited among the military and established a special military section. Several of its members joined the Free Officers, most importantly Ahmad Hamrush and Yusuf Siddiq, who was also a member of the RCC. Ahmad Fu'ad, judge and liaison between the military section of HADITU and the Free Officers, even became one of Gamal Abd al-Nasser's most important advisers and sided with the military when the relations with HADITU soured in January 1953.[83] Before the coup d'état Ahmad Fu'ad and Khalid Muhyi al-Din had helped the Free Officers draw up, print, and distribute their pamphlets, giving them a distinctly left-wing flavor.[84] Along with the Muslim Brotherhood and some liberals, HADITU too had been informed of the coup d'état in advance. HADITU's good relations with the Free Officers initially partly account for its warm reception of the military immediately after the takeover. Similarly, the rejection of the coup d'état by the CPE only days after the event can be ascribed to their total lack of relations with the military.

All the same, ideological factors were crucial to the attitude of the communist organizations towards the Free Officers. HADITU's strategy of the broad nationalist democratic front made a more flexible approach to the Free Officers possible, in contrast with the more doctrinaire, Stalinist attitude of the CPE, in which the proletariat formed the vanguard. Without a front strategy HADITU would never even have made contact with the Free Officers. The primary ideological factor in HADITU's analysis of the military takeover is the role that is assigned to the middle classes. In the following years the theoretical question that was to preoccupy the Egyptian-Marxist analysis of the revolution and the military was whether the middle classes constituted a revolutionary factor as a part of the alliance of the forces against imperialism or whether it was a part of the counter-alliance of the big bourgeoisie and feudal landowners with imperialism.

For the CPE the character of the military takeover had been decided with the Kafr al-Dawwar strike on 12 August, which had led to the suppression of the workers' movement and the hanging of the workers Khamis and al-Bakri on 7 September. The hesitant attitude of the regime during the banishment of the King, whom the CPE had wanted to bring to court and have hanged, and the installation of a Regency Council had already evoked suspicion about the character of the military leaders, who were now quickly condemned as "fascist."[85] Although the Workers' Vanguard was much more flexible, for them too the Kafr al-Dawwar incident marked a turning point.

In contrast, HADITU retained relations with the military until the beginning of 1953. This happened in spite of the publication of a pamphlet printed on 23 July in which HADITU demanded the immediate resumption of the armed struggle along the Suez Canal, the return of the dissolved Wafd parliament, the formation of a government based on a united national front consisting of all nationalist political forces, and the immediate release of all prisoners.[86] At this time, HADITU believed that the military belonged to the "petty bourgeoisie," which favored a revolutionary transition and was opposed to the alliance of the indigenous feudal and financial interests with imperialism. This attitude began to change under the influence of the anti-democratic policy of the military against own members. The temporary arrest of Ahmad Hamrush in January 1953, the resignation of Yusuf Siddiq from the RCC, and the suppression of *al-Malayin, al-Wajib, al-Katib*, and other organs of the communist movement spelled the end of the honeymoon. In addition, there were the excellent relations that the RCC entertained with the American ambassador, Jefferson Caffery, who made it clear that the United States preferred a military dictatorship to a return to democracy and the risk of a further spread of communism.[87]

Confrontation

The beginning of the confrontation between the military and the communists is reflected in pamphlets that designated the Free Officers as the "henchmen of imperialism within the army" and "enemies of the people."[88] Another pamphlet lists the main objections against the regime in a critique of Muhammad Naguib:

Naguib has unveiled his fascist face by severing his ties with the people. He promised to defend the constitution but abrogated it, he announced the return of parliamentary life but disbanded it, he promised to respect to civil liberties but executed Khamis and al-Baqri and arrested liberals. He declared his respect for political parties but dissolved them and announced the establishment of a one-party system and imposed the Liberation Rally.[89]

The pamphlet ends with a comparison of the military to the previous minority governments under the monarchy, declaring: "We will work together to destroy it and make it fall, as we have done before with the enemies of the people, and the enemies of the constitution, Sidqi, al-Nuqrashi, Abd al-Hadi, and Faruq ... forwards towards a united front."

In January 1953, *al-Tali'a*, an internal publication meant for the cadres of HADITU, published a class analysis of the position of the Free Officers and its consequences for the democratic, national revolution. It is interesting to see how this analysis differs from Rashid al-Barrawi's, made a few months earlier in *The Military Coup in Egypt*, and from those of other liberals who used the same terminology. The radical liberals had described the military as the representatives of the self-conscious and vigorous "new middle classes," which were the vanguard of history. But HADITU takes a perspective reminiscent of

Mau Zedong's view of the national bourgeoisie in China and calls the petty bourgeoisie "one of the weakest points in the fortification of the block against the enemies of the people." As a result, Anglo-American imperialism could "transform the military from a movement with a popular character to a military dictatorship hostile to the people."

The petty bourgeoisie in a colonial Egypt is in general a revolutionary class whose economic interests differ from those of imperialism. On the other hand, on account of its position between the two main classes in the country – the workers and the capitalists – it does not have the ability to find its own independent ideological orientation. Therefore it does not have an independent position from these two classes. [Within this class] there exists a current that is influenced by the attitudes of the workers' class and its parties, that is, our positions, while another current is influenced by the bourgeois parties and the upper classes of society.

The writer draws the following conclusions for a new strategy of the front:

The present struggle is not in its essence a struggle between the people and the military; it is not a struggle between the working class and the petty bourgeoisie. Nor is it a struggle between the people and a section of this class represented in the RCC of the military movement. In fact it is essentially a struggle with the purpose of isolating the RCC from the influence of imperialism and the parties of the big bourgeoisie.[90]

During the months of March and April 1953 HADITU tried to establish the National Democratic Front (Jabha Wataniyya Dimuqratiyya) together with the Wafd. One of its activities was to organize a campaign for its National Charter (al-Mithaq al-Watani), which consisted of five demands concerning the immediate return of the 1923 Constitution and the rejection of all military alliances.[91] Later these points, which the party shared with the Wafd, were confirmed in the statement (*bayan*) of the National Democratic Front.[92] The front's support for Mustafa al-Nahhas, the leader of the Wafd, was remarkable. He was now, once again, seen as the symbol of the nationalist movement.[93] The front had little influence on the course of events and lasted until November 1953, when most of its members were arrested together with almost all of the members of the Central Committee of HADITU.

By then, HADITU itself had suffered a fundamental ideological crisis that led to several splits into factions. The first occurred after the first wave of arrests in January 1953, when a small group of members formed the Communist Unity (Wahdat al-Shuyu'iyya), while others joined the CPE and the Workers' Vanguard. On 28 June a more serious struggle led to the division of the Central Committee ending in the founding of HADITU-Revolutionary Wing (HADITU al-Tayyar al-Thawri) by Sayyid Sulayman Rifa'i.[94] As with the previous division in 1948, this split was the result of the fundamental dilemma within the communist movement between its maximum and its minimum program.

This last splinter group not only condemned the military and HADITU's policy with regard to the new regime, but even criticized the entire strategy that HADITU had pursued during the past years. HADITU-Revolutionary Wing considered the party's attitude towards the bourgeoisie as the reason for the current predicament of the Egyptian communist movement. By concentrating on forming a national front, the group claimed, HADITU had taken over bourgeois thinking and adopted "in general a legalist, reformist struggle" (*kifah islahi qanuni fi al-ghalib*). This strategy had been wrong, they asserted, because "opinions circulating among the middle classes defend basically the return to parliamentary life and the reign of the bourgeoisie." Instead, HADITU-Revolutionary Wing proposed the one-stage revolution, not based "on the support of the bourgeois powers," but aimed at "hastening the establishment of the people's power with the working class at its helm." The final nail driven into the coffin of the strategy of the national democratic revolution was the condemnation of all democratic procedures and coalitions with ambivalent anti-imperialist forces. The pamphlet concluded with the statement that a true revolutionary strategy could only be carried out by the workers and peasants and had to be based on the *armed struggle* against the regime. Secret worker and peasant committees had to be established to pursue such a policy.[95]

Although HADITU did not adopt the strategy of the one-stage socialist revolution, Zaki Murad, one of the remaining members of the CC of HADITU, was forced to formulate a riposte in a booklet published in commemoration of Khamis and al-Baqri, *On 7 September Khamis Did Not Die*. In the introduction the leadership of HADITU acknowledges that its former policy was erroneous.[96] In January 1954 Zaki Murad finally drew the conclusion that the military had formed an alliance with imperialism based on the same class analysis: "We recognize that we have made mistakes in the analysis of the military movement and in its description as the representative of the petty bourgeoisie ... Time has confirmed this analysis. The military movement takes the side of the large bourgeoisie and represents clearly a traitorous disposition."[97] At the end of 1953 and during the March Crisis, the communist movement would be completely opposed to the military regime, which it now generally described as "fascist." By regarding the military as a tool of the bourgeoisie instead of an authentic (middle-class) political movement in its own right, the communist movement alienated itself fully from the new regime until 1955.

The March Crisis

The final round

The March crisis was the final round in the political and ideological struggle between the regime and its democratic, reformist opponents, in the form that it had existed since July 1952. For the opposition, the crisis offered the last hope of reintroducing the multi-party system and sending the military back to the barracks after the 1923 Constitution had been abrogated and a one-party system had been established in January 1953.

The immediate cause for the March crisis was the conflict between Muhammad Naguib, who had become President of the Republic in June 1953, and the RCC with Gamal Abd al-Nasser as its leader. The outcome of the conflict was the dismissal of Naguib on 25 February 1954 and his reinstatement two days later, after huge demonstrations in the streets in favor of Naguib and the return to democracy had forced the military to reconsider their previous decision. In the following week, the RCC was compelled to make further concessions to Naguib. This led to the famous 5 March Declaration, which stated that a constituent assembly would be elected on 23 July, which would be the first step towards a return to a multi-party system.[98]

The simultaneous termination of press censorship unleashed a storm of criticism of the military that had been pent-up since it had been instated in October 1952. *Al-Misri* triumphantly took the lead in the frontal attack on the regime, mobilizing all the support it could muster. On 7 March it printed an interview with Khalid Muhyi al-Din, who championed democratic reformism in the RCC and had been instrumental to bringing about the March Declaration. In the interview he calls the end of press censorship "a beneficial step to increase democratic life," adding, "I believe only in one thing:

democratic parliamentary life." Ahmad Abu al-Fath wholeheartedly supported the March Declaration in his editorial, reinterpreting it in as liberal a sense as possible. He prophesies that 5 March would become a national holiday and, therewith confirming the liberal platform, he enumerates the main points of the declaration: complete freedom of the press; the election of the constituent assembly (instead of its appointment); the return of political parties; the participation of the military in politics only in their capacity as civilians; the unity of the people and the military against imperialism and in defense of democracy; and the non-political task of the military as defenders of the nation.[99]

"Retracing our steps"

These homilies directed towards the military served to hide the widespread feeling among liberal reformers that the continued role of the military in politics had been a major mistake. Wahid Ra'fat expressed these feelings in a devastating article in *al-Misri*. He writes that he regards the past year and a half as a waste of time. The step that had been taken with the 5 March Declaration should, he argues, have been taken immediately after the banishment of King Faruq on 26 July: "If developments had proceeded in a natural way since the beginning, then the call for an elected constituent assembly to draw up a new constitution would have been the immediate step after the success of the movement of 23 July 1952." He asserts that sovereignty should return to the people and claims that it will not be until the constituent assembly has been elected that the "new era" can really begin. Finally, Wahid Ra'fat calls upon the presumed liberal victors to forgive the military for its mistakes and aggression, in order to obtain a new national unity, instead of being grateful.[100] Later, Ahmad Abu al-Fath articulated the same sentiments: "It is my conviction that the military movement will have proven its worth and will have been of service to the people at the moment when Egypt experiences free elections."[101]

The idea that events had taken a wrong turn was not exclusive to liberals like Wahid Ra'fat, who represented the liberalism of the Society of National Renaissance. A leftist like Yusuf Siddiq, a former RCC-member who had been member of HADITU, likewise advocated a return to the past in order to take a different road, in an open letter to Muhammad Naguib. He represented the new position of HADITU, which now regarded the decision to employ "revolutionary jurisprudence" and to refrain from calling back the dissolved Wafdist parliament a mistake. He urged for a return to this point in time because "after it has become clear that we have taken a wrong turn we can only correct the situation by retracing our steps to the place where we went wrong and taking the right path." This would mean either the recall of the Wafdist parliament or the formation of a coalition government with – of all people – Wahid Ra'fat as Prime Minister.[102]

Earlier, Khalid Muhyi al-Din had repeated the main ideas of HADITU with regard to democracy. He rejected the arguments of the pro-regime press that the Egyptian people were unfit to govern themselves because feudalism and imperialism would succeed again in manipulating their votes if democracy was reinstated. Instead, he argued that with the banishment of the King and the implementation of the land reform, feudalism and imperialism could not reclaim their former power. In fact, he stated, democracy was a precondition for liberation and only a greater degree of participation by the people in government could end imperialist domination.[103] Khalid Muhyi al-Din was himself strongly partisan to the founding of a political party by the military so that it could participate in the coming elections. He wanted to defend the revolution but within a democratic context.[104] Furthermore, he pointed to the RCC's tendency to depend on "experts" rather than relying on the people's trust.[105]

Ihsan Abd al-Quddus adopted a similar stance in this debate, but he was more careful to incorporate the military into the new democratic structure as a part of the new ruling middle class and as the "executive" of the revolution. Thus, he denied the military its special character and regarded it as a continuation of the nationalist movement led by the Wafd. However, Ihsan Abd al-Quddus also attacked the military fiercely in his famous article "The Secret Association that Governs Egypt." Looking back over the past year and a half, he criticizes the military for not having formed a political party to defend the principles of the revolution in free elections. By retaining its secretive character, he writes, the military has alienated itself from the people and has become isolated, disregarding advice and resorting to terror by establishing the revolutionary courts.[106] In his last article, written when he was already in hiding, he compares the military to the minority governments of the monarchy.[107]

In practical terms, the struggle against the dictatorship was fought on different fronts. During the March crisis, an essential part of the campaign of *al-Misri* was to insure that the constituent assembly was indeed elected and not appointed. "They must be representatives of the people," an editorial stated at the beginning of its campaign.[108] Other concerns were the immediate abrogation of martial law and the release of all political prisoners.[109] Similarly, the call for the direct election of a parliament was often heard. The idea behind this was that the sooner a parliament was installed, the sooner the counterbalancing forces against the military would be institutionalized. A parliament, rather than a much more limited and therefore pliable constituent assembly, could then decide on a new constitution.[110] All of these issues can be seen in light of the liberal interpretation of Egyptian history, that it had been the people who had toppled the regime and that therefore arguments for paternalistic surveillance and the abeyance of civil rights, even temporarily, were illegitimate and uncalled-for.[111]

In the end, the liberal forces did not succeed in tipping the balance. On 25 March the RCC not only announced that it would lift the ban on political parties and allow the constituent assembly to be elected, it also declared that it would dissolve itself on 24 July and end the revolution. With this ploy the RCC regained the initiative and forced a choice between the revolution and the continuation of military rule on the one hand and democracy and a return to the *ancien régime* on the other. Despite this stark choice, many of the organizations that had strengthened civil society since the 1930s supported the democratic demands of the opposition. Most of the trade unions did not heed the call of the RCC to strike.[112] The bar association took the side against the military as well as the teachers' union, the journalists' syndicate, and many of the university students.[113]

The latter choice was supported in demonstrations in favor of the RCC. The trade unions, which proclaimed a general strike on 27 March, played a crucial role in the counterattack. They had been brought over to the side of the military regime through the promise of workers' job security. The neutrality of the Muslim Brotherhood made another important contribution to the eventual success of the military. Finally, the Liberation Rally proved its worth as a political organization in these decisive moments by mobilizing the supporters of the regime and organizing mob violence.[114] In the backlash that followed the democratic upsurge, *al-Misri* was banned and closed down, while Ihsan Abd al-Quddus was held prisoner for a month. In the subsequent months, organizations that had withstood the military, such as the journalists' syndicate, were gradually included in the new corporatist state.

Conclusion

From 1950 to 1954 liberal reformers were presented with different political opportunities to realize their ideas, all of which ended in failure. The opportunity for democratic self-reform as a precondition for a general political and social overhaul of the monarchy and Egyptian society had presented itself when the Wafd was elected into government in 1950. It had been unsuccessful because the Wafd was incapable of reforming itself and conservative forces prevailed. The option of popular mobilization, which became viable during the guerrilla struggle along the Suez Canal, turned into an even greater fiasco when the people set Cairo on fire on 26 January 1952, which triggered the dismissal of the Wafd government. Of the subsequent minority governments in the last months of the monarchy only Ali Mahir's wetted the fantasy of the reformers, but his position was not strong enough to reach the stage of serious implementation; his second chance under the military proved to be a disappointment.

In these changing circumstances the reformers had to make crucial decisions on strategies and consider these new options, while trying to maintain as much ideological consistency as possible. However, as time went on, the opportunities for reform by democratic means faded and the predicament of the liberals worsened, until they finally ended up supporting the "benevolent dictatorship." This was an option all reformers eventually adopted, even those who were in favor of a return of the military to the barracks during the March crisis. They differed widely with regard to benevolent dictatorship, however, once the military had seized power in July 1952, banished the King, drafted a land reform law, and imposed a political reform program that included the "purification" of the old party leadership by authoritarian means. Their attitude towards these measures depended on a combination of their ideological make-up and their political and social connections. The choice was hardly ever clear-cut. The basic difference between the reformers was their trust in the military to eventually return to the barracks. None expected them to stay in power indefinitely, not even Rashid al-Barrawi, who chose the side of the military at an early stage. In the case of almost every reformer studied here, the attitude towards social reform and especially towards social engineering ultimately decides whether he supports the regime or opposes it. The opportunity to bring about reform "from above" was for these reformers too good to let pass and finally overrode any doubts they may have had.

Interestingly, the most liberal institution for reform, the Society of National Renaissance, was split. Two of its members, Mirrit Butrus Ghali and Ibrahim Bayumi Madkur, who had drawn up the Society's plans for social change, joined the new regime to help devise its reform program, first as ministers under Ali Mahir, and later as advisors and members of the reform councils. However, Wahid Ra'fat, who had a purely legal background, opposed the regime during the March Crisis and demanded a reinstatement of a multi-party system once the minimum conditions for its functioning, the banishment of the King and land reform, had been met. This group, to which Ahmad Abu al-Fath and Ihsan Abd al-Quddus belonged, eventually included the majority of the liberals, who came out decisively in favor of a multi-party system and opposed the role of the military in politics. That this group formed the majority of the reformers shows that in 1954 the basic democratic principles were still upheld by Egypt's liberal intellectuals. Only a few, like Rashid al-Barrawi, had joined the regime to help formulate a new modernist ideology of authoritarian social and economic developmentalism in which to couch the revolution. This ideology would eventually supplant the democratic principles most reformers had resisted. Once the military had captured the state after March 1954 and gained the full authority to enforce the new policy, it could win over the "new middle classes" and give its technocratic "experts" and opinion makers (*ashab al-ra'y*) a prominent place as modernizers of the new state.

Notes

1. Suhayr Iskandar, *Jaridat al-Misri wa-l-qadaya al-wataniyya* (Cairo: Mu'assasat Sijill al-'Arab, 1986), 32–3.
2. Suhayr Iskandar, *al-Sihafa al-Misriyya wa-l-qadaya al-wataniyya, 1946–1954* (Cairo: al-Hay'a al-Misriyya al-'Amma li-l-Kitab, 1992), 78–83; 134–7; 148–52; 161–4; 177–8; 185–8; 192–6; 208–16; 231–9; 249–51; 259–64; 272–5.
3. Robert Vitalis, *When Capitalists Collide: Business Conflict and the End of Empire in Egypt* (Berkeley: University of Califronia Press, 1995), 151–9.
4. Robert Bianchi, *Unruly Corporatism: Associational Life in Twentieth-Century Egypt* (New York and Oxford: Oxford University Press, 1989), 75.
5. Isma'il Muhammad Zayn al-Din, *al-Tali'a al-Wafdiyya wa-l-haraka al-wataniyya, 1945–1952* (Cairo: al-Hay'a al-Misriyya al-'Amma li-l-Kitab, 1991), 61.
6. Ahmad Abu al-Fath, *Jamal 'Abd al-Nasir* (Cairo: al-Maktab al-Misri al-Hadith, 1991).
7. For a description of the conflict between the Wafd and *Ruz al-Yusuf*, see Fatima al-Yusuf, *Dhikrayyat* (Cairo: Kitab Ruz al-Yusuf, 1953), 155–216.

8 Amira Abu al-Futuh, *Ihsan 'Abd al-Quddus ... yatadhakkar* (Cairo: al-Hay'a al-Misriyya al-'Amma li-l-Kitab, 1982), 70–4.
9 Personal interview with Salah al-Din Namiq on 27 October 1989.
10 James P. Jankowski, *Egypt's Young Rebels "Young Egypt": 1933–1952* (Stanford: Hoover Institution Press, 1975), 108–9.
11 Joel Beinin, "Islamic Responses to the Capitalist Penetration of the Middle East," in *The Islamic Impulse*, edited by Barbara Freyer Stowasser (Washington DC: Center for Contemporary Arab Studies, 1987), 96–100.
12 Sayyid Mar'i, *Awraq siyasiyya*, 2 vols. (Cairo: al-Maktab al-Misri al-Hadith, 1978).
13 Rashid al-Barrawi, "Hadha sawt al-sha'b fa-istami'u ilayhi," *al-Ahram*, 11 January 1950; Rashid al-Barrawi, *Ara' Hurra* (Cairo: Maktabat al-Nahda al-Misriyya, 1949).
14 Muhammad Zaki 'Abd al-Qadir, *Mudhakkirat ... wa dhikrayyat* (Cairo: n.p., n.d.), 114.
15 Joel Gordon, "The False Hopes of 1950: The Wafd's Last Hurrah and the Demise of Egypt's Old Order," *International Journal of Middle East Studies* 21 (1989): 198–214.
16 'Abd al-Futuh, 97–108.
17 This was in particular the image that Ahmad Baha' al-Din presents of the whole affair in his book *Faruq malikan* (Cairo: Kitab Ruz al-Yusuf, 1952), 85–101. Recent research has shown that this image is highly exaggerated. See 'Abd al-Mun'im al-Disuqi al-Jami'i, *al-Asliha al-fasida wa dawruha fi harb filastin 1948* (Cairo: al-Hay'a al-Misriyya al-'Amma li-l-Kitab, 1990).
18 Ihsan 'Abd al-Quddus, *Ruz al-Yusuf* No. 1217 (9 October 1951). Cited in 'Abd al-Futuh, 129–30.
19 See for instance Rashid al-Barrawi, "Radd hadi" 'ala Atcheson," *al-Zaman*, 19 October 1951.
20 Ihsan 'Abd al-Quddus, "al-Hukuma ma'ana ... am 'alayna," *Ruz al-Yusuf* No. 1225 (4 December 1951). Cited in Abd al-Futuh, 134.
21 Rashid al-Barrawi, "al-Isti'mar ... huwa mas'ul," *al-Zaman*, 27 January 1952.
22 Ihsan 'Abd al-Quddus, "al-Rajul al-wahid alladhi yu'minu bi-bara'at al-sha'b," *Ruz al-Yusuf* No. 1234 (4 February 1952): 3.
23 Rashid al-Barrawi, "al-Islah wa-l-tatawwur fi al-duwal al-mustanira," *al-Zaman*, 23 August 1951.
24 Bianchi, 72–3.
25 Rashid al-Barrawi, "al-Isti'mar ... huwa mas'ul," *al-Zaman*, 27 January 1952.
26 Ihsan 'Abd al-Quddus, "al-Rajul al-wahid alladhi yu'min bi-bara'at al-sha'b," *Ruz al-Yusuf* No. 1234 (4 February 1952): 3.
27 Ihsan 'Abd al-Quddus, "Inna misr fi haja ila diktatur ... fa-hal huwa Ali Mahir?," *Ruz al-Yusuf* No. 1235 (11 February 1952): 3.
28 For a discussion of this issue see also Joel Gordon, "The Myth of the Savior: Egypt's "Just Tyrants" on the Eve of Revolution, January–July 1952," *Journal of the American Research Centre in Egypt* 16 (1989): 223–38.
29 Ihsan 'Abd al-Quddus, "Laysa al-fasad hukamat al-wafd wahdaha!!," *Ruz al-Yusuf* No. 1238 (3 March 1952): 3.
30 Ihsan 'Abd al-Quddus, "Ayna ma'alim al-tariq ... wa ila ayna al-masir?!," *Ruz al-Yusuf* No. 1243 (6 April 1952): 3.
31 Ihsan 'Abd al-Quddus, "Man yu'alliq al-jaras fi raqabat al-qitt al-kabir," *Ruz al-Yusuf* No. 1253 (16 June 1952): 3.

32 Ihsan 'Abd al-Quddus, "Himayat al-hukuma ... himayat al-sha'b," *Ruz al-Yusuf* No. 1255 (30 June 1952): 6–7.
33 Rashid al-Barrawi, 'Law ansha'tu hizban siyasiyyan,' *al-Zaman*, 23 March 1952.
34 Rashid al-Barrawi, 'Da'wa khatira yajib al-qada' 'alayha,' *al-Zaman*, 5 April 1952.
35 Rashid al-Barrawi, 'al-Ahzab al-siyasiyya ka'inat hayya,' *al-Zaman*, 12 June 1952.
36 Rashid al-Barrawi, "Mashru'at yajib an takhruj ila hayyiz al-tanfidh," *al-Zaman*, 6 August 1951.
37 Ahmad Abu al-Fath, *Jamal 'Abd al-Nasir* (Cairo: al-Maktab al-Misri al-Hadith, 1991), 78.
38 See for reproductions of some of the pamphlets of the Free Officers: Khalid Muhyi al-Din, *Wa al-ana atakallam* (Cairo: Markaz al-Ahram li-l-Tarjama wa-l-Nashr, 1992), 91. For the most extensive account of the pamphlets of the Free Officers, see Kamal al-Din Rif'at, *Mudhakkirat: Harb li-l-tahrir al-wataniyya bayna ilgha' mu'ahadat 1936 wa-ittifaqiyyat 1954* (Cairo: Dar al-Kitab al-'Arabi li-l-Tiba'a wa-l-Nashr, 1978).
39 See especially for this whole period Joel Gordon, *Nasser's Blessed Movement: Egypt's Free Officers and the July Revolution* (Oxford: Oxford University Press, 1992).
40 Rashid al-Barrawi's article is cited in 'Abd al-'Azim Ramadan, *'Abd al-Nasir wa azmat maris 1954* (Cairo: Maktabat Ruz al-Yusuf, 1977), 229–31.
41 Interview with Rashid al-Barrawi in Ramadan, 325–7.
42 Mirrit Butrus Ghali, *Taqrir 'an al-azma al-iqtisadiyya al-ijtima'iyya* (Cairo: n.p., 1952), 5–17.
43 Butrus Ghali, 23–5.
44 Butrus Ghali, 44–53.
45 Ramadan, 57.
46 Rashid al-Barrawi, "Shurut awwaliyya li-najah al-islah," *al-Misri*, 5 September 1952, 5.
47 Rashid al-Barrawi, "Hadhihi al-thawra al-islahiyya ... man hum a'da'uha al-haqiqiyyun?," *al-Misri*, 12 September 1952, 8.
48 Ihsan 'Abd al-Quddus, special appendix on the coup d'état, *Ruz al-Yusuf* No. 1259 (28 July 1952): 2–3.
49 Ihsan 'Abd al-Quddus, "al-Dustur lam ya'zil al-malik, wa lam yutahhir al-ahzab," *Ruz al-Yusuf* No. 1260 (4 August 1952): 3.
50 Rashed El-Barawy, *The Military Coup in Egypt: An Analytic Study* (Cairo: The Renaissance Bookshop, 1952). The English translation of the book was published in December. The first printing of the Arabic original, *Haqiqat al-inqilab al-akhir fi misr*, was brought out by the same publisher in October 1952, while the second was published in December. See chapter three.
51 El-Barawy, *Military*, 21.
52 Ahmad Baha' al-Din, *Faruq malikan* (Cairo: Kitab Ruz al-Yusuf, 1952).
53 Baha' al-Din, *Faruq*, 48.
54 'Abd al-Mughni Sa'id, *An libadha al-sha'b an yafham!* (Cairo: Dar al-Kitab al-'Arabi, 1952).
55 Sa'id, 35–7.
56 Sa'id, 47.
57 Sa'id, 53–62.
58 Sa'id, 78–9.

59 See Ihsan 'Abd al-Quddus' description of this episode in *Ruz al-Yusuf* No. 1264 (2 September 1952): 3 and 30.
60 Ihsan 'Abd al-Quddus, "Faruq lam yakun al-wahid alladhi taqarrar an natakhallas minhu," *Ruz al-Yusuf* No. 1261 (11 August 1952): 3.
61 Ihsan 'Abd al-Quddus, "al-Dustur lam ya'zil al-malik, wa lam yutahhir al-ahzab," *Ruz al-Yusuf* No. 1260 (4 August 1952): 3.
62 Ihsan 'Abd al-Quddus, "al-Jaysh yantazir al-sha'b, wa-l-sha'b yantazir al-jaysh," *Ruz al-Yusuf* No. 1263 (25 August 1952): 3.
63 Ihsan 'Abd al-Quddus, "Mata ya'ud al-dustur, wa mata tajri al-intikhabat?!" *Ruz al-Yusuf* No. 1266 (15 September 1952): 3.
64 Ahmad Baha' al-Din, "Fi zill al-dustur," *Ruz al-Yusuf* No. 1259 (28 July 1952): 9.
65 Ahmad Baha' al-Din, "al-Dustur bayna al-'arsh wa-l-sha'b," *Ruz al-Yusuf* No. 1260 (4 August 1952): 22–3.
66 Ahmad Baha' al-Din, "al-'Askariyyun ... wa-l-madaniyyun," *Ruz al-Yusuf* No. 1265 (8 September 1952): 5.
67 Ahmad Baha' al-Din, "Hadha al-qanun ... raj'i," *Ruz al-Yusuf* No. 1268 (29 September 1952): 5.
68 Ahmad Baha' al-Din, "al-Hizb al-wahid," *Ruz al-Yusuf* No. 1269 (6 October 1952): 5.
69 Ibrahim Tal'at, "Falsafat al-inqilab (I). Kayfa nabni al-dawla," *al-Misri*, 16 August 1952. The other two parts of the series were published on 17 and 20 August.
70 Ahmad Abu al-Fath, "Mabadi' al-jaysh," *al-Misri*, 22 August 1952.
71 Ahmad Abu al-Fath, "Ila ayna?" *al-Misri*, 7 September 1952.
72 Ahmad Abu al-Fath, "Ila ayna?" *al-Misri*, 9 September 1952.
73 Ahmad Abu al-Fath, "Ila ayna?" *al-Misri*, 12 September 1952.
74 Gordon, *Movement*, 71.
75 Rashid al-Barrawi, "Hadhihi al-thawra al-islahiyya ... man hum a'da'uha al-haqiqiyyun?" *al-Misri*, 12 September 1952, 8.
76 Rashid al-Barrawi, "Himayat al-thawra," *al-Misri*, 26 September 1952, 5 See also Rashid al-Barrawi, "Kuttabuna ... wa harakat al-tahrir," *al-Misri*, 4 October 1952.
77 Ihsan 'Abd al-Quddus, "Ghadan lan tastaqirr illa idha taharrarna min 'aqliyyat al-'abid," *Ruz al-Yusuf* No. 1267 (22 September 1952): 3; and Ihsan 'Abd al-Quddus, "Mata ya'ud al-dustur, wa mata tajri al-intikhabat," *Ruz al-Yusuf* No. 1266 (15 September 1952): 3.
78 Ihsan 'Abd al-Quddus published on this issue a series of four articles: "Kayfa nurid an tuhkam Misr?!" *Ruz al-Yusuf* Nos. 1270, 1271, 1272, and 1273 (13, 20, 27 October, and 3 November 1952): 3.
79 Ihsan 'Abd al-Quddus, "Ru'us al-masa'il awwalan thumma al-tafasil," *Ruz al-Yusuf* No. 1275 (17 November 1952): 5.
80 'Abd al-'Azim Anis, "Wa min ajli adab waqi' aydan," *al-Misri*, 17 January 1954; 'Abd al-'Azim Anis, 'Ma'sat 'al-zaman' 'inda Tawfiq al-Hakim," *al-Misri*, 24 January 1954; 'Abd al-'Azim Anis and Muhammad Amin al-'Alim, "'Abqariyyat al-'Aqqad," *al-Misri*, 7 March 1954; 'Abd al-'Azim Anis, "al-Adab wa-l-hurriyya," *al-Misri*, 21 March 1954. Later these articles as well as others published elsewhere were collected as a one of the most important Marxist theoretical contributions to Egyptian literature: 'Abd al-'Azim Anis and Muhammad Amin al-'Alim, *Fi al-thaqafa al-Misriyya* (Cairo: Dar al-Fikr al-Jadid 1955; Cairo: Dar al-Thaqafa al-Jadida, 1988).

81 Ahmad Abu al-Fath, "Hurriyya fi kull al-bilad," *al-Ghad* I (May 1953): 20–2. And Ahmad Baha' al-Din, "Imbiraturiyyat Zifta," *al-Ghad* I (May 1953): 35–45.
82 Muhammad Mandur, *al-Dimuqratiyya al-siyasiyya* (Cairo: Kitab al-Muwatin, 1953) and 'Abd al-Raziq Hasan, *Azmatuna al-iqtisadiyya* (Cairo: Kitab al-Muwatin, 1953). Interestingly, Muhammad Mandur also translated from the French a history of the declaration of the human rights: *Tarikh islah huquq al-insan* (Cairo: the Arab League, 1950).
83 On the relations between the communist movement and the Free Officers see: Selma Botman, "Egyptian Communists and the Free Officers: 1950–54," *Middle Eastern Studies* 22 (1986): 350–66.
84 See for the best account of this episode: Muhyi al-Din, *Wa al-ana*, 78–96.
85 Ramadan, 77; and Selma Botman, *The Rise of Egyptian Communism in Egypt, 1939–1970* (Syracuse, NY: Syracuse University Press, 1988), 123.
86 Ramadan, 81.
87 Muhammad Abd el-Wahab Sayed-Ahmad, *Nasser and American Foreign Policy 1952–1956* (Cairo: The American University in Cairo Press, 1989), 51–70.
88 Cited in al-Sa'id, *Munazzamat al-yasar al-Misri, 1950–1957* (Cairo: Dar al-Thaqafa al-Jadida, 1983), 106–7.
89 Cited in al-Sa'id, 107–8.
90 Cited in al-Sa'id, 111–2.
91 Al-Sa'id, 149–50.
92 Al-Sa'id, 152–4.
93 Al-Sa'id, 155.
94 For a full account of the internal struggle in HADITU see al-Sa'id, 112, 137, and 199–205.
95 Internal publication of HADITU, "al-Tayyar al-Thawri," *al-Kadir* No. 5 (November 1953). Cited in al-Sa'id, 199–202.
96 *7 Sibtambir Khamis lam yamut*. Cited in al-Sa'id, 116–7.
97 Internal report written by Zaki Murad, *'An harakat al-jaysh: naqd dhati li-tahlil harakat al-dubbat wa mawqifina minhu*. Cited in al-Sa'id, 137.
98 Gordon, *Movement*, 127–43.
99 Ahmad Abu al-Fath, "Khutwa muwaffaq ...," *al-Misri*, 7 March 1954.
100 Wahid Ra'fat, "al-'Ahd al-jadid," *al-Misri*, 8 March 1954.
101 Ahmad Abu al-Fath, "Siyadat al-sha'b," *al-Misri*, 15 March 1954.
102 Open letter written by Yusuf Siddiq, published in *al-Misri* on 24 March 1954.
103 Interview with Khalid Muhyi al-Din printed on the front page of *al-Misri*, 11 March 1954.
104 Muhyi al-Din, *Wa al-ana*, 289–94 and 251–61.
105 Khalid Muhyi al-Din, "Usturat al-kafa'at fi misr," *Ruz al-Yusuf* No. 1344 (15 March 1954): 8.
106 Ihsan 'Abd al-Quddus, "al-Jam'iyya al-sirriyya allati tahkum misr!!," *Ruz al-Yusuf* No. 1345 (22 March 1954): 3–5.
107 Ihsan 'Abd al-Quddus, "Masir al-thawra ... wa masir rijal al-thawra!!?," *Ruz al-Yusuf* No. 1346 (29 March 1954): 3–5.
108 "Kalimat al-Misri," *al-Misri*, 9 March 1954.
109 Ahmad Abu al-Fath, "Hukm al-sha'b," *al-Misri*, 9 April 1954 and "Sayha ... liss!!" *al-Misri*, 21 March 1954.
110 Ihsan 'Abd al-Quddus, "Barlaman ... la jam'iyya ta'sisiyya," *al-Misri*, 16 March 1954.

111 "Kalimat al-Misri," *al-Misri*, 11 March 1954.
112 Marsha Pripstein Posusney, *Labor and the State in Egypt: Workers, Unions, and Economic Restructuring* (New York: Columbia University Press, 1997), 53–55.
113 See Gordon, *Movement*, 136; Robert Springborg, "Professional Syndicates in Egyptian Politics, 1952–1970," *International Journal of Middle East Studies* 9 (1978), 281–2; Donald Reid, "The Rise of Professions and Professional Organization in Egypt," *Comparative Studies in Society and History* 16 (1974), 54–55.
114 Gordon, *Movement*, 134–6.

◆ CHAPTER FIVE ◆

Towards a Modern Society, 1955–57

Introduction

During the second half of the 1950s Egypt witnessed a complete reversal of the position of its government. Still a widely suspected regime in 1954, it quickly gained a tremendous amount of popularity. Nasser became the foremost national reformer and an unassailable, charismatic leader of the Arab world. The reforms propagated by the new regime promised to change Egypt from a corrupt, "feudal," and "backward" country to a modern, integrated society. How could a regime that had lost its legitimacy and had been so unpopular acquire such a wide following in such a short time? More specifically, why did the liberal, socialist, and communist intellectuals who had defended a discourse of democratic transformation support the regime and accept its authoritarian modernization program?

The answer must be sought both in the regime's successful implementation of the program of the radical nationalist movement and in its effective formulation and dissemination of an authoritarian discourse of modernization. The discourse of democratic reformism was never completely erased, but it was pushed into a defensive position. In the changed political circumstances after 1955, it gradually lost its relevance and could no longer be employed effectively in opposition to the dominant authoritarian discourse, which increasingly set the terms for political, economic, and cultural debate.

Several factors contributed to the establishment of the hegemony of authoritarian modernism. The rise of the discourse of authoritarian modernism was greatly enhanced by the regime's use of repression and intimidation. Once the regime had definitively established its authority after the March Crisis in 1954, it was clear that the nature of political contest had been drastically altered. Press censorship and martial law were reinstated, and the doors to an open debate closed. The instatement of a multi-party system was firmly ruled out. Equally consequential to Egypt's history in the long run perhaps was the brutal and total elimination of the Muslim Brotherhood in October 1954. Thus, the regime not only removed its fiercest rival from the political scene, it also suppressed the discourse of Islamist authenticity as an alternative discourse until well into the 1970s. Although the government used Islam for the purpose of gaining authority, it was subordinated to and put in the service of the discourse of authoritarian modernism domestically and of pan-Arabism internationally. Repression, however, does not suffice as an explanation for the regime's popularity. After all, the hegemony of any discourse must be based on popular acceptance.

By far the most conspicuous means the Nasser government employed to harness its position was foreign policy. From 1955 the regime redirected its foreign policy away from the United States towards neutralism and anti-imperialism. The rejection of the Baghdad Pact at the beginning of 1955, Nasser's prominent role during the Bandung Conference in April, the Czech Arms Deal in September of the same year, the Suez Canal Crisis from July to December 1956, and finally the unification with Syria in February 1958, all these feats not only brought about and asserted Egypt's political independence; they also propelled Egypt to the center of the regional as well as the international stage.

By fulfilling the demands of the radical nationalist movement in such a spectacular manner, the regime swept its former opponents off their feet. On the ideological level, this enabled the regime to appropriate the vocabulary of national liberation used by the radical nationalist movement, to incorporate it into its own discourse of authoritarian modernism. Democratic reformist arguments with respect to the establishment and endorsement of such a foreign policy seemed absurdly feeble and childish, if not treacherous, in the dramatic circumstances in which Egypt fought for its liberation in the face of Western imperialist aggression. Consequently, the central tenet of democratic modernism, that independence and social and economic reform can only be attained by democratic means and through the mobilization of the population, was fundamentally undermined by the authoritarian implementation of the program of the radical nationalist movement. Needless to say, with this defeat of the democratic trend in the reformist movement, the struggle for the independence of civil society lost its momentum entirely.

Yet, the purpose of the struggle for independence had been not just to get rid of British political and economic domination, but also to develop Egypt economically and accomplish far-reaching social and economic reforms. The regime could only attain legitimacy if it could realize the two broader goals of the nationalist movement: national emancipation through economic and social development and the formation of a modern nation-state. Having broken the power of patronage and clientalism of the *ancien régime* and eliminated a corrupt political society, the new leaders would have to realize a program of reform to "modernize" Egypt further. At the same time, they would have to enhance their own power by carrying out this program through state institutions based on an authoritarian modernist program of reform from above.

The High Dam and the Suez Canal crisis provided an opportunity for doing both. The High Dam was of course one of the key projects that symbolized the high modernism of the new regime. Typically, the rejection of offers from the United States and Great Britain to finance the High Dam played a central part in the rise of the discourse of authoritarian modernism and the establishment of the regime's authority. By asserting Egypt's universal right to "modernize" itself, the regime took the opportunity to expand its control over the economy to an unprecedented degree. Not only did it nationalize what had always been regarded by the nationalist movement as the quintessential symbol of foreign imperialism and impediment of national development – the Suez Canal Company – the state also sequestrated all French and British assets, arguing that state control was crucial. Moreover, the regime reasserted a state ideology of modernization that had been carefully prepared from the beginning of the takeover of power, while expanding the number of technocratic institutions needed to carry out its policies.

The ideological centerpiece of the new technocratic modernism was state planning, which had already been established before the Suez Canal crisis. As explained in previous chapters, the terminology of planning was expressed in the Arabic terms *tawjih*, *tarshid*, and *takhtit* and had strong connotations of authoritarian supervision, direction, and control. Planning and its corollary, technocracy, had been institutionalized in economic organizations that had been founded in 1952 and 1953.[1] Although the economic significance of planning and of these institutions in particular has been subject to debate, their political and ideological implications have been neglected. Before 1955 and "Bandung," the regime had little legitimacy, and the state was in charge of economic and social reform. Ideology was a crucial asset in the political struggle with its opponents. 1954 had been a particularly bad year for the regime. After the March Crisis, the regime had damaged its reputation even further by signing a treaty with Great Britain concerning its military bases along the Suez Canal in October. In the eyes of intellectuals, planning and state-initiated social and economic transformation was the regime's only redeeming feature in this period, but because of its authoritarian character, this policy was still widely distrusted. Many accepted the new foreign policy as a sign of the changed direction of the new regime, because it appealed to the authoritarian strain in their own reformist program. The successful foreign policy in 1955 and 1956 reinforced the domestic policy of authoritarian modernization and the ideology that supported it, ensuring that the two would be linked. A large number of former opponents came to accept the general developmentalist slogan that the regime launched to celebrate its victory over the opposition: after the "stage of stabilization" (*marhalat al-istiqrar*) Egypt had now entered a "stage of construction" (*marhalat al-bina'*).

The implementation of the radical program of the nationalist movement explains in part why reformist intellectuals accepted the new setup and abandoned the democratic road to modernization. The subsequent incorporation of the new generation of reformist intellectuals into the new state structures as molders of public opinion – a process already started with Rashid al-Barrawi, Mirrit Butrus Ghali, and Ibrahim Bayumi Madkur in 1952 – further contributed to the hegemony of authoritarian modernism. The intellectuals were given a new role as "experts," "engineers," and in general as "ideologues" in newly established economic, political, and cultural institutions. These institutions replaced those of the *ancien régime* and the grand families (*buyutat*) that were associated with political favoritism, elitism, patronage, cultural decadence, and economic extravagance.

Once these intellectuals had accepted the authoritarian road to modernity between 1955 and 1958, they were assigned the position of opinion makers (*ashab al-ra'y*), a position they had demanded since the radicalization of the nationalist movement after the Second World War. The regime gave them the room and the authority they needed to help formulate, support, and disseminate a new hegemonic ideology, making them feel part of the modernization program. The incorporation of the intellectuals – eventually fully realized with the nationalization of the national press in 1961 and the dissolution of the Egyptian Communist Party in 1964 – was accompanied by the gradual replacement of the old guard of liberal intellectuals who had failed to fulfill to bring about the cultural, political, and economic renaissance they had envisioned. The position of the new regime improved further as a result of the rise to power of a young generation of intellectuals who derived their influence from their claim to be modernizers. Now reformist intellectuals could accomplish their original goals of "integrating" new social groups and classes into the nation-state and "deepening" their political participation in its political institutions. What was new in 1955 was that these institutions had become authoritarian and the ambivalence of the intellectuals towards the regime had largely dissolved.

The liberal and social intellectuals supported the regime not merely on the basis of opportunist and materialist motives. This is clear from the intellectual and imaginative challenges and opportunities the new regime opened up for them in the second half of the 1950s. Although the regime blocked off certain avenues for intellectual discourse on the defense of political individual rights, it also opened up completely unprecedented and exciting new imaginative inroads in other fields. These highly stimulating developments made it easier for intellectuals to adjust their ideas to take up the challenge of mapping and stretching the geographical, historical, and cultural boundaries of the new dimension Egypt was entering. They had the constructivist, modernist feeling that they were "building" a new society. As a result of this intellectual enthusiasm, the political literature of the 1950s reflects an unprecedented exhilaration and a boundless optimism that compensated for all the failures and frustrations of the mass mobilization and the democratic reformism of the previous decade.

In the following paragraphs the gradual rise and establishment of the discourse of authoritarian modernism is traced by exploring some of the many ways in which it was disseminated to all parts of Egyptian society. In the first section, I focus on the significance of economic planning as the centerpiece of authoritarian modernism. The rise of the discourse of planning is regarded here as the main alternative to the discourse of democratic development. I will demonstrate how it provided the terminology of state development and helped middle-class intellectuals to become the opinion makers of the new regime. The ascendancy of planism is described through the ideological works and political career of Rashid al-Barrawi. In the second section, I examine the changing perceptions of the new regime in the liberal weekly *Ruz al-Yusuf* between 1955 and 1958. The third section deals with the gradual change in the communist movement's attitude towards the regime, which moved from total rejection to far-reaching support. It will also demonstrate the role of planning in the changed attitude towards the regime.

The next chapter takes up the influence of the concept of planning on democracy, the role of the intellectual as servant of the state, the concept of time, historiography, philosophy, and travel literature. In all these fields, we can witness the exhilaration of modernism.

Economic Planning

The origins of planning

Most experts on the Egyptian economy hold the view that the beginning of serious economic planning started after the Suez Crisis, when the state sequestrated most of the French and British assets, acquiring a stake of 12 percent of the G.N.P. It was not until then that the state was induced to draw up sectional plans in preparation of the first five-year plan, to be implemented in 1958.[2] This does not mean, however, that before that time planning was not well established, albeit in the more modest form of larger state interference in the economy. More importantly, planning as an ideology seems already to have occupied a central place in political discourse before 1956 and could be put into practice when the occasion arose. The difference was that at this point the regime still believed in co-operation with the foreign and indigenous capitalist private sector. State planning was meant to induce the private sector to increase its investments, which had declined since 1950. In addition, the state was assigned the responsibility for projects that the private sector could not take on, such as creating an infrastructure and building a heavy industry. But even these etatist goals were ideologically induced. Prestigious, large-scale projects like the establishment of the Iron and Steel plant in Helwan and the building of the Aswan High Dam paved the way for high modernism and future overall planning. This is evident in the reception of these schemes and in the spread of the discourse of planning in the press.

In this transitional period, no one was identified with planning as much as Rashid al-Barrawi. Although it is impossible to ascertain the exact extent of his influence within the councils of state, he became in a sense the personification of the new policy in its early stages. In October 1952 the new regime decided to found the Permanent Council for the Development of National Production (PCDNP; al-Majlis al-Da'im li-Tanmiyat al-Intaj al-Qawmi). Reflecting the policy of co-operation with the Egyptian entrepreneurial class, businessman Husayn Fahmi was appointed president. Among its specialized members were Ibrahim Bayumi Madkur and the economist Ali al-Gritli, while Khalid Muhyi al-Din became the liaison with the RCC. In accordance with the new fixation on research and scientific rationality, the PCDNP had to draw up a survey of the national economy, set priorities, identify fields for private investment, and advise and collaborate with private capital in fulfilling the goals that it had decided on. All of this had to be done within a year. The council was given a great degree of independence and its own budget with which it could carry out those plans that were not passed on to the ministries.

The immediate response to the foundation of the Council was enthusiastic. Indeed, from the very start it was clear that it would have important ideological and political implications.[3] Opening the Council in January 1953, Muhammad Naguib described its tasks in the early military rhetoric of the revolution as part of the "reform struggle" (*ma'rakat al-islah*), emphasizing the need for "a plan for reform and renaissance" (*khitta li-l-islah wa-l-nuhud*) and calling for "sacrifice" for the sake of economic development. In true modernist spirit, he claimed that the council would help organize production on "a national, scientific and economic basis."[4] In his founding speech, Husayn Fahmi stressed the supporting role of the Council, using the more neutral terms "co-ordination" (*tansiq*) and "organization" (*tanzim*) to describe its tasks.[5]

In the following year, when the Council was primarily preoccupied with drawing up its survey, it stayed out of the limelight. In this period its most important act was to propose a complete reorganization of the Industrial Bank, which had been founded in 1949 but had not played the role that had been assigned to it. Rashid al-Barrawi became the Bank's new president on 1 November 1953. With the Industrial Bank, the regime had created the first institution that would actively promote the technocratic ideology of production and planning. The press coverage of al-Barrawi's appointment was very favorable; *al-Misri* printed an article entitled "The Mission of the Industrial Bank," in which it called for an active industrial policy and the expansion of industrial credit.⁶ It was argued that £E60 million should be invested in industry every year and that the state should reorganize the relations between the Central Bank and the Industrial Bank in order to expand its credit facilities. On the other hand, *al-Misri* clearly saw it as the mission of the Industrial Bank to promote small industries and put in place a policy that would draw the savings of the middle and lower classes towards industry.⁷ In the same month the Permanent Council for Social Services (al-Majlis al-Da'im al-Khadamat al-Ijtima'iyya), the social counterpart of the production council, was established, at which Aziz Sidqi (b. 1920), the future Minister of Industries, started his career.⁸

An alternative discourse

Thus, in 1954, the year in which the democratic opposition was defeated by the regime, the stage was set for the rise of an alternative discourse through its institutionalization and the appointment of some of its foremost proponents. In this year the more right-wing newspapers of the *Akhbar al-Yawm* group especially provided extensive coverage of the economic policies of the regime. Husayn Fahmi of the Production Council, interviewed on his way to India for an investigation into that country's industrial development, was quoted as saying, "Egypt will become an industrial country."⁹ Later, a trip of the members of the Production Council to the Soviet Union was covered, on which occasion they proclaimed that Egypt would introduce a five-year plan in the near future.¹⁰ The new year also saw the beginning of the customary rituals of a planned economy: contracts were signed, first stones laid, and new factories opened. High officials and eventually Nasser himself figured prominently at these and other highly visible ritual events, which were reported on in the newspapers daily. Most of the important industries that the Industrial Bank had helped establish and finance received this treatment. For instance, the media hailed the contract with the German Steel Company for the founding of the Iron and Steel plant in Helwan as an economic victory of the revolution. Commonly seen as the cornerstone of a complete and therefore independent economy, the Iron and Steel plant inaugurated the new era in industry, just like the High Dam inaugurated the new era in agriculture. Other newly established industries, less spectacular, but considered essential because they were believed to reduce imports, were a rubber factory, a salt industry, and a fertilizer plant.

Besides serving as propaganda for industrialization and for support of both foreign and indigenous private capitalist interests, the growing involvement of the state shifted attention away from private enterprise towards the state and its economic achievements. This shift became all the more obvious as private interests hardly responded to the industrialization drive promoted by the regime. Despite the repeal of Law 138 of 1947, which stipulated a 51 percent Egyptian participation in enterprises, and other stimulating measures like the provision for repatriation of profits and tax cuts, neither foreign nor indigenous capital responded positively to the state's initiatives. In fact, they even de-invested during this period. In 1956 private gross investments amounted to nearly a third of its 1950 level. Rather than being re-invested, profits were distributed among shareholders, as was the case with Misr Mahallat al-Kubra Spinning and Weaving Company where the distribution of dividends reached 78 percent of profits in 1952, then decreased to 62 percent in 1954, but rose again to 81 percent in 1958.[11] While private industrial investment stagnated at about £E30 million from the early 1950s, in urban real estate it rose from £E40 million in 1954 to £E59 million in 1958.[12]

The frustration of the state with private initiative was reflected in the gradual encroachment of the Industrial Bank on the private sector and its director's enthusiasm for organizing firms on the basis of his socialist ideas. Typical of the new structure that the Industrial Bank was promoting in this period was the establishment of the Egyptian Salt Company, which the Industrial Bank helped finance and put together in March 1955. The new company was formed through the merger of several smaller ones, which had been former competitors. Previously, they did not have the capital to renovate and survived by exploiting their workers. In contrast, Rashid al-Barrawi boasted, the new company had been able to acquire new machinery through a loan of the Industrial Bank, had become efficient, ran at a profit, was able to pay its workers reasonable wages, and could even export its product. An important characteristic of the new deal, stressed by al-Barrawi, was the fact that a 51 percent majority of shares belonged to the Industrial Bank. This had changed its economic attitude: "The company by virtue of its origin, looks at the problem [of production] from a higher level than its own interest; it is concerned with this first of all from the viewpoint of "Egyptian salt," as part of the national economy."[13] Majority participation became the rule in most of the large projects in which the Industrial Bank participated, as was for instance the case in a porcelain factory, which it took over and reorganized,[14] and the metallurgical company in which the Industrial Bank participated.[15] All the same, in all its projects the Industrial Bank was careful to stress private participation, and sixty percent of the capital of the Iron and Steel complex in Helwan was in the hands of private citizens.[16]

An economic philosophy for the revolution

In 1955 another important step towards the institutionalization of planning was taken. The PCDNP produced its final report, which provided the state with an inventory of the national economy and the means for controlling it.[17] Having served its purpose, the PCDNP was supplanted by the newly established National Planning Committee, which was entrusted with the task of "drafting a national comprehensive plan for social and economic development."[18] Ideologically, the economic policy of the regime was spelled out in more detail by Rashid al-Barrawi. At the height of his power as spokesman of the PCDNP and director of the Industrial Bank, he substantiated the trend toward etatist modernization in his book *The Economic Philosophy of the Revolution*.[19] Reflecting a still lingering hope of establishing an independent middle class (as opposed to a salaried one) that would carry the revolution, al-Barrawi divided the policy of the regime into three categories. The first, entitled "economic democracy," was intended to enhance the middle classes in the private sector. Not only would new measures open up different sources of investment for the new middle class; they would also establish a strong link between this class and the state, which depended on its savings for establishing heavy industries. The second category, "mobilizing surplus value," which in practical terms meant the introduction of a progressive income and inheritance tax, had the same intention: it supported the middle classes by diminishing class differences on the one hand and increased state revenue and power on the other. The last category of state policy entitled "economic planning" (*al-tawjih al-iqtisadi*) was meant to justify greater state interference in general. Key terms in this section are "organization" (*tanzim*) of limited resources, "supervision" (*ishraf*), "control" (*raqaba*), and "co-ordination" (*tansiq*) of common efforts to prevent "waste" (*israf*) and "chaos" (*fawda*).[20]

Remarkable in *The Economic Philosophy of the Revolution* is not al-Barrawi's use of this vocabulary in itself, but the fact that it had acquired semi-official status and was incorporated in official policy.

Rashid al-Barrawi had been forced to make considerable concessions, especially with regard to his acceptance of the American Point Four Aid Program, which the left generally regarded as a form of imperialism.[21] Nonetheless, it is clear that planning and etatism were in the ascendant. To promote the trend towards harnessing science to economics and to enhance the state's claim to objectivity and efficiency, Rashid al-Barrawi founded a research center for the Industrial Bank to which he appointed Abd al-Raziq Hasan as chief. Abd al-Raziq Hasan was to play an exceedingly important role in this period, not only in his capacity at the research center, but also in propagating the concept of planning as editor of the professional journal of the national organization of Egyptian economists, *al-Iqtisad wa-l-Muhasaba*.[22] In this journal, he attacked the regime's policy of attracting foreign investment and emphasized the indissoluble link between etatist planning, industrialization, economic independence, and economic development and prosperity, which became the hallmark of the later 1950s.[23]

The role of the Industrial Bank

The Industrial Bank put this new formula for economic development in practice by expanding its activities immensely from 1955 onward and implementing the policy that had been drawn up by the PCDNP in the previous two years. Its annual reports, written by Rashid al-Barrawi and traditionally published in the national newspapers in March and April, were meant as propaganda for the "new philosophy of the state" and provided a counterweight to the increasing anxiety voiced by Ali al-Shamsi, then still director of the National Bank, who warned against etatist encroachments in his annual report.[24]

In the first annual report written under his directorship in April 1955, Rashid al-Barrawi already claimed that he was proud to announce that the total amount of activities (i.e. loans, subsidies, and shares) during the past year had almost superseded those since the foundation of the Industrial Bank in 1949, amounting to a total of £E1,711,401 over the year 1954. In accordance with the idea that "it is necessary that the state gives an example by playing a positive role by industrializing in accordance with a distinct plan (*li-khitta marsuma*)," al-Barrawi enumerated all the projects in which the Industrial Bank had begun to participate, such as the Egyptian Salt Company and the Iron and Steel plant. He reported that the total participation of the Industrial Bank in these companies in shares had risen more than tenfold from in £E50,000 in 1953 to £E598,000 in 1954. Another indication of the bank's new orientation was the shift from short- to middle- and long-term loans, reaching 59.9 percent in 1954 from 26.5 percent in 1953.[25]

In the following years this trend continued. Credits, advances, and letters of credit showed an increase of 77 percent in 1955 compared with the previous year, whereas in the same period direct participation almost doubled to £E857,000. Credit released to the more traditional industrial sector, the textile industry, was slashed in half to 23.5 percent.[26] The biggest change, however, occurred in 1957, when credit amounted to £E3.1 million and the nominal capital of the establishments had multiplied by eight number to £E29 million. Foremost among the beneficiaries of the bank were what were considered "essential industries," especially metal and mechanical industries, whose total share exceeded £E1 million, or 40.7 percent of all loans and credits granted by the bank. The greater importance of the Industrial Bank was also reflected in the loans the state was willing to guarantee. Whereas the state's guarantee for loans by the Industrial Bank from the National Bank had been limited to £E1 million in December 1953, in March 1955 it rose to £E5 million, reaching £E7 million by the end of 1956.[27]

Institutionalization of planning

By this time, the discourse of planning had been fully sanctioned and institutionalized. The new constitution, instated in January 1956, stipulated in article 7 that the "national economy shall be organized in accordance with predesigned plans which provide for social justice and aim at promoting production and raising the standard of living." In addition, article 9 stated, "capital must be exploited for the benefit of the national economy, [and] the methods of this exploitation should not conflict with the general interests of the people."[28] These intentions were translated into policy during a major cabinet reorganization in June 1956 when the Ministry of Trade and Industry was divided and a separate Ministry of Industries was established with Aziz Sidqi, the future "industrial Czar," at its head. The technocratic character of the regime can also be seen in the creation of the office of Minister of State for Planning as well as the appointments of Sayyid Mar'i as Minister of Agriculture and Land Reform and Mustafa Khalil as Minister of Transport. Abd al-Mun'im al-Qaysuni had already been appointed as the Minister of Finance in August 1954.

These young and dynamic ministers embodied, as it were, the modernism of the new regime. They promoted the discourse of technocratic transformation with a vigor that helped consolidate the regime as much as it justified the expansion of their own ministries. And although al-Qaisuni was a more conservative Minister of Finance, he made major contributions to the industrialization drive, for instance by supplying the Industrial Bank with credit and mobilizing other resources for that purpose. In March 1956 he let it be known that the government was conducting negotiations with the Suez Canal Company to invest part of its profits in productive projects in Egypt.[29] That industrialization had become a top priority was also clear from a speech on the topic by Nasser on 18 June. Characteristically, the newspaper *al-Akhbar* welcomed the ministerial reorganization eleven days later as symbolic of the new stage of history that Egypt had entered. By demoting the Ministry of Trade, which was associated with Egypt's dependence on cotton export, imperialism, and the decadence of the *ancien régime*, and by creating a Ministry of Industry, with its connotations of independence, development, and a new, modern society, the regime had taken a major step in leaving the past behind and building a new future.[30]

The consolidation of the industrialization drive and sectorial planning is suggested by the influence of the Arabic terms *takhtit* and, to a lesser extent, *tarshid*, which points far more strongly towards purposeful, rational control and power than the term *tawjih*. An indication of the magic of these new terms is the appointment of Aziz Sidqi as Minister of Industries who had written his PhD on *takhtit*. From the start, Sidqi was a virtuoso at employing the vocabulary of planning and its modernizing implications. In his first interview as a Minister, he stated that Egypt needed an "industrial revolution" (*thawra san'iyya*) and that government policy would insure the transformation of the countryside through "industrialization" (*tasni'*). Confirming the imperative nature of planning, he went on to say, "it is necessary to mobilize the material, financial, and human potential in accordance with a distinct program that has clear objectives." In the familiar terminology of planism, etatist "direction" (*irshad*) and "supervision" (*ishraf*) were regarded as essential elements of "long-term planning" (*al-takhtit al-tawil*). Historically, Aziz Sidqi legitimizes the authoritarian modernist argument by referring to Nasser's speech on industrialization, which upheld the view that Egypt had now entered the "stage of construction" (*marhalat al-bina'*) after it had passed through the "stage of stabilization" (*marhalat al-istiqrar*), the regime's euphemism for the phase of repression of the liberal opposition.[31] Thus, before the nationalization of the Suez Canal Company in July 1956, the institutions, ideology, and personnel were in place to realize and put forward the concept of planning. Planning provided an important alternative technocratic discourse of power and legitimization during the March Crisis, before regime's foreign policy successes.

Reorientation of the Liberals

New horizons: from Bandung to the Suez Canal crisis

The journalists of *Ruz al-Yusuf* regarded the policy of the government between 1955 and 1958 as proof of the final realization of the program of the radical nationalist movement of the 1940s. As such, this was for them a period of exuberance. They believed that Egypt had found its rightful place in the world, and that the principles of the radical nationalist program guaranteed a glorious future. The years 1955 and 1956 can be seen as a transitional period in this respect.

In January 1955 Ihsan Abd al-Quddus expressed ambivalence about the goals of the revolution, showing himself to be divided on foreign and domestic policy, as was typical of the reformists at this time. He argued that land reform had had some good results, but "the Egyptian countryside remains to this day in the power of the great families (*buyutat*)," even if they were in decline. On the other hand, the influence of capital in society had diminished, because, he stated, the leadership was "convinced of the necessity of the balance (*tawazun*) between capital and labor." Proof of the more even-handed policy of the government was the instatement of labor laws, a type of legislation that would have been impossible if the government had been dominated by capital. The industrialization program of the government as well as the High Dam project and the Tahrir Province land development project demonstrate, he argues, the same concern for the people.[32]

Such qualified support for the regime already marked a significant change in the development of liberal socialist thought and partly showed the effects of the regime's reformist program. The real turning point would come in the first months of 1955 as the regime rejected the Baghdad Pact and its independent policy towards the United States became more pronounced.[33] Nasser's prominent role at the Bandung Conference in April caused a complete reversal of the liberal socialists' previous critical attitude towards the regime, sparked by the signing of the Anglo-Egyptian Treaty in October 1954. Ihsan Abd al-Quddus, who traveled with the Egyptian delegation to Indonesia, described Nasser's contacts with Nehru, Chou En Lai, and Sukarno in glowing terms. He greeted Nasser's adoption of "positive neutralism" with alacrity.[34] Furthermore, *Ruz-al-Yusuf* hailed Nasser's endorsement of the conference resolutions as the first step towards Egypt's adoption of a position of leadership in the emancipation of the Afro-Asian peoples, together with India, Indonesia, and Yugoslavia.[35] Likewise, the journal recognized the Soviet Union's backing of positive neutralism and acceptance of non-communist nationalism as a breakthrough in the relations between the Soviet Union and the emerging, newly independent Afro-Asian countries.[36] Finally, the Czech Arms Deal, which was closed in September, was regarded as a confirmation of the new era of co-operation. This change in its political, military, and economic policies (trade with the East preceded the political relations) marked Egypt's reorientation towards the East and its growing independence from the West.[37]

In all these matters, Ihsan Abd al-Quddus clearly perceives a relation between the regime's foreign policy and its domestic economic and political program. He states that the building of the High Dam, land reform, the abdication of King Faruq, and the Czech Arms Deal are all part of the same struggle for independence. Together, he writes, they spell the end of the three afflictions of Egypt, ignorance (*jahl*), poverty (*faqr*), and disease (*marad*). Bandung represented a major step in this process, because that is where Nasser "confirmed the independent Egyptian personality."[38] *Ruz al-Yusuf* also caught on to the drive for industrialization, claiming, "the real mission of our generation is to industrialize."[39]

We can thus clearly see the intellectuals' enthusiasm for the regime's new orientation reflected in the changed attitude of prominent journalists at *Ruz al-Yusuf*. It is also apparent in the re-establishment of the old coalition between the intellectuals of the middle class and those of the communist movement, who were given space in the weekly to declare their support for the regime's policies. Their contributions to *Ruz al-Yusuf* served both to convince the communist movement to alter its stance towards the regime and to give the regime's policies a more left-wing interpretation than seemed warranted. Indirectly and covertly these articles were meant to express the communist intention to establish a "national front" with the regime on the basis of the radical nationalist program of the 1940s, a strategy fully endorsed by *Ruz al-Yusuf* so long as the communists remained in a subordinate position.

In the articles that came out at the end of 1955 and in 1956, Mahmud Amin al-Alim (b. 1924) praises the government's neutralism, its refusal to enter military alliances, and its expansion of trade with the East Bloc. He argues that the regime supports world peace, the common communist stamp of approval of the times.[40] In all of his articles, he stresses that the radical nationalist program links political independence with economic development. He sums up this view after the Czech Arms Deal has been signed as follows: "If weapons can protect us against a military threat, then heavy industry will protect us against economic pressure and political encirclement." Conversely, he claims that the concentration on agriculture in the United States Point Four Program only indicates its imperialist intention of keeping Egypt backward.[41] Anwar Abd al-Malik expresses similar views in his articles on the principles of the Bandung conference and Soviet foreign policy.[42]

"A period of miracles": from Suez to the unity with Syria

While we see increasing communist and liberal socialist praise for Nasser during the entire period between 1955 and 1958, the Suez Crisis was indicative of another stage in the integration of the intellectuals through their acceptance of authoritarian modernism. Just after the nationalization of the Canal on 26 July 1956, Ihsan declared, "22 million Egyptians are unified as one heart, one mind, and one will... They have given it the name of Jamal Abd al-Nasir." He felt that this new unity prevented any attempt to split the nation and banned such traitors as had been present in Iran or in Egypt before the revolution. He proclaimed that there were no Adenauers, no Chang Kai Cheks, and no Mendereses in Egypt: "Before the revolution Great Britain only had to rescind its trust in a Prime Minister to cause a cabinet to fall and have it replaced. After the revolution the people decide for themselves. If Eden wants to negotiate with Egypt, he will have to negotiate with Nasser." In this elated article, Ihsan Abd al-Quddus also prophesied that Israel would do the bidding of the imperialist powers, now that its internal allies had been suppressed.[43]

Although Egypt's political victory during the Suez Canal crisis was a high point for the country, the real climax of this period was the unification with Syria in February 1958. These two events are seen as evidence of the realization of the nationalist movement and the interconnectedness of internal and external policy measures. Previously, Mahmud Amin al-Alim expressed his enthusiasm over the article in the new 1956 Egyptian constitution that states, "Egypt is an Arab state and the Egyptian people are part of the Arab nation."[44] Fathi Khalil, a new journalist on the staff of *Ruz al-Yusuf*, who had been appointed because of his outspoken Nasserist sympathies in 1956, welcomes the rapprochement with Syria even before the nationalization of the Suez Canal as "the first step" and "the cornerstone in the wall that can keep imperialism outside." Capturing the euphoric mood of the times, he declares that, "it would be a miracle if Egypt and Syria would unify, and this can happen faster than we can imagine. We live in a period in which nations produce miracles. Imperialism is incapable of obstructing this."[45]

Ahmad Baha al-Din and Ihsan Abd al-Quddus saw the unification of Egypt and Syria in February 1958 in the United Arab Republic (UAR) as not just a major political event, but also a meeting of two peoples and two governments on the basis of a common program of neutralism, industrialization, and anti-imperialism. Despite their doubts over its feasibility, they regarded it as a victory of mind over matter, justice over oppression, unity over diversity, and in short as the fulfillment of history. Above all, they write that unity had been realized on the basis of modern political principles and common interests, and not on the basis of some vague ideas concerning shared traditions, a common language, or religion. The victory was all the more sweet as previous "reactionary" attempts at unification by Hashemites had failed. Therefore, the unification vindicated the radical nationalist modernist program.[46]

All this did not mean that intellectuals had completely given in to the regime. Although the regime had achieved complete dominance by the end of 1956 and during the Suez Canal Crisis, which was consolidated in 1958, it had done so by reason of the principles of the radical nationalist program, which the middle class intellectuals regarded as their own. That program was not limited to foreign policy, for ultimately the internal transformation of society was the radical nationalist movement's goal. Foreign policy would be judged on the modernism of the concomitant domestic program. This did mean, however, that intellectuals had accepted the basic authoritarian principles of the regime. By agreeing with its policies, they agreed to their authoritarian implementation. As part of the *ashab al-ra'y*, they could comment on and try to debate the issues, but the regime made all the decisions.

Reorientation of the Communists

Background

The gradual reorientation of the Egyptian communist movement towards the regime during the second half of the 1950s was a more arduous process than that of the liberals, and it took longer to accomplish. First, the movement had to extract itself from the ideological corner it had maneuvered itself into by defining the Nasserist regime as "fascist." As we have seen in previous chapters, however, there were certain ideological loopholes that allowed the communists to accept the new regime once it had fulfilled part of the demands of the radical nationalist movement. Second, their reorientation was complicated by the organizational and ideological unification of the communist movement. HADITU merged with its factions to form the Unified Egyptian Communist Party in February 1955 (UECP, in Arabic: al-Hizb al-Shuyu'i al-Misri al-Muwahhad). In July 1957, these groups united with the CPE in the United Egyptian Communist Party (al-Hizb al-Shuyu'i al-Misri al-Muttahid). Finally, in January 1958, the Workers' Vanguard joined the United Egyptian Communist Party and together they became the Communist Party of Egypt (al-Hizb al-Shuyu'i al-Misri).

Within the communist movement, acceptance of the new regime partly depended on the outcome of the debate between upholders of the "minimum program" and upholders of the "maximum program." While the first supported a broad national front of all progressive forces, the second maintained that only a revolutionary vanguard of workers, without the national bourgeoisie, could lead such a front. Even the vindication of the upholders of the minimum program left the main ideological debate and the movement's position in relation to the military undecided. The failure to decide on the movement's attitude towards the regime was due to the vagueness of the concept of the national bourgeoisie. When the question to which "side" the officers belonged was finally settled during the Suez Canal crisis, the regime was accepted as part of the progressive national bourgeoisie. Only then it was incorporated into the national front. The theoretical fiction that the working class was the leader of this front barely masked the unequal power relations between the communist movement and the state.

Ultimately, the authoritarian modernist strain in the new regime was primarily responsible for its positive evaluation by the communist movement. Despite the fact that communists remained in two minds about the regime's class character and its repressive policies, they accepted the high modernist ideology of the state as a means to realizing the radical nationalist program and bringing Egypt into the modern age. Although the independence struggle and the Suez Canal crisis played an important part in this acquiescence, the purpose to which independence was put and the way in which it was consolidated were as important as independence itself. As was the case for the radical liberals of *Ruz al-Yusuf* and socialists like Rashid al-Barrawi, the hegemony of the discourse of authoritarian modernism in the communist movement found its clearest expression in the movement's support for economic planning and social reform. Through these means the regime could bring Egypt to a higher phase of historical development.

Acceptance of the regime

The first attempts at unifying the communist movement at the end of 1953 meant a complete victory for the supporters of the maximum program. The HADITU-Revolutionary Wing and other radical groups had previously condemned the minimum program of HADITU as the source of the movement's weakness. A preliminary program was drawn up in the terms of the radical maximum agenda. In it, Egypt was described as "semi-feudal" and "semi-colonial," and the political line was that "the Egyptian working class under the leadership of the Egyptian Unified Communist Party supports the people's armed struggle to liberate our country from Anglo-American imperialism." The program called for a united front of four classes against feudalism and imperialism, following the Chinese model. The present regime was denounced as "merely an instrument in the hands of imperialism."[47]

A later policy document, drawn up to determine the tactics that the Unified Communist Party should follow in 1955, states, "Anglo-American imperialism has succeeded in imposing a dictatorial military government." The document downgrades land reform, treating it as inconsequential, and it calls for "a democratic nationalist front" composed of all progressive social layers of society, political parties, and "personalities opposed to the dictatorship." It ends by asserting, "the cause of democracy cannot be won without destroying the present military gang and establishing a national democratic government. We need a government that is based on a republican parliamentary system that implements the program of the front."[48]

The movement accepted neither of these documents. The regime's resistance to the Baghdad Pact, its support for the Bandung Conference, and the acceptance of the Czech arms deal had outdated them. All the same, on account of the past rejection of the regime, the communist reorientation in light of the new policies lagged behind the events by almost a year. Most communists were still in prison during these events in 1955 and would stay there until the Suez Canal crisis in the fall of 1956, or even longer. Official external publications by the Unified Egyptian Communist Party long remained highly critical of the regime. For instance, a leaflet published on 1 May 1955 still called the July Revolution a military coup and claimed that the working class "was the first national group to become conscious of the truth of this imperialist conspiracy."[49] Even after the Czech arms deal in September of the same year, the official external publication of UECP, *Kifah al-Sha'b* (*The Struggle of the People*) condemned the regime's pro-American policy, accusing it of preferring the harsh terms of the World Bank in financing the High Dam to the generous offers by the Soviet Union.[50]

It was left up to Zaki Murad (d. 1979), a member of the Central Committee of the UECP, to force a breakthrough. In the regime's new foreign policy he found a confirmation of HADITU's original view of the military as part of the national front. He rejected the notion that Egypt was semi-colonial and semi-feudal and recognized that the government was a forerunner in the struggle for the political, military, and economic liberation of Egypt from imperialism.[51] He saw the nationalization of the Abbud group in 1955–56, the quintessential monopoly in the eyes of the Egyptian left, as well as the new laws on the limitation of the number of board members in companies as "clear indicators that the power of the big capitalists, both foreign and Egyptian, is receiving ever greater blows, day after day." The same applied to "feudalism."

Yet, the most important part of Zaki Murad's argument on this topic is his emphasis on the links between the regime's foreign and domestic policy, which established its overall progressive character:

> All of us know that feudalism in Egypt has received enormous blows since 26 July 1952, when the king was banished and the agrarian reform law as well as the agrarian labor laws [were

adopted] ... This was followed by the sequestration of the possessions of the royal family in November 1953, and the ending of feudalism was taken up as one of the prime goals in the constitution ... All these measures have destroyed the feudal system ... as we knew it in the past. If a few of this system's traits still remain in existence, this is natural because the struggle continues and the termination of all the vestiges of the feudal system cannot be accomplished all at once.

Murad concludes, "Egyptian society has experienced profound changes. After having been a society with a semi-feudal character, today it is becoming independent and democratic."[52] This analysis calls for a complete reversal of the strategy of the communist movement towards the regime, which would have to be directed once again at its incorporation into the national front. In February 1956 Zaki Murad and other members of the UECP sent a letter from prison camp, in which they describe the policies of the regime as "the crowning of the long-lasting struggles of the Egyptian people."[53] To support this view, the letter explicitly mentions the Bandung Conference, Nasser's role in formulating and later implementing its resolutions, the regime's condemnation of the Baghdad Pact, and the promulgation of the new constitution in January, which guaranteed every citizen the right to work and social security.

The Workers' Vanguard had changed its position toward the military regime even earlier. In January 1955, the party announced in one of its pamphlets that it would support the regime as soon as it severed its ties with "Anglo-American imperialism" and adopted an independent policy of neutrality.[54] After Bandung and the start of new relations with the East Bloc, the Workers' Vanguard wrote an open letter to Prime Minister Abd al-Nasser, proclaiming its endorsement of the "new steps" in the regime's foreign policy. At the same time, however, the letter includes demands for civil liberties based on human rights and calls for greater efforts to achieve Arab unity.[55] And in a historical analysis of the nationalist movement published in September 1955, the Workers' Vanguard still called Egypt a "semi-feudal," "semi-colonial" country dominated by foreign monopoly capital with a "dictatorial government that does not fulfill the demands of the radical nationalist movement."[56]

The UECP officially declared its support for the regime in March 1956 in *The Line of the Unified Egyptian Communist Party*.[57] This document gives a detailed evaluation of the regime as well as an overview of the UECP's ideas on Egypt's general political and economic situation at the time, concluding,

> the Nasserist government has taken the road toward independent political and economic development of our country, which entails the gradual liberation of our country from the imperialist market and the weakening of the political power of imperialism and the strengthening of economic, political, and cultural links with the socialist camp.[58]

In agreement with the general communist reorientation towards the emerging independent countries of the Third World after Bandung, the official *Line* regarded the Nasserist regime as part of the international independence struggle of "the big ruling bourgeoisies of India, Indonesia, Burma, Syria, Lebanon, and the Sudan." The general view of the bourgeoisie in these different countries was that industrialization is an absolute precondition for national development. It knew that while the "imperialist camp" obstructed industrialization, especially in the form of the establishment of heavy industry, and tried to concentrate on supporting agriculture, the socialist camp was willing to provide economic and military aid at reasonable prices and to further world peace.[59]

Zaki Murad confirms this line of reasoning in his report *On the Class Nature of the Government of the Officers*, written in July 1956.[60] His central argument is that the Free Officers' Movement is "one of the political organizations of a section of the national bourgeoisie in Egypt. More specifically, it is an organization that expresses the interests of the middle and lower ranks of the officers and opposes the absolute power of imperialism and feudalism over the army and the officers."[61] However, both the official *Line* and Murad's report still contain the ambivalence that characterizes the communist movement's relation with the new regime.[62] In April 1956, the official *Line* of the UECP was made public in an article in *Sawt al-Fallahin* (*The Voice of the Peasants*), which called for a broad nationalist front as a first step towards the unification of the Arab countries against imperialism.[63] Furthermore, the official declaration *Imperialism Is the Main Enemy* encouraged the mobilization of "all the nationalist forces, calling on millions of workers, peasants, students, writers, artists, tradesmen, small, middle and large industrialists to resist the imperialist onslaught."[64]

The Workers' Vanguard's support of the regime was much less conditional and cautious than the UECP's, although it too was ambiguous due to the regime's affiliations with national bourgeoisie. The party analyzed the class character of the military in relation to its neutralism, which was regarded as a policy adopted by many leaders of semi-colonial and colonial countries, like Nasser, Nehru, and Sukarno, in order to liberate their countries from the domination of imperialism. Thus, the Workers' Vanguard declared:

> Our support of the government is not negative. It means that not only will we refrain from attacking the government in its foreign policy, but we will also make widely known the nationalist and peaceful policy that the government has adopted recently, and we shall collect signatures and urge the trade unions and other influential organizations to adopt resolutions in support of that policy. In addition, we will work together with the Liberation Rally to propagate this political line, and co-operate with and support the policy of Abd al-Nasser. Moreover, we will support the government against coups d'état that imperialism will try to organize against the government.[65]

Both organizations' changed position towards the regime led to greater freedom of expression and the release of most of the members of the communist movement. The most tangible result of the rapprochement between the two sides was the foundation of the evening paper *al-Masa'* on 6 October 1956, with Khalid Muhyi al-Din as editor-in-chief. *Al-Masa'* would grow into the most important left-wing mass organ. It would also voice the most enthusiastic support of economic planning. In the same liberal period, several left-wing publishing houses were established, such as Dar al-Fikr and Dar al-Nadim.[66]

A common front

Ambivalence towards the regime would diminish as the regime acquired legitimacy during the Suez crisis and as the discourse of authoritarianism came to dominate. This had important consequences for the communist movement. While its ideological pretensions to leading the nationalist movement were jeopardized, it lost the means of forming an alternative to the regime once the other opposition parties had been eclipsed or completely suppressed. These dramatic developments forced the UECP and the Workers' Vanguard to seek a coalition with a government in which they were very much the junior partner.[67] Their subordinate position strengthened the authoritarian trend within the movement itself. The more the communist movement became tied to the regime, the more infrequent and the less tenacious their democratic demands were. Even if such demands were made, they were often adjusted to the new authoritarian structures. As was true in the case of the liberals and liberal socialists of *Ruz al-Yusuf*, the new corporatist state increasingly determined the rules of the game and the content of political discourse.

For the communists, the immediate result of the Suez Crisis was their total support of the government. As early as in January 1956, the Workers' Vanguard founded a special bulletin, *al-Muqawama al-Shaʿbiyya* (*Popular Opposition*), in which it proclaimed that a united front against imperialism had "overriding national priority over all particular interests."[68] The UECP declared the crisis a chance to prove the communist movement's nationalism:

> This struggle presents for us Egyptian communists – and for the members of the UECP in particular – a golden opportunity to establish our credentials, not only as leaders of the workers and the peasants, but also as the leaders of Egypt as a whole in its sacred endeavor to preserve its independence and guarantee its victory and progress toward true democracy and socialism ... It is our duty as members of the UECP to prove ourselves the most pure and consistent nationalists in defense of the freedom of our people and our national independence.[69]

This ascendancy would take the form of the United Nationalist Front (al-Jabha al-Muttahida al-Wataniyya), which differed from the previous fronts in that it was directed against imperialism and not against the government. As it had during the struggle over the Suez Canal in 1951, the UECP now called for the organization of civilians in armed battalions and the erection of committees in villages and cities. These committees would have "the task of protecting the nationalist gains (*al-makasib al-wataniyya*) that the government of Gamal Abd al-Nasser has realized." In addition, they would "protect his government and develop and realize new gains in domestic and foreign policies." Their membership would consist of "the broadest possible masses," and members of the UECP were advised not to dominate these committees or let them be dominated by communist sympathizers at first.[70]

The united front seemed to provide a new opportunity for mobilizing the population in the type of grass-roots resistance organizations that the communists could influence or perhaps come to dominate. When a front did emerge during the Suez Canal Crisis, it was established in Port Sa'id after that city had been occupied by the British and French troops and after it had been completely cut off from the authority of the central Egyptian government. The united front organized demonstrations and protest against the foreign occupation.[71] In accordance with the previously established strategy, its mouthpiece, *al-Intisar* (*Victory*), recognized Nasser as "our leader" (*za'imuna*) and proclaimed,

> our united front will continue its battle. Its continuous support is the first guarantee of the realization of new victories ... This is a long road ... The only guarantee [of its success] is the rallying of the people, the government, and the army around *our* goals and around the leader (*al-qa'id*), Gamal Abd al-Nasser, the symbol of our popular resistance ... forwards![72]

The regime prohibited the organization of committees of popular resistance, and after the foreign occupiers had left, *Kifah al-Sha'b* reported that only a few had been established in Cairo.[73] It remained, nonetheless, one of the UECP's most important experiments in mobilizing the people and establishing its own channels of influence while showing its support for the regime. When the Eisenhower Doctrine was proclaimed in January 1957, the UECP adopted the same strategy:

> No doubt the popular resistance committees that sprang up from the armed nationalist struggle against imperialism are the most appropriate organizational form for the masses to execute this task. Other mass organizations of the trade unions and federations can be formed in complete unity around them, and thus, a united nationalism will be directed against the conspiracies of imperialism.[74]

The party claimed that Egypt had to wage a permanent war against the United States in order to preserve its own independent economic policy. This required arming the population, setting up training centers, and organizing popular militias.

Another reason for this strategy was that the postponed parliamentary elections demanded a selection of the party's candidates. Popular resistance committees could weed out "opportunistic, hesitating or treacherous elements ... and help cut off the head of conspiracies." Finally, these committees could help mobilize the population for the immanent unification of Egypt and Syria against imperialism. Even on other occasions, the Port Sa'id model was held up as a national, organizational model of popular resistance. It was stressed that all existing organizations in society should join the popular resistance committees, in particular the professional organizations, the trade unions, and even the Liberation Rally. A Higher Committee would be established to supervise the activities of the local and regional committees.[75]

Planning and the communist movement

The communist movement was relatively late in appreciating the importance of planning to the regime's policy. Not until the nationalization of foreign assets during the Suez Canal crisis and the introduction of the first Five-Year Plan in 1957, did the communists realize the extent of the prior reforms leading to state control and economic change. Once they had become aware of the impact of the new measures, they vigorously advocated planning as the only means to achieve modernization. Like the radical liberals and socialists, the communists saw planning as central to achieving modernity and building a rational and ordered society. For them, the new technocratic institutions the regime set up evoked the image of a society based on "science" and run by "experts" who carefully draw up integrated, comprehensive plans instead of letting market forces squander the nation's wealth and social strife dissipate its resources. The communist support for planning in the pages of the newspaper *al-Masa'* spread the new gospel highly effectively.

The communists saw the establishment of a heavy industry and large public projects like the High Dam as crucial to economic independence and development. They applauded all measures that directed the economy away from Western imperialism, such as increasing trade with the East Bloc, and criticized the regime's encouragement of foreign investments. Later, however, the communist movement would come around to supporting the regime wholeheartedly in this respect. Its reticence vanished with the nationalization of the Suez Canal Company on 26 July 1956 and the subsequent sequestration of British and French possessions in Egypt in November 1956. The establishment of the Economic Organization in January 1957, which took over most of the sequestered British and French property, as well as the foundation of the National Planning Council and a National Planning Committee in the same month, greatly stimulated the general tendency towards planning. This trend was confirmed when Minister of Industry Aziz Sidqi announced a Five Year Industrial Plan in April 1957, worth £E114 million, of which £E24 million would be provided by the state.[76]

The communists viewed planning, admired as a Soviet invention, as the supreme expression of economic rationalism. The newfound control over the country's own destiny not only led to optimism for the economic future of Egypt, it also inspired new visions for the future in general. Recently acquired power over such symbols of foreign oppression as the Suez Canal Company and huge foreign banks like Barclays sparked the idea that Egypt had entered into a stage of modernity in which rationalism and state-led planning prevailed over greed, class exploitation, and waste. The economic editor of *al-Masa'*, Abd Al-Raziq Hasan, appointed head of the research department of the Industrial Bank by Rashid al-Barrawi, lost no time in promoting the concept of planning with the utmost vigor. A long list of economists and non-specialist ideologues of planning were mobilized to support a veritable campaign for the concept of planning in all its forms.

Nationalization or "Egyptianization" (*tamsir*) was presented in *al-Masa'* as a precondition for planning.[77] It was pointed out that the nationalization of the Suez Canal Company revealed that monopolies, and especially foreign monopolies, were the root of Egypt's economic problems. These monopolies, it was claimed, controlled the Egyptian capital market, exploited its mineral wealth, and held Egyptian industry in its grip.[78] The establishment of the Economic Organization (al-Mu'assasa al-Iqtisadiyya) was seen as the next step towards "scientific planning" (*al-takhtit al-'ilmi*) and the creation of an economy that would be beneficial for the whole nation and the "majority of the population."[79] The founding of the EO was, moreover, regarded as the realization of the articles in the constitution that stated that the national economy should be based on "drawn-up plans" (*al-khitat al-marsuma*).[80] Finally, the formation of the Higher Council of Planning (al-Majlis al-A'la li-l-Takhtit al-Qawmi) with Nasser at its head confirmed the essentiality of planning.[81] *Al-Masa'* prophesied that the chaos of capitalism would be a thing of the past and that national productivity and individual potential would be maximized now that the new era of "complete planning" (*takhtit shamil*) had begun.[82] The new era would bring "progress" (*taqaddum*) and "independence" (*istiqlal*), and the Higher Council of Planning would organize the economy in accordance with "the general interest" (*al-salih al-'amm*).[83] By breaking the hold of imperialism, which had kept Egypt backward, planning would free the Egyptian national potential,[84] which would lead to a "stable, permanent development."[85]

The announcement of the Industrial Five-Year Plan in early 1957 gave further impetus to the debate on planning in *al-Masa'*. Most of its authors pleaded for a larger share of state capital in the projects included in the plan. They rightly predicted that the still large share of private Egyptian capital in these projects would lead to another round of nationalizations.[86] The proponents of etatist planning used the recent lack of enthusiasm for investing in Egypt on the part of private capital to argue for the expansion of state-led development.[87] In this light, they expressed their approval for the 1956 Annual Report of the Industrial Bank, which announced an increase in the percentage of investments and loans to the heavy chemical industry.[88] Only rarely did they raise their voices in warning against greater state intervention, the concomitant growth of an inefficient bureaucracy, and the increase in authoritarian rule.[89] By the second half of 1957, the Industrial Five Year Plan had become one of the sanctified principles of the revolution, "the cornerstone of political independence," as one commentator put it, which could only be criticized by "reactionaries."[90] Planning had come to be regarded as the only way of catching up with the West and of eventually surpassing it.[91] During the unification with Syria, planning was regarded as an appropriate method of integrating the two economies.[92]

Crucial to the new technocratic ideology, expounded by the left in *al-Masa'*, was an absolute faith in the science that supported planning. If the magic of laying the first stone and opening factories was meant to impress modernism on the population, the establishment of economic institutes, councils, and especially of higher councils was meant to entice the intellectuals. Apart from new employment opportunities, for them, these temples of science symbolized the entrance of Egypt into the modern age. As in heavy industry and in planning, the Soviet Union was again to be emulated. The writers for *al-Masa'* ascribed its rapid technological progress, for instance, to its ability to turn out scientists at three times the rate of the United States. The launching of the Sputnik as the first satellite into orbit proved the Soviet Union's scientific superiority.[93] The efficacy of science was given expression in numbers, and especially climbing numbers, with their mesmerizing effects. Anticipating the numerical mania of the Industrial Five-Year Plan once it took effect, *al-Masa'* interpreted the past increase in the budget of the Permanent Council for the Development of the National Production (PCDNP) and the

Industrial Bank as indicators of Egypt's progress that could be extrapolated into the future.[94]

The commentators for *al-Masa'* located the highest form of scientific revolution in the scientific planning of science itself. What was true for the fields of economy and culture was also true for science and scientific production. They too could be subjected to *takhtit*. In the march to modernity, the establishment of the National Center of Research (al-Markaz al-Qawmi li-l-Buhuth) and the Higher Council for the Sciences (al-Majlis al-A'la li-l-'Ulum) were the first steps towards "planning of scientific research" (*takhtit al-bahth al-'ilmi*).[95] Although there had been research before the revolution, now, through direct intervention of a state that worked for the benefit of the people, science could be "applied to society so that scientific research can move society forward."[96] Moreover, these authors saw science as a means of drawing the universities into supporting government policies.[97] According to one article, which called for a five-year Plan for science, the investment of one percent of the national income in science would result in its rise by ten percent.[98] The highest efficiency could be reached, this author claimed, when "science was organized" (*al-tanzim al-'ilmi*) in one huge institute, like in the Soviet Union.

Conclusion

The reasons why liberals, socialists, and communists supported the new regime began to resemble each other over the course of this period. We can see this clearly in the specific expressions of their backing for the regime and the authoritarian modernism on which it was based. All of these currents had the same mechanistic image of society and imagined its progress in uniform stages of development ending in modernity. Modernity is defined as massive industrialization leading to migration to modern cities, while land reforms and development schemes are thought to lead to the disappearance of the peasant class. Symbols of the new society were the huge public projects such as the High Dam, the Iron and Steel complex at Helwan, and the Tahrir Province land development project. These projects were a sign that Egypt had emancipated itself from imperialism because it could combine science and knowledge with the power to transform society and the economy to the benefit of its population as a whole. The premise was a far-reaching rationalization of society in which the state would play a preponderant role. Economic planning and social and civil engineering would combine to make the new society a success.

Many intellectuals who upheld a discourse of modernism began to support the regime when it became clear they shared the same model of a modern society. In the face of the onslaught of the new institutions and the success of the regime's foreign policy, they abandoned their past ambivalence about state-led economic and social reform free from the checks of a strong civil society and direct supervision by a reformed political society. As a result, they gave up their endeavors to create a politically educated, critical citizenry, as well as the attempt to establish independent social and economic associations and institutions that would support an independent civil society as a counter-weight to state power. Instead, the press was put into the service of the state, trade unions were advised to join the nationalist struggle, and intellectuals were taken up with the new challenges the regime offered them. This change of attitude was not only, or even primarily, the result of fear; more importantly it was part of the authoritarian modernism most intellectuals upheld in their writings even before the July Revolution. National independence, economic development, social change, and a more equal distribution of income and wealth guaranteed by the state were deemed more important than individual political rights or the rights of professional groups and associations. Individualism had been vanquished by a new collectivism and conformism, in which the intellectuals acquiesced and which they apparently even welcomed. Overawed by the struggle over the Suez Canal and intimidated by the huge public projects, they were enchanted by the promise of collective modernization leading to a truly homogenized, well-ordered and socially structured nation-state that the more pluralistic monarchy had not been able to produce. Rationalization of society by the state seemed preferable to the uncertainty of civil society. The elimination of the discourse of Islamic authenticity only seemed to confirm the modernity of the regime and the correctness of their project.

In many ways this complex of institutions, the ideology that supported it, and their pervasiveness in society are reminiscent of what James Scott calls high modernism: civil society is repressed and rational planning has become all powerful. Scott also points to the combination with science and the authority and legitimization it gives to the economic and social transformation of society. In the next chapter we will see how these concepts are applied to other fields of intellectual activity.[99]

Notes

1 See for the technocratic character of the regime, Nazih N. M. Ayubi, *Bureaucracy & Politics in Contemporary Egypt* (London: Ithaca Press, 1980), Chapter 3, "New Political, New Organizational facts," 157–253. See for the rise of engineering profession and technocracy, Clement Henry Moore, *Images of Development: Egyptian Engineers in Search of Industry* (Cambridge: The MIT Press, 1980).
2 There are two sets of ideas about Egyptian economic development in this period. Patrick O'Brien presents the majority view, according to which Egypt's new rulers did not have a particular economic ideology. In this view the continuity with the pre-revolutionary period is stressed. See Patrick O'Brien, *The Revolution in Egypt's Economic System: From Private Enterprise to Socialism, 1952–1966* (London: Oxford University, 1966), 68–70 and 82–3. Robert Mabro, on the other hand, presents the minority view. He regards the year 1952 as a turning point in Egyptian economic history. Mabro states that despite a certain measure of continuation, "the Revolution committed itself very early in the day to rapid industrialization and a deepening of the industrial structure; and the period is dominated by attempts to carry through this program. The steel mill symbolized the commitment and the National Production Council paved the way for planning and strong government intervention in industry." Further, Mabro argues, "a new orientation was taken, involving a large measure of state intervention both in agriculture and in industry, and later steps – e.g. *planning and nationalization – followed logically from this earlier commitment*. The suggestion is not that these steps were inevitable but that we can discern, with hindsight, a *consistent purpose throughout the period.*" See Robert Mabro, *The Egyptian Economy, 1962–1972* (Oxford: Clarendon Press, 1974), 5. Italics added. Recently this opinion has been supported by Robert Vitalis, *When Capitalists Collide: Business Conflict and the End of Empire in Egypt* (Berkeley: University of California Press, 1995), 161–4. My view is that even if the new institutions did not make a crucial difference economically, they did pave the way for greater intervention ideologically. As we shall see, the whole concept of planning became the centerpiece of the modernism and developmentalism of the 1950s.
3 "Qararat majlis al-intaj al-qawmi fi 'alat al-muwafaqa 'ala qanun al-sharikat al-jadida," *al-Misri*, 3 January 1953. "Arkan harb al-hukuma fi midan al-intaj al-qawmi," *al-Musawwar*, 9 January 1953. For the early enthusiasm in *al-Ahram* for the new economic policy of the state with regard to the PCDNP, steel, planning, and the scientific control of the economy, see: "Bina' al-mujtama' al-Misri," *al-Ahram*, 18 September 1952; "Marsum bi-insha' Majlis li-Tanmiyat al-Intaj al-Qawmi," *al-Ahram*, 3 October 1952; "Bi-madha nabda'?," *al-Ahram*, 6 January 1953; "al-Ba'th al-'ilmi fi khidmat al-thawra," *al-Ahram*, 24 January 1953; "al-Takhtit wa-l-tansiq al-qawmi," *al-Ahram*, 26 January 1953. For articles on the PCDNP in *al-Ahram al-Iqtisadi*, see "Intajuna," *al-Ahram al-Iqtisadi*, November–December 1953, 1–5 and 16–7.
4 *al-Akhbar*, 4 January 1953.
5 *al-Musawwar*, 23 January 1953.
6 "Risalat al-Bank al-Sina'i," *al-Misri*, 1 November 1953, 4.
7 Ahmad Abu Isma'il, "Tamwil al-sin'a fi Misr yatatallab insha' Bank Sina'i jadid," *al-Misri*, 15 March 1954.

8   Kalimat al-Misri, *al-Misri,* 15 November 1953, 5.
9   "Satakun Misr baladan sina'iyyan," *Akhbar al-Yawm,* 30 January 1954.
10 *al-Akhbar,* 20 April 1954.
11 Mourad Magdi Wahba, *The Role of the State in the Egyptian Economy: 1945–1981* (Houndsmill: MacMillan, 1993), 75.
12 John Waterbury, *The Egypt of Nasser and Sadat: The Political Economy of Two Regimes* (Princeton: Princeton University Press, 1983), 62.
13 "Najah li-siyssat hukumat al-thawra," *al-Akhbar,* 24 March 1955, 3.
14 "al-Sharika al-'Amma li-intaj al-harariyyat wa-l-fakhkhar," *al-Akhbar,* 13 September 1956.
15 *al-Akhbar,* 19 September 1956.
16 Annual Report of the Iron and Steel Company at Hilwan, *al-Akhbar,* 16 March 1956.
17 *al-Majlis al-Da'im li-Tanmiyat al-Intaj al-Qawmi* (Cairo: n.p., 1955).
18 Mabro, 113.
19 Rashid al-Barrawi, *al-Falsafa al-iqtisadiyya li-l-thawra min al-nahiyatayn al-nazariyya wa-l-'ilmiyya* (Cairo: Maktabat al-Nahda al-Misriyya, 1955).
20 Al-Barrawi, *Falsafa,* 164.
21 Rashid al-Barrawi, *al-Nuqta al-rabi'a fi al-mizan* (Cairo: Maktabat al-Nahda al-Misriyya, 1953).
22 Personal interview with 'Abd al-Raziq Hasan on 2 October 1989.
23 'Abd al-Raziq Hasan, "Ittifaqat sharikat Kunurada al-Muttahida li-l-bahth 'an al-bitrul wa-istighlalihi fi al-Sahra' al-Gharbiyya," *al-Iqtisad wa-l-Muhasaba* No. 75 (15 April 1954): 14–5; 'Abd al-Raziq Hasan, "Imtiyaz sharikat Kunurada al-Muttahida li-l-Bitrul," *al-Iqtisad wa-l-Muhasaba* No. 76 (1 May 1954): 14–8; 'Abd al-Raziq Hasan, "Aswaq al-awraq al-maliyya wa-l-'awamil allati tatahakkam fiha," *al-Iqtisad wa-l-Muhasaba* No. 86 (1 January 1955): 11–3 and 21; 'Abd al-Raziq Hasan, "Tahlil al-dakhl al-qawmi al-Misri 'an sana 1953," *al-Iqtisad wa-l-Muhasaba* No. 87 (1 February 1955): 26–32.
24 'Ali al-Shamsi, Annual Report of the National Bank (*al-Bank al-Ahli*), *al-Misri,* 25 March 1954.
25 Rashid al-Barrawi, Annual Report of the Industrial Bank 1954 (in Arabic), *al-Akhbar,* 14 April 1955: 8–9.
26 *The Industrial Bank: Report of the Sixth Ordinary General Meeting 1955* (Cairo: 1956).
27 *The Industrial Bank: Report of the Seventh Ordinary General Meeting 1957* (Cairo: 1958).
28 *The Industrial Bank: Report 1957,* 28.
29 *al-Akhbar,* 22 March 1956, 4.
30 Kalimat al-Yawm, *al-Akhbar,* 1 July 1956.
31 Press conference of Aziz Sidqi, *al-Akhbar,* 4 July 1956, 7 and 9.
32 Ihsan 'Abd al-Quddus, "Hisab al-ahdaf la hisab al-hawadith," *Ruz al-Yusuf* No. 1386 (3 January 1955): 6–7.
33 Ahmad Baha' al-Din, "al-Istiqlal al-tamm ... huwa ma nurid," *Ruz al-Yusuf* No. 1389 (24 January 1955): 12–3.
34 Ihsan 'Abd al-Quddus, "Ihsan 'Abd al-Quddus yaktub min Bandunj," *Ruz al-Yusuf* No. 1402 (25 April 1955): 6–7.
35 Ahmad Baha' al-Din, "Hadha al-sabah ... fi bandunj!," *Ruz al-Yusuf* No. 1401 (18 April 1955): 5.
36 Ahmad Baha' al-Din, "Da'wat al-hiyad ...," *Ruz al-Yusuf* No. 1407 (30 May 1955): 5.

37 Ahmad Baha' al-Din, "Ihtikar al-siyasa," *Ruz al-Yusuf* No. 1426 (10 October 1955): 5.
38 Al-Muwatin al-Misri, "al-Rajul alladhi bana al-Sadd al-'Ali," *Ruz al-Yusuf* No. 1435 (12 December 1955): 3.
39 Al-Muwatin al-Misri, "Kayfa nashab al-ard min taht isra'il?," *Ruz al-Yusuf* No. 1444 (13 February 1956): 3.
40 Mahmud Amin al-'Alim, "Mistir Dulles yatahaddath 'an al-sa'ada," *Ruz al-Yusuf* No. 1421 (5 September 1955): 5.
41 Mahmud Amin al-'Alim, "Likay nahmi ... intitasaran," *Ruz al-Yusuf* No. 1427 (17 October 1955): 5.
42 Anwar 'Abd al-Malik, "ma huwa al-ta'uyush al-silmi?" *Ruz al-Yusuf* No. 1466 (16 July 1956): 22–23. The five principles on which both were based are: mutual respect for national sovereignty, non-aggression, non-interference in internal affairs, equality, and peaceful co-existence.
43 Ihsan 'Abd al-Quddus, "Hadha al-rajul huwa al-sha'b," *Ruz al-Yusuf* No. 1468 (30 July 1956): 3.
44 Mahmud Amin al-'Alim, "Wataniyyatuna," *Ruz al-Yusuf* No. 1462 (18 June 1956): 6–7.
45 Fathi Khalil, "Suriya khatwa ula," *Ruz al-Yusuf* No. 1465 (9 July 1956): 5.
46 See for the unity with Syria the following articles: Ahmad Baha' al-Din, "Suriya wa Misr..bi-shaja'a," *Ruz al-Yusuf* No. 1545 (20 January 1958): 3–4; Ahmad Baha' al-Din, "Sulta markaziyya wahida tunaffidh al-wahda," *Ruz al-Yusuf* No. 1546 (27 January 1958): 3 and 38; Ahmad Baha' al-Din, "Mujtama' taqaddumi ... li-l-dawla al-muttahida," *Ruz al-Yusuf* No. 1547 (3 February 1958): 8–9; Ahmad Baha' al-Din, "Athar tarattabat 'ala mawlid al-Jumhuriyya al-'Arabiyya al-Muttahida," *Ruz al-Yusuf* No. 1553 (17 March 1958): 3–4; Ihsan 'Abd al-Quddus, "Mashakil," *Ruz al-Yusuf* No. 1546 (27 January 1958): 6–7; Ihsan 'Abd al-Quddus, "Alladhina yu'aridun al-wahda ... bi-labaqa," *Ruz al-Yusuf* No. 1547 (3 February 1958): 3–5; Fathi Khalil, "Himayat al-wahda," *Ruz al-Yusuf* No. 1548 (10 February 1958): 10; Fathi Ghanim, "Alladhina yastafidun min al-wahda," *Ruz al-Yusuf* No. 1548 (10 February 1958): 8–9. Fathi Ghanim, "Fatrat al-intiqal," *Ruz al-Yusuf* No. 1553 (17 March 1958): 5.
47 *al-Khutut al-ra'isiyya li-barnamij al-Hizb al-Shuyu'i al-Misri al-Muwahhad*. Cited in Rif'at al-Sa'id, *Munazzamat al-yasar al-Misri, 1950–1957* (Cairo: Dar al-Thaqafa al-Jadida, 1983), 256.
48 *Mashru' taktik al-Hizb al-Shuyu'i al-Muwahhad*. Cited in Rif'at al-Sa'id, 257–9.
49 Cited in Rif'at al-Sa'id, 267.
50 *Kifah al-Sha'b* No. 9 (December 1955): 1.
51 Zaki Murad, *Hawla wajibina iza'a Misr al-mustaqilla*. Cited in Rif'at al-Sa'id, 268.
52 Murad, *Hawla wajibina*, 269.
53 Cited in Rif'at al-Sa'id, 273.
54 *Bayan min Tali'at al-'Ummal ila al-sha'b al-Misri*. Leaflet published in January–February 1955.
55 *Min Tali'at al-'Ummal. Khitab maftuh ila ra'is al-wuzara'*. Leaflet published between April and September 1955.
56 *al-Haraka al-wataniyya fi marhalat al-intisar 'ala al-isti'mar wa-l-raj'iyya*. Pamphlet published in September 1955.
57 *Khittat al-hizb al-shuyu'i al-Misri al-muwahhad*. Leaflet published in March 1956.
58 *Khitta*, 1.

59 *Khitta*, 2.
60 Zaki Murad, "Hawla al-tabi'a al-tabaqiyya li-hukumat al-dubbat," *al-Kadir* No. 21 (May 1957): 1–15. The report was written in July 1956 and only printed in the internal cadre bulletin of the UECP in May 1957, as is stated on the front page of the issue.
61 Murad, "Hawla al-tabi'a," 2.
62 Murad, "Hawla al-tabi'a," 5. See also *Khitta*.
63 "Nahwa jabha wataniyya wasi'a," *Sawt al-Fallahin* No. 8 (April 1956): 1–3.
64 *al-Isti'mar huwa al-'aduw al-awwal*.
65 *al-Hiyad*, "Matbu'at Tali'at al-'Ummal" (January 1956).
66 Anouar Abdel-Malek, *Égypte société militaire* (Paris: Éditions du Seuil, 1962), 120–1.
67 See also Joel Beinin, "The Communist Movement and Nationalist Political Discourse in Nasirist Egypt," *The Middle East Journal* 41 (Autumn 1987): 568–84.
68 *al-Muqawama al-Sha'biyya* No. 1 (9 January 1956): 1. See also Ahmad Sadiq Sa'd's brochure written in support of the regime against the foreign invasion: Ahmad Sadiq Sa'd, *As'ila wa ajwiba hawla al-mawqif al-hadir* (Cairo: n.p., 1956).
69 "Jabha wataniyya muttahida shamila," *al-Kadir* No. 13 (October 1956): 1.
70 "Jabha wataniyya," 8.
71 See for a more detailed account of the communist resistance at Suez: Ahmad Rifa'i and 'Abd al-Mun'im, *Ayyam al-intisar* (Cairo: Dar al-Dimuqratiyya al-Jadida, 1957).
72 "Tariquna tawil ... wa 'aduwuna ghadir," *al-Intisar* (19 December 1956): 1–2.
73 "Lijan al-muqawama al-sha'biyya tuwasilu nash'ataha," *Kifah al-Sha'b* No. 23 (December 1956): 2.
74 (title of the article unreadable) *Kifah al-Sha'b* No. 24 (January 1957): 1.
75 "al-Jabha al-muttahida hiyya al-sabil al-wahid amama Misr," *Kifah al-Sha'b* No. 28 (February 1957): 3.
76 Roger Owen, "The Economic Consequences of the Suez Crisis for Egypt," in *Suez 1956: The Crisis and its Consequences*, edited by W.M. Roger Louis and Roger Owen (Oxford: Clarendon Press, 1989), 367.
77 'Ali al-Shalaqani, "al-Takhtit al-iqtisadi ... ma'raka siyasiyya," *al-Masa'*, 3 February 1957, 5.
78 'Abd al-Raziq Hasan, "Iqtisaduna qabla wa ba'da al-ma'raka," *al-Masa'*, 29 December 1956.
79 Khalid Muhyi al-Din, "Qawanin al-taharrur al-iqtisadi," *al-Masa'*, 16 January 1957.
80 Al-Iqtisadi, "al-Mu'assasa al-iqtisadiyya wa dawruha fi al-iqtisad al-Misri," *al-Masa'*, 16 January 1957, 5.
81 Al-Iqtisadi, "al-Mu'assasa al-iqtisadiyya wa dawruha fi al-iqtisad al-Misri," *al-Masa'*, 1 January 1957, 5.
82 'Adil Thabit, "Usus al-takhtit al-qawmi al-shamil," *al-Masa'*, 27 January 1957, 5.
83 'Ali al-Shalaqani, "al-Takhtit al-iqtisadi ... ma'raka siyasiyya," *al-Masa'*, 3 February 1957, 5.
84 'Ali al-Shalaqani, "Asbab al-takhtit al-qawmi wa madkhal al-dawla," *al-Masa'*, 6 February 1957, 5.
85 Al-Iqtisadi, "Ziyadat al-kifa'a al-intajiyya fi sabil iqtisad mustaqirr mutatawwir," *al-Masa'*, 9 May 1957, 5.

86 Nahid Abu Zahra, "Tamsir al-sharikat al-musahama," *al-Masa'*, 6 March 1957, 5.
87 'Ali al-Shalaqani, "Ba'da 3 sanawat musahamat al-hukuma fi al-tasni'i," *al-Masa'*, 27 March 1957, 5.
88 'Ali al-Shalaqani, "Nashat al-Bank al-Sina'i fi 'am," *al-Masa'*, 3 April 1957, 5.
89 Al-Iqtisadi, "Mashru' qanun al-tanzim al-sina'i," *al-Masa'*, 9 April 1957.
90 'Ali al-Shalaqani, "Mashru' al-sanawat al-khams. Ba'd al-i'tibarat al-siyasiyya," Part I, *al-Masa'*, 2 December 1957, 5.
91 'Ali al-Shalaqani, "Mashru' al-sanawat al-khams. Ba'd al-i'tibarat al-siyasiyya," Part IV, *al-Masa'*, 10 December 1957, 5.
92 Husayn Kamal al-Din, "al-Bahth al-'ilmi fi al-jumhuriyya al-'arabiyya al-muttahida," *al-Masa'*, 17 February 1958.
93 Rashid al-Barrawi, "al-Janib al-mansi min al-mushkila al-jami'iyya," *al-Masa'*, 15 October 1957.
94 'Ali al-Shalaqani, "Mashru' al-sanawat al-khams. Ba'd al-i'tibarat al-siyasiyya," Part V, *al-Masa'*, 15 December 1957, 5.
95 Husayn Kamal al-Din, "al-Bahth al-'ilmi fi Misr," Part I, *al-Masa'*, 5 January 1958, 5.
96 Husayn Kamal al-Din, "al-Bahth al-'ilmi fi Misr," Part II, *al-Masa'*, 6 January 1958, 5.
97 'Adil Thabit, "Tanzim al-buhuth al-'ilmiyya bi-l-wizarat," *al-Masa'*, 11 January 1958, 5.
98 'Adil Thabit, "Tamwil al-buhuth al-'ilmiyya: takhsis nisba min al-dakhl al-qawmi aw masrufat al-mujtama'," *al-Masa'*, 2 March 1958, 5.
99 James C. Scott, *Seeing Like a State: How Certain Schemes to Improve the Human Condition Have Failed* (New Haven: Yale University Press, 1998), 87–102.

◆ CHAPTER SIX ◆

The Hegemony of Authoritarian Modernism, 1958

Introduction

This chapter further explores the way in which liberal, socialist, and communist intellectuals supported and helped formulate the discourse of authoritarian modernism in the second half of the 1950s. In analyzing their thought, it is important to realize that their backing of this discourse was not a result of their fear of the repressive power of the new regime. As we have seen in the previous chapter, authoritarian modernism was already part of the reformist ideology of these intellectuals, which made it less difficult to help develop this discourse. The discourse itself was still in the process of being formed and had not been officially sanctioned or rigidly drawn up, as would be the case under Arab socialism in the 1960s. For this reason, these intellectuals could still fulfill their mission as "opinion makers" (*ashab al-ra'y*) more independently. Censorship existed, and the state was to show its repressive face in 1959 when the members of the communist movement would once again be incarcerated. Nonetheless, the press was still largely independent, and the scope of civil society was narrow, but not destroyed. If room for criticism was limited, one was not forced to show enthusiasm to the degree that the intellectuals did in the period from 1955 to 1958. The discourse of authoritarian modernism gained its position of hegemony because of their acceptance of many of its features and their willingness to support and expand it. In many ways it was their creation. Unwittingly, however, they also strengthened the authoritarian strain within their own discourse and undermined its democratic content.

As we have seen in the previous chapter, one of the central elements in authoritarian modernism is economic planning. Economic planning and social engineering in the form of land reform were symbolic of the rationalization of society as a whole and had far-reaching implications. Planning legitimated extensive state penetration into many new fields of activity. Once the state had freed itself of the control of "special interests," Egyptian reformist intellectuals saw it as the main benefactor of society. They treated the state as a neutral force that stood above society and could order it efficiently and disinterestedly. Many believed that only the state had the power to achieve the goals of the nationalist movement and the capacity to hire expertise and put it to good use, as was apparent in economic planning institutions and the five-year plans. After the nationalization of the Suez Canal Company, a boundless trust emerged in the institutionalization of science, expertise, and planning together with the belief that such institutionalization would automatically lead to progress.

The reformist intellectuals began to apply the concept of planning in all its formulations (*tawjih, takhtit, tarshid*) to culture, political education and political debate, the idea of democracy itself, and other fields of activity previously outside the state's purview. This and other features of the discourse of authoritarian modernism had large implications. The emphasis on quantity and output instead of quality and authenticity meant that progress could be expressed in production and output statistics — it was tangible and measurable. Moreover, it could be controlled by the state. Conversely, if progress could not be measured, officially controlled, and sanctioned, it was considered suspect and subversive. This positivist, etatist perception of progress turned out to be all the more limiting when it was combined with nationalism and associated with national liberation and the defense of the "national mind" (*al-'aql al-watani*). The consequences of this type of reasoning for other discourses are apparent in the debate on culture that was held even before the Bandung period, in 1954–55. It was believed that, much like economic planning, "cultural production" (*intaj al-thaqafa*) could be guided by the state, which could produce "books of guidance" (*kutub al-tawjihiyya*). Besides controlling the national culture, the state was also assumed to be able to protect it from foreign "dumping" practices, which undermined the "national mind" (*al-'aql al-watani*) very much in the same way that the unbridled importation of foreign competitive goods undermined the national economy.

Politics itself, the heart of the democratic strain in the secular liberal, socialist, and communist reform programs of the 1940s, was seriously affected by the discourse of economic planning. The conception of politics as a means of solving social, economic, and political conflict through rational debate had been central to the struggle of the secular intellectuals against the monarchy. This view was substituted by a new technocracy of planning, arrogated to state institutions. As had been true under monarchical rule, public opinion once again became a political factor to be controlled and directed, not respected and encouraged through education. The difference with the earlier period is that public opinion was no longer manipulated through patronage or mobilized by populism. Supported by the ideology of "building" and "construction" (*bina'*), politics was now to be geared to creating national unity and mobilizing the population.

Discipline, in the sense of honesty, frugality, dedication, and accountability, had always been an integral part of the liberal reformist program of groups like the Society of National Renaissance. Now, however, the intellectuals associated discipline increasingly with the state — it was seen as part of the job of the central bureaucracy, in agreement with its specific logic. Democracy became the purpose of national liberation and social transformation, both of which were firmly in the hands of the state and subordinated to the policy of the new leadership. The intellectuals' high regard for the "rationalization" of society also encouraged the application of materialist and realist concepts to art, historiography, and philosophy. On the whole, therefore, the secular intellectual worldview in this period became increasingly mechanistic and objectivistic. The strong developmentalist strain in political and cultural discourse gave rise to an economically reductionist perspective on society, history, and politics.

Another crucial feature of the discourse of authoritarian modernism was the tendency to think in dichotomous terms. The idea that Egypt had reached modernity, or was in the process of reaching it, enabled reformist intellectuals to posit an exaggerated contrast with the previous "stage" of history. In accordance with the modernist streak in their historical thinking, they treated the past as binary opposite, in negative terms, of the present.[1] As we have seen in previous chapters, the reformists argued that politicians of the past era were "corrupt," its political system "traditional," its feelings of coherence based on "tribal solidarity" (*asabiyya*). Its rulers were considered "feudal" and its economy "monopolistic." "Compromise" (*tahadun*) and an "understanding" (*tafahum*) with imperialism had

210

undermined the nationalist struggle for independence. And while society as whole had been afflicted by "mental stagnation" (*rukud al-fikri*), which derived in part from its "Eastern mentality" (*al-'aqliyya al-Sharqiyya*) and "superstition" (*khurafat*), imperialism had deepened the backwardness of society by "dividing" (*taftit*), "corrupting" (*tazyif*), and "fragmenting" (*tamziq*) its national personality. The new, modern society was, of course, painted in bright colors.

By creating this dichotomy between traditional and modern, backward and developing, intellectually stagnant and progressively evolving, intellectuals legitimated not only the new regime, but also their own role in the process of modernization. In much the same way as the economic planners, they saw themselves directing the nation to a bright future from their elevated position of authority as the intellectual vanguard. They claimed to have obtained the authority for this task on account of their superior knowledge, which enabled them to lead the nation to "renewal" (*tajdid*) and bring about a "renaissance" (*nahda*), a "mission" (*risala*) the past generation had not accomplished. As modern intellectuals, they believed they were capable of fathoming the "national mind" (*al-'aql al-watani*) and creating with that knowledge a new "collective personality" (*shakhsiyyat majmu'*) that was appropriate to the new era. As politicians, they could educate the citizens and instill in them a new revolutionary discipline and "consciousness" (*wa'y*). And while as historians they could evaluate the nation's historical past, analyze its historical laws, and determine its "mission" (*risala*), as philosophers they could provide the country with a "rational, scientific philosophy" (*al-falsafa al-'aqliyya al-'ilmiyya*).

A fascinating aspect of the new role of the intellectuals was that they were not only to determine the domestic road to modernity and define its enemies, but also to navigate Egypt past international obstacles to modernity. This explains the appearance in the 1950s of the new genre of the travelogue. Travelogues were written by Egyptians who, like modern-day Ibn Batutas, discovered an emerging world of countries like Egypt that had rid themselves of their colonizing masters and faced the same problems of modernization. In the constructivist era of the period between 1955 and 1958, characterized by its conviction that society was malleable, the reformist intellectuals of the 1940s felt as if they had become "engineers of the human mind" (*muhandisin al-'aql al-insaniyya*). This would finally allow them to bring the nation "in accordance with the spirit of the times."

A Modern Democracy

"A guided democracy"

The intellectual support for the regime's foreign and economic policy and the new self-consciousness that accompanied it had direct consequences for the conception of democracy that was to prevail in the second half of the 1950s. If the general trend was towards independence and the realization of a separation between capitalism and communism in the fields of economics and foreign policy, the same applied to democracy.

This new development was already discernable in May 1955, when Ihsan Abd al-Quddus stated, "in principle democracy is international and applicable to all times and circumstances ... but democratic systems must always have local variations that comply with the nature of the people and the local circumstances and must develop in accordance with the natural development of the people."[2] The new constitution with its economic and social guarantees and its corporatist structure was promulgated in January 1956. Ihsan Abd al-Quddus welcomed it as the logical outcome of the long nationalist struggle for independence and democracy waged since Urabi, thereby incorporating the revolution into Egypt's national history. He contrasted the 1923 Constitution, which had been at the mercy of imperialist manipulation and provided it with the opportunity to extend its control over the country by proxy, with the new constitution, which was guarded by "the army as the revolutionary spiritual vanguard of the nation."[3] Moreover, the new constitution guaranteed "a democracy that emanates from its own history, heritage (*turath*) and belief system,"[4] while it provided for "economic democracy without which democratic experiments cannot flourish."[5]

That Ihsan Abd al-Quddus recognized the nature of the new situation is apparent from his support for Nasser's presidency in June 1956. Just like at the beginning of the revolution, he stresses that the social basis of the regime consists of a coalition of peasants, workers, and the middle classes, the progressive forces that had led all Egyptian revolutions. The army, he writes, had chosen the side of the people throughout the nationalist struggle and had become its representative, while Nasser had become its "leader" (*za'im*). He points out that the position of "leader" and not just president involves well-defined responsibilities towards the people: "The difference is that a president simply holds an office, while a leader has principles." The principles to which Nasser was now obliged to abide were, in al-Quddus's view, neutralism, ending the power of capital, socialism, Pan-Arabism, and democracy.[6]

Under the monarchy, modernist intellectuals had called for circumscribing the powers of the executive and expanding the powers of the legislative. Now, the infiltration of their discourse by the terminology of authoritarian modernism limited this possibility. Increasingly, democratic discourse was eroded by technocratic arguments and by the terminology of efficiency and authoritarian organization. Authority and hierarchy, as well as privileged knowledge and expertise, were gaining importance as the state itself was expanding. Even if the modernists wanted to enlarge the powers of parliament at the expense of the powers of the president, they believed that parliamentary powers had to be subject to regimentation and disciplined by means of a cadre party to form a counterbalance to the president and defend the revolution.

By the time parliamentary elections were held in June 1957, belated on account of the Suez Canal Crisis, technocratic efficiency and revolutionary fervor had become the overriding principles of political thought. Ihsan Abd al-Quddus applied them first of all to the new state-led party, the National Union, which he argued had to be grounded in a firm revolutionary ideology. He pinned his hopes on a new generation that would be able to adopt a new political consciousness, and he argued for new schoolbooks and the establishment of "popular political schools" (*madaris siyasiyya sha'biyya*), at which the principles of the revolution would be taught and which would be able to consolidate the authority of the regime and the revolution further. Similarly, a school for all higher officials would groom them for their tasks and strengthen the revolutionary mentality.[7] Like the economy, politics would have to be "guided."

In a modern Egyptian society, the application of the principles of controlled democracy to parliament meant its members must have a higher education. But unlike in the reform program of the Society of National Renaissance, politicians now had a more distinctive professional purpose: they were to support the revolution and the ideas behind it. Ihsan Abd al-Quddus believed that after five years, in which the social revolution had been carried out by force from above, the time had come to delegate power to parliament, which should become a responsible institution. He sums up the idea of "guided democracy" by stipulating, "[t]hese currents become part of democracy as long as they endorse the principles of the revolution."[8]

He immediately uses this principle in his discussion of co-operative socialism. Not in favor of state socialism, he pleads for divesting the new state property to private persons and thus creating co-operative socialism. Income and profit, he argues, should be produced by labor. Planning (*takhtit*) will see to it that this is accomplished in an orderly fashion.[9]

The extent to the notion of a planned economy had infiltrated the vocabulary of politics is perhaps even more apparent in the complex writings of Ahmad Baha al-Din, who points out the dangers that democracy faces in a state-dominated economy. He defends the "guided democracy" with the argument that political society in Egypt under the monarchy had been deplorable. Society overall had been dominated by a class that regarded it as its own "estate" (*'izba*), political parties were only interested in coming to power by whatever means necessary, and widespread poverty had made social justice imperative. Consequently, he argues, justice has to prevail over the sanctity of private property, and industrialization demands a certain measure of coercion: "To force some people to relinquish their privileges and others to guide their investments (*tawjih mustathmirihim*) presupposes a guided democracy (*tawjih al-dimuqratiyya*)."[10]

All the same, Ahmad Baha al-Din shows his awareness of the dangers of "planning" (*tawjih*) turning into "tutelage" (*wisaya*). He argues that a guided democracy presupposes the same rules as a Western democracy: both the state and the citizen should be subject to the law. Further, he criticizes those who completely reject the Western model of democracy: "We must study the subject, like all democratic experiments, in the light of our circumstances and the interests we pursue. However, we must keep in mind what it means that the people rule themselves." True democracy, he claims, entails training and a long period of experience. It would therefore be impossible to implement a democracy by undemocratic means, "because you cannot construct a democracy like a building or a factory behind a wall to unveil it suddenly."[11]

In another article, however, democracy is clearly subordinated to social and economic "progress" and planning. This becomes the case when Ahmad Baha al-Din defines modernity no longer as the dissemination of democratic discourse among the whole population, but begins to see the spread of technocracy throughout society as its prerequisite:

> We will buy from abroad machinery and factories that are based on the language of modernity. But the acquisition of

these machines and factories and having the engineers to run them is not enough. It is important that we acquire the mind that has created and built these machines. A mentality that respects science and expertise and applies scientific methods to everything that obstructs the development of that mind.

He adds that the essential criteria that differentiate barbarism from civilization are expertise and organization, or in other words the capacity to build and develop. Respect for science, says Ahmad Baha al-Din, should expand to include "all sectors of life."[12]

This infiltration of democratic discourse with technocratic concepts would become a common pattern, in spite of resistance from liberal intellectuals like Ahmad Baha al-Din himself and Fathi Ghanim. For instance, Fathi Ghanim criticized the etatist concept of planning, pointing out the tensions as a result of the growing power of the state and its increasing interference in the life of the individual. Through planning (*takhtit*) of education and labor, the state was increasingly directing (*tawjih*) the personal life of the individual. But although he was aware of the dangers, Fathi Ghanim did not object to this greater degree of state intervention in and of itself. In his eyes, it was permissible as long as the state convinced the people of its necessity, and this could only be done if it allowed them a larger measure of participation.[13] In this way, corporatism, which would become the overriding principle, crept into the discourse of democratic modernism.

A vote for modernity

Eventually, the communist movement joined the discourse of guided democracy. The elections of June 1957 definitively established the subordination of the communist movement to the regime. The regime disbanded the Liberation Rally and founded the National Union in its stead, but the new party bore no resemblance to the popular committees of resistance envisioned by the communist movement. On the contrary, although the founding of the National Union marked a conspicuous shift towards the middle classes, which the regime favored, it was not a political organization that was meant to mobilize the population.

Despite these handicaps the communist movement joined the elections enthusiastically. It had become almost impossible to pose democratic demands since the elections had become so fully enmeshed in the whole social and economic modernization program, which the regime defended against foreign intervention. This logic is evident in *Kifah al-Sha'b*'s pronouncement in March that these elections would be the most important in the parliamentary history of Egypt because they presented an opportunity for "the broad masses to unify all nationalist forces in the united front on the basis of a certain program."[14] Or, as was declared in one of the following issues, "the coming elections are a struggle against imperialism, and this struggle should concentrate on the eviction of the reactionary henchmen of imperialism and the election of nationalist elements in the coming parliament, so that it reflects the peaceful, independent, progressive politics that Egypt pursues."[15]

The same attitude can be found in articles in *al-Masa'* that were written to show the support of the different communist organizations for the regime. Abu Sayf Yusuf, member of the Central Committee of the Workers' Vanguard, explicitly states that the elections are first and foremost a vote of confidence in the revolution – a vote for independence, national sovereignty, peace, and Arab unity. He claims that the elections are also directed against internal reactionary elements.[16] The prominent communist intellectual Abd al-Azim Anis argues that the call for opposition is unnecessary and even treacherous in the present circumstances, in which Egypt is under threat from the United States and the Eisenhower Doctrine. Although he maintains that members of parliament should exert "supervision" (*raqaba*) over the government, he agrees with the regime that this task should be based on "positive criticism" (*fikrat al-naqd al-ijabi*), not on "aggressive criticism" (*fikrat al-hujum*).[17] This entailed control and surveillance of new members. To eliminate the possibility of treacherous elements joining the elections, candidates would have to be forced to present their program.[18]

Perhaps the most important commentary on the elections published in *al-Masa'* was written by Fu'ad Mursi. As Secretary-General of the CPE, which had recently joined the Unified Egyptian Communist Party to form the United Egyptian Communist Party, his support meant an important shift away from the former policy of his organization, which had called the regime "fascist" in the past. In *al-Masa'* he conveys clearly how the communist movement had put itself in the service of the authoritarian modernization program of the regime. He introduces his series of articles by stressing the enormous progress that Egypt had made:

Today Egypt is going through a complete renaissance (*nahda shamila*) represented in these fundamental transformations, which have been obtained and continue to be obtained in our social, economic, and political structure and our international position. These transformations, expressed in the last instance in the complete revolution in our means of living, reveal forcefully this deep-seated will of ours for renovation (*tajdid*) and the pursuit of human perfection.[19]

Although Mursi is critical of the coming elections, he compares the present form of Egyptian democracy to the "traditional" forms of democracy as they evolved after the French revolution. These forms knew opposition, but this was not always necessary, for, he claims, "democracy is not a goal in itself, rather it is a *means* to wage the struggle for social progress." This instrumental concept of democracy is enhanced by his relativist philosophy of particular circumstances:

> Democracy is realized in every country *in accordance with its social, economic, and political level of development* and is commensurate with the purpose of the political struggle that its sons, one generation after the other, wage for progress. Democracy is realized to the degree that all of the people participate in realizing the historical mission that a *particular* country has set itself at a *particular* time.[20]

At this stage in Egyptian history, Mursi asserts, democracy is a channel through which the peasants, workers, and intellectuals can express their historical mission; "it is the freedom to express their historical goals and organize themselves to realize them." This freedom applies to the majority and not to the minority, and it does not necessarily involve the existence of "divided opinion" (*inqisam al-ra'y*), a "multi-party system" (*ta'addud al-ahzab*), or the "establishment of an opposition" (*qiyam al-mu'arada*). Democracy, he writes, means the protection of the majority by the government.[21] Before, democracy had protected colonialism, despotism, and feudalism, but now, says Mursi, "for the first time in our modern history the Egyptian people enjoy the freedom to express their nationalist goals and organize themselves internally to realize them." Therefore, there is no need for an opposition as there was in the past, when democracy worked to the advantage of imperialism.[22]

Having identified themselves to such a large extent with the government, the members of the communist movement turned against their former, ambiguous "allies" whom they had tried to organize in the National Democratic Front in 1953–54. Following the policy of weeding out "opportunistic, hesitating or treacherous elements ... and [helping to] cut off the head of conspiracies," their attention was directed at spotting these plots. Candidates who posed a threat to the revolution typically did not have any political program, and their electorate was based on money and "patronage" (*'asabiyya*). Their purpose, it was revealed, was to divide the "nationalists" (*al-wataniyyun*) and destroy the revolution.[23]

The new internal publication of the United Egyptian Communist Party, *Hayat al-Hizb*, included an extensive, generally positive evaluation of the elections.[24] Their purpose had been "not simply to establish a parliament, but to elect a revolutionary parliament that has as its task the preservation of the revolution; not to terminate it but to extend it."[25] To a large degree, *Hayat al-Hizb* concludes, the elections seemed to have fulfilled these hopes. Despite the weak representation of the workers in parliament, a future task for the UECP, the report argues, "the working class is beginning to occupy its political place in our country and participate in the revolution, giving it direction."[26] The same applies to the peasants: "for the first time the peasant has liberated himself from the power of feudalism to go to the ballot box to choose."[27]

The Role of the Intellectual

Planning a new collective personality

A significant indication of the changing relationship of the middle class intelligentsia with the new regime as well as their trust in state planning and the adoption and further development of the modernization paradigm was their increasing dependence on the state for realizing their cultural agenda. This is clearly reflected in the debate on the "Egyptian personality" (*al-shakhsiyya al-Misriyya*), to which Ihsan Abd al-Quddus contributed in the form of a series of articles in *Ruz al-Yusuf*.

In his first article Ihsan Abd al-Quddus explains the issue and defines the "collective personality" (*shakhsiyyat majmuʿ*) as consisting of the totality of Egyptian culture, its houses, social relations, traditions, belief systems, music, and art. According to Ihsan Abd al-Quddus, this collective personality is in a state of crisis as a result of its disintegration into a "bewildering fluidity" (*ma'i'a ha'ira*). As a consequence, it has lost its particular characteristics and coherence, and solidarity has been replaced by individualism. He ascribes this crisis to the ages of imperialist domination, which have separated thought from emotions. While reason (*'uqul*) follows Western models in thought and custom, the emotions of Egyptians have resisted these models, with widespread alienation as result. In his view, there are two ways to counter this alienation: following religion or following science. Religion has failed because it relies completely on emotions and religious education has not attained modern standards. Therefore, he argues, science and rationalism remain as the only solution.[28]

In a second article, Ihsan Abd al-Quddus continues this line of argument, repeating his desire for the formation of a totally new personality and citing Turkey under Atatürk and India during the time of Gandhi's leadership of the Congress Party as examples. The Turkish experiment in particular fascinates him. He is interested in this type of radical Westernization program to produce a new personality, but says that it could take decades before such a program would take root among the population. In the Egyptian situation, however, he claims that such a total transformation would be problematic. In the past, that road has been blocked by the aristocracy, which has been completely assimilated with the colonial dominant culture. First adopting Turkish and then Western high culture, the Egyptian aristocracy has never developed nationalist credentials and has acted as a pawn in the hands of imperialism. To al-Quddus, the one authentic class is the Egyptian *fallahin* (peasant), the only class that has remained "untarnished" by Western influences and has kept thousand-year-old traditions intact. In between these two cultures stand the middle classes – the real subject of Ihsan Abd al-Quddus's series. Torn between modernism and tradition, rationality and emotions, as the most dynamic and progressive class, the middle classes are in a crisis that affects society as a whole. For that reason, he concludes, "stabilization" (*istiqrar*) of the personality of this class and the adoption of stable, clear models and ideals will insure stability and progress for Egyptian society as a whole.[29]

In his third article Ihsan Abd al-Quddus provides his readers with his populist, romantic solution in which the *fallahin* are the source of an authentic personality, while the middle classes have the task of transforming the old traditions to form a modern personality:

> It is important that we take the traditions of the *fallahin* as the basis of the search for the modern Egyptian personality because

they possess the only traditions that have been conserved in an exceptional and strong personality that has succeeded in resisting Western cultures. We cannot build something unless we base ourselves on our own *turath* ... the tradition that contains in itself new directions, our experience, and our pride.[30]

According to Ihsan Abd al-Quddus, a "renaissance" (*nahda*) consists in bringing about "harmony" (*tawfiq*) between international ideas and ideas that are developed in one's own country. International ideologies, he writes, should be adapted and pressed into the service of national interests, which are determined by the specific circumstances. As in the case of the peasant culture as a source of national culture, it is the task of the middle classes to construct such a common culture for society within an international context.[31]

Ahmad Baha al-Din formulates the tasks of the middle classes in a much more clear-cut, reformist political terminology within the model of the national front and its class coalition. His main contention is that the declining power of the "feudal class" and the weakness of the industrial class and the proletariat leave the middle classes as the only social category that can lead Egypt to national liberation and progress. Its enlightened members, the intellectuals, students, professors, and members of the liberal professions, who are the most eager to accept new ideas, form the most revolutionary group: "If the feudalists are the bulwark of conservatism, then this group constitutes the engine of innovation and resistance." It is the task of this group to spread ideas and further national consciousness. Furthermore, it must defend freedom and social justice, and see to it that national capital remains independent. By assuming these responsibilities, he writes, this group will enlighten the other classes of the front and lead Egypt to progress and development.[32]

For Ahmad Baha al-Din, just like for Ihsan Abd al-Quddus, the role of the middle classes as the vanguard of the nationalist movement also implies their cultural hegemony and imposes on them the task of defining the Egyptian collective personality. A greater internationalist than Ihsan Abd al-Quddus, Ahmad Baha al-Din was forced to balance his Egyptian cultural nationalism with his strong international sympathies and his admiration for international political models, especially the British Labour Party, on which he wrote numerous articles. His major contribution to the former enterprise was his book on Egyptian history, *Historical Days*.[33]

Characteristically, Ahmad Baha al-Din looked to the state to shield national culture in the same way it protected the national economy. His anxiety concerned in particular Western low culture, that is, magazines, such as *Readers' Digest*, and cheap books, which were translated into Arabic and, he claims, heavily subsidized. He compares the import of these publications to Japanese dumping practices and demands that the state take measures to protect the "national mind" (*al-'aql al-watani*) against this onslaught. He argues for a protectionist cultural policy, writing, "the citizen who clothes himself in a British suit made of American textile for which he pays a few pounds does not have grave consequences ... but the citizen who acquires a British or an American mind we have lost forever." He concludes that, while liberals should support freedom of the press and encourage foreign translations, Western cultural influence should be controlled and conditional:

> We need Western translations on condition that the mind (*'aql*) that translates them is Egyptian and the hand that translates them is Egyptian and the money that finances them is Egyptian ... We only want Egyptians to know as much about Urabi as Napoleon, as much about the struggle for the constitution in Egypt as the liberation of slaves in America. We only want to retain our Egyptian interpretation of the world.[34]

The debate on national culture had deep roots among the nationalist coalition and reflects its attempts to control nationalist, modernist discourse. Communists like Mahmud Amin al-Alim took up the issue in *Ruz al-Yusuf* in 1955, more than a year after Ahmad Baha al-Din wrote this. He demands in much stronger terms that the state pass "legislation that will protect our national existence against the all-consuming attacks that the American press has launched against us." Three unnamed weeklies and four monthly journals translated into Arabic were cause for alarm:

> If they are translated into our Arabic language they form a severe strain on the modern, nationalist spirit (*wijdan*) ... The translation of American magazines and their publication in Arabic means the introduction of a non-nationalist element in our modern nationalist culture. It means that we renounce the idea that our press has the function of mirroring national opinion.[35]

However, in their theoretical work on Egyptian culture, Mahmud Amin al-Alim and Muhammad Anis reject the central premise of the discourse of authenticity, i.e. that there is a chasm between a "Western mentality" (*al-'aqliyya al-gharbiyya*) and an "Eastern mentality" (*al-'aqliyya al-sharqiyya*). They maintain that there exists only one human mentality and that wherever national differences are in evidence, they are based on social circumstances that have been produced by imperialism. They write that because imperialism has blocked Egyptian cultural development, just like its economic development, "our social praxis consists of the continuous struggle to liberate ourselves from imperialism, economically, politically and culturally." The true "Egyptian cultural personality" (*al-shakhsiyya al-thaqafiyya al-Misriyya*) could only come about if it was integrated into the nationalist struggle and supported that struggle.[36]

In essence, all these views on Egyptian culture and the Egyptian renaissance were modernist. Whether they harped back to the mythical Egyptian "cultural heritage" (*al-turath*) or looked to the middle classes themselves or to the praxis of the revolutionary, nationalist struggle, these writers intended to create or defend a completely new Egyptian collective personality that would sever its ties with a past associated with the *ancien régime* and its cosmopolitan higher culture. This trend gained momentum as all proponents of the new Egyptian personality looked to the state to impose the supremacy of the middle classes, to instill a certain ideology in the other classes, or to defend the country against foreign, cultural penetration. In the latter half of the 1950s, *takhtit* of culture became as common a term as *takhtit* of the economy. Culture was something that could now be planned and practiced. As Muhammad Awda put it, reflecting the increasingly technocratic strain of nationalist discourse, "The intellectual is the engineer of the human mind. It is his mission to liberate it from all its limitations in order that possibilities will present themselves for the construction of life."[37] In the new symbiosis of the state and the middle classes, the intellectuals of the middle class could provide this service.

Fulfillment of the historical mission

An important factor in the communist movement's acceptance of the regime was the communist idea of national history. Although theoretically it involves the predominance of the working class, in its authoritarian reformist stance, this view of history leads to authoritarian modernism. After the movement had begun to support the regime in 1956, a number of books were published by some of the best-known intellectuals of the communist movement. They include *The Development of the Egyptian Nationalist Movement, 1882–1956* by Shuhdi Atiyya al-Shafi'i (1912–1960),[38] *Studies in the Political History of Egypt from the Mamluk Period* by Fawzi Girgis (1914–1986),[39] and *The Land and the Peasant: The Agrarian Problem in Egypt*[40] as well as *The Nationalist Revolution*[41] by Ibrahim Amir (1922–1976). These works represent a revolution in Egyptian historiography. The traditional, mostly conservative academic historiography of the time was authored by Shafiq Ghurbal (1894–1961) and others who had been appointed during the monarchy and often wrote in praise of the king.[42] Communist historiography, by contrast, was a highly analytical and powerful expression of the ideas of the radical nationalist movement of the 1940s. Although none of these authors would gain official state sanction, they exerted a tremendous influence on the younger generation of academic historians like Muhammad Anis (1921–1986), who was to incorporate many of the concepts he found in their standard work on the Egyptian revolution.[43] These writings expanded on the modernist interpretation of Egyptian history that had been initiated by Rashid al-Barrawi, also a non-academic historian, in his *The Military Coup in Egypt*.[44] Although the communist movement had rejected al-Barrawi's work at the time, their historical studies of the 1950s came very close to his conclusion that the coup d'état was a revolution.

Egyptian Marxist historiography of the 1950s is characterized by a synthesis of economic determinism and the nationalist master narrative of emancipation of the nation. These works' support for nationalist modernization is apparent in their teleological analysis of Egyptian history as a process of continuous unfolding of national potential, growing enlightenment, and expanding "consciousness" (*wa'y*), based on the advances in cultural and political awareness and in scientific knowledge. The end of this historical process is complete independence, national redemption, and modernity. Marxists introduced into this nationalist master narrative the theme of class struggle, which moves in stages from feudalism to capitalism and eventually to socialism, each stage being represented by a dominant class and ending with the triumph of the working class. Not only is the working class regarded as the embodiment of the highest stage of consciousness and enlightenment, it is also the only class capable of achieving independence. Yet, at the same time, as we have seen, communist theory is thoroughly shot through with contradictions, manifested in the concept of the front and the ambivalence towards the national bourgeoisie, while at the same time it contains strong authoritarian, etatist, and reformist elements. Part of the task of Egyptian Marxist historiography therefore was to clarify the rise of the new authoritarian state and justify their acceptance of it by mapping the peculiar Egyptian road to modernity.

The communist historians explain the specific, "distorted" character of Egyptian history by pointing to the early absence of a (national) bourgeoisie in Egypt that would fulfill its task as the carrier of enlightenment and democracy. This absence thwarted a "natural" capitalist development. They account for this partly through the class and state formation that existed in Egypt before the French campaign. Based on the plunder and exploitation of the peasantry as well as the discouragement of trade, the Ottoman Empire or, according to Ibrahim Amir, Oriental despotism precluded the rise of an independent capitalist class that could lead the country towards development. It was not until after the old formations had been broken down by Napoleon's campaign that Egypt's modern history began and the country embarked on its convoluted road to modernity. The absence of an indigenous bourgeois capitalist class in combination with the interference of imperialism led to the domination of the large landowning class and foreign imperialist interests. Whether Egypt had become at the end of the nineteenth century "semi-feudal, semi-colonial," as Fawzi Girgis maintains, whether it remained feudal, as Shuhdi Atiyya holds, or whether it had become capitalist, as Ibrahim Amir argues, the country had been set on an "unnatural" course.

In the view of the Marxists, this unnatural economic substructure would determine to a large extent how the country's spirit of national awakening unfolded. Adopting the nationalist historiography, they maintain that the full national potential of Egypt had lain dormant. Fawzi Girgis argues, for instance, that despite centuries of oppression and invasions Egypt had always retained its "authentic Egyptian traditions," which had covered its nationalism under "a thin veil of religion" (al-ghilala al-diniyya al-raqiqa). It was the French campaign that worked "as a spark that set us on fire and released the deep revolutionary spirit."[45] This revolutionary spirit, the Marxists claim, was democratic and completely dedicated to political, economic, and cultural independence. It was a result of the distorted economic structure that this revolutionary nationalist "consciousness" (al-wa'y) had not evolved as might have been expected. These historians find evidence of the "immaturity" of the nationalist movement in its failure to achieve independence and democracy during revolts such as the 1805 uprising led by shaykh Umar Makram against Muhammad Ali, the Urabi Revolution of 1881–82, the resistance of the Nationalist Party in 1907 against the British, and the 1919 Revolution led by the Wafd.

Fawzi Girgis writes that in spite of the "distorted" economic structure, the nationalist movement did evolve into a broader and more radical movement at the beginning of the twentieth century. "Consciousness" of the true situation in which Egypt found itself expanded. Marxist historians see this for example in the public attention devoted to the necessity of industrialization and education by the leader of the Nationalist Party, Muhammad Farid (1868–1919), as well as in his concern for the rising working class movement.[46] Similarly, they regard the dissemination of the "bourgeois mentality" (*al-'aqliyya al-burjwaziyya*) among certain sections of the large landowners as a sign of progress.[47] The stronger the nationalist movement became, they find, the more frequent and forceful the demand for a constitution was. Likewise, the increasingly bolder demands for democracy and independence are seen as the expression of the growing strength of the nationalist movement.[48] Eventually, says Shuhdi Atiyya al-Shafi'i, this progressive trend was reflected in the rise of the Wafd and the eruption of the Revolution of 1919, in which, for the first time, the workers and the *fallahin* fully participated.[49]

The rise of the national bourgeoisie is another important feature of the Revolution of 1919 to which Marxist historians draw notice. They claim that the strength and the weakness of the national bourgeoisie, represented by the Wafd, determined Egyptian politics until 1952. Its strength was reflected in the gains of the revolution. These gains are listed as: the move toward independence; the beginning of the termination of the absolute power of large landowners and the king; the limitation of the power of imperialism; the introduction of a parliament; the establishment of national unity between Copts and Muslims; the creation of the right circumstances for the expansion of indigenous industry and trade; the expansion of education, and the cultural renaissance.[50] The Marxists describe the weakness of the national bourgeoisie as: the reliance on "peaceful legal means" of negotiation with the British instead of the mobilization of the masses; the resulting "compromise" (*tahadun*) with imperialism, as witnessed in the 1936 Treaty; the continuing power of feudalism, whose interests were defended by the Party of the Liberal Constitutionalists; and the failure of indigenous industrial interests to act independently from foreign capitalist interests with which they eventually formed monopolies.[51]

Fawzi Girgis describes how feudal, financial, and imperialist interests succeeded together in blocking the proper working of the parliamentary system and frustrating the nationalist movement in the attainment of its goals. As a result, fascism and fascist-oriented organizations like Young Egypt and the Muslim Brotherhood sprang up.[52] Shuhdi Atiyya al-Shafi'i writes that the Wafd was impotent as the representative of the national bourgeoisie in the face of these forces because the "class that led the national movement was weak economically, politically, and unclear ideologically. It did not realize the laws of development and could not use these laws to push the nationalist movement forward."[53]

The Marxist historians ascribe the radical stage of the nationalist movement after 1936 to the failure of the Wafd as well as to the enormous industrial expansion and the concomitant growth of the working class, especially during the Second World War. With growing social inequality, these developments led to a new "national consciousness that began to acquire a clear scientific basis, which penetrated the ranks of the intellectuals and certain sections of the Egyptian working class."[54] Although the new movement did not succeed in pushing its revolution through in 1946, the Second World War is seen as a turning point in the history of the nationalist movement, after which it acquired a completely new content. The new direction was adopted by the time of the revolution of July 1952. In this latest stage of the nationalist movement, the historians contend, economic development and full "consciousness" will finally be realized.

International circumstances further vindicated and reinforced the progressive concept of Egyptian history that was upheld by Marxist historians. The increasingly socialist orientation of Egypt and its closer ties with the East Bloc gave rise to the idea that the country was entering a stage in its history that matched the history of socialist countries. The parallel developments of the establishment of the Soviet Union and the rise of the nationalist movements in the 1920s, followed by the victory of the Soviet Union during the Second World War, the expansion of the East Bloc, the victory of the Chinese Communist Party in 1949, and the continuing de-colonization were all seen as part of the advancement towards a new civilization. To historians like Shuhdi Atiyya al-Shafi'i, the Bandung Conference and "peaceful coexistence" meant a further integration of the non-capitalist forces and the shrinkage and ultimate demise of imperialism and capitalism.[55] Even Fawzi Girgis and Ibrahim Amir, who were more critical of the new regime, believed that the increasing ties with the East Bloc and the Soviet Union would guarantee a "deepening" of the revolution. The new regime, they claimed, spelled the end of feudalism and of the power of monopoly capital. It would develop Egypt's economic potential, especially through heavy industry. Eventually, they affirmed, with further industrialization and modernization, a working class would arise that would take over the leadership of the nationalist movement and turn it into a socialist revolution.

A new philosophy for a new society

The euphoria of the Bandung period had a widespread effect on all sections of the Egyptian intelligentsia, but few intellectuals have been capable of expressing the new exuberance as well as Anwar Abd al-Malik.[56] His ideas not only convey the quest for modernity that held the radical nationalist movement in its grip; they were also couched in the discourse of authoritarian modernism that had come to dominate the second half of the 1950s. A positivistic faith in science and etatist reform, as well as the belief that Egypt had entered a new *rational* civilization when it oriented itself towards the East form the ingredients of Abd al-Malik's new philosophy. These ideas were expressed in combination with the most conspicuous characteristic of his thought: the pervasive notion of progress.

First and foremost, Abd al-Malik's faith in progress comes to the fore in the idea that his generation is superior to the previous one. In accordance with the notion of history as a progressive line, he admits that the generation of Salama Musa (1887–1958), Tawfiq al-Hakim (1899–1987), Ahmad Amin (1886–1954), Ali Abd al-Raziq (1888–1966), and Sayyid Darwish (1892–1923) contributed to Egyptian history and the rise of "modern culture/renaissance" (*al-nahda*), but at the same time did not understand the real meaning of "renewal" (*tajdid*). Typically, Abd al-Malik describes the previous stage of the nationalist movement as an intermediate, unfulfilled stage of Egyptian history.

In contrast, Abd al-Malik writes, his own generation has linked the city to the countryside, the worker to the peasant, and has created the national front that brought workers, peasants, the national bourgeoisie, and progressive intellectuals together.[57] By basing life on humanist values and science, his generation presents an "ethical model" (*qudwa akhlaqiyya*) to the rest of the nation.⁵⁸ The main source of strength of the new generation is that it is based on principles as opposed to "compromise" (*tahadun*) and a collaborationist "understanding" (*tafahum*) with imperialism.⁵⁹ He sees positive neutralism, the Bandung conference, industrialization, and an independent economy as the practical achievements of this philosophy. However, he points out three problems that, in his view, make the task of "building" (*bina'*) after Bandung a daunting one. Firstly, there is the problem of the Egyptian mentality, which he sees as still overwhelmingly backward. Secondly, the country has not yet been fully integrated into the rest of the non-capitalist world. And thirdly, the new specifically Egyptian philosophy on which the new society should be based is not yet completed.⁶⁰

Anwar Abd al-Malik ascribes the backwardness of the Egyptian mentality to the overwhelmingly agrarian character of the country. He states that Egypt still finds itself in a period of "mental stagnation" (*'ahd al-rukud al-fikri*), in which the "belief in legends" (*al-'aqliyya al-usturiyya*) predominates.⁶¹ Accordingly, he writes, Egyptian is still dominated by the "Eastern mentality" (*al-'aqliyya al-sharqiyya*), which is characterized as a state of mind "that is incapable of independent, critical thought and creativity, and that is only capable of execution, obedience (*idh'an*), and transmission (*al-naql*)." Other negative features of the Eastern mentality are that it "sanctifies that which is written" (*taqdis al-maktub*) and reproduces knowledge by heart, without the development of critical, positive faculties."⁶² Imperialism, Anwar Abd al-Malik argues, has reinforced the Eastern mentality by neglecting to carry out a broad educational policy. As a result it has "helped spread superstition (*khurafat*), idle prattle (*abatil*), and myths (*asatir*), which have undermined the capacity of the Egyptian to believe in his own mental faculties and to dominate the forces of nature and society."⁶³

Moreover, Abd al-Malik believes that imperialism has destroyed the positive qualities of the Egyptian mind. It has done this with the aim to "completely crush the personality of the subjected peoples, wipe out their distinctive characteristics, and destroy everything that could help them to develop themselves in their specific way." Colonialism has led to the "division (*taftit*), corruption (*tazyif*), and fragmentation (*tamziq*) of the national spirit in its rational and psychological aspects, with the aim to mold the colonized people as if it has no personality." As a result the "national heritage" (*al-turath al-qawmi*) of those countries that have been subjected to imperialism has become a "fragmented and broken culture" (*turath mabtur mutaqqati'*). Finally, imperialism has cut national culture off from the East, which could have nourished it.⁶⁴

The renaissance that Anwar Abd al-Malik proposes to initiate is eclectic. It borrows from both the West and the East and is based on the *turath* (national cultural heritage) at the same time. It is the task of the new generation of intellectuals to construct a philosophy on which this renaissance can be built:

> This means that the goal of philosophy is to make man more conscious in order that he works according to the principles that lead him little by little to raise existence to the essential level, that is, raise history and society to the essential humanist level by enabling him to dominate nature and the factors of social development. In this way he will become a human in control of his destiny and leave the period prior to history in which we live and enter conscious history (*al-tarikh al-wa'y*).⁶⁵

This can be achieved by following a "rational, scientific philosophy" (*al-falsafa al-'aqliyya al-'ilmiyya*) that elevates life from the level of spontaneity to the level of consciousness.⁶⁶ The modernist imagery Anwar Abd al-Malik uses to describe the renaissance derives largely from positivism and is presented in an economic vocabulary. For instance, he states that a precondition for a *nahda* is the "cultural production" (*al-intaj al-thaqafa*) of superior strategic "books of direction" (*kutub al-tawjihiyya*) on politics, culture, and economics, which deal with pressing problems and therefore stand at the top of the hierarchy of national culture. These scientific books of direction have only one goal, to obtain "objective truth" (*al-haqiqa al-mawdu'iyya*), which is described as the closest approach to "reality" (*al-waqi'*). The purpose of science, then, is "to give a more exact and faithful representation of reality by respecting its objective truth without subjective distortions."⁶⁷

In conclusion, Anwar Abd al-Malik contends that at this stage of civilization, the first goal of Egyptian intellectuals is to "liberate the Egyptian mind from its mythical orientation and direct it towards the scientific one."⁶⁸ The second aim is the "purification" (*takhlis*) of Egyptian thought and "spirit" (*wijdan*) from all imperialist influences. The two will lead to

> a revival of the national heritage (*al-turath al-qawmi*), which imperialism has buried, a revival of all the elements that can

help our new society, [which includes] the search for the sources of popular culture and arts in the cities and the villages; to feel the characteristics of the contemporary Egyptian personality and give expression to them by all known means; study our specific problems scientifically and by Egyptian methods ... for the progress of our people and a contemporary humanistic civilization (*turath al-khadara al-insaniyya al-mu'asira*).[69]

After having ended the "crisis of thought" (*azmat al-fikr*), Anwar Abd al-Malik states, Egyptians must create a new personality, in the same manner in which they construct heavy industry and are now able to irrigate thousands of *faddan*.[70] In this endeavor, he argues, Egypt can and must take advantage of the progress that has been made in other countries, even if they are Western. The crucial difference in Anwar Abd al-Malik's Enlightenment project is not between Western and Egyptian culture, but between imperialist and "popular Egyptian culture." He points to the importance of learning to distinguish between the reactionary and the progressive elements in Western civilization.[71]

Joining a Modern Civilization

A new dichotomy

The idea of a new civilization was not only represented as entering a new imaginary era in time, as a socioeconomic transition, and a philosophical transformation; it also implied a shift in identity geographically. In its successful struggle for independence, Egypt supposedly cut its ties with its colonial masters and made new relations and associations with other, often socialist countries in Eastern Europe, Asia and Africa. To the radical intellectuals, these new relations reinforced their optimistic faith in having entered modernity.

If for many Egyptian secular modernists the West had continued to function as an important model in their rejection of the Islamic discourse of authenticity, after the Bandung conference in April 1955, an Eastern model of civilization started to supplant the Western one as a source of inspiration. To these thinkers, the East was not the seat of spiritual purity in opposition to Western materialism, as the previous generation of Egyptian intellectuals had maintained.[72] Rather, it had become the model of a superior socialist rationality, inherited by the East from the West. In the East, it was believed, rationality would reach a higher stage, finally superseding and conquering the declining Western civilization, which was based on outmoded models of organization.

The new civilization was a constructed concept. The features of the new civilization presented more an ideal than a reality on account of their highly generalized form. Often the differences between countries were minimized, while the similarities were overemphasized. On the whole, the highly abstracted signs of progress were deemed constitutive of the newly imagined community. This was enhanced by the linear concept of history, according to which all the countries belonging to the new civilization went through the same stages of development to reach "modernity." By using only such categories of analysis as "feudalism," "imperialism," "the national bourgeoisie," and "national liberation," differences were erased and the feelings of common destiny and solidarity enhanced. For example, the failure to mention the existence of a communist party, downplaying its importance, or transforming the communist party simply into an abstract modernizing force were conspicuous ways of creating solidarity between the communist and non-communist countries. If the repression of democratic opinion by communist regimes was mentioned at all, it was presented as a temporary lapse and not as inherent in the system itself. Stressing the positive elements of the East also had the purpose of describing an ideal that the new Egyptian regime should pursue, instead of attempting to give a realistic picture of the East itself. The common theme of all these countries was their will to modernize. The nationalist element, always in evidence, had the purpose of highlighting the new nation-state and its endeavor to exceed the West. Culture and national character were important signs of distinction, but they functioned more as a way to give a specific coloring to the process of modernization than to assert essential differences.

By positing the East against the West, however, a new dichotomy was created. The relationship between the two was portrayed as a perpetual struggle for dominance between a socialist, rational, civilized, peaceful, and developing East versus a capitalist, imperialist, irrational, aggressive, competitive, decadent, and declining West. Reflecting the new collectivist direction, it was asserted that in Eastern society social harmony and a unified cohesive social structure prevailed, while in Western society an individualistic and divisive social structure reigned supreme. Likewise, the West as a whole was treated as parasitic and exploitative, living off the rest of the world, while the East was presented as energetic, self-effacing, self-reliant, and compassionate. The modernist intellectuals argued that this contrast was apparent, for instance, in the difference in the character of nationalism in both civilizations. Whereas Western nationalism was based on repression and aggression, Eastern nationalism was liberating and emancipating.[73] As in internal politics, planning was regarded as an important criterion of distinction between a "progressive," "rational," and future-oriented society based on science on the one hand and "reactionary," "backward" society based on special interests and exploitation on the other.

If deviations appeared in the image of the East and its darker, repressive side showed through, they were justified as necessary to defend the East against foreign aggression. These left-wing thinkers invoked relativism and the special circumstances of the new civilization to counter the universalism of Western pretensions. The dichotomy between the two civilizations was, however, not essentialist and permanent because in the end it was believed that socialism would be victorious or that the world tended towards one collectivist system.[74] To underline their universalist pretensions, Egyptian left-wing intellectuals always pointed to the existence of positive examples in the West. Dar al-Nadim, for instance, published numerous translations of books written by Harold Laski. Nevertheless, these highly regarded socialist individuals often confirmed the image of a decadent West.

The Soviet Union

The dichotomy between West and East was especially pertinent in the travel stories of Egyptian intellectuals, who had started to "discover" the East in the 1950s. The countries that attracted special attention were the Soviet Union, China, India, Eastern Europe, and to a lesser extent Africa and other Asian countries.

In his wonderful account of his trip to the Soviet Union, Ahmad Baha al-Din puts this country forward as the embodiment of rationality.[75] He sums up the rational quality of the Soviet Union by showing how personal and institutional interests are subordinated to principles:

> Russia is not ruled by the ministry that Bulganin runs, nor is it ruled by the red army that Zukhov commands, nor by the communist party that Khrushchev leads as Secretary-General ...

Russia is ruled by theory (*nazariyya*)!

If someone thinks it is an exaggeration that the power of theory stands above the power of the party, the ministry, or the army, I can tell him that this theory reaches the level of religion. Like religion it has a holiness that raises it above that of any human being.[76]

With his comparison between ideology and religion, Ahmad Baha al-Din expresses his fascination for the power of thought and abstraction in the Soviet Union. He concludes that theory dominates "all forms of life, in the sense that it not just organizes the relations between people, but that it also gives them a new culture."[77] Although Ahmad Baha al-Din condemns Stalinist terror, he qualifies his condemnation with the remark, "freedom can take on many forms in the course of time," adding, "every form of freedom has its own characteristics." In France freedom is individualistic; in Russia it is collectivistic.[78] All people in the Soviet Union, he continues, are aware of the general idea that gives purpose to their lives. Even the artist is subjected to the common goal: "As the peasant produces the specific crops that the country demands and is not at liberty to grow what he wants, [...] the artist also must write for the needs of the country according to a plan."[79] According to Ahmad Baha al-Din, another indication of the rational quality of the Soviet Union is found in the harmony that has been obtained between the past and the present, which has been brought about by means of statues, operas and theater. These keep the past alive and help its citizens to "remember the national spirit."[80] Furthermore, women enjoy equal rights and have to perform less arduous work than men, while minorities enjoy equal rights in addition to a large measure of autonomy.[81]

Muhammad Mandur similarly voiced his admiration for the Soviet Union and Rumania after he visited these countries in 1956.[82] As was the case for Ahmad Baha al-Din, Mandur's trip was intended to disprove myths about socialist countries. His writings convey his admiration and fascination with the political and social order he found there. Characteristically, he was in awe of the collective farms he visited.[83] The strictness of the regime reminded him of Wahhabism and Protestantism.[84] He denies any evidence of repression of opinion, giving examples of personal experiences that showed that freedom of speech did exist.[85] His most important aim, however, was to hold the cultural policy of the socialist countries up as an example to the new Egyptian regime and emphasize the role of the intellectual in giving "direction" (*tawjih*) to policy matters for the numerous institutes and ministries involved with the production of culture.[86]

Even Abd al-Mughni Sa'id, who always tried to strike a balance between the discourse of modernism and the discourse of authenticity, showed himself impressed with the Soviet Union when he visited it in 1958.[87] To him the Soviet Union proved the possibility of establishing a modern industrialized country that was based on the most advanced economic techniques (i.e. planning) and the most progressive ideology, while retaining its authentic cultural values. This was apparent for instance in the structure of the Russian family. While Ahmad Baha al-Din and Muhammad Mandur had been careful to refute the idea, commonly held in the Middle East, that communism leads to sexual indulgence and the dissolution of the family, Abd al-Mughni Sa'id is elated to find the Soviet family positively traditional.[88] He ascribes the superiority of the Soviet Union over Western society to the balance between its modern economic and political system and its authentic cultural values that were untouched by the "hypocrisy" (*nifaq*) and "decay" (*inhilal*) of the West.[89]

The Soviet Union's foreign policy since the Bandung conference and its support for Egypt during the Suez Canal crisis greatly added to the standing of communism. It was more proof of the notion that Egypt had entered a new era. Like its domestic policy, the Soviet Union's foreign policy seemed to be based on a rational system and was therefore described as "principled." As was typical of these writings, the non-communist Ihsan Abd al-Quddus contends that the principles of the Soviet Union's foreign policy "are not related to communism, but are connected with the liberation from egoism and international ambition, and [are based on] the belief in humanity."[90] Communists only encouraged this idea. In *Ruz al-Yusuf*, Anwar Abd al-Malik argues that the acceptance of the principle of peaceful coexistence strengthens the positive side of the Soviet Union's foreign policy.[91] Kamil Zuhayri underlines the ideological convergence of the Soviet Union and the Arab countries in light of the Soviet Union's recognition of the legitimacy of different routes to socialism and the increasingly socialist orientation of the Arab countries.[92] Although some criticized Soviet repression of the Hungarian uprising, the Workers' Vanguard quickly produced a booklet in which it was defended as a measure against imperialist intervention.[93]

China

The same evocation of the dawn of a new civilization can be seen in the case of China. Part of the reawakened interest in China since the Bandung conference was based precisely on its relationship with the Soviet Union, that is on the Soviet Union's respect for the specific route other countries were taking in their development towards a new civilization. The book *The People's China*, by Muhammad Awda, reflects this preoccupation.[94] Although not a communist, Awda reassures the Egyptian reader that the Soviet Union respects China's individual character by upholding the principle "that the revolution cannot be exported or lent and that every society should create and realize the revolution that is in accordance with its special circumstances."[95] Awda's book also reflects a continuing interest in the role of the national bourgeoisie. The massacre of the communists at Shanghai in 1927 is described as a betrayal of revolutionary change by "big bourgeoisie" and "feudalists." The bourgeoisie, writes Awda, "had not only betrayed the people and the revolution, but also the bourgeoisie's mission (*risala*) in history, which was to end imperialism and feudalism and establish a nationalist, democratic, capitalist, enlightened society."[96] Nowhere does Awda refer explicitly to the Egyptian situation, but the comparison with Egypt is easy to make. If the Wafd is the betrayer of the bourgeois revolution, the new regime is its fulfillment. It can carry the revolution through by taking the initiative and forcing the national bourgeoisie to support its industrialization program.

That China was indeed believed to resemble Egypt in more ways than one is clear in numerous articles in *Ruz al-Yusuf*, whose staff Muhammad Awda joined. Ihsan Abd al-Quddus, who obviously did not care for Awda's implicit comparison between China and Egypt,[97] nevertheless sent one of his journalists to report on the situation in China. The reports that were sent back reinforced the idea that China and Egypt should be regarded as two distinct, but nevertheless comparable modernist experiments with nationalism and socialism. In his first report, Muhammad Bili writes, "what happened in China is not a completely communist revolution." In fact, he explains, capitalism in China helped build socialism; ninety percent of the shops were still privately owned and factory owners were elected to parliament.[98] Another article stresses the cooperation between the national bourgeoisie and the regime in implementing five-year plans.[99] Muhammad Awda later confirmed this view by remarking that in China "capitalists have been transformed into socialists and [have become] convinced of the value of coexistence and cooperation with other classes."[100]

India, Pakistan and Turkey

As a consequence of their modernist outlook, Egyptian left-wing liberals and communists looked towards China as well as India, Yugoslavia, and Indonesia, long before the government embarked on its neutralist foreign policy in 1955. Special attention was paid to India under Nehru, who compared favorably with the weak Egyptian political leaders for a long time. Nehru's secular outlook, independent foreign policy, and centrally guided industrial program were held up as a model for Egypt. For someone like Ahmad Baha al-Din, Nehru embodied the right mixture of westernization and nationalism. In contrast, Pakistan, under the leadership of Premier Muhammad Ali, was regarded as the worst example. Not only did he sign a military pact with the United States directed against India, China, and the USSR, he also tried to entice Egypt to join the Islamic League, which Rashid al-Barrawi had already described in 1951 as an attempt to get Egypt to adopt a foreign policy based on religious "fanaticism."[101] Pakistan, together with Turkey, the other "traitor" of the anti-imperialist front, were named "the greatest reactionary countries in the region."[102] Turkey moved in the opposite direction from Egypt after its free elections in 1950, dismantling its centrally organized, etatist economy while joining NATO in 1954 and the Baghdad Pact in February 1955. For these reasons, Turkey was considered the greatest non-Arab, non-Western foe of Egypt and the modernist principles of the radical nationalist movement. The modernists claimed that Turkey sold its independence out of an exaggerated fear of the Soviet Union and had relinquished its opportunities for economic development to American imperialism, becoming once again a backward, agrarian country. In short, wrote Ihsan Abd al-Quddus, Turkey was losing its "personality."[103] Likewise, Pakistan's new policy was described as based on "religious miracles and American dollars."[104]

The Arab world

Ruz al-Yusuf's adherence to the regime as regards foreign policy can be explained by the regime's realization of the general radical nationalist program of the 1940s, which treated political, economic, and cultural independence as the preconditions for development. In foreign affairs, this program led to neutralism, which had been Egypt's policy since the last Wafd government. It was primarily directed against military alliances with the West, which were regarded as infringing national sovereignty and therefore hampering national development. Economically, neutralism became more and more closely linked to the idea that developing countries should take a separate road, independent of capitalism and communism, and that their economical and social structure was in based on their specific circumstances. Increasingly, counter-alliances had to join independent countries that were fully detached from the West and imperialism. Moreover, they had to be based on secular principles. In sum, neutralism oriented Egypt towards countries that were regarded as comparable in terms of their stage of development, both socially and economically. In its extreme form and in line with the common historical notion of stages of development, it was assumed that these countries formed the vanguard of the international liberation movement and had entered a new, higher level of civilization.

The same principles were at the heart of *Ruz al-Yusuf*'s views on Pan-Arabism. Pan-Arabism was seen as not in itself a goal to be pursued and only relevant so long as it supported modernization. This notion is clearly at the heart of a series entitled "Egypt First," written by Ihsan Abd al-Quddus in 1953, when Egypt was still completely entangled in its domestic problems. In this series, Ihsan Abd al-Quddus warns against being swept up by the emotions of pan-Arab solidarity, mocking "Arab wisdom."[105] He criticizes the main pan-Arab argument that divisions within the Arab world had been imposed by imperialism, arguing that they had far deeper historical roots, which predated colonial domination. Those traits that the Arab world did have in common, like language, religion, and social and cultural traditions, were not sufficient to warrant a common policy. The only basis for a common policy, he argues, is self-interest. This did not mean that Arab countries should not join together in a common goal. On the contrary, provided it is based on common interests, Ihsan Abd al-Quddus welcomes co-operation, but it is obvious that he does not really believe that there are common interests.[106] Under attack for his views, he points to India as an example of a country that is based on common interests instead of a common religion or language.[107]

Ahmad Baha al-Din agreed with Ihsan Abd al-Quddus in seeing religion and language as insufficient in themselves as a basis for a foreign policy. He does point, however, to another element that may be grounds for unity: the common historical experience of the Arab countries. All Arab countries had suffered Turkish Ottoman rule as well as European domination. During their resistance to foreign repression, they had become more and more integrated, especially after World War II. Ahmad Baha al-Din explains that this continuing process of integration is in the interest of Egypt, which could function as the center of the Arab world on account of its more advanced position in science and culture. In addition, the Arab countries provided Egypt with a market for its new industrial products.[108]

Left-wing political thought subsumed the Arab world and Pan-Arabism into the same modernist model. From World War II, the communist movement had valued Arab integration only if it was carried by the people, led to socioeconomic reform, and resisted imperialism.[109] Accordingly, the left supported the regime's policy of Arab cooperation from Bandung onwards. The Suez Canal crisis further strengthened the Pan-Arab feelings of the communist movement and the left in general. Nevertheless, Pan-Arabism remained for the left on the whole a strategy for achieving certain goals; it was never a goal in itself. To left-wing thinkers, the continuing integration of the Arab world and the greater solidarity against imperialism reinforced the idea that Egypt was entering modernity.

This is especially true for one analysis of Arab nationalism, which was written by the young historian Muhammad Anis for *al-Masa'* on the occasion of the Egyptian-Syrian unification in 1958. In contrast to the Pan-Arabists, Anis does not dwell on the cultural, linguistic, and economic arguments for Arab unity. Instead, he portrays Arab unification in a detached, academic manner as the inevitable outcome of the historical process of modernization. In a later lecture in which he returned to the subject, Anis declares explicitly that Arab unification should be divested of its irrational features based on primitive political slogans and whimsical feelings of sympathy and solidarity. These should be substituted by objective, scientific studies that reveal history's inner laws and logic.[110] In this manner, Anis links Arabism to Progress and Fate, which destines it to conquer all those forces that have obstructed its mission. He argues that all attempts to keep the Arab East backward, exploited, and divided, first by the Ottoman Empire, then British and French imperialism, Israeli aggression, and American imperialism, were doomed to failure. He emphasizes the inevitable, objective, scientific, and progressive character of Arabism by linking its blossoming to higher stages of socioeconomic development and an ever-greater degree of economic integration of the Arab world. This route of development is confirmed, he finds, by the failure of earlier, less developed and reactionary forms of Arab unification, such as those of the Hashimites of Jordan and Iraq. Finally, Muhammad Anis sees further proof of the progressive character of Arabism in its secular character.[111]

The decadent West

Over and against the general progressive march of history in which Egyptian and Arab potential is realized, supported by the larger context of the new civilization, stands its opposite: the decadent and declining forces that in spite of their weakness try to prevent this new civilization from emerging. The left-wing thinkers find the most obvious confirmation of this view in the decline of the old imperialist powers, Great Britain and France. The Suez Canal crisis, with the absolute humiliation of the West and the total victory of the East, undermined the last remains of their credibility. In subsequent years, accounts of travels to the West further deepened the sense of moral, economic, and social crisis in which the West was bogged down. For instance, Ahmad Baha al-Din described France during the Algerian crisis in 1958 as a country that had lost its direction. From a powerful empire it had declined, he wrote, to a country "at the margin of life" (*hala hamish al-hayah*). Its provinciality was expressed in the indifference of its intellectuals, the senselessness of its youth culture, and the bankruptcy of its economy. Facing "catastrophe" (*karitha*), France had declined politically, he believed, from the height of its heroic struggle against fascism during the Second World War to the depth of the current general malaise and "despair" (*ya's*).[112] Ahmad Baha al-Din saw the triumphant take-over of power by Charles de Gaulle and the end of the Fourth Republic as the confirmation of the datedness of the multi-party system.[113]

By the second half of the 1950s, however, the greatest enemy of the left-wing Egyptian intellectuals was the United States. Since the end of the 1940s, the United States had come to be regarded as heir to the old imperialist powers. The increasing American intervention in the region in light of the Truman doctrine, its support for Israel, and its constant attempts to build military alliances, followed by the American refusal to help finance the Aswan High Dam, and finally the Eisenhower doctrine in 1957, all of this made the United States the main political opponent of Egypt. Numerous texts were published that showed the imperialist intentions of the United States. These books, which derived their overall model directly from

Lenin's work on imperialism, traced the imperialist tradition of the United States back to the end of the nineteenth century.[114]

But the animosity for the United States cannot be explained through its foreign policy alone. The unfamiliarity and distance of the United States as well as the fact that the United States were the most powerful adversary of the Soviet Union probably led to its demonization by many Egyptian left-wing intellectuals. The most extreme case is *In Defence of Arab Culture: The Ideological War That Imperialism Wages Against Our Arab East* (1959) by Fathi Khalil.[115] The book is a direct, but a much more shrill continuation of the debate on the preservation of national culture, which had been initiated by Ahmad Baha al-Din. Fathi Khalil sees American institutes, such as the Franklin Institute, as "centers of ideological American poison."[116] He portrays American culture as completely artificial, produced, and manipulated by monopolies. Hollywood is cast as the "key to the ideological war" because American movies turn the world upside down: criminals become heroes, thieves and gamblers are made attractive, and women evoke the worst animal instincts.[117] The typical accusation made against the United States was that its philosophy was based on pragmatism and that its lack of principles led to adventurism, war, and the denial of objective truths, such as the existence of Arab nationalism.[118] In his other work, *America 1958: Seven Million Unemployed, Five Billion Dollars for War*,[119] Khalil tries to refute the idea that the United States is the land of freedom and human rights. Instead, he states, "war is the oxygen of its existence."[120] He claims that war has always been the engine of the American economy and will remain so now that unemployment is rising. In addition, it has been a means of diverting attention from the class character of American society.[121] Every topic is embraced that might embarrass the pretensions of the United States to be the leader of the "free world." Another favorite subject for Egyptian intellectuals was the humiliating position of blacks in the United States. Tahir Abd al-Hakim, for instance, wrote a booklet entitled *The Suppression of the Negroes in America* (1958), which recounts the history of African Americans from slavery to the recent emancipation movement.[122]

Notes

1 This was, of course, the central historiographical legitimization of the regime. See especially Anwar el-Sadat, *Révolte sur le Nil* (Paris: Pierre Amiot, 1957) and also his *Ma'na al-Ittihad al-Qawmi* (Cairo: n.p., 1958).

2 Ihsan 'Abd al-Quddus, "al-Nizam al-dimuqratiyya ... sina'a mahalliyya," *Ruz al-Yusuf* No. 1406 (23 May 1955): 6–7.
3 Al-Muwatin al-Misri, "Alladhina waqafu makan Jamal 'Abd al-Nasir," *Ruz al-Yusuf* No. 1440 (16 January 1956): 3.
4 Al-Muwatin al-Misri, "al-Haqiqa allati yatajahaluha Eden wa Eisenhower," *Ruz al-Yusuf* No. 1442 (30 January 1956): 2.
5 Al-Muwatin al-Misri, "Alladhina waqafu makan Jamal 'Abd al-Nasir," *Ruz al-Yusuf* No. 1440 (16 January 1956): 3.
6 Ihsan 'Abd al-Quddus, "Ba'da al-jala' ... kayfa nuhasib Jamal 'Abd al-Nasir?" *Ruz al-Yusuf* No. 1462 (18 June 1956): 3–4.
7 Ihsan 'Abd al-Quddus, "al-Bahth 'an za'im jadid," *Ruz al-Yusuf* No. 1516 (1 July 1957): 6–7.
8 Ihsan 'Abd al-Quddus, "Kay la nakhaf al-dimuqratiyya," *Ruz al-Yusuf* No. 1536 (18 July 1957): 3–5.
9 Ihsan 'Abd al-Quddus, "Mujtama' ishtiraki ta'awuni," *Ruz al-Yusuf* No. 1538 (2 December 1957): 3–4.
10 Ahmad Baha' al-Din, "Kayfa nuwajjih al-dimuqratiyya?" *Ruz al-Yusuf* No. 1538 (2 December 1957): 6–7.
11 Ahmad Baha' al-Din, "Kayfa nuwajjih al-dimuqratiyya?" *Ruz al-Yusuf* No. 1538 (2 December 1957): 6–7.
12 Ahmad Baha' al-Din, "Mujtama' taqaddumi ... li-l-dawla al-muttahida," *Ruz al-Yusuf* No. 1547 (3 February 1958): 8–9.
13 Fathi Ghanim, "Mas'uliyyat al-dawla, wa hurriyyat al-fard," *Ruz al-Yusuf* No. 1545 (20 January 1958): 8.
14 "Jabha wahida 'idd al-isti'mar," *Kifah al-Sha'b* No. 32 (March 1957): 2.
15 "Hawla al-intikhabat al-qadima," *Kifah al-Sha'b* No. 34 (13 April 1957): 3.
16 Abu Sayf Yusuf, "Ma'raka wataniyya fi al-mahall al-awwal," *al-Masa'*, 21 May 1957.
17 'Abd al-'Azim Anis, "al-Ma'raka al-intikhabiyya," *al-Masa'*, 7 June 1957.
18 'Abd al-'Azim Anis, "Hadhihi al-baramij al-intikhabiyya," *al-Masa'*, 17 July 1957.
19 Fu'ad Mursi, "al-Dimuqratiyya fi Misr," *al-Masa'*, 13 July 1957, 5.
20 Mursi, "al-Dimuqratiyya." Italics added.
21 Mursi, "al-Dimuqratiyya."
22 Fu'ad Mursi, "al-Dimuqratiyya fi Misr – dimuqratiyyatuna al- haliyya?" *al-Masa'*, 14 July 1957, 5.
23 "Ba'd asalib al-raj'iyya fi al-ma'raka al-intikhabiyya," *Kifah al-Sha'b* No. 39 (23 May 1957): 3.
24 "Dalalat al-ma'raka al-intikhabiyya," *Hayat al-Hizb* No. 1 (August 1957): 18–42.
25 "Dalalat," 18–9.
26 "Dalalat," 27–8.
27 "Dalalat," 29.
28 Ihsan 'Abd al-Quddus, "al-Shakhsiyya al-Misriyya allati da'at ... ayna najiduha?!," *Ruz al-Yusuf* No. 1350 (26 April 1954): 3.
29 Ihsan 'Abd al-Quddus, "al-Shakhsiyya al-Misriyya," *Ruz al-Yusuf* No. 1366 (16 August 1954): 6–7.
30 Ihsan 'Abd al-Quddus, "alladhin lam yatalawwathu bi-madaniyyat al-atrak wa la bi-madaniyyat al-ingiliz!," *Ruz al-Yusuf* No. 1396 (14 March 1955): 6–7.

31 Ihsan 'Abd al-Quddus, "Hal anta 'alami, am anta watani?!," *Ruz al-Yusuf* No. 1395 (7 March 1955): 6–7.
32 Ahmad Baha' al-Din, "al-Iqta'iyyun ... wa-l-ra'smaliyyun ... al-muthaqqafun ... wa-l-'ummal!," *Ruz al-Yusuf* No. 1353 (17 May 1954): 6.
33 Ahmad Baha' al-Din, *Ayyam laha tarikh* (Cairo: Kitab Ruz al-Yusuf, 1954).
34 Ahmad Baha' al-Din, "Lahum al-dunya ... wa lana al-akhira," *Ruz al-Yusuf* No. 1343 (8 March 1954): 19.
35 Mahmud Amin al-'Alim, "Sihafat al-wataniyya fi khatr," *Ruz al-Yusuf* No. 1431 (14 November 1955): 19.
36 'Abd al-'Azim Anis and Mahmud Amin al-'Alim, *Fi al-thaqafa al-Misriyya* (Cairo: Dar al-Fikr 1955. Cairo: Dar al-Thaqafa al-Jadida, 1988), 27.
37 Muhammad 'Awda, "Thawrat tahtaj ilayha Misr," *Ruz al-Yusuf* No. 1464 (2 July 1956): 10–11.
38 Shuhdi 'Atiyya al-Shafi'i, *Tatawwur al-haraka al-wataniyya al-Misriyya, 1882–1956* (1957; Cairo: Dar Shuhdi, 1983).
39 Fawzi Jirjis, *Dirasat fi tarikh Misr al-siyasi mundhu al-'asr al-mamluki* (Cairo: Matb'at al-Dar al-Misriyya, 1958).
40 Ibrahim 'Amir, *al-Ard wa-l-fallah. al-Mas'ala al-zira'iyya fi Misr* (Cairo: Matb'at al-Dar al-Misriyya, 1958).
41 Ibrahim 'Amir, *Thawrat Misr al-qawmiyya* (Cairo: Dar al-Nadim, 1956).
42 See for instance Muhammad Shafiq Ghurbal, *Tarikh al-mufawadat al-Misriyya al-Britaniyya. Bahth fi al-'alaqat al-Misriyya al-Britaniyya min al-ihtilal ila 'aqd mu'ahadat al-tahaluf* (Cairo: Maktabat al-Nahda al-Misriyya, 1952).
43 Muhammad Anis and al-Sayyid Rahab Hiraz, *Thawrat 23 yulyu 1952 wa usuluha al-tarikhiyya* (Cairo: Dar al-Nahda al-'Arabiyya, 1965). See also Muhammad Anis, *Tatawwur al-Mujtama' al-Misri min al-iqta' ila thawrat 23 yulyu sanat 1952* (Cairo: Matb'at al-Jablawi, 1965).
44 Rashed El-Barawy, *The Military Coup in Egypt: An Analytic Study* (Cairo: The Renaissance Bookshop, 1952). This is a translation of the Arabic version: Rashid al-Barrawi, *Haqiqat al-inqilab al-akhir fi Misr* (Cairo: Maktabat al-Nahda al-Misriyya, 1952). See Chapter 2.
45 Jirjis, 25–6.
46 Jirjis, 122–3.
47 Jirjis, 131.
48 al-Shafi'i, 22–3.
49 al-Shafi'i, 28–9.
50 Jirjis, 147; al-Shafi'i, 54–60; 'Amir, *Thawra*, 60.
51 See for instance the work of al-Shafi'i.
52 Jirjis, 173.
53 al-Shafi'i, 72.
54 al-Shafi'i, 95.
55 al-Shafi'i, 129.
56 Most of Anwar 'Abd al-Malik's articles were published in *al-Masa'*; others were published in *al-Hadaf*. Later, these articles were collected and published as Anwar 'Abd al-Malik, *Dirasat fi al-thaqafa al-wataniyya* (Beirut: Dar al-Tali'a, 1967). For this chapter, the articles in the book have been used, but reference will be made to the original source.
57 'Abd al-Malik, "Ihtiyajat al-shabab fi marhalat al-bina'," *Dirasat*, 80–1. Original in *al-Masa'*, 4 February 1958 and 12 February 1958.

58 'Abd al-Malik, "al-Shabab al-Misri wa-l-thaqafa," *Dirasat*, 72. Original in *al-Masa'*, 14 August 1957.
59 'Abd al-Malik, "Min ajli nahda fikriyya," *al-Masa'*, *Dirasat*, 121–2. Original in *al-Masa'*, 17 September 1957.
60 'Abd al-Malik, "al-Isti'mar wa thaqafatuna al-wataniyya," *Dirasat*, 55. Original in *al-Masa'*, 17 September 1957 and 7 February 1958.
61 'Abd al-Malik, introduction, *Dirasat*, 15.
62 'Abd al-Malik, "al-Itar al-'amm li-wad' al-mas'ala," *Dirasat*, 37–8. Original in *al-Hadaf*, January 1957, 42–4.
63 'Abd al-Malik, "Min ajli nahda fikriyya," *Dirasat*, 120. Original in *al-Masa'*, 17 September 1957.
64 'Abd al-Malik, "Min ajli tarikhina al-qawmi," *Dirasat*, 114. Original in *al-Masa'*, 9 June 1957.
65 'Abd al-Malik, introduction, *Dirasat*, 19.
66 'Abd al-Malik, "Ihtiyajat al-shabab fi marhalat al-bina'," *Dirasat*, 83. Original in *al-Masa'*, 4 February 1958 and 12 February 1958.
67 'Abd al-Malik, introduction, *Dirasat*, 15–27.
68 'Abd al-Malik, introduction, *Dirasat*, 26.
69 'Abd al-Malik, "Min qadaya al-bina' al-thaqafa," *Dirasat*, 99. Original in *al-Hadaf*, December 1956, 34–47.
70 'Abd al-Malik, "Madha wara'a hadhihi al-hamla," *Dirasat*, 107. Original in *Ruz al-Yusuf* No. 1467 (23 July 1956).
71 'Abd al-Malik, "al-Itar al-'amm li-wad' al-mas'ala," *Dirasat*, 36. Original in *al-Hadaf*, January 1957, 42–4.
72 See for the concept of "Easternism" as significant to the previous generation of Egyptians and expressed in the 1930s: Israel Gershoni and James P. Jankowski, *Redefining the Egyptian Nation, 1930–1945* (Cambridge: Cambridge University Press, 1995), 35–53.
73 Tahir 'Abd al-Hakim, "Bayna al-qawmiyya al-'Arabiyya wa-l-harakat al-qawmiyya fi urubba," *al-Masa'*, 1 September 1958, 5.
74 Ahmad Baha' al-Din, "'Asr al-ishtirakiyya," *Ruz al-Yusuf* No. 1416 (1 August 1955).
75 Ahmad Baha' al-Din, *Shahr fi Rusiya* (Cairo: Dar al-Nadim, 1955). The book was originally serialized in *Ruz al-Yusuf* from 12 September to 14 November 1955.
76 Baha' al-Din, *Shahr*, 79.
77 Baha' al-Din, *Shahr*, 79.
78 Baha' al-Din, *Shahr*, 102.
79 Baha' al-Din, *Shahr*, 103.
80 Baha' al-Din, *Shahr*, 26.
81 Baha' al-Din, *Shahr*, 43.
82 Muhammad Mandur, *Jawla fi al-'alam al-ishtiraki* (Cairo: Dar al-Tiba'a al-Haditha, 1957).
83 Mandur, 21.
84 Mandur, 32–4.
85 Mandur, 30–2.
86 Mandur, 59.
87 'Abd al-Mughni Sa'id, *al-Ittihad al-Sufyati kama ra'aytuhu* (Cairo: Dar al-Fikr, 1958).

88 'Abd al-Mughni Sa'id, 18.
89 'Abd al-Mughni Sa'id, see the chapter "al-Takhtit wa bina" al-nizam al-ishtiraki," 75–103.
90 Ihsan 'Abd al-Quddus, "Tahiyya ila Rusiya, nasiha li-Amrika, saf'a li-Birataniya," *Ruz al-Yusuf* No. 1470 (13 August 1956): 3.
91 Anwar 'Abd al-Malik, "Amrika ... wa-Rusiya," *Ruz al-Yusuf* No. 1491 (7 January 1957): 18–9.
92 Kamil Zuhayri, "Kayfa iltaqayna ma'a Rusiya. Wa kayfa iltaqat al-ishtiraki ma'a al-qawmiyya al-'Arabiyya?," *Ruz al-Yusuf* No. 1560 (5 May 1960): 3 and 33.
93 Muhammad Hilmi Yasin, *al-Isti'mar yuhzam fi al-Majar*, (Cairo: al-Mu'assasa al-Qawmiyya li-l-Nashr wa-l-Tawzi', n.d.).
94 Muhammad 'Awda, *al-Sin al-sha'biyya* (Cairo: Dar al-Nadim, 1955).
95 'Awda, 67.
96 'Awda, 99.
97 Ihsan 'Abd al-Quddus, "Misr fi tarikh al-Sin," *Ruz al-Yusuf* No. 1432 (21 November 1955): 6.
98 Muhammad Bili, "Awwal tahqiq sahafi 'an al-Sin al-sha'biyya!" *Ruz al-Yusuf* No. 1435 (12 December 1955).
99 Fathi Khalil, "Qantarat al-janna," *Ruz al-Yusuf* No. 1470 (13 August 1956): 24–5.
100 Muhammad 'Awda, "Ra'smaliyyun wa shuyu'iyyun ma'an," *Ruz al-Yusuf* No. 1463 (25 June 1956): 10–1.
101 Rashid al-Barrawi, *Mashru'at al-difa' 'an al-Sharq al-Awsat* (Cairo: Maktabat al-Nahda al-Misriyya, 1952) 70.
102 'Adil Thabit, "Mu'amarat al-difa'... fi al-Sharq al-Awsat," *Ruz al-Yusuf* No. 1347 (5 April 1955): 18–9.
103 Al-Muwatin al-Misri, "Wasiyyat Kamal Ataturk li-khulafa'ihi," *Ruz al-Yusuf* No. 1454 (23 April 1956): 3.
104 "Ayna taqif bakistan?" *Ruz al-Yusuf* No. 1475 (17 September 1956): 16–7.
105 Ihsan 'Abd al-Quddus, "Ma zilt aqul ... Misr awwalan," *Ruz al-Yusuf* No. 1325 (2 November 1953): 3.
106 Ihsan 'Abd al-Quddus, "Misr awwalan ... wa amrika awwalan," *Ruz al-Yusuf* No. 1326 (9 November 1953): 3.
107 Ihsan 'Abd al-Quddus, "Man yumaththil al-shu'ub al-'arabiyya fi mu'tamar al-shu'ub," *Ruz al-Yusuf* No. 1333 (28 December 1953): 3.
108 Ahmad Baha' al-Din, "(Misr wa 'arab) kilta awwalan," *Ruz al-Yusuf* No. 1335 (11 January 1954): 18–9.
109 See for instance for the period just after World War II: Ahmad Sadiq Sa'd, 'Jami'at al-Duwwal al-'Arabiyya 'ala daw' mawqifiha min masalat Suriya wa Lubnan," *al-Fajr al-Jadid* No. 14 (1 July 1945). Republished in Ahmad Sadiq Sa'd, *Safahat min al-yasar al-Misri fi a'qab al-harb al-'alamiyya al-thaniya 1945–1946* (Cairo: Matktabat Madbuli, 1976), 224–6; Shuhdi 'Atiyya al-Shafi'i and Muhammad 'Abd al-Ma'bud al-Jubayli, *Abdafuna al-wataniyya* (Cairo: Matba'at Risala, 1945), 32–6. The Egyptian communist movement showed itself also in favor of greater Arab unity during the 1950s, but mostly it believed that it should take the form of federalism, not a merger between Arab countries.
110 Muhammad Anis, *Dirasat al-qawmiyya al-'Arabiyya min al-nahiyatayn al-nazariyya wa-l-tarikhiyya* (1959; Cairo: Dar al-Jabal, 1963), 3.

111 Anis, *Dirasat*, 11. See for the series Muhammad Anis wrote in *al-Masa'*: Muhammad Anis, "Suriya wa-l-wahda al-'Arabiyya," *al-Masa'*, 10 and 11 February 1958; Muhammad Anis, "al-Wahda al-'Arabiyya amama al-tarikh, "*al-Masa'*, 20 and 22 February 1958; Muhammad Anis, "al-Jaysh al-Iraqi wa-l-haraka al-wataniyya," *al-Masa'*, 20 and 26 July 1958.
112 Ahmad Baha' al-Din, "Hakadha ta'ish Baris fi harb al-Jaza'ir," *Ruz al-Yusuf* No. 1554 (24 March 1958): 16–7.
113 Ihsan 'Abd al-Quddus, "Hazuma ukhra li-l-dimuqratiyya al-hizbiyya," *Ruz al-Yusuf* No. 1565 (9 June 1958): 6.
114 For instance see: Mishil Kamil, *Amrika wa-l-Sharq al-'Arabi* (Cairo: Dar al-Fajr, n.d.); 'Ali Dali, *Amrika wa-l-'udwan 'ala Misr* (Cairo: Dar al-Fikr, 1957); Tahir 'Abd al-Hakim, *al-Amrikiyyun kharij biladihim* (Cairo: Matba'at al-Ma'rifa, n.d.).
115 Fathi Khalil, *Difa' 'an al-thaqafa al-'Arabiyya. al-Harb al-fikriyya allati yudiruha al-isti'mar fi Sharqina al-'Arabi* (Cairo: Dar al-Fajr al-Jadid, 1959).
116 Khalil, *Difa' 'an al-thaqafa*, 41.
117 Khalil, *Difa' 'an al-thaqafa*, 57.
118 Khalil, *Difa' 'an al-thaqafa*, 75–6.
119 Fathi Khalil, *Amrika 1958: 6 Milyun 'atil, 50 bilyun dular li-l-harb* (Cairo: Dar al-Fikr, 1958).
120 Khalil, *Amrika 1958*, 41.
121 Khalil, *Amrika 1958*, 112.
122 Tahir 'Abd al-Hakim, *Idtihad al-zunuj fi Amrika* (Cairo: Dar al-Fikr, 1958).

Conclusion

This study has focused on the role secular intellectuals and political currents of the 1940s played in the transition from the pluralist political system of the monarchy to the authoritarian regime of the Nasserist era. Two questions are central to this topic. The first is why so many prominent intellectuals joined the new regime in the second half of the 1950s, even though most of them had laid the ideological and institutional foundations for a pluralist civil society in the 1930s and 1940s. And the second is how these intellectuals helped shape the ideology of the reformist regime in the years between 1955 and 1958.

The political ideas of this period have been analyzed in the context of two developments I regard as essential to this period: the rise of civil society on the one hand and the emergence of the sovereign state on the other. Although the concept of civil society is usually considered to be valid only to later periods in Egyptian history, it is more appropriately applied to the monarchy. Not only does the existence of civil society account for the rise of these movements; their proponents also refer to it indirectly in their works. Room for the development of a civil society had been created since British rule had restricted the absolutist power of the monarchy. By the 1940s Egypt had seen the emergence of a rich variety of associations ranging from private cultural salons, clubs, and independent publishing houses to trade unions and professional organizations. In addition, the country had witnessed the development of a political society with its own rules, including a multi-party system and a liberal tradition of law. The power of civil organizations was further enhanced by the autonomy and protection of different national and ethnic minorities, each with their own rules and community life. In this diverse and vibrant civil society, freedom of expression found its institutionalization in a powerful press and a public opinion.

Paradoxically, civil society came into being in a political environment that was not altogether conducive to its growth. It is clear that despite the relatively liberal atmosphere of Egyptian society in the 1920s, it contained major drawbacks. The British occupation limited the sovereignty of the Egyptian state and prevented the formation of an integrated nation. Its domination of politics led to the economic and political discrimination of Egyptian nationals, thereby undermining the expansion of democracy it had encouraged as a means to curtail the power of the monarchy. The deficiencies that characterized the political system on the Egyptian side were equally important. Patronage and clientalism kept subordinate classes and social groups dependent on an elite that monopolized political power and prevented the necessary reforms. Eventually, these factors barred the transformation of Egypt into a homogeneous, coherent nation-state based on universal education, general political participation, and a more equitable social system. It is therefore not surprising that when the middle and working classes started to organize themselves, they revolted against the prevalent political culture of patronage and the privileged socioeconomic and political system it kept intact. They adopted more abstract, less personalized political concepts that were more appropriate for mass politics and the challenges Egypt faced at the time.

The other important feature of this period was the rise of the sovereign Egyptian state. The national state had gradually come into being, starting with the introduction of a parliamentary system in 1923 (sovereignty of internal politics), the attainment of Tariff freedom in 1930 (economic sovereignty), the endorsement of the Anglo-Egyptian Treaty in 1936 (partial military sovereignty), and the abolition of the Capitulations in 1937 (sovereignty over foreign and ethnic minorities). These international agreements resulted in a host of measures, such as the Arabization of business language, the Egyptianization of business itself, and the homogenization of education. Such developments worked only partially to benefit the middle classes and their new civil institutions because the elite used the state to try to repress the increasingly radicalized and politicized civil society. The deadlock in the relations between the more independent civil society and the emerging sovereign state led to successive violent clashes between the state and the left in 1945–46 and between the state and the Islamist movement in 1948–49. It ended with the popular uprising in January 1952, a prelude to the military takeover in July 1952. While civil society was unable to enforce reform, the state was incapable of transforming society and achieving independence due to the conservatism of the elite. This book has argued that the general context in which reformist movements operated, and in which they should therefore be understood, is formed by the tension between civil society (along with political society) and the state in the 1940s. The political culture of patronage explains the content of the reformist programs.

After setting up this context, my next task was to define the thought of the three political currents under analysis. I use the term modernism to describe the ideology that came to dominate these currents in the 1930s. In contrast to previous theories of modernity, the modernism of the 1930s and 1940s was based on a new concept of society as a social, economic, and political entity that can be reformed. Due to this optimistic belief in the malleability of society, we see calls for social engineering and economic planning. Moreover, the modernist program employed a new sense of time and space based on a perceived dichotomy between past and present, or "traditional" and "modern." These thinkers often condemn the past as outdated and accept the future as marked by boundless opportunities. Another essential element of modernism is a view of progress as a universal linear process of passing through consecutive and increasingly complex economic and social stages of greater perfection and rationalization. Further, the achievement of modernity was consistently associated with the rise of a new class and the modern values associated with it: the middle classes for the liberals and socialists, the working class for the communist movement. Other than through carefully planned reforms, the transition to modernity was believed to come about by massive industrialization and the application of new technologies. Nationalism and the struggle for independence were important to the quest for modernity not so much in determining the country's identity and gaining independence as such, but in acquiring complete sovereignty and the opportunity to determine Egypt's future. They were also treated as instrumental to the creation of a nation-state that, for the first time, would include the entire nation and not just the elite. Finally, an essential characteristic of this brand of modernism was the concept of the intellectual as the vanguard. Based on their knowledge of science and the laws of history, intellectuals were able to construct a new society, establish a new economy, and explore the new international borders. As the molders of public opinion (*ashab al-ra'y*), they were to lead the nation to modernity.

This study has aimed to determine how, during the transitional period between 1945 and 1958, the modernist political currents were affected by the existence of a civil society on the one hand and the gradual emergence of a sovereign state on the other. My general conclusion for the period until the March Crisis of 1954 is that the tension between the two was expressed in an extreme ambivalence about the way in which society should be transformed. The central thinkers of these political currents supported the independence of civil society's organizations (free press and independent publishing houses, autonomous clubs and associations, and a plurality of political organizations) and further democratization (reform of the multi-party parliamentary system). Their leaflets, pamphlets, and more theoretical publications argued for a further deepening of civil society and freedom of expression. At the same time, however, they envisioned an authoritarian transformation of society by the state, and authoritarian reform was increasingly regarded as the only means of achieving progress. Affected by the continuing radicalization and repression, many of these movements also showed a weakness in the field of "civil virtues." They show a strong intolerance for other movements. This was especially true of the communist movement's attitude towards the Muslim Brotherhood and the idea of false consciousness, but it was also apparent in the work of a socialist like Rashid al-Barrawi. The main dilemma, between authoritarian and democratic reform, however, was largely muted and contained under the monarchy because the state was basically in the hands of the conservative elite. It was not until after the failure of the Wafd's internal reforms in 1950–52 and the popular revolution that these intellectuals were tempted by more authoritarian modes of reform.

The reformist dilemma is most apparent in the writings of the Society of National Renaissance. Liberals concentrated on reforms that would turn political parties into permanent organizations to be led by professional and responsible politicians who would regard themselves as representatives of the people, learn their needs, and be elected on the basis of their political program and specific interests rather than their patronage relations. To this end and to let public opinion become a decisive force, the population as a whole would have to take part in politics, which meant that large scale social reforms would have to raise to an acceptable level its standard of living, its general education, its political consciousness, and its awareness of its national identity. At a later stage, liberals called for land reform without eliminating the landed class entirely. The problem with these measures was that they were so far-reaching that the state would have to become the main instrument of reform, thereby undermining the liberal goal of creating a balance between civil society and the state. Frustrated with the inability of existing political parties to reform themselves, the liberals looked more and more to a "benevolent dictator" to do their bidding in 1952. It was this authoritarianism that initially led them to support the military takeover and brought some of the members of the Society of National Renaissance to take part in the regime's new institutions of reform, the Permanent Council of Social Services (PCSS) and the Permanent Council for the Development of National Production (PCDNP). During the March Crisis of 1954, once it became clear that the military were there to stay, the liberals turned around and once again defended their earlier notion of civil society, calling for the election of the constituent assembly and the return of the military to their barracks.

I have examined the socialist road to modernity by concentrating on the writings of Rashid al-Barrawi. Rashid al-Barrawi adopted a less sanguine view of social reform through existing channels and called for a complete overhaul. A true authoritarian modernist, he pinned his hopes on massive industrialization, land reform, and the capacity of the state bureaucracy to transform Egypt into a modern society. Planning as a principle of rationalization and bringing Egypt "in accordance with the spirit of the times" found in Rashid al-Barrawi its first advocate. All the elements of authoritarian modernism come together in his work, which is pervaded by a distrust of politics and an absolute faith in the power of social and economic planning. This faith was supported by a historical, linear conception of progress that would end in the supremacy of technocracy and the rule of "experts." More so than the liberals, al-Barrawi turned his reform program into an ideology that was buttressed by a clearly defined concept of history that entailed the emergence and eventual victory of the middle classes as the main modernizing force.

Remarkably, once the new regime had come to power, Rashid al-Barrawi was able to carry out many of the reforms he had promoted in his dual capacity as ideologue and reformer. As director of the Industrial Bank and spokesperson for the PCDNP, he formulated and helped realize the new technocratic ideology of planism and state intervention. With the initiation of many of these projects, he also helped establish a new ideology of authoritarian modernization just after the March Crisis, when the new regime was in need of recognition as a "rationalist" state. From its reception in the press and in the writings of liberal and communist intellectualsm, it appears that for several years before the Suez Canal crisis planning had already been essential to the legitimization of the new regime. Rashid al-Barrawi was an important representative of the technological ideological strain in Egyptian political thought of the 1940s and the 1950s, upheld by a highly diverse set of personalities, including Aziz Sidqi, the Minister of Industry, the labor expert and advisor Abd al-Mughni Sa'id, and the more nationalist politicians like Fathi Radwan and Ibrahim Shukri.

Of the three currents that are the subject of this book, the communist movement shows the greatest contradictions in its attempts to negotiate between the varying demands of democratic and authoritarian reform. In practice the communists enhanced the expansion of civil society by endorsing the trade unions' struggle for independence. Due to the tactic of the national and popular front, the movement also favored the rise of a national bourgeoisie and took part in the parliamentary elections and the political reorganization of the existing system, with the aim to reform it from within. Communist publications called for the independence of civil society and injected into the public debate a healthy criticism that challenged the prevailing political culture of patronage and the social and economic inequality on which it was based. Yet, its more radical tactics, which led to a concentration on the workers' and proletarian revolution as well as the condemnation of the parliamentary system and of bourgeois culture in its entirety, were irrational and desperate in their isolationism. In the end, however, the social vision of the communist movement, aiming for an authoritarian, modernist transformation of society, should be regarded as the basis for its support of the regime in 1955. Planning in all its forms, including strong etatist leanings, represented in five-year plans, the "guided democracy," and state control of culture and ideology, enhanced the movement's support of an authoritarian, modernist political structure. The few "dissidents" who warned against the dangers of collectivism and etatism as it had evolved in the Soviet Union were ostracized as "Trotskyites."

In the course of events between 1950 and 1958, I regard the March Crisis as the final opportunity for democratic modernism. By that time most of the reformist platform had been realized. King Faruq had been banished, and land reform had eliminated the political power of the landed classes and the monarchy as well as the main source of the political culture of patronage. A new constitutional commission was drawing up a more inclusive constitution that would have led to greater political participation. Most political parties had also been purged of their corrupt and populist leadership. In the meantime, the middle classes had gained greater influence and a new generation of intellectuals could have taken over. This is supported by the writings that came out of the three currents. They all called for the military's withdrawal from politics, and many liberals and communists supported the election of a constituent assembly, one of the main issues at the time. The organizations of civil society – trade unions and the journalists' and the lawyers' syndicates – openly backed democratic demands.

In the period from 1955 to 1958, this trend was completely reversed, and the authoritarian strain in political thought became hegemonic. As a result, the ideas of the different secular currents began to resemble each other. Liberals and communists now adopted the same ideas that Rashid al-Barrawi had propounded since World War II. Partly, this was a consequence of the foreclosure of other possibilities after the March Crisis; partly it was the product of the authoritarian programs of the intellectuals themselves. Although dramatic political circumstances such as the Suez Canal crisis stimulated the authoritarian strain in secular thought, it is clear from their writings that the intellectuals willingly supported the new regime and that they did not defend it simply on the basis of its struggle for independence, let alone its pan-Arabist program. A new ideological trend had come about in the promotion of the regime. We can see this in numerous publications, including major newspapers, like *al-Akhbar*, *al-Ahram*, the liberal paper *al-Misri*, and especially the leftist *al-Masa'*, as well as in the leftist and liberal weekly *Ruz al-Yusuf*, the internal and external publications of the communist movement, and the publications of the newly established publishing houses of the left (such as Dar al-Nadim and Dar al-Fikr). I have called this new ideology, which has its origins in the revolt against the paternalism, patronage, and clientalism of the 1930s and 1940s, authoritarian modernism. Once a reformist movement had taken control of the state in the second half of the 1950s, many intellectuals were willing and able to back it. In fact, the prominence of the new state as the only focus for support along with the emergence of its new institutions and the expansion of bureaucracy provided the intellectuals with the opportunity to adopt the position of "experts" and "modernizers" they had aspired to for so long.

Ideologically, authoritarian modernism combines several elements that champion what James Scott has called "high modernism." The main feature of authoritarian modernism is a view of the state as in charge of the rationalization of society. In itself the increased focus on the state as agent of change was not surprising after eighty years of British domination. During the Suez Canal crisis Egypt had finally rid itself of British imperialism and had established for the first time a sovereign state that could implement the necessary reforms from above and create a nation. What is surprising is that we see intellectuals providing political, or at least ideological, justification for the suppression of civil society. In many respects they put forward a view of civil society as an obstacle to progress. They accepted the position that civil society causes social and political division, encourages compromises and inefficiency, enhances "special interests," and allows for the development of divergent cultural ideas. Furthermore, they acknowledged the state as the ultimate arbiter and appealed to it to defend the national culture and help establish a national identity. Essential to this shift in orientation on the part of the intellectuals was the substitution of a discourse of political rights and emancipation by an economic discourse of efficiency, rationalization, and collective rights of development. Planning became particularly influential and was seen as a means of state control, the basis of technocracy, and, in light of its emphasis on quantity above quality, part of a new ideology of production. Henceforth, specialized institutions had to guide democracy, culture, and a national philosophy, just like the newly controlled economy was managed by specialists, experts, and others who were educated to lead the nation to modernity. This was seen as the only way for Egypt to reach a higher stage of development. Contemporary travel literature underlines the importance of authoritarian modernism by reflecting an interest in comparable experiments in modernization conducted in other countries. From its pervasiveness in political and cultural discourse and the image the intellectuals had of themselves as the vanguard of the nation, it is clear that the 1950s were marked by a distinct ideology.

From a historical perspective, the authoritarian modernism of this period has to be seen as a prelude to its "deepening" in the 1960s when state control reached new heights. The nationalization of the press and the Egyptian firms, the importance of a centrally led economy and the five-year plans, the role of the intellectuals as the vanguard of the nation, and the final dissolution of the Egyptian

Communist Party in 1964, all had their roots in the 1950s. The difference was that in the 1960s state control became complete, so that the state dominated the ideological debates that supported authoritarian modernism. In the 1950s these debates were mostly carried out by the intellectuals, who were responsible for formulating this ideology. It was not until the 1970s that a new opposition against the state made itself heard. In the following decades, this opposition gradually took charge of the civil society that had been largely abandoned by the secular currents. In its struggle against authoritarian modernism, the Islamist movement could now lay claim to the issue of identity and the expansion of the free market.

Bibliography

Interviews

'Abd al-Mughni Sa'id, 28 November 1990.
Ibrahim Hilmi 'Abd al-Rahman, 10 December 1990.
Sa'd Zahran, 1 October 1987.
'Abd al-Raziq Hasan, 2 October 1989.
Salah al-Din Namiq, 27 October 1989.
Anwar 'Abd al-Malik, 1 November 1990.
Mustafa Tiba, 3 December 1990.
'Adil Thabit, 12 November 1990.
Muhmud Amin al-'Alim 20 October 1990.

Newspapers and Periodicals

al-Ahram, 1949–53.
al-Ahram al-Iqtisadi, 1952–56.
al-Akhbar, 1952–56.
al-Fajr al-Jadid, 1945–46.
al-Fusul, 1949–1952.
Hayat al-Hizb, 1957.
al-Intisar, 1956.
al-Iqtisad wa-l-Ijtima', 1945.
al-Iqtisad wa-l-Muhasaba, 1952–54.
Kifah al-Sha'b, 1955–57.
al-Kadir, 1957.
al-Masa', 1956–58.
al-Misri, 1952–54.
al-Musawwar, 1953.
Ruz al-Yusuf, 1952–1959.
Sawt al-Fallahin, 1956.
al-Zaman, 1951–52.

Collections of documents

Private collection of leaflets and pamphlets of Rif'at al-Sa'id.
Collection of Tali'a al-'Ummal (International Institute of Social History, Amsterdam).
Collection of Group de Rome (International Institute of Social History, Amsterdam).

Books and Articles in Arabic

'Abbas, Ra'uf. *Jama'at al-Nahha al-Qawmiyya.* Cairo: Dar al-Fikr li-l-Dirasat wa-l-Nashr wa-l-Tawzi', 1986.
'Abd al-Hakim, Tahir. *al-Amrikiyyin kharij biladihim.* Cairo: Matba'at al-Ma'rifa, n.d.
———. *Idtihad al-zunuj fi Amrika.* Cairo: Dar al-Fikr, 1958.
'Abd al-Malik, Anwar. *Dirasat fi al-thaqafa al-wataniyya.* Beirut: Dar al-Tali'a, 1967.
———. *al-Shari' al-Misri wa-l-fikr.* Cairo: al-Hay'a al-Misriyya al-'Amma li-l-Kitab, 1989.
'Abd al-Qadir, Muhammad Zaki. *Mihnat al-Dustur, 1923–1952.* Cairo: Kitab Ruz al-Yusuf, 1954.
———. *Aqdam 'ala al-Tariq.* Cairo: al-Mu'assasa al-Misriyya al-'Amma li-l-Ta'lif wa-l-Nashr, 1967.
———. *Mudhakkirat ... wa dhikrayat.* Cairo: N.p., n.d.
Abu al-Fath, Ahmad. *Jamal 'Abd al-Nasir.* Cairo: al-Maktab al-Misr al-Hadith, 1991.
Abu al-Futuh, Amira. *Ihsan 'Abd al-Quddus ... yatadhakkar.* Cairo: al-Hay'a al-Misriyya al-'Amma li-l-Kitab, 1982.
Ahmad, Muhammad Hasan. *al-Ikhwan al-muslimun fi al-mizan.* Cairo: N.p., n.d.
'Amir, Ibrahim. *al-Ard wa-l- fallah: al-Mas'ala al-zira'iyya fi Misr.* Cairo: Matba'at al-Dar al-Misriyya, 1958.
———. *Thawrat Misr al-qawmiyya.* Cairo: Dar al-Nadim, 1956.
Anis, 'Abd al-'Azim and Mahmud Amin al-'Alim. *Fi al-thaqafa al-Misriyya.* Cairo: Dar al-Fikr al-Jadid, 1955. Cairo: Dar al-Thaqafa al-Jadida, 1988.
Anis, Muhammad and al-Sayyid Rajab Hiraz. *Thawrat 23 yulyu 1952 wa usuluha al-tarikhiyya.* Cairo: Dar al-Nahda al-'Arabiyya, 1965.
Anis, Muhammad. *Dirasat al-qawmiyya al-'Arabiyya min al-nahiyatayn al-nazariyya wa-l-tarikhiyya.* 1959. Cairo: Dar al-Jabal, 1963.
———. *Tatawwur al-mujtama' al-Misri min al-iqta' ila thawrat 23 yulyu sanat 1952.* 1965. Cairo: Matba'at al-Jabalawi, 1977.
'Awda, Muhammad. *al-Sin al-sha'biyya.* Cairo: Dar al-Nadim, 1955.
Baha' al-Din, Ahmad. *Faruq malikan, 1936–1952.* Cairo: Kitab Ruz al-Yusuf, 1952.
———. *Ayyam laha tarikh.* Cairo: Kitab Ruz al-Yusuf, 1954.
———. *Shahr fi Rusiya.* Cairo: Dar al-Nadim, 1955.
Barakat, 'Ali. "Fi tariq ila madrasa ijtima'iyya fi kitabat tarikh Misr al-hadith." *al-Fikr* 5 (1985): 56–61.
Barakat, Baha al-Din. *Safahat min tarikh.* Cairo: Dar a-Hilal, 1960.
al-Barrawi, Rashid and Muhammad Hamza 'Ulaysh. *al-Tatawwur al-iqtisadi fi Misr fi al-'asr al-hadith.* 1944. Cairo: Maktabat al-Nahda al-Misriyya, 1945.
al-Barrawi, Rashid and Ahmad Nazmi 'Abd al-Hamid. *al-Nizam al-Ishtiraki: 'Ard, wa-l-tahlil, wa naqd.* Cairo: Maktabat al-Nahda al-Misriyya, 1946.

al-Barrawi, Rashid. *Nahwa 'alam jadid aw tatawwur al-fikra al-duwaliyya.* Cairo: Maktabat al-Nahda al-Misriyya, 1945.
———, trans. *al-Isti'mar a'li marahil al-ra'smaliyya.* By V.I. Linin. Cairo: Maktabat al-Nahda al-Misriyya, 1945.
———, trans. *al-Iqtisad al-siyasi.* By A. Liyuntif. Cairo: Maktabat al-Nahda al-Misriyya, 1946.
———, trans. *al-Tafsir al-ishtiraki li-l-tarikh: Mukhtarat min Fridrik Injilz.* By Fridrik Injilz. Cairo: Maktabat al-Nahdda al-Misriyya, 1947.
———, trans. *Ra'smal.* By Karl Markis. Cairo: Maktabat al-Nahda al-Misriyya, 1947.
———. *Mashru' Siriya al-kubra.* Cairo: Maktabat al-Nahda al-Misriyya, 1947.
———. *Halat Misr al-iqtisadiyya fi 'ahd al-Fatimiyyin.* Cairo: Maktabat al-Nahda al-Misriyya, 1948.
———. *Mashru'at al-sanawat al-khams min al-nahiyatayn al-nazariyya wa-l-tatbiqiyya.* Cairo: Maktabat al-Nahda al-Misriyya, 1948.
———. *Mushkilatuna al-ijtima'iyya: al-Faqr, al-fallah, al-ta'mim, al-'ummal.* Cairo: Maktabat al-Nahda al-Misriyya, 1948.
———, ed. *Mushkilat al-Sharq al-Awsat.* Cairo: Maktabat al-Nahda al-Misriyya, 1948.
———. *Ara' hurra.* Cairo: Maktabat al-Nahda al-Misriyya, 1949.
———. *al-Tariq ila al-salam: Bahth fi tanzim al-'alaqat al-duwaliyya.* Cairo: Maktabat al-Nahda al-Misriyya, 1949.
———. *Harb al-bitrul fi al-Sharq al-Awsat.* Cairo: Maktabat al-Nahda al-Misriyya, 1950.
———, trans. *al-Dawla wa al-nuzum al-iqtisadiyya fi al-Sharq al-Awsat.* By A. Buni. Cairo: Maktabat al-Nahda al-Misriyya, 1950.
———, ed. *Dirasat fi al-Sudan wa iqtisadiyyat al-Sharq al-Awsat.* Cairo: Maktabat al-Nahda al-Misriyya, 1951.
———. *al-Kutla al-Islamiyya.* Cairo: Maktabat al-Nahda al-Misriyya, 1952.
———. *Mashru'at al-difa' 'an al-Sharq al-Awsat.* Cairo: Maktabat al-Nahda al-Misriyya, 1952.
———. *Haqiqat al-inqilab al-akhir fi Misr.* Cairo: Maktabat al-Nahda al-Misriyya, 1952.
———. *Majmu'at al-watha'iq al-siyasiyya: al-Markaz al-duwali li-Misr wa-l-Sudan wa Qanat al-Suways.* Cairo: Maktabat al-Nahda al-Misriyya, 1952.
———. *Libiya wa-l-mu'amara al-Britaniyya.* Cairo: Maktabat al-Nahda al-Misriyya, 1953.
———. *al-Nuqta al-Rabi'a fi al-mizan.* Cairo: Maktabat al-Nahda al-Misriyya, 1953.
———. *al-Falsafa al-iqtisadiyya li-l-thawra min al-nahiyatayn al-nazariyya wa-l-'aqliyya.* Cairo: Maktabat al-Nahda al-Misriyya, 1955.
———. *al-Nizam al-ishtiraki min al-nahiyatayn al-nazariyya wa-l-'amaliyya.* 1951. Cairo: Maktabat al-Nahda al-Misriyya, 1956.
———. *Min hilf Baghdad ila al-hilf al-Islami.* Cairo: Maktabat al-Nahda al-Misriyya, 1958.
———. *Fi al-iqtisad al-Islami.* Cairo: Kitab al-Hurriyya, 1986.
Birnz, Ilinur. *al-Isti'mar al-Britani fi Misr.* Translated by Ahmad Rushdi Salih. Cairo: Dar Qarn al-'Ishrin, 1946.
al-Bishri,Tariq. *al-Haraka al-siyasiyya fi Misr, 1945–1952.* Cairo: Dar al-Shuruq, 1982.
———. *al-Muslimun wa-l-aqbat fi itar al-jama'a al-wataniyya.* 1980. Beirut: Dar al-Wahda, 1982.
———. *Dirasat fi al-dimuqratiyya al-Misriyya.* Cairo: Dar al-Shuruq, 1987.
———. *al-Dimuqratiyya wa nizam 23 yulyu, 1952–1970.* Beirut: Mu'assasat al-Abhath al-'Arabiyya, 1987.

BIBLIOGRAPHY

Butrus Ghali, Mirrit. *Siyasat al-ghad: Barnamij siyasi wa iqtisadi wa ijtima'i*. Cairo: Matba'at al-Risala, 1938.
——. *al-Islah al-zira'i: al-Milkiyya, al-ijar, al-'amal*. Cairo: Dar al-Fusul, 1945.
——. *Taqrir 'an al-azma al-iqtisadiyya al-ijtima'iyya*. N.p:. N.p., 1952.
Butrus Ghali, Mirrit and Ibrahim Bayyumi Madkur. *al-Adab al-Hukumiyya: Nizam jadid, hayah jadida*. Cairo: Dar al-Fusul, 1945.
Dali, 'Ali. *Amrika wa-l-'udwan 'ala Misr*. Cairo: Dar al-Fikr, 1957.
al-Disuqi, Asim. *Kibar mallak al-aradi al-zira'iyya wa dawruhum fi al-mujtama' al-Misri, 1914–1952*. Cairo: al-Hay'a al-Misriyya al-'Amma li-l-Kitab, 1975.
al-Disuqi al-Jami'i, 'Abd al-Mun'im. *al-Asliha al-fasida wa dawruha fi harb Filastin 1948*. Cairo: al-Hay'a al-Misriyya al-'Amma li-l-Kitab, 1990.
al-Ghazali, 'Abd al-Mun'im. *Indunisiya al-mujahida*. Cairo: Dar al-Fajr, n.d.
Ghurbal, Shafiq. *Muhammad 'Ali al-Kabir*. Cairo: Dar al-Ihya' li-l-Kutub al-'Arabiyya, 1944.
——. *Tarikh al-mufawadat al-Misriyya al-Britaniyya: Bahth fi al-'alaqat al-Misriyya al-Britaniyya min al-ihtilal ila 'aqd mu'ahadat al-tahaluf*. Cairo: Maktabat al-Nahda al-Misriyya, 1952.
Hasan, 'Abd al-Raziq. *Azmatuna al-iqtisadiyya*. Cairo: Kitab al-Muwatin, 1953.
Ibrahim, Ahmad. *al-Bank al-Markazi*. Cairo: Dar al-Fusul, 1949.
Iskandar, Suhayr. *Jaridat al-Misri wa-l-qadaya al-wataniyya*. Cairo: Mu'assasat Sijill al-'Arab, 1986.
——. *al-Sihafa al-Misriyya wa-l-qadaya al-wataniyya, 1946–1954*. Cairo: al-Hay'a al-Misriyya al-'Amma li-l-Kitab, 1992.
Jirjis, Fawzi. *Dirasat fi tarikh Misr al-siyasi mundhu al-'asr al-mamluki*. Cairo: Matba'at al-Dar al-Misriyya, 1958.
Jritli, 'Ali. *Tarikh al-sina'a fi Misr fi al-nisf al-awwal min al-qarn al-tasi' 'ashar*. Cairo: Dar al-Ma'arif bi-Misr, 1952.
Kamil, Anwar and Lutfallah Sulayman. *Ukhruju min al-Sudan*. Cairo: Matbu'at al-Duhama', 1947.
Kamil, Anwar. *Afyun al-Sha'b*. Cairo: Matba'at al-Risala, 1948.
Kamil, Mishil. *Amrika wa-l-Sharq al-'Arabi*. Cairo: Dar al-Fajr, n.d.
Khalil, Fathi. *Amrika 1958. 6 milyun 'atil, 50 bilyun dular li-l-harb*. Cairo: Dar al-Fikr, 1958.
——. *Difa''an al-thaqafa al-'Arabiyya: al-Harb al-fikriyya allati yudiruha al-isti'mar fi Sharqina al-'Arabi*. Cairo: Dar al-Fajr al-Jadid, 1959.
Lahita, Muhammad Fahmi. *Tarikh Fu'ad al-Awwal al-iqtisadi: Misr fi tariq al-tawjih al-kamil*. 3 vols. Cairo: Maktabat al-Nahda al-Misriyya, 1945–46.
——. *al-Nizam al-naqd bayna al-ra'smaliyya wa al-ishtirakiyya*. 2 vols. Cairo: Maktabat al-Nahda al-Misriyya, 1950.
Madkur, Ibrahim Bayumi. *Ma'a al-ayyam: Shay' min al-dhikriyyat*. Cairo: Kitab al-Hilal, 1990.
Mandur, Muhammad. *al-Dimaqratiyya al-siyasiyya*. Cairo: Kitab al-Muwatin, 1953.
——. *Jawla fi al-'alam al-ishtiraki*. Cairo: Dar al-Tiba'a al-Haditha, 1957.
Mar'i, Sayyid. *Awraq siyasiyya*. 3 vols. Cairo: al-Maktab al-Misr al-Hadith, 1978.
Maw Tsi Tunj. *al-Dimuqratiyya al-jadida*. Translated by Yusuf Ahmad. Cairo: Dar al-Nadim, 1957.
Muhyi al-Din, Khalid. *Wa al-ana atakallam*. Cairo: Markaz al-Ahram, 1993.
Mursi, Fu'ad. *Tatawwur al-ra'smaliyya wa kifih al-tabaqat fi Misr*. 1949. Cairo: Kitabat al-Misr al-Jadid, 1990.

Musa, Salama. *Hurriyyat al-'aql fi Misr.* Cairo: Dar al-Fajr, 1945.
Ramadan, 'Abd al-'Azim. *'Abd al-Nasir wa azmat maris 1954.* Cairo: Maktabat Ruz Yusuf, 1977.
———. *Tatawwur al-haraka al-wataniyya fi Misr min sanat 1918 ila sanat 1936.* Cairo: Maktabat Madbuli, 1983.
Rif'at, Kamil al-Din. *Mudhakkirat: Harb li-l-tahrir al-wataniyya bayna ilgha' mu'ahadat 1936 wa-l-ittifaqiyyat 1954.* Cairo: Dar al-Kitab al-'Arabi li-l-Taba'a wa-l-Nashr, 1978.
Rifa'i, Ahmad and 'Abd al-Mun'im. *Ayyam al-intisar.* Cairo: Dar al-Dimuqratiyya al-Jadida, 1957.
Sa'd, Ahmad Sadiq. *Mushkilat al-fallah.* Cairo: Dar al-Qarn al-'Ishrin, 1945.
———. *Ma'sat al-tamwin.* Cairo: Dar al-Qarn al-'Ishrin, 1945.
———. *As'ila wa ajwiba hawla al-mawqif al-hadir.* Cairo: N.p., 1956.
———. *Safahat min al-yasar al-Misri fi a'qab al-harb al-'alamiyya al-thaniya, 1945–1946.* Introduction by 'Abd al-'Azim Ramadan. Cairo: Maktabat al-Madbuli, 1976.
Sa'id, 'Abd al-Mughni. *al-'Alam ba'da harbayn.* Cairo: Dar al-Nil li-l-Tiba'a, 1947.
———. *Nahwa al-rushd al-iqtisadi. Dirasa shamila li-nazariyyat al-tarshid wa wasa'ilihi.* Cairo: Dar al-Nil li-l-Tiba'a, 1950.
———. *An lihadha al-sha'b an yafham.* Dar al-Kitab al-'Arabi, 1952.
———. *al-Ittihad al-Sufyati kama ra'aytuhu.* Cairo: Dar al-Fikr, 1958.
———. *Asrar al-siyasa al-Misriyya fi rub' qarn.* Cairo: Kitab al-Hurriyya, 1985.
al-Sa'id, Rif'at. *Tarikh al-munazzamat al-yasariyya al-Misriyya, 1940–1950.* Cairo: Dar al-Thaqafa al-Jadida, 1976.
———. *al-Sihafa al-yasariyya fi Misr, 1925–1948.* Cairo: Maktabat al-Madbuli, 1977.
———. *al-Sihafa al-yasariyya fi Misr, 1950–1952.* Cairo: Dar al-Thaqafa al-Jadida, 1982.
———. *Munazzamat al-yasar al-Misri, 1950–1957.* Cairo: Dar al-Thaqafa al-Jadida, 1983.
———. *Hasan al-Banna mu'assis jama'at al-ikhwan-al-muslimin. Mata . . . Kayfa . . . limadha?* 1977. Cairo: Dar al-Thaqafa al-Jadida, 1983.
———. *Tarikh al-shuyu'iyya al-Misriyya: al-Wahda, al-inqisam, al-hall, 1957–1965.* Cairo: Sharikat al-Amal, 1986.
Salih, Ahmad Rushdi. *Krumir fi Misr. Safahat min tarikh Misr al-hadith.* Cairo: Dar Qarn al-'Ishrin, 1945.
———. *Mas'alat al-Sudan.* Np:. N.p., n.d.
———. *Funun al-adab al-sha'bi.* Cairo: Dar al-Fikr, 1956.
al-Sayyid, Mustafa Kamil. *al-Mujtama' wa al-siyasa fi Misr. Dawr jama'at al-masalih fi al-nizam al-siyasi al-Misri, 1952–1981.* Cairo: Dar al-Mustaqbal al-'Arabi, 1983.
al-Shafi'i, Shuhdi 'Atiyya and Muhammad 'Abd al-Ma'bud al-Jubayli. *Ahdafuna al-wataniyya.* Cairo: Matba'at Risala, 1945.
al-Shafi'i, Shuhdi 'Atiyya. *Tatawwur al-haraka al-wataniyya al-Misriyya, 1882–1956.* 1957. Cairo: Dar Shuhdi, 1983.
al-Sharqawi, 'Abd al-Rahman. *Bandunj wa-l-salam al-'alami.* Cairo: Dar al-Fikr, 1955.
Shilaq, Ahmad Zakariyya. *Hizb al-Ahrar al-Dusturiyyun, 1922–1953.* Cairo: Dar al-Ma'arif, 1982.
al-Siba'i, Bashir. "Hawla ma yussama bi 'al-Trutskiyya al-Misriyya' bayna 'amay 1938–1948." In *Tarikh Misr bayna al-manhaj al-'ilm wa l-sira' al-hizbi.* Edited by Ahmad 'Abdallah. Cairo: Dar Shuhdi, 1987.
Tiba, Mustafa. *al-Haraka al-shuyu'iyya al-Misriyya 1945–1965. Ru'ya dakhiliyya.* Cairo: Sina li-l-Nashr, 1990.

Yasin, Muhammad Hilmi. *al-Isti'mar yuhzam fi al-Majar.* Cairo: al-Mu'assasa al-Qawmiyya li-l-Nashr wa-l-Tawzi', n.d.
Yusuf, Abu Sayf. *Hawla al-falsafa al-markisiyya, Radd 'ala al-'Aqqad.* Cairo: Dar al-Qarn al-'Ishrin, 1946.
al-Yusuf, Fatima. *Dhikrayat.* Cairo: Kitab Ruz al-Yusuf, 1953.
Zahran, Sa'd. *Fi usul al-siyasa al-Misriyya: Maqal tahlili naqdi fi al-tarikh al-siyasa.* Cairo: Dar al-Mustaqbal al-'Arabi, 1985.
Zayn al-Din, Isma'il Muhammad. *al-Tali'a al-Wafdiyya wa-l-haraka al-wataniyya, 1945–1952.* Cairo: al-Hay'a al-Misriyya al-'Amma li-l-Kitab, 1991.

Books and Articles in European languages

Abdalla, Ahmad. *The Student Movement and National Politics in Egypt.* London: Saqi Books, 1985.
Abdel Malek, Anouar. *Égypte société militaire.* Paris: Éditions du Seuil, 1962.
Alexandrian, Sarane. *Georges Henein.* Paris: Éditions Seghers, 1981.
Anderson, Benedict. *Imagined Communities: Reflections on the Origins and Spread of Nationalism.* 1983. London: Verso, 1993.
Anderson, Lisa. "Democracy in the Arab World: A Critique of the Political Approach." In *Political Liberalization and Democratization in the Arab World.* Vol. I: *Theoretical Perspectives.* Edited by Rex Brynen, Bahgat Korany, and Paul Noble. Boulder: Lynne Rienner, 1995. 77–92.
Awad, Louis. "Cultural and Intellectual Developments in Egypt Since 1952." In *Egypt Since the Revolution.* Edited by P.J. Vatikiotis. London: George Allen and Unwin, 1968. 143–61.
Ayalon, Ami. "Egyptian Intellectuals versus Fascism and Nazism in the 1930." In *The Great Powers in the Middle East 1919–1939.* Edited by Uriel Dann. New York: Holmes & Meier, 1988. 391–404.
———. *The Press in the Arab Middle East: A History.* Oxford: Oxford University Press, 1995.
Ayubi, Nazih N. M. *Bureaucracy and Politics in Contemporary Egypt.* London: Ithaca Press, 1980.
Badrawi, Malak. *Isma'il Sidqi 1875–1950: Pragmatism and Vision in Twentieth-Century Egypt.* Richmond: Curzon Press, 1996.
Baer, Gabriel. "Egyptian Attitudes Towards Land Reform, 1922–1955." In *The Middle East in Transition: Studies in Contemporary History.* Edited by W. Laqueur. London: RKP, 1958. 80–99.
Barakat, Magda. *The Egyptian Upper Class between Revolutions, 1919–1952.* Reading: Ithaca Press, 1998.
Barawy, Rashed El-. "The Agrarian Problem in Egypt." *Middle Eastern Affairs* 2 (1951): 75–84.
———. *The Military Coup in Egypt: An Analytic Study.* Cairo: The Renaissance Bookshop, 1952.
Baron, Beth. *The Women's Awakening in Egypt: Culture, Society, and the Press.* New Haven: Yale University Press, 1994.
Bauman, Zygmunt. *Legislators and Interpreters: On Modernity, Post-modernity and Intellectuals.* Cambridge: Polity Press, 1987.
Beattie, Kirk J. *Egypt During the Nasser Years: Ideology, Politics and Civil Society.* Boulder: Westview Press, 1994.

Beilharz, Peter. *Labour's Utopias: Bolshevism, Fabianism, Social Democracy.* London: Routledge, 1992.

Beinin, Joel and Zachary Lockman. *Workers on the Nile: Nationalism, Communism, Islam, and the Egyptian Working Class, 1882–1954.* Princeton: Princeton University Press, 1988.

Beinin, Joel. "The Communist Movement and Nationalist Political Discourse in Nasirist Egypt." *Middle East Journal* 41 (1987): 568–84.

———. "Labor, Capital, and the State in Nasirist Egypt, 1952–1961." *International Journal of Middle East Studies* 21 (1989): 71–90.

———. *Was the Red Flag Flying There? Marxist Politics and the Arab–Israeli Conflict in Egypt and Israel, 1948–1965.* London: I.B. Tauris, 1990.

———. "Exile and Political Activism: The Egyptian-Jewish Communists in Paris, 1950–59." *Diaspora* 2 (1992): 73–94.

Bellamy, Richard. *Liberalism and Modern Society: An Historical Argument.* Cambridge: Polity Press, 1992.

Berger, Morroe. *Islam in Egypt Today: Social and Political Aspects of Popular Religion.* Cambridge: Cambridge University Press, 1970.

Berman, Marshall. *All That Is Solid Melts into Air: The Experience of Modernity.* London: Verso, 1991.

Bianchi, Robert. *Unruly Corporatism: Associational Life in Twentieth-Century Egypt.* New York: Oxford University Press, 1989.

Binder, Leonard. *Islamic Liberalism: A Critique of Development Ideologies.* Chicago: University of Chicago Press, 1988.

Botman, Selma. "Egyptian Communists and the Free Officers: 1950–54." *Middle Eastern Studies* 22 (1986): 350–66.

———. *The Rise of Communism in Egypt, 1939–1970.* Syracuse: Syracuse University Press, 1988.

———. *Egypt from Independence to Revolution, 1919–1952.* Syracuse: Syracuse University Press, 1991.

Boullata, Issa J. *Trends and Issues in Contemporary Arab Thought.* Albany: State University of New York Press, 1990.

Boutros Ghali, Mirrit. *The Policy of Tomorrow.* Translated by Isma'il R. el-Faruqi. Washington DC: American Council of Learned Societies, 1953.

Burns, Elinor. *British Imperialism in Egypt.* Colonial Series. No. v. London: The Labour Research Department, 1928.

Bryant, Christopher G. A. "Civic Nation, Civil Society, Civil Religion." In *Civil Society: Theory, History, Comparison.* Edited by John Hall. Cambridge: Polity Press, 1995. 136–57.

Brynen, Rex, Bahgat Korany, and Paul Noble, eds. *Political Liberalization and Democratization in the Arab World.* Vol. I: *Theoretical Perspectives.* Boulder: Lynne Rienner, 1995.

Carr, E. H. *Twilight of the Comintern, 1930–1935.* New York: Pantheon Books, 1982.

Carter, B. L. *The Copts in Egyptian Politics.* London: Croom Helm, 1986.

Chatterjee, Partha. *Nationalist Thought and the Colonial World: A Derivative Discourse?* London: Zed Books, 1986.

———. *The Nation and Its Fragments: Colonial and Postcolonial Histories.* Princeton: Princeton University Press, 1993.

Choueri, Youssef M. *Arab History and the Nation-State: A Study in Modern Arab Historiography 1820–1980.* London: Routledge, 1989.

Claudin, Fernando. *The Communist Movement: From Comintern to Cominform.* London: Peregrine Books, 1975.
Collini, Stefan. *Public Moralists: Political Thought and Intellectual Life in Britain, 1850–1930.* Oxford: Clarendon Press, 1991.
Crabbs, Jack A. *The Writing of History in Nineteenth-Century Egypt.* Cairo: The American University in Cairo Press, 1984.
Crouchley, A. E. *The Investment of Foreign Capital in Egyptian Companies and Public Debt.* Cairo: Government Press Bulaq, 1936.
———. *The Economic Development of Modern Egypt.* London: ****, 1938.
Davis, Eric. *Challenging Colonialism: Bank Misr and Egyptian Industrialisation, 1920–1941.* Princeton: Princeton University Press, 1983.
———. "The Concept of Revival and the Study of Islam and Politics." In *The Islamic Impulse.* Edited by Barbara Freyer Stowasser. Beckenham: Croom Helm, 1987. 37–58.
Deeb, Marius. *Party Politics in Egypt: The Wafd and Its Rivals, 1919–1939.* London: Ithaca Press, 1979.
Deane, Herbert A. *The Political Ideas of Harold Laski.* Hamden, CT: Archon Books, 1972.
Delanty, Gerard. *Social Theory in a Changing World: Conceptions of Modernity.* Cambridge: Polity Press, 1999.
———. *Modernity and Postmodernity: Knowledge, Power and the Self.* London: Sage Publications, 2000.
Denoeux, Guilain. *Urban Unrest in the Middle East: A Comparative Study of Informal Networks in Egypt, Iran and Lebanon.* Albany: State University of New York Press, 1993.
al-Din al-Hadidy, Alaa. "Mustafa al-Nahhas and Political Leadership." In *Contemporary Egypt through Egyptian Eyes: Essays in Honour of P.J. Vatikiotis.* Edited by Charles Tripp. London: Routledge, 1993. 72–88.
Egger, Vernon. *A Fabian in Egypt: Salamah Musa and the Rise of the Professional Classes in Egypt.* Lanham: University Press of America, 1986.
Ehrenberg, John. *Civil Society: The Critical History of an Idea.* New York: New York University Press, 1999.
Erlich, Haggai. *Students and University in Twentieth-Century Egyptian Politics.* London: Frank Cass, 1989.
Fahmy, Khalid. *All the Pasha's Men: Mehmed Ali, His Army and the Making of Modern Egypt.* Cambridge: Cambridge University Press, 1997.
Featherstone, Mike, Scott Lash, and Roland Robertson, eds. *Global Modernities.* London: Sage Publications, 1995.
Foucault, Michel. *Power/Knowledge: Selected Interviews and Other Writings, 1972–1977.* Edited by Colin Gordon. New York: Pantheon Books, 1980.
Gellner, Ernest. *Nations and Nationalism.* Oxford: Basil Blackwell, 1983.
Gershoni, Israel. *The Emergence of Pan-Arabism in Egypt.* Tel Aviv: Shiloah Center for Middle Eastern and African Studies, 1981.
———. "Egyptian Intellectual History and Egyptian Intellectuals in the Interwar Period." *Asian and African Studies* 19 (1985): 333–64.
———. "The Muslim Brothers and the Arab Revolt in Palestine, 1936–39." *Middle Eastern Studies* 22 (1986): 367–97.
———. "Rejecting the West: The Image of the West in the Teachings of the Muslim Brotherhood, 1928–1939." In *The Great Powers in the Middle East 1919–1939.* Edited by Uriel Dann. New York: Holmes and Meier, 1988. 370–90.

———. "Imagining the East: Muhammad Husayn Haykal's Changing Representation of East-West Relations, 1928–1933." *Asian and African Studies* 25 (1991): 209–51.
Gershoni, Israel and James P. Jankowski. *Egypt, Islam, and the Arabs: The Search for Egyptian Nationhood, 1900–1930*. Oxford: Oxford University Press, 1986.
———. *Redefining the Egyptian Nation, 1930–1945*. Cambridge: Cambridge University Press, 1995.
Goldberg, Ellis. "Bases of Traditional Reaction: A Look at the Muslim Brothers." *Peuples Méditerranéens* 14 (1981): 79–93.
———. *Tinker, Tailor and Textile Worker: Class and Politics in Egypt, 1930–1952*. Berkeley: University of California Press, 1986.
Goldschmidt, Arthur Jr. "The Egyptian Nationalist Party: 1992–1919." In *Political and Social Change in Modern Egypt: Historical Studies from the Ottoman Conquest to the United Arab Republic*. Edited by P.M. Holt. Oxford: Oxford University Press, 1968. 308–33.
———. *Modern Egypt: The Formation of a Nation-State*. Boulder: Westview Press, 1988.
Gordon, Joel. "The False Hopes of 1950: The Wafd's Last Hurrah and the Demise of Egypt's Old Order." *International Journal of Middle East Studies* 21 (1989): 193–214.
———. "The Myth of the Savior: Egypt's Just Tyrants" on the Eve of Revolution, January–July 1952." *Journal of American Research Centre in Egypt* 26 (1989): 223–38.
———. *Nasser's Blessed Movement: Egypt's Free Officers and the July Revolution* New York: Oxford University Press, 1992.
Greenleaf, W. H. "Laski and British Socialism." *History of Political Thought* 2 (1981): 573–91.
———. *The British Political Tradition*. Vol. I. London: Methuen, 1983.
El-Gritly, A. A. I. "The Structure of Modern Industry in Egypt." *L'Égypte Contemporaine* 38 (1948): 364–582.
Habermas, Jürgen. *The Structural Transformation of the Public Sphere: An Inquiry into a Category of Bourgeois Society*. Translated by Thomas Burger. Cambridge: Polity Press, 1989.
Haithcox J. P. *Communism and Nationalism in India: M. N. Roy and Comintern Policy, 1920–1939*. Princeton: Princeton University Press, 1971.
Hall, John, ed. *Civil Society: Theory, History, Comparison*. Cambridge: Polity Press, 1995.
Harris, Christina Phelps. *Nationalism and Revolution in Egypt: The Role of the Muslim Brotherhood*. The Hague: Mouton, 1964.
Harris, José. *William Beveridge: A Biography*. Oxford: Clarendon Press, 1977.
Harvey, David. *The Condition of Postmodernity: An Inquiry into the Origins of Cultural Change*. Oxford: Basil Blackwell, 1989.
Haslam, Jonathan. "The Comintern and the Origins of the Popular Front, 1934–1935." *Historical Journal* 22 (1979): 673–91.
Hettne, Bjorn. *Development Theory and the Three Worlds*. Burnt Mill: Longman, 1990.
Hobsbawm, E. J. *Nations and Nationalism since 1780: Programme, Myth, Reality*. Cambridge: Cambridge University Press, 1992.
Hossseinzadeh, Esmail. *Soviet Non-Capitalist Development*. New York: Praeger, 1989.
Hourani, Albert. *Arabic Thought in the Liberal Age, 1798–1939*. Oxford: Oxford University Press, 1962.
Hudson, Michael C. "The Political Culture Approach to Arab Democratization: The Case for Bringing It Back in, Carefully." In *Political Liberalization and*

Democratization in the Arab World. Vol. I: *Theoretical Perspectives.* Edited by Rex Brynen, Bahgat Korany, and Paul Noble. Boulder: Lynne Rienner, 1995. 61–76.
Hussein, Taha. *The Future of Culture in Egypt.* New York: Octagon Books, 1975.
Ibrahim, A. Ibrahim. "Salama Musa: An Essay on Cultural Alienation." *Middle Eastern Studies* 15 (1979): 346–57.
Ibrahim, Saad Eddin. "Civil Society and the Prospects for Democratization in the Arab World." In *Civil Society in the Middle East.* Edited by Augustus Richard Norton. Leiden: Brill, 1995. 27–54.
Ismael, Tareq Y and Rifa'at el-Sa'id. *The Communist Movement in Egypt, 1920–1988.* Syracuse: Syracuse University Press, 1990.
Jackson, Julian. *The Popular Front in France: Defending Democracy, 1934–38.* Cambridge: Cambridge University Press, 1988.
Jankowski, James P. *Egypt's Young Rebels "Young Egypt": 1933–1952.* Stanford: Hoover Institute Publications, 1975.
Kazziha,Walid. "The Jaridah-Umma Group and Egyptian Politics." *Middle Eastern Studies* 13 (1977): 373–85.
Keane, John. *Democracy and Civil Society: On the Predicaments of European Socialism, the Prospects for Democracy, and the Problem of Controlling Social and Political Power.* London: Verso, 1988.
Kedourie, Elie. *The Chatham House Version and Other Middle-Eastern Studies.* Hanover: University Press of New England, 1984.
Kelidar, Abbas. "The Political Press in Egypt, 1882–1914." In *Contemporary Egypt: Through Egyptian Eyes: Essays in Honour of P.J. Vatikiotis.* Edited by Charles Tripp. London: Routledge, 1993. 1–21.
Kitroeff, Alexander. *The Greeks in Egypt, 1919–1937: Ethnicity and Class.* Oxford: Ithaca Press, 1989.
Krämer, Gudrun. *The Jews in Modern Egypt 1914–1952.* London: I.B. Tauris, 1989.
Laski, Harold. *A Grammar of Politics.* London: George Allen and Unwin, 1925.
Lenin, V. I. *Imperialism, the Highest Stage of Capitalism. Selected Works.* Vol. I. Moscow: Foreign Language Publishing House, 1946. 643–740.
Lia, Brynjar. *The Society of the Muslim Brothers in Egypt: The Rise of an Islamic Mass Movement, 1928–1942.* Reading: Ithaca Press, 1998.
Linz, Juan J. and Alfred Stepan. *Problems of Democratic Transition and Consolidation: Southern Europe, South America, and Post-Communist Europe.* Baltimore: The John Hopkins University Press, 1996.
Lockman, Zachary. "The Social Roots of Nationalism: Workers and the National Movement in Egypt, 1908–1919." *Middle Eastern Studies* 24 (1988): 445–59.
Lutfi al-Sayyid-Marsot, Afaf. *Egypt's Liberal Experiment: 1922–1936.* Berkeley: University of California Press, 1977.
Mabro, Robert. *The Egyptian Economy, 1962–1972.* Oxford: Clarendon Press, 1974.
Mahmoudi, Abdelrashid. *Taha Husain's Education: From the Azhar to the Sorbonne.* Richmond: Curzon Press, 1998.
Mau Tse-Tung. "On New Democracy." *Selected Works of Mau Tse-Tung.* Vol. 2. Peking: Foreign Language Press, 1965. 339–84.
Mayfield, James B. "Agricultural Cooperatives: Continuity and Change in Rural Egypt." In *Egypt from Monarchy to Republic: A Reassessment of Revolution and Change.* Edited by Shimon Shamir. Boulder: Westview Press, 1995. 81–102.
McCrone, David. *The Sociology of Nationalism: Tomorrow's Ancestors.* London: Routledge, 1998.

Meijer, Roel. "History, Authenticity, and Politics: Tariq al-Bishri's Interpretation of Modern Egyptian History." *MERA Occasional Paper* 4 (September 1989).
———. "Authenticity in History. The Concepts al-Wafid and al-Mawruth in Tariq al-Bishri's Reinterpretation of Modern Egyptian History." In *Amsterdam Middle Eastern Studies*. Edited by Manfred Woidich. Wiesbaden: Dr. Ludwig Reichert Verlag, 1990. 68–83.
———. "Postmodernism and Egyptian Political Thought." In *Changing Stories: Postmodernism and the Arab-Islamic World*. Edited by Inge Boer, Annelies Moors, and Toine van Teeffelen. Amsterdam: Orientations No. 3, 1995. 69–90.
———. "Liberal Reform: The Case of the Society of National Renaissance." In *Entre reforme social et mouvement national: Identité et modernisation en Egypte (1882–1962)*. Edited by Alain Roussillon. Cairo: CEDEJ, 1995. 129–62.
———, ed. and introd. *Cosmopolitanism, Identity and Authenticity in the Middle East*. Richmond: Curzon Press, 1999.
———, ed. and introd. *Alienation or Integration of Arab Youth: Between Family, State and Street*. Richmond: Curzon Press, 2000.
Mitchell, Ritchard P. *The Society of the Muslim Brothers*. London: Oxford University Press, 1969.
Mitchell, Timothy. *Colonising Egypt*. Cairo: The American University in Cairo Press, 1989.
Moore, Barrington, Jr. *Social Origins of Dictatorship and Democracy: Lord and Peasant in the Making of the Modern World*. Boston: Beacon Press, 1967.
Moore, Clement Henry. "Authoritarian Politics in Unincorporated Society." *Comparative Politics* 6.2 (1974): 193–218.
———. *Images of Development: Egyptian Engineers in Search of Industry*. Cambridge: The MIT Press, 1980.
Morgan, K. O. *Labour in Power, 1945–1951*. Oxford: Clarendon Press, 1984.
Mouzelis, Nicos. "Modernity, Late Development and Civil Society." In *Civil Society: Theory, History, Comparison*. Edited by John Hall. Cambridge: Polity Press, 1995. 224–49.
Nederveen Pieterse, Jan. *Empire and Emancipation: Power and Liberation on a World Scale*. London: Pluto Press, 1990.
———. "Dilemmas of Development Discourse: The Crisis of Developmentalism and the Comparative Method." *Development and Change* 22 (1991): 5–29.
Nisbet, Robert A. *The Sociology of Emile Durkheim*. London: Heinemann Educational, 1975.
Norton, Augustus Richard. "The Future of Civil Society in the Middle East." *Middle East Journal* 47 (1993): 205–16.
———. ed. and introd. *Civil Society in the Middle East*. Vol. I. Leiden: E. J. Brill, 1995.
O'Brien, Patrick. *The Revolution in Egypt's Economic System: From Private Enterprise to Socialism, 1952–1966*. London: Oxford University Press, 1966.
Owen, Roger. *The Middle East in the World Economy, 1800–1914*. London: Methuen, 1981.
———. "The Ideology of Economic Nationalism in its Egyptian Context: 1919–1939." *Intellectual Life in the Arab East, 1890–1939*. Edited by M. R. Buheiry. Beirut: American University of Beirut Press, 1981. 1–9.
———. "The Economic Consequences of the Suez Crisis for Egypt." In *Suez 1956: The Crisis and its Consequences*. Edited by W. M. Roger Louis and Roger Owen. Oxford: Clarendon Press, 1989. 363–76.

Perrault, Gilles. *Un homme à part*. Paris: Bernard Barrault, 1984.
Pérez-Díaz, Víctor. "The Possibility of Civil Society: Traditions, Character and Challenges." In *Civil Society: Theory, History, Comparison*. Edited by John Hall. Cambridge: Polity Press, 1995. 80–109.
Peters, Rudolph. *Islam and Colonialism: The Doctrine of Jihad in Modern History*. The Haque: Mouton, 1979.
Philipp, Thomas. "Copts and Other Minorities in the Development of the Egyptian Nation-State." In *Egypt from Monarchy to Republic: A Reassessment of Revolution and Change*. Edited by Shimon Shamir. Boulder: Westview Press, 1995. 131–50.
Pocock, J. G. A. *Politics, Language and Time: Essays on Political Thought and History*. New York: Atheneum, 1971.
Pripstein Posusney, Marsha. *Labor and the State in Egypt: Workers, Unions, and Economic Restructuring*. New York: Columbia University Press, 1997.
Reid, Donald, M. "The Rise of Professions and Professional Organizations in Modern Egypt." *Comparative Studies in Society and History* 10 (1974): 24–57.
———. "Fu'ad Siraj al-Din and the Egyptian Wafd." *Journal of Contemporary History* 15 (1980): 721–44.
———. *Cairo University and the Making of Modern Egypt*. Cambridge: Cambridge University Press, 1990.
———. "Archeology, Social Reform and Modern Identity among the Copts." In *Entre réforme sociale et mouvement national: Identité et modernisation en Egypte (1882–1962)*. Edited by Alain Roussillon. Cairo: CEDEJ, 1995. 311–36.
Rothstein, Theodore. *Egypt's Ruin: A Financial and Administrative Record*. London: Cliffords Inn, 1910.
Safran, Nadav. *Egypt in Search of Political Community: An Analysis of the Intellectual and Political Evolution of Egypt, 1804–1952*. Cambridge, MA: Harvard University Press, 1961.
Sayed-Ahmad, Muhammad Abd el-Wahab. *Nasser and American Foreign Policy 1952–1956*. Cairo: The American University in Cairo Press, 1989.
al-Sayyid, Mustapha Kamil. "A Civil Society in Egypt." *Middle East Journal* 47 (1993): 229–43.
Scott, James C. *Seeing Like a State: How Certain Schemes to Improve the Human Condition Have Failed*. New Haven: Yale University Press, 1998.
Seligman, Adam B. "Animadversions upon Civil Society and Civic Virtue in the Last Decade of the Twentieth Century." In *Civil Society: Theory, History, Comparison*. Edited by John Hall. Cambridge: Polity Press, 1995. 200–23.
Schram, Stuart. *Mau Tse-tung*. Harmondsworth: Penguin Books,1967.
———. *The Political Thought of Mau Tse-tung*. Harmondsworth: Penguin Books, 1969.
Schrand, Irmgard. *Louis Awad: Ein ägyptischer Kritiker und Denker des 20. Jahrhunderts: Streiter für einen säkularen Staat*. Münster/Hamburg: Lit Verlag, Hamburger Islamwissenschaftliche und Türkologische Arbeiten und Texte, 1994.
Schulze, Reinhard. *Die Rebellion der ägyptischen Fallahin 1919*. Berlin: Baalbek Verlag, 1981.
Sharabi, Hisham. *Neopatriarchy: A Theory of Distorted Change in Arab Society*. Oxford: Oxford University Press, 1988.
Shepard, William. "The Dilemma of a Liberal: Some Political Implications in the Writings of the Egyptian Scholar, Ahmad Amin (1886–1954)." In *Modern Egypt: Studies in Politics and Society*. Edited by Elie Kedourie and Sylvia Haim. London: Frank Cass, 1980. 84–97.

Shils, Edward. *The Virtue of Civility: Selected Essays on Liberalism, Tradition, and Civil Society.* Edited by Steven Grosby. Indianapolis: Liberty Fund, 1997.
Smart, Barry. *Postmodernity.* London: Routledge, 1993.
Smith, Anthony. *National Identity.* London: Penguin Books, 1991.
Smith, Charles D. "The "Crisis of Orientation': The Shift of Egyptian Intellectuals to Islamic Subjects in the 1930s." *International Journal of Middle East Studies* 4 (1973): 382–410.
——. "4 February 1942: Its Causes and Its Influence on Egyptian Politics and on the Future of Anglo-Egyptian Relations, 1937–1945." *International Journal of Middle East Studies* 10 (1979): 453–79.
——. "The Intellectual and Modernization: Definitions and Reconsiderations: The Egyptian Experience." *Comparative Studies in Society and History* 22 (1980): 513–33.
——. *Islam and the Search for Social Order in Modern Egypt: A Biography of Muhammad Husayn Haykal.* Albany: State University of New York Press, 1983.
Springborg, Robert. "Sayed Bey Marei and Political Clientalism in Egypt." *Comparative Political Studies* 42 (1979): 259–88.
——. "Patterns of Association in the Egyptian Political Elite." In *Political Elites in the Middle East.* Edited by G. Lenzsowski. Washington DC: American Enterprise Institute, 1975. 83–108.
Stephens, Robert. *Nasser: A Political Biography.* Harmondsworth: Penguin Books, 1971.
Terry, Janice. *The Wafd, 1919–1952: Cornerstone of Egyptian Political Power.* London: Third World Centre, 1982.
Therborn, Göran. "Routes to/through Modernity." In *Global Modernities.* Edited by Mike Featherstone, Scott Lash, and Roland Robertson. London: Sage Publications, 1995. 124–39.
Thieck, Jean Pierre. "Communistes et mouvement national en Égypte (1945–1946)." *Passion d'Orient.* Paris: Éditions Karthala, 1992. 71–109.
Tignor, Robert L. "The Egyptian Revolution of 1919: New Directions in the Egyptian Economy." *Middle Eastern Studies* 12 (1976): 41–67.
——. "Equity in Egypt's Recent Past: 1945–1952." In *The Political Economy of Income Distribution in Egypt.* Edited by Gouda Abdel Khalek and Robert Tignor. New York: Holmes and Meier, 1982. 20–55.
——. *State, Private Enterprise and Economic Change in Egypt, 1918–1952.* Princeton: Princeton University Press, 1983.
——. "Decolonization and Business: The Case of Egypt." *Journal of Modern History* 59 (1987): 479–505.
——. *Egyptian Textiles and British Capital, 1930–1956.* Cairo: The American University in Cairo Press, 1989.
——. "Foreign Capital, Foreign Communities, and the Egyptian Revolution of 1952." In *Egypt from Monarchy to Republic: A Reassessment of Revolution and Change.* Edited by Shimon Shamir. Boulder: Westview Press, 1995. 103–130.
Toledano, Ehud. *State and Society in Mid-Century Egypt.* Cambridge: Cambridge University Press, 1990.
Turner, Bryan S., ed. *Theories of Modernity and Postmodernity.* London: Sage Publications, 1990.
Vatikiotis, P. J. *The History of Egypt from Muhammad Ali to Sadat.* 1969. London: Weidenfeld and Nicolson, 1980.
——. *Nasser and His Generation.* London: Croom Helm, 1978.

Vitalis, Robert. "On the Theory and Practice of Compradors: The Role of Abbud Pasha in the Egyptian Political Economy." *International Journal of Middle East Studies* 22 (1990): 291–315.

———. *When Capitalists Collide: Business Conflict and the End of the Empire in Egypt.* Berkeley: University of California Press, 1995.

Wahba, Mourad Magdi. *The Role of the State in the Egyptian Economy: 1945–1981.* Houndsmills: MacMillan Press, 1993.

Wall, Irwin M. *French Communism in the Era of Stalin: The Quest for Unity and Integration, 1945–1962.* Westport, CT: Greenwood Press, 1983.

Wallwork, Ernest. *Durkheim: Morality and Milieu.* Cambridge, MA: Harvard University Press, 1972.

Walzer, Michael, ed. and introd. *Toward a Global Civil Society.* Providence: Berghahn Books, 1995.

———. "The Concept of Civil Society." In *Toward a Global Civil Society.* Edited by Michael Walzer. Providence: Berghahn Books, 1995. 7–28.

Warren, Bill. *Imperialism Pioneer of Capitalism.* London: Verso, 1980.

Warriner, Doreen. *Land and Poverty in the Middle East.* London and New York: Royal Institute of International Affairs, 1948.

Waterbury, John. *The Egypt of Nasser and Sadat: The Political Economy of Two Regimes.* Princeton: Princeton University Press, 1983.

———. "Democracy without Democrats?: The Potential for Political Liberalization in the Middle East." In *Democracy without Democrats? The Renewal of Politics in the Muslim World.* Edited by Ghassan Salamé. London: I.B. Tauris, 1994. 23–47.

Webb, Sidney and Beatrice Webb. *Soviet Communism: A New Civilisation.* London: Longman, 1935.

Wendell, Charles. *The Evolution of the Egyptian National Image: From Its Origins to Ahmad Lutfi al-Sayyid.* Berkeley: University of California Press, 1972.

Wild, Stefan. "'Das Kapital' in arabischer Übersetzung." In *Festgabe für H. Wehr.* Edited by Wolfdietrich Fischer. Wiesbaden: Otto Harrassowitz, 1969. 97–111.

Wittig, Peter. *Der englische Weg zum Sozialismus: Die Fabier und ihre Bedeutung für die Labour Party und die englische Politik.* Berlin: Duncker and Humblot, 1982.

Zaki, Moheb. *Civil Society and Democratization in Egypt, 1981–1994.* Cairo: Konrad Adenauer Stiftung and The Ibn Khaldun Center, 1995.

Index

Abbas II, Khedive, 14
Abbud, Ahmad, 17
Abbud group, 192
Abdallah, Isma'il Sabri, 121
Abd al-Hakim, Tahir, 240
Abd al-Malik, Anwar: and Copts and communism, 104; designer of a new philosophy, 227–230; as intellectual, 5; and the Soviet Union, 234; as editor of *al-Jamahir*, 120
Abd al-Hamid, Ahmad Nazmi, 69
Abd al-Nasser, Gamal, 86, 162, 173, 185, 187, 188, 195, 197, 212
Abd al-Qadir, Muhammad Zaki: background of, 42–44; and elections of 1950, 141; ideological influences on, 46–7; influence on *Ruz al-Yusuf*, 61, 139
Abd al-Quddus, Ihsan (*see also Ruz al-Yusuf*): and Ali Mahir, 144, 153; appointment as editor-in-chief of *Ruz al-Yusuf*, 139; and arms deal, 141; and armed struggle along the Suez Canal, 142; and Bandung conference, 187; and "benevolent dictatorship", 145–6; and Cairo fire, 143; on China, 235; on Constitution of 1923, 145; and debate on "Egyptian personality", 218–9; and democracy, 167, 212–3; and his imprisonment, 165; on India, 237; and industrialization, 186; on Israel, 188; and March Crisis, 164–5; and Naguib al-Hilali, 144–6; and nationalization of Suez Canal Company, 188; on Pakistan, 236; on Pan-Arabism, 237; on a political party for the military, 156; and reorientation toward new regime, 186–8; and Society of National Renaissance 61, 136; on the Soviet Union, 234; in support of the revolution, 150–1; and temporary dictatorship, 144–6; torn between modernity and tradition, 219; on Turkey, 236; on unification with Syria, 189; and Wafd, 153
Abd al-Raziq, Ali, 18, 227
Abd al-Raziq, Mustafa, 43
Abu al-Fath, Ahmad: on agrarian reform law, 149; on armed struggle along Suez Canal, 142; and authoritarian reform, 146; and "benevolent dictatorship", 154; and the Wafd, 155; and democracy, 167; as editor-in-chief of *al-Misri*, 138; and March Declaration, 163; and political purification, 154–5; and relations with Gamal Abd al-Nasser, 138, 140; and relations with liberals, 61, 136; and relations with Wafd, 140; and communist periodicals, 157
Abu al-Fath, Mahmud, 138
Afifi, Hafiz, 87
Africa, 232
Ahmad, Muhammad Hasan, 118–9
al-Ahram, 15, 42, 139
Akhbar al-Yawm, 156, 180

269

INDEX

Ali, Muhammad, 81, 110, 143, 225
al-Alim, Mahmud Amin, 139, 157, 188–9, 221–2
Amin, Ahmad, 17, 43, 20, 227
Amir, Ibrahim, 223–7
Anglo-Egyptian Treaty, 23–24, 87, 112, 115, 247, 142
Anis, Abd al-Azim, 157, 214, 221–2
Anis, Muhammad, 157, 338
al-Aqqad, Abbas Mahmud, 17, 107
Art et Liberté, 103, 124
Aswan High Dam, 175, 178, 187, 192, 201, 239
Ataturk, 154, 219
authenticity: and communist critique of, 107–8; and defense of culture, 218–22; and discourse on, 21, 24; and Egyptian communism, 96–97; and Egyptian communist historiography, 224; and identity, 5–6
Awda, Muhammad: 222, 235–6
Azhar university, 18
Aziz, Da'ud, 122

Baghdad Pact, 186, 193, 236
Baha al-Din, Ahmad: defense of democracy, 153–4; on France, 239; joining staff of *Ruz al-Yusuf*, 139; and military takeover, 151–2; on Nehru, 236; on Pakistan, 236; on Pan-Arabism, 237–8; on political purification, 154; on planning, 214–5; and Society of National Renaissance, 61, 152; on state protection of national culture, 221, 240; and trip to the Soviet Union, 232–3; on unification with Syria, 189; on the tasks of the middle classes, 220; and writing in *al-Ghad*, 157
Bandung conference, 70, 186, 227, 234
Bank Misr, 4, 17, 112
Barakat, Magda, 15
Barakat, Baha al-Din, 42
al-Barrawi, Rashid: and agrarian reform, 82–85, 148–9; and Ali Mahir, 144, 148; and authoritarian modernism 67, 88–90, 191, 250–2; and Beveridge Plan, 74–75; biography of, 68–70; and British socialism, 70–75; and civil society, 66–67; and collectivism, 72; and contacts with Free officers, 148–9; and contacts with Gamal Abd al-Nasser, 148; and communist historiography of Egypt, 109; and democracy, 145–6; and democratic socialism, 73–4; and economic philosophy, 182; and *effendiyya*, 88–89, 167; and Egyptian economic historiography, 80–81; and high modernism, 78–79, 90; and historical laws of development, 77–80; and Industrial Bank, 150, 180–2; and industrialization, 80, 90; on Isma'il Sidqi, 146; and July revolution, 85–88, 150–1, 155, 166–7; and large landowners, 75, 81, 148; and Leninism, 76; and Marxism, 72; on Muhammad Ali, 143; and patronage, 67; and nationalization, 75; and Permanent Council for the Development of National Production, 150, 179; on political reform, 136, 147–8; promotor of economic planning, 67, 72–73, 79, 88, 178, 180–4; representative of new reformist currents, 26; and the Soviet Union, 78–79, 84; and technocracy, 67; and welfare state, 74–75; and writing in *al-Zaman*, 139, 145
Beinin, Joel, 7
Bentham, Jeremy, 46, 71
Beveridge, William, 74
Bili, Muhammad, 235
Blunt, Wilfred Scawen, 108
Bolshevism, 123
Botman, Selma, 7, 116
Burma, 194
Burns, Elinor, 108

Caffery, Jefferson, 159
Cairo fire, 143, 146, 166
Capitulations, 15, 247
Chiang Kaishek, 103, 188
China: and comparison with India, Indonesia and Yugoslavia, 236; and Egyptian communist movement, 102–3; and Egyptian travel literature, 28, 232, 235–6; and national bourgeoisie, 160

INDEX

Chou En Lai, 187
civil society: and bourgeoisie, 8; and communism, 98; and demise of, 9, 23; and emergence of, 11–14, 246–7; flaws of, 12; and ideology of, 9; and large landowners, 15; and middle classes, 13, 247; and new generation of intellectuals, 17; and patronage, 8, 16; and planning, 22; and political society, 8–9; and post-World War II, 137–40; and the press, 15; and private *ahli* organizations, 12; and Rashid al-Barrawi, 90; and scholarly debate on 7–11; and theory of, 6–9; and threats to, 7; and trade unions, 14, 252; and values of, 7; and welfare associations, 17; and working class, 22, 247; and support of after the July revolution, 156; and repression of during the July revolution, 175; and revival, 254
Cleland, W., 85
collectivization, 79
Comintern, 100–3, 106, 112
Comité du Rassemblement Populaire, 102
Commission of Commerce and Industry, 15
Communist Party of China (CPC), 103, 191, 226
Communist Party of Egypt (CPE): and dissolution of, 177, 254; and foundation of, 103; and reestablishment of, 121–123; and rejection of military takeover, 158; and role of, 127; and unification of, 161, 190
Communist Party of France (CPF), 101–2, 122
Communist Unity, 161
Comte, Auguste, 71
Conference of Montreux, 24
Constitution of 1923: communist movement on, 99, 160; and democracy, 6; and Ihsan Abd al-Quddus on, 145, 212; and multi-party system, 17; and Society of National Renaissance on, 37, 39, 49; and Rashid al-Barrawi on, 87, 145; and *Ruz al-Yusuf* on, 61; after July revolution, 147; and Wafd, 137

Constitution of 1956, 212
Copts, 15, 119, 225
Cromer, Lord (Evelyn Baring), 108–9
Crouchley, A.E., 68, 80
Curiel, Henri, 104, 116, 120
Curiel, Raoul, 104
Czech arms deal, 187

al-Damir, 117
Dar al-Abhath al-'Ilmiyya, 105, 117
Dar al-Fajr, 106
Dar al-Fikr, 195
Dar al-Nadim, 102, 195, 232
Dar al-Qarn al-'Ishrin, 106, 108, 117
Darwish, Sayyid, 227
Darwish, Yusuf, 104
al-Da'wa, 142
Democratic Movement for National Liberation, DMNL (al-Haraka al-Dimuqratiyya li-l-Taharrur al-Watani, HADITU): and Constitution of 1923, 160; and CPE, 121–3; and establishment of, 119–20; and July revolution, 148, 157–61; and National Democratic Front, 160; and religion, 126; and splits within, 120–1, 161–2; and unification of, 190; and the Wafd, 158
Democratic Movement for National Liberation-Revolutionary Wing (HADITU-al-Tayyar al-Thawri), 161, 191
Democratic Union, 104
Descombes, Paul Jacot, 104
Dimitrov, Georgi, 101
Don Quichotte, 103
Durkhem, Emile, 46–47
Duwayk, Raymond, 104, 115

Easternism, 24, 97, 230–2
Economic Organization, 198–9
economic society, 7, 15
Eden, Anthony, 188
effendiyya: and progress 70; and Rashid al-Barrawi 66–67, 88–89; and revolt against elite, 4, 22; and rise of, 22; and Society of National Renaissance, 40
L'Effort, 103, 124

271

INDEX

Egyptian Communist movement: and agrarian reform, 110–11, 127; and Aswan High Dam, 198; and authoritarian modernism, 99, 191; and Bandung Conference, 193; and civil society, 98–99, 136, 251; and Comintern, 100–103; communist dissidents, 123–6, 251; and democracy 113–114, 215–8; and economic planning, 111–13, 198–200; and economic reform, 111–113; and "Egyptianization", 105; and false consciousness, 106–8; and founding of the CPE, 121–3; and high modernism, 127; and historiography, 108–9, 222–7; and industrialization, 99, 111–13, 194; and Jews, 103–4; and July revolution, 136, 159, 190–201, 251; and laws of history, 106, 222–7; and maximum program, 99, 136–7, 190–1; and minimum program, 99–100, 136, 190; and minorities, 97; and modernism, 96–100, 126–8; and modernization, 97; and Muslim Brotherhood, 117–19, 126, 249; and national bourgeoisie, 194–5, 224–7; and nationalism, 104–5, 107, 113–117; and Pan-Arabism, 238; and paradigm of the front, 99–100, 106–18; and patriarchy, 97; and patronage 97; and politics of identity, 96–97; and the Popular Front, 98; and Port Said, 197; and "proletarization", 105; and national bourgeoisie, 99, 127, 190; as representative of new reformist currents, 26; and its second wave, 103–6; and splits within, 119–121; and the Soviet Union, 123, 124–5, 127; and Suez Canal crisis, 192, 194–8; and surrealism, 103; and trade unions, 136; and Wafd, 113–117, 122–3; and Westernism, 97
Egyptian Federation of Industries (EFI), 14
Egyptian historiography: contemporary liberal current, 3; contemporary Marxist current, 3; Marxist current of the 1940s, 108–9, 122–3; Marxist current under the new regime, 222–7; linear concept of history and new civilization, 231; and Rashid al-Barrawi, 80–82, 85–88; under new regime, 210–1; progressive march of Egyptian history, 239
Egyptian identity: and Anwar Abd al-Malik, 228–9; and debate on "Egyptian personality", 218–9; and discourse of authenticity, 19; and "Easternism", 19; and intellectuals of 1920s, 15; and the Muslim Brotherhood, 18; and secular reformist movement of 1930s, 20
Egyptian Movement for National Liberation, EMNL, (al-Haraka al-Misriyya li-l-l-Taharrur al-Watani, HAMITU), 104–6, 116–9
Eisenhower doctrine, 197, 216, 239
Enlightenment: and Anwar Abd al-Malik, 230; and Egyptian communism, 108; and generation of 1930s, 22; and Society of National Renaissance, 48

Fabian Society, 71, 86
Fahmi, Aziz, 140
Fahmi, Husayn, 179–80
al-Fajr al-Jadid, 104, 115, 117, 118
fallahin, 16, 85, 219–20, 227
Farid, Muhammad, 225
Faruq, King, 20, 25, 143, 146, 151, 251
fascism: Egyptian communism and Islamism, 117–9; and Nasserist regime, 190; and Rashid al-Barrawi, 77–78
February incident, 25
France, 239
Franklin Institute, 240
Free Officers, 125–6, 157
Fu'ad, Ahmad, 125, 157
al-Fusul, 42, 61

Gandhi, Mahatna, 219
Gershoni, Israel, 4, 6, 22
Ghali, Mirrit Butrus (*see also* Society of National Renaissance): and agrarian reform, 57–59, 83, 110–11, 149; background of, 42; on democracy, 47–51; ideological influences on,

272

46–7; and the military, 167; incorporation into the new regime, 176; and national unity, 55–57; and social reform, 51–55
Ghurbal, Muhammad Shafiq, 80, 223
Ghanim, Fathi: joining the staff of *Ruz al-Yusuf*, 61, 139; critique of planning, 215
Girgis, Fawzi, as communist Copt, 104, and Egyptian historiography, 223–7
Great Britain, 14–15, 17, 143, 239
al-Gritli, Ali: as economic historian, 76–77; as economist 80; as member of the Permanent Council for the development of National Production, 179

al-Hakim, Tawfiq, 227
Hamrush, Ahmad, 148, 157, 159
Hamza, Abd al-Qadir, 17
Hasan, Abd al-Raziq, 157, 183, 199
Hashimities, 239
Harb, Tal'at, 17
Hayat al-Hizb, 218
Haykal, Muhammad Husayn: and Society of National Renaissance, 38; as ideologue of Party of the Liberal Constitutionalists, 20; as member of new generation, 18; relations with Muhammad Zaki Abd al-Qadir, 43
Henein, George, 103–4, 124
Higher Council for Sciences (al-Majlis al-A'la li-l-'Ulum), 201
al-Hilali, Naguib, 144–6, 154
Hitler, Adolf, 101
hizbiyya, 24, 49–50
Hollywood, 240
Husayn, Taha: and new generation of intellectuals, 17; and political modernism, 20; and the Azhar, 18

Imari, Abd al-Jalil, 148
India, 129, 187, 194, 219, 232, 236
Indonesia, 187, 194
Industrial Bank: and appointment of Rashid al-Barrawi as president, 26, 179; and establishment of new firms by, 181–2; promotor of economic planning, 183–4, 201; promotor of technocracy,

179; and new research department, 183; and Abd al-Raziq Hasan, 199; and Annual Reports of, 200
intellectuals: and authoritarian modernism, 14, 188, 213, 246, 252; and enthusiasm for new regime, 177, 187, 252; first generation, 12, 16–7, 20–21; new generation, 2–3, 6, 25–28, 175–8; as opinion makers (*ahl al-ra'y* and *ashab al-ra'y*), 16, 89, 156, 176, 249; rejection of civil society, 253; replacement of the previous generation, 177; role in new regime, 211; second generation, 12–13, 18
al-Intisar, 197
al-Iqtisad wa-l-Muhasaba, 183
Iraq, 239
Iron and Steel plant in Helwan, 178, 180, 201
al-Ishtiraki, 142
Iskra, 104–5, 111–13, 116, 118–20, 125
Islamic League, 236
Israel, 188
Israel, Marcel, 104, 124, 238

al-Jamahir, 120
Jankowski, James, 4, 6, 22
Jews, 119
Jordan, 239
journalists' syndicate, 138
al-Jubayli, Muhammad Abd al-Ma'bud, 106
July revolution: and authoritarian modernism, 191; and "benevolent dictatorship", 146–7; and communist movement after 1955, 190–201; and economic planning, 178–186; and high modernism, 191, 201; and intellectuals after March crisis, 186–190; and Marxist historiography, 226; and military takeover, 25; and Rashid al-Barrawi, 69–70, 73; and repression of civil society, 202; and state reform, 210

Kafr al-Dawwar, 158
Kamil, Anwar, 103, 112, 124–5
Kamil, Fu'ad, 103, 125
Kamil, Mustafa, 16–17

INDEX

al-Katib, 142, 159
Keane, John, 9
Khalil, Fathi, 189, 240
Khalil, Mustafa, 184
Khattab, Muhammad, 60
al-Khuli, Amin, 43
Kifah al-Sha'b, 192, 197, 216

Lahita, Muhammad Fahmi, 80
large landowners, 15, 19, 75, 81
Laski, Harold, 70, 73–74, 232
Lebanon, 194
Lenin, V.I.: and Egyptian communism, 112; and Egyptian communist radicalism, 121; and imperialism in Egypt, 75–76, 240; and Rashid al-Barrawi, 69, 78
Liberation of the People (Tahrir al-Sha'b), 104
Liberation Rally, 159, 165, 198
Lique Pacifique, 104
al-Liwa, 15
Lockman, Zachary, 7
Lutfi al-Sayyid Marsot, Afaf, 3
Lutfi al-Sayyid, Ahmad: elitist political ideas of, 16; influence on the Party of the Liberal Constitutionalists, 20; contemporary Marxist critique of, 3; relations with the Society of National Renaissance, 42

Madkur, Ibrahim Bayumi (*see also* Society of National Renaissance): background, 42–43; and agrarian reform, 60; and incorporation into the new regime, 176; as member of Permanent Council for the Development of National Production, 179; as member of Permanent Council of Social Services, 150; and the military, 167; as minister, 149; and political reform, 47–51
Mahir, Ali: critique by Rachid al-Barrawi, 87; as Head of the Royal Diwan, 18; as prime minister, 144, 146, 166; opposed to Rashid al-Barrawi, 148; as reformer, 43– 44; and Young Egypt, 118

Mahmud, Muhammad, 43, 146
Makram, Umar, 225
al-Malayin, 142, 159
Mandur, Muhammad: elected to parliament, 140; as leader of the Wafdist Vanguard, 115; publishing *Kitab al-Muwatin* series, 157; and trip to the Soviet Union, 233–4
March Crisis, 5, 26–27, 135, 137, 157, 162–165, 176, 249–51
Mar'i, Sayyid, 90, 184
Marxism: and Egyptian communist movement, 105; and Egyptian communist historiography, 108–9, 223–7; and Rashid al-Barrawi 69, 72, 86
al-Masa', 195, 198–200, 216, 238
Mau Zedong, 102–3, 160
Mazhar, Isma'il, 17
Menderes, Adnan, 188
middle classes (see also *effendiyya*): CPE on the role of, 123; and the communist movement, 97; Rashid al-Barrawi on, 66–67, 87–89, 167; and revolt against patronage, 247; Society of National Renaissance on, 40
Mill, John Stuart: influence on Ahmad Lutfi al-Sayyid, 16; influence on the Society of National Renaissance, 46
al-Misri (*see also* Ahmad Abu al-Fath): and attack on the military, 162; banning of, 165; and campaign against the palace, 142; and Industrial Bank, 179–80; and March Crisis, 164; and Society of National Renaissance, 61, 136, 138–40; and struggle along the Suez Canal, 142
Mitchell, Timothy, 4
modernization, 5, 175
modernism: and Anwar Abd al-Malik, 227–30; and authoritarianism, 2, 173–8, 189–91, 208–13, 252; concept of, 2, 5–6, 11–12, 248–9; dichotomy with tradition, 211; and the East, 230–40; and economic planning, 12; and Egyptian communism, 96–100, 191; and communist historiography, 222–7, 250; and emancipation, 10; and

Fabian socialism, 71; and heavy industry, 198–200; and high modernism, 13, 191, 195, 253; and identity, 10; and intellectuals of 1930s, 11, 14, 22, 27; and intellectuals of 1950s, 7, 201–2; ministers as embodiment of, 184–5; and new civilization, 231–2; and planning, 208–211; and political ideologies, 12; and progress, 13; and Rashid al-Barrawi, 67, 88–90, 250; and science, 200; and social constructivism, 12; and social engineering, 10; and Society of National Renaissance, 37–41, 250; and state ideology, 13; and technocracy, 22, 213; and technology, 200

Montreux conference, 87
al-Mu'ayyad, 15
Muharram, Uthman, 153
Muhyi al-Din, Khalid: as editor-in-chief of al-Masa', 195; and HADITU 157; and Iskra, 125; and March crisis, 162, 164; and Permanent Council for the Development of National Production, 179
Murad, Zaki, 161, 192–4
Mursi, Fu'ad: on HADITU, 121, 123; on "guided democracy", 216–7; on nationalist movement, 122–3
Musa, Salama: and Anwar Abd al-Malik, 227; and Enlightenment, 18; and new generation of intellectuals, 18; and political modernism, 20; and Rashid al-Barrawi, 66, 89
Muslim Brotherhood: and Egyptian communist movement, 98, 107–8; and Islamic welfare associations, 17; and Marxist historiography, 3–4, 226; and political moralism, 19; and political patronage, 22; and repression by the July revolution, 174; and revolt against modernism, 21; and socialist tendency within, 140; and Society of National Renaissance, 44
al-Muqattam, 15
al-Muqawama al-Sha'biyya, 196
al-Muqtataf, 15

Naguib, Muhammad, 149, 159, 162, 179
nahda, 217, 220, 227
al-Nahhas, Mustafa, 160
Napoleon, Bonaparte, 224
National Center of Research (al-Markaz al-Qawmi li–l-Buhuth), 201
National Committee (al-Lajna al-Qawmiyya), 118
National Democratic Front (al-Jabha al-Wataniyya al-Dimuqratiyya), 160, 218
National Planning Committee, 198
National Planning Council, 198
Nationalist Party, See also Watani Party, 15–17, 225
National Committee of Students and Workers (NCWS), 114, 117
NATO, 236
Nehru, Jawaharlal, 187, 195, 236
neutralism, 237
New Dawn group (see also al-Fajr al-Jadid and Workers' Vanguard): and Ahmad Abu al-Fath, 138; foundation of, 104–5; ideas of, 110–17; and repression of, 121; and splits ithin communist movement, 120
al-Nuqrashi, Mahmud Fahmi: 43–4, 115, 122

Oriental despotism, 224

Pakistan, 236
PanArabism, 4, 6, 174, 213, 237
Pan-Islamism, 16
Party of the Liberal Constitutionalists (Hizb al-Ahrar al-Dusturiyyun), 20, 43, 112, 225
patriarchy, 97
patronage: and civil society, 8–11; and communism, 97; and modernism 2–4; under the monarchy, 16–28; 175–6, 247, 252; and Mustafa Kamil, 13; and the Society of National Renaissance, 37
People's Liberation (Tahrir al-Sha'b), 104, 124
Permanent Council for the Development of National Production, PCDNP (al-Majlis al-Da'im li–Tanmiyat al-Intaj al-Qawmi): and authoritarianism, 250;

INDEX

influence on planning, 180, 200; report of, 183; and Rashid al-Barrawi, 26, 69, 150, 179–181
Permanent Council of Social Services, PCSS (al-Majlis al-Da'im al-Khadamat al-Ijtima'iyya), 150, 250
planning Arabic terminology of, 79, 175, 185, 209, 222; and authoritarian modernism, 7, 14, 177–86, 187, 198–201, 208–9, 214, 250, 253; communist movement on, 198–200; and culture, 209, 218–22; and 'guided' democracy, 210, 214; and the Economic Organization, 198; and economic organizations, 175; and five year plans, 72, 199–200; and the Higher Council of Planning, 199; and Industrial Bank, 180–2, 199–200; institutionalization of, 184, 198–200; and intellectuals, 176, 195–201; and the National Planning Committee, 198; and the National Planning Council, 198; and the new regime, 27, 178–86, 198–202; and Rashid al-Barrawi, 79, 87, 178, 250; and science, 200–1; and state philosophy, 182–4; and technocracy, 7
political culture, 11
Popular Front, 98
populism: 8, 15
Port Said, 197–8
positivism, 71
progress, 88, 231, 248, 253
public opinion, 6, 12, 14, 18
public sphere, 7, 15
purification, 144–6, 152, 166

Qaysuni, Abd al-Mun'im, 184
Qutb, Sayyid, 139

Rabitat al-Shabab, 138
Radical Party, 102
Radwan, Fathi, 149, 251
Ra'fat, Wahid, 44, 61, 163–4, 167
Rassemblement Universel pour la Paix, 104
Readers' Digest, 221
Renaissance (*nahda*), 44, 50, 211, 217, 220, 227

Revolution of 1919, 17, 225
Revolutionary Bloc (al-Takattul al-Thawri), 120, 127
Ricardo, David, 110
Rifa'i, Sayyid Sulayman, 161
Rothstein, Theodore, 108
Roy, M.N., 100
Russian revolution, 78, 87
Russian Socialist Party, 121
Ruz al-Yusuf (*see also* Ihsan Abd al-Quddus): and armed struggle, 142; and arms deal, 141; and authoritarian modernism, 191; and campaign for a political party for the military, 156; and changing attitude toward the new regime, 178; and civil society, 138–9; and debate on "Egyptian personality", 218–9; and defense of national culture, 22; as promoter of liberal reform, 61, 136; in support of new regime, 187–8; and Wafd, 139

Sa'd, Ahmad Sadiq, 104, 110–12;
Sa'di Party, 140
Safran, Nadav, 3
Sa'id, Abd al-Mughni: critique of communist movement, 124–6; critique of the Muslim Brotherhood, 126; as modernizer, 251; reaction to the military takeover, 152; and planning, 152; trip to the Soviet Union, 234
Salih, Ahmad Rushdi, 80, 108–10
Sawt al-Fallahin, 194
Sawt al-Umma, 115
Schwarz, Hillel, 104
Scott, James, C., 13, 202, 253
al-Shafi'i, Shuhdi Atiyya: as historian, 223–7; as member of the communist movement, 105–6; and splits within the communist movement 120–1
al-Shamsi, Ali, 42, 183
Shubra, 23
Shubra al-Khayma, 117
Shukri, Ibrahim, 251
Sid Ahmad, Muhammad, 120
Siddiq, Yusuf, 157, 159, 163–4
Sidqi, Aziz: and Five Year Plan, 199; and ideology of planning, 185, 251; as member of the Permanent Council of

Social Services, 180; as Minister of Industries, 184–6
Sidqi, Isma'il: as industrialist, 17; and Muslim Brotherhood, 118; and al-Nuqrashi, 115–6; and political elitism, 20; and Rashid al-Barrawi, 87, 146; and repression of the communist movement, 117; and Society of National Renaissance 44
Siraj al-Din, Fu'ad, 115, 147, 153
Sirri, Husayn, 146
Social Darwinism, 20
social engineering, 40, 47, 89, 209
Socialist Party, 102
Society of National Renaissance (Jama'at al-Nahda al-Qawmiyya) (*see also* Mirrit Butrus Ghali and Ibrahim Bayumi Madkur): and agrarian reform, 57–59, 250; and background of members, 42; and civil society, 46; and Constitution of 1923, 37, 39, 49; and ideological influences, 8–9; and liberal dilemma, 40, 46, 52; and military takeover, 167; and nationalist movement, 39, 60–61; and origins of, 41–44; and patronage, 37, 45, 249; and previous liberal generation, 37–38; political reform program of, 44–51; as new reformist current, 25, 249; and social integration, 38; and social reform of, 51–59: and new regime, 149–50, 210; and older generation of liberals, 42–44); and *Ruz al-Yusuf*, 61
Soviet Union: and Egyptian communist agrarian reform, 111; and economic planning, 199; and high modernism, 28, 78–79; in Egyptian Marxist historiography, 226; and Rashid al-Barrawi, 72, 78; and scientific planning, 201; and Egyptian travel literature, 232,–4; and the United States, 240
Sputnik, 200
Sudan, 194
Suez Canal, 142
Suez Canal Company, 112, 175, 185, 198–9;
Suez Canal crisis, 175, 190–1, 195–8, 234, 239, 251–2

Sukarno, 187, 195
Syria, 189, 194, 197, 200

Tahrir Province, 201
Tal'at, Ibrahim, 154
al-Tali'a, 159
Tali'a al-Wafdiyya, 61, 140
Tarraf, Nur al-Din, 149
al-Tatawwur, 103, 125
technocracy: discourse of, 185; and discourse of planning, 209–10; and intellectual discourse, 213; and July revolution, 175; and Rashid al-Barrawi, 67; and Society of National Renaissance, 40
Thabit, Adil, 157
Therborn, Göran, 11
Tiba, Mustafa, 122
Tilmisani, Kamil, 103
trade unions: and civil society, 8; and Egyptian communist movement, 99, 116, 251; independence of, 22; and March Crisis; and popular resistance committees, 198
travel literature, 211–212, 230–40
turath, 220, 228–30
Turkey, 219, 236

Ulaysh, Muhammad Hamza, 80–83
Umm Durman, 117
Umma Party, 15, 20
Unified Egyptian Communist Party, UECP (al-Hizb al-Shuyu'i al-Misri al-Muwahhad): on Baghdad Pact, 192; on Bandung Conference, 194; on Czech arms deal, 192; on democracy, 192; and the new regime, 190–200; and national bourgeoisie, 194; on World Bank and the Aswan High Dam, 192;
United Egyptian Communist Party, UECP (al-Hizb al-Shuyu'i al-Misri al-Muttahid), 190, 218
United Nationalist Front, UNF (al-Jabha al-Muttahida al-Wataniyya), 196
United Nations, 85
United States, 123, 197, 216, 236, 239–40
Urabi revolution, 109, 225

INDEX

Vatikiotis P.J., 3
Voice of the Opposition (Sawt al-Mu'arada), 121, 127

Wafd: abrogation of the Anglo–Egyptian Treaty, 142; and *Akhbar al-Yawm*, 157; call for return of, 164; communist strategy toward, 99–100, 113–117, 120–1, 123, 127; comparison with Chinese nationalists, 235; conflict with King Fu'ad 17; and decline of monarchy, 2; and electoral victory, 135–6, 140; front with communists, 160; in government 1950–52 141–3, 166; and Isma'il Sidqi, 20; in Marxist historiography, 225–6; and neutralism, 237; and party politics, 20; and patronage, 18–19; and repression of, 146–7; and resistance against reform, 39; Society of National Renaissance on 48
al-Wafd al-Misri, 61, 115, 117
Wafdist Vanguard (al-Tali'a al-Wafdiyya), 115–6, 117, 138, 140
al-Wajib, 159
Watani Party (*see also* Nationalist Party and Mustafa Kamil), 16, 225
Warriner, Doreen, 85
Waterbury, John, 10
Webb, Sidney and Beatrice, 70–72, 73, 75, 79
Western civilization, 231

Workers' Vanguard (Tali'a al-'Ummal) (*see also* Fajr al-Jadid group, Ahmad Sadiq Sa'd, Ahmad Rushdi Salih, Abu Sayf Yusuf): and civil society, 247; and "guided democracy", 216; foundation of 121; and Hungarian uprising, 234; and national bourgeoisie, 195; open letter to Gamal Abd al-Nasser, 193–5; changing position towards the new regime, 190, 193; and front with new regime, 195–8; working class: rise of, 19, 190, 223; revolt against patronage, 247
World Bank, 113, 192

Yahya, Amin, 17
Young Egypt: Egyptian communist movement on, 98, 107, 118; Marxist historiography on, 226; and Rashid al-Barrawi on, 88; and revolt against modernism, 21; changing into the Socialist Party of Egypt (SPE), 140
Young Men's Muslim Association (YMMA), 17
Yunan, Ramsis, 103, 104
Yugoslavia, 187
Yusuf, Abu Sayf, 107–8, 118, 216
al-Yusuf, Fatima, 139

al-Zaman, 69, 145
Zahran, Sa'd, 120–1
Zuhayri, Kamil, 234

278

For Product Safety Concerns and Information please contact our EU representative GPSR@taylorandfrancis.com
Taylor & Francis Verlag GmbH, Kaufingerstraße 24, 80331 München, Germany